Writing Law Dissertations

An Introduction and Guide to the Conduct of Legal Research

Michael Salter
Professor of Law

and

Julie Mason
Senior Lecturer

Lancashire Law School
University of Central Lancashire

PEARSON

Longman

Harlow, England • London • New York • Boston • San Francisco • Toronto • Sydney • Singapore • Hong Kong
Tokyo • Seoul • Taipei • New Delhi • Cape Town • Madrid • Mexico City • Amsterdam • Munich • Paris • Milan

Pearson Education Limited

Edinburgh Gate
Harlow
Essex CM20 2JE
England

and Associated Companies throughout the world

Visit us on the World Wide Web at:
www.pearsoned.co.uk

First published 2007

ISBN: 978-0-582-89435-8

British Library Cataloguing-in-Publication Data
A catalogue record for this book is available from the British Library

Library of Congress Cataloging-in-Publication Data
Salter, Michael, 1957-
    Writing law dissertations : an introduction and guide to the conduct of legal research /
  Michael Salter and Julie Mason.
      p. cm.
    ISBN-13: 978-0-582-89435-8
    ISBN-10: 0-582-89435-2
    1. Legal research–Great Britain. 2. Legal composition. 3. Dissertations,
  Academic–Great Britain. I. Mason, Julie. II. Title.

  KD392.S25 2007
  808'.06634–dc22

                                                                    2006052532

10 9 8 7 6 5 4 3 2 1
10 09 08 07

Typeset in 9/12pt Interstate by 35
Printed in Great Britain by Henry Ling Ltd., at the Dorset Press, Dorchester, Dorset

The publisher's policy is to use paper manufactured from sustainable forests.

Brief Contents

Contents

Acknowledgements

To our families and friends (too numerous to mention) for enduring months of our trials and tribulations. To our colleagues and in particular to Andrew Harries and Bogusia Puchalska for their support, encouragement and constructive feedback. To Dr Peter Billings and Charlotte Smith for reviewing the book and supplying us with helpful commentary. To Rebekah Taylor for her patience and enthusiasm. To Andrea Coles for administering 'first aid' to the injured draft. Finally to all our students – you provided the inspiration for this book.

With special thanks to my father Henry Ormerod – a man of honour, humanity and truth. *'Who dared won'*. Julie.

Publisher's Acknowledgements

We are grateful to the following for permission to reproduce copyright material:

Extracts from the website of the Law Office of Walter Wm. Hofheinz: http://www. hofheinzlaw.com/LANLSYS.php#anchor47300 reproduced by permission of Walter Wm. Hofheinz; Extracts from 'Exploring the Limits of Formalism: AI and Legal Pedagogy' in *Law Technology Journal*, Peritz, R.J. 1991; Extracts from Campbell, D., 'Socio-Legal Analysis of Contract', Hillyard and Sim, 'The Political Economy of Socio-Legal Research', Jolly, S., 'Family Law', Bradshaw, A., 'Sense and Sensibility: Debates and Developments in Socio-Legal Research Methods', Wheeler, S., 'Company Law', Shaw, J., 'Socio-Legal Studies and the European Union' from © *Socio-Legal Studies* edited by Thomas, P., 1997, Ashgate-Dartmouth; Material from the University of New South Wales website, the University of New South Wales, Australia: www.law.unsw.edu.au/Course/course_guide/ LAWS4128.doc accessed July 2005, reproduced by permission of Leon Wolff; Extracts from 'Reconciling Process And Policy: Sentence Discounts In The Magistrates' Courts', Henham, R., in 15 *Criminal Law Review* (2000) June pp. 436–51, reproduced by permission of Sweet & Maxwell; Extracts from Douglas, G., and Ferguson, N., 'The Role of Grandparents in Divorced Families', in *International Journal of Law, Policy and the Family*, 2003, 41, by permission of Oxford University Press; 483 words total, pp. 20, 25 by Brigit Hutter & Sally Lloyd-Bostock, pp. 240–241 by John Eekelaar, pp. 178, 196–7 by McBarnet & Whelan, pp. 121–150 by William Felstiner, p. 65 by Robert Baldwin from *The Human Face of Law: Essays in Honour of Donald Harris* (1997) edited by Hawkins, K. Free Permission, by permission of Oxford University Press.

In some instances we have been unable to trace the owners of copyright material, and we would appreciate any information that would enable us to do so.

Introduction

● Why Should You Read This Book?

Since you have opened this book, it is probably safe for us to assume that you are either thinking about researching, or have already started to write a research project or a dissertation. At the outset, we need to point out that this book, in common with all textbooks, cannot guarantee you success in terms of your results. However, what it can do is provide you with advice and guidance, which we hope will make the process of writing your dissertation a more enjoyable and rewarding learning experience.

Students undertake research projects for various reasons. For example, you may be required by your degree regulations to write a dissertation, i.e. it is a compulsory element of your course. Alternatively, you may have certain motivations for opting to engage in research. Perhaps you like the idea of self-managed study with the added bonus that you do not have to turn up for lectures or prepare for seminars! There is nothing intrinsically wrong in choosing to do a dissertation for tactical reasons; it is now a fact of life that students have to 'juggle' numerous demands (academic, domestic and employment related) and therefore need to apportion their available time. However, irrespective of the impetus for your research project, you must accept that it will be necessary to devote *at least* the same amount of time to researching materials and writing drafts, as you would do in seminar preparation and assessment revision for any 'taught' module.

Our overall aim in this book is to provide you with help and guidance in understanding the *process* of constructing a dissertation. This includes, choosing an appropriate way of conducting your research and maintaining a productive relationship with your supervisor. Throughout the book, we shall also point out some of the common pitfalls that you should aim to avoid. Engaging in research is a very individual undertaking. *You* choose the topic and methodology, manage the available study time and, at the end of the day, are responsible for the entire research project (and the mark that it ultimately achieves). Such individuality will necessarily generate diversity and in many respects the advice we give in this book is generic, i.e. of general applicability to all dissertation research and writing. In saying that, it will be easy for you to adapt the advice given in the chapters to fit your own particular study circumstances and choice of topic.

If you need some encouragement at this early stage, here are a number of positive aspects of dissertation writing. Firstly, in terms of academic success, we have found that generally, students achieve higher marks in courseworks and dissertations, as compared to unseen examinations. In some respects this may be due to the fact that whilst dissertation research does require students to locate and analyse relevant legal materials, it does not require that all this information be committed to memory. Secondly, on the whole, students rise to the challenge of undertaking a project which is very much within their control in terms of the choice of topic, time-management and creativity. In other words, students tend to enjoy the academic freedom that dissertation writing brings. Thirdly, when engaged in their research, students often discover wider and more controversial dimensions of the law, including cultural, economic and political aspects, that taught modules and courses may not necessarily highlight. Students often find these wider aspects of the law to be particularly stimulating and thought-provoking, at least with respect to a topic in which they are personally interested.

In addition, there are many personal benefits to be derived from undertaking and completing a dissertation. Assuming the responsibility for producing a piece of work which is based on one's own research, as distinct from rote-learning materials handed out by lecturers, can help to generate or improve academic confidence and self-esteem. Furthermore, the process of writing a dissertation hones time-management skills and fosters the ability to be self-motivated and disciplined.

In summary, successful completion of a dissertation reveals evidence of the ability to:

- identify a subject which actually warrants research;
- undertake research on an issue by carrying out a literature-based search and/or fieldwork;
- locate pertinent sources and select, organise and prioritise information from those sources;
- formulate and analyse various arguments contained within the available academic literature;
- write in a clear, critical and logically structured fashion;
- analyse data (quantitative and qualitative);
- present a persuasive argument.

These transferable skills are highly valued by many employers and you can legitimately include references to their acquisition in your curriculum vitae. Indeed, you should consider the ability to carry out legal research, and to bring your research project to a successful conclusion, to be an essential skill with a much wider scope than the academic context.

● Why Did We Write This Book?

As experienced supervisors, we wanted to produce a book that would provide students with a realistic picture of what dissertation writing actually involves in practice, both generally and also specifically in terms of the implications of adopting one methodology rather than another. One key aspect of this book is that the advice proffered is not based on a tutor's perspective alone but, rather, on the 'real life' views of a sample of our students, whose individual dissertation diaries[1] contained accounts of their feelings, worries and exhilarations as they experienced the process of writing their dissertations. We should add that, in accordance with the principle of 'informed consent',[2] students who

---

[1] During the academic year 2002–2003, a number of volunteer students in Lancashire Law School completed 'diaries' in which they were asked to record their experiences as they researched and compiled their dissertations. The students were given complete freedom in this respect. Many of the students used this as an opportunity not only to comment upon the technicalities of dissertation research but also to describe their feelings (anxieties, exhilarations, etc.).

[2] Informed consent relates to 'the procedures in which individuals choose whether to participate in an investigation after being informed of facts that would be likely to influence their decision'. E. Diener and R. Crandall, (1978) *Ethics in Social and Behavioral Research*. University of Chicago Press. Cited in L. Cohen and L. Manion, (1994) *Research Methods in Education*. Routledge Press, at page 350.

chose to participate in our research were advised that we would publish verbatim extracts from their diaries but would do so in a manner that guaranteed anonymity.

Our experiential research indicated that a major problem which students experienced whilst writing a dissertation was not a lack of commitment or academic ability or motivation; instead, many of the perceived problems lay rather in students' unfamiliarity with planning and adopting a strategy for writing a longer piece of work, including the choice of overall approach. Given this, we highlight tactics that you can adopt, and measures that you can take, to ensure that you are better prepared to undertake the long haul, particularly with respect to avoiding some of the methodological pitfalls!

● Why Is There a Need for This Book?

Although there are many books on different aspects of legal research skills, this book aims to be different in terms of its scope. It focuses on the practicalities of dissertation research and includes guidance on adopting an appropriate method and methodology. Further, we have based a great deal of the material on our experiences of supervising undergraduate and postgraduate dissertation students, together with the results of our research into this aspect of legal education. This book therefore incorporates a real-life dimension and, as a consequence, you may find that you are able to identify with some of the dilemmas, issues, and high and low points revealed throughout.

Ideally, we would like you to read this book at the very moment you start thinking about doing a dissertation since we have included practical advice on *choosing* a research topic. On the other hand, we would hope that the chapters on specific methodologies will be of use at different stages of your research, including those periods when you reflect upon the implications and limits of any methodological approach you choose to adopt. This particular aspect of your research is important in relation to avoiding claims that overstate the implications of your findings, i.e. as if those findings were produced from the ultimate perspective to end all perspectives!

Chapter 1 is devoted to some of the more practical elements of dissertation writing. Included in this chapter are a series of activities. These are designed to help you focus on and address specific points in the research process. Engaging in these activities will enable you to build a 'reflective journal' in which you will be able to see how your research skills and academic profile develop as you progress through the dissertation. You may find this information helpful in terms of charting your personal achievements, and particularly useful when completing applications for further study or employment. Chapter 2 discusses the importance of setting up the supervision relationship in a manner that best allows you to get the most out of such guidance. There are activities throughout the chapter to help you in this respect. It also addresses an equally important issue: that of negotiating a productive relationship with your supervisor in which both sides are aware of each other's likely expectations.

Chapter 3 discusses the importance of dissertation students reflecting upon and justifying their choice of methodologies. It emphasises the importance of explaining and justifying the approach you have decided to take to the conduct of your dissertation research. In other words, you must select the most appropriate way of setting up relevant questions, defining the scope of the topic and analysing various issues. Chapters 4 and 5 contrast two different research methods and methodologies that you can adopt and adapt to the demands of your particular dissertation topic: traditional black-letter and more recently developed sociolegal studies approaches to the conduct of legal research. Each of these methodologies is defined and then discussed in some detail, with particular emphasis on their requirements and limitations, whilst the general strengths and weaknesses of each are summarised. Some but not all of the strengths and weaknesses will apply to their possible application to your particular topic. The final chapter, Chapter 6, discusses the nature, and pros and cons, of adopting comparative and historical approaches to the conduct of dissertation research. It considers those types of historical analysis that are compatible to both black-letter and sociolegal approaches to legal research.

It is important to note that different universities will have different requirements for dissertations, e.g. with respect to a bibliography and citation styles, which students should familiarise themselves with. We strongly advise you to check with your own department/supervisor for information on custom, practice and guidelines relating to these particular requirements. Many institutions supply students with a handbook in which such guidance is given.

In summary, writing a dissertation may initially seem to be a formidable task. In your taught modules, you will probably have been given reading lists which direct you to the relevant primary and secondary sources. By contrast, when writing a dissertation you will be responsible for locating and prioritising relevant and up-to-date materials. Depending upon your choice of methodology, this can require you to consult a certain type of relevant primary and secondary source. It may be necessary to locate and analyse policy issues and theoretical arguments. You may also choose to carry out small-scale empirical research on how one aspect of law is actually operating in practice.

Given the personal effort involved, it is not surprising that many students develop a strong 'bond' with their dissertation. To illustrate, using the words of one of our students when handing in the completed dissertation, '*it was like sending my child off to school for the first time*'. However, you do need to be able to 'stand back' from your work from time to time. This is necessary in order to engage in critical reflection on your propositions and arguments and, also, on how your approach to the conduct of research is assisting you in making and supporting your overall argument. It has to be said that this is *always* easier said than done! This book aims to help you with this reflective work and various other difficulties that you may encounter, e.g. when selecting your methodology, and in carrying out and writing up dissertation research. In conclusion, by the time you have finished your dissertation, you will have developed your own unique style of engaging in and managing your research. This is a skill which can be utilised in many aspects of your future academic and employment careers.

Just one final point, we would both like to wish you every success with your adventure into legal research. **Enjoy!**

Michael Salter and Julie Mason

1 How to Begin

To be honest, I did not know where to start and the efforts I made did not seem useful. It was all very demoralising.

I changed my plan umpteen times before starting my dissertation. I think that I was just putting it off; scared to start.

● Introduction

This chapter examines a number of the more practical elements of dissertation writing and is supported by exercises designed to help you focus on, and address, specific points in the process of your dissertation research. These exercises will enable you to build a 'reflective journal' which chronologically charts the development of your research skills and academic profile as you progress through the dissertation. This chapter also clarifies the meaning of research and provides some guidance concerning the crucial issue of selecting a viable dissertation topic. It makes suggestions as to how to overcome the familiar problem of not knowing where to begin and – once you have chosen an appropriate topic – it provides some help with the question of identifying relevant issues, some of which could provide useful internal sub-headings. Finally, this chapter provides some guidance on drafting and redrafting successive chapters, bearing in mind that no first draft is likely to be of a standard worth submitting as a finished piece of work.

As indicated by the above quotations, many of our students felt 'daunted' by the prospect of months and months engaged in research and writing up their dissertations. A number of reasons were cited. Firstly, many students were acutely aware of the fact that their dissertation would be the largest piece of written work they had undertaken so far in their academic careers. Secondly, dissertation writing requires students to motivate themselves, manage their own study and take full responsibility for their efforts (or lack of effort). These are demands which a student may not have experienced to such a degree. As a result of the responses to our research, we felt that in this initial chapter, we should help to ease you into dissertation writing by focusing on a number of preliminary issues (see below) and at the same time, try to allay any anxieties you may have in relation to starting your research.

- What is 'research'?
- What is a 'dissertation'?
- How to choose your dissertation topic.
- Specific suggestions for getting you started.
- Identifying key issues within your chosen topic (what are 'core' and 'marginal' issues?).

- Is the research viable in practice?
- Putting pen to paper.

By the end of this chapter, you should feel confident that you are now at the stage where you are able to:

- choose a suitable and appropriate dissertation topic in a structured and logical manner;
- begin the process of identifying the key issues within your topic;
- be confident that your topic is actually researchable;
- begin researching!

● What is 'Research'?

'Research' signifies the systematic study of a topic. 'Research' seeks to define, describe and explain what the topic is and how it has come to be distinct from other similar phenomena. Research requires the ability to access and then critically assess the various debates and issues that the topic has generated. Research is usually assessed (graded/marked) in terms of its accuracy, the scope and depth of appropriate reading, explanatory power, and the extent to which it has developed a suitably critical analysis of both the explicit claims and implicit assumptions which currently prevail regarding the topic.

● What is a 'Dissertation'?

Although the dictionary[1] provides a succinct definition of a 'dissertation', i.e. 'a written thesis, often based on original research, usually required for a higher degree', this really does not give us any indication of the 'ingredients' which are necessary to create a successful dissertation. We are assuming that you have probably submitted many pieces of coursework but, as yet, no piece of work that could be defined as a 'dissertation'. One of the key issues at the outset is to identify the differences between a piece of coursework and a dissertation so that you are prepared for what will be expected of you. Some of our students identified (with hindsight) certain benefits which they attributed to the process of researching for a dissertation – benefits which did not seem to be linked to the preparation of courseworks.

> Doing the dissertation has been of great help to me. I have especially learned that as an independent learner you have to manage time and prioritise your work. Organised students don't face difficulties.

> The style we had to write in was different. It wasn't the same as other courseworks. The dissertation was supposed to be very critical, other people's opinions were needed as well as my own. It turned out to be more difficult than I thought and the amount of reading I had to do was tremendous. But I think that my research skills have improved especially with online sources and less traditional sources.

> I am pleased with my dissertation because I have completed a substantial piece of work. My writing ability has improved in terms of quality, structure and referencing.

---

[1]*Collins Softback English Dictionary*, (New York: Harper Collins, 1991).

This was an invaluable experience. I felt that I had gained a kind of specialism in the area. I am pleased that my work was not descriptive but mainly analytical and critical. This is probably the most significant piece of work that I have produced as an undergraduate student.

The dissertation has made me seek a wider range of sources of information than other modules where one can find much of the information in textbooks. So this module is more challenging but also more fulfilling.

The obvious distinction between a piece of coursework and a dissertation is its length. An average piece of coursework is often within the region of 3,000 to 4,000 words – a dissertation at LLB or LLM level can require you to write anything from 10,000 to 20,000 words. This may seem formidable (or even impossible!), but as you will be breaking the dissertation down into chapters or sections it may help you to think of each one of them as a 'mini' coursework (with discernable links between each so as to maintain continuity).

The next issue to consider in terms of the difference between a coursework and a dissertation is that of 'originality'. In this context, originality means examining something that *you* have deemed to be interesting rather than being directed to the topic by one of your course tutors. It is for *you* to decide upon the pertinent issues and for *you* to locate the relevant sources – do not expect, or ask, to be supplied with a reading list. Aim to be inventive and creative. You will also be required to sift through your research and discard any irrelevant materials – often easier said than done when these materials have made a significant dent in your photocopying budget.

The final difference is narrative structure – your dissertation is essentially an argument, therefore in the introduction you must show *what* you are going to investigate, *why* it is worthy of investigation and *how* you will attempt to investigate it. Remember that your tutors are not interested in your general knowledge of an area of law but in the argument that you wish to develop and debate in your dissertation.

If you are feeling a little anxious about commencing work, remember that there are distinct advantages to preparing a dissertation (as opposed to sitting an examination). As highlighted in the introduction to this book, students tend to achieve higher marks in research-based assessments (such as courseworks and dissertations). This may be because students respond more positively to the challenge of undertaking a task that is very much within their control. When writing up a dissertation, students have continuous access to resources – there is no need to rely on memory. Furthermore, during the process of writing a dissertation, students will receive periodic assistance from their supervisors and there may be opportunities for staged feedback which can then be reflected upon and, if appropriate, can be incorporated into the research.

At this stage it may be helpful, for you to spend the next five minutes jotting down some responses to the question, 'what is the purpose of a dissertation'? This exercise will help to focus your mind on the task and the process ahead of you. For example, try to imagine how writing your dissertation will differ from essay writing. You may also like to think about the type of activities you will be engaged in; the degree of support you will expect to receive; how long you intend to spend on information gathering; how long you envisage the writing up stage will take and finally, any concerns that you have at this early stage.

. . . .
. . . .
. . . .
. . . .
. . . .
. . . .
. . . .
. . . .

Try to complete this exercise with a fellow student. At the end of the five minutes, swap your notes and see if either of you identified any issues which the other had omitted.

Now compare your views to those put forward by a tutor. Cottrell[2] identifies what she considers to be some of the key opportunities afforded to a student by completing a dissertation.

● To be able to undertake a substantial piece of independent academic study.

● To be able to pursue in much greater depth a relevant topic that is interesting.

● To be able to develop a personal specialism.

● To be able to put a personal stamp on a piece of work.

● To be able to explore the literature on a chosen topic.

● To be able to refine and extend skills in finding, selecting and critically analysing information.

● To be able to refine skills in decision-making, task management and problem solving.

● To be able to refine skills in summarising and presenting findings.

Cottrell[3] also highlights a number of factors which in many respects are particular to researching for, and writing, a dissertation.

● 'Independence' (in terms of controlling the nature and scope of the dissertation);

● 'Personal involvement' (in terms of personal commitment and responsibility);

● 'Time' (in terms of quantity required and the need for careful management of);

● 'Self management and motivation' (in terms of the need to adopt appropriate strategies);

● 'Literature search' (in terms of being more extensive and therefore more complicated; also, in relation to the need to maintain accurate records of all references);

● 'Presentation' (in terms of the need for comprehensive proofreading and also, com-plying with relevant regulations on the submission of completed dissertations).

The above information should help you to put dissertation writing into context along-side your other academic commitments. In short, you should be *prepared* to approach

---

[2]Stella Cottrell, *The Study Skills Handbook*, (London: Palgrave MacMillan, 2003), at page 201.
[3]*Ibid.*

dissertation writing as a *process* which will require of you a great deal of time, determination and enthusiasm. In saying that, it will provide you with an opportunity to develop and pursue a novel line of argument and give you the freedom to express your (reasoned) opinions. Your research and analytical skills will improve and your completed dissertation may even act as a springboard to additional publishable research.

● How to Choose your Dissertation Topic

Many of our students indicated to us that choosing the subject matter for their research was one of the most challenging aspects of the dissertation.

> I spent a few weeks collecting and reading information on my topic. However, I felt bogged down with all the information, it was overwhelming.

> I spoke to two lecturers to get their opinions on a few ideas. I also went to the library to get out some textbooks and to do some initial reading. I felt that this was a good start but in the end, I was confused and could not think of an original idea for my dissertation.

> I went to see my supervisor and after I explained to him my aims he said that I must change my subject because it is a massive area and I should be very specific. The choice he offered me was to either forget all about the original topic or narrow it down to a concrete area. I decided to follow the first option although that was rather devastating when I realised that I must disregard everything I had in mind up till then.

Perhaps you are sitting there thinking, 'I have absolutely no idea of what to write about. I don't know where to look for inspiration'. Your initial strategy must be to think of a 'suitable' subject area. By 'suitable' we mean something that *can* be researched and which will fire your imagination. Consider the modules you have studied to date. Are there any aspects which you found particularly interesting or controversial? Are there any issues in the news that you feel may or indeed should impact on an area of law? In our experience, it is unusual (but not unheard of) for a student to have no ideas at all. In fact the opposite is frequently the problem, i.e. too many ideas and uncertainty as to which direction to take. If you encounter any of the above problems, our advice is that you should approach a tutor with some expertise in the subject area(s) you have earmarked. He/she may be able to direct you to controversial or topical aspects which have been highlighted in recent academic articles and furthermore, will be able to tell you whether any of your ideas have the *potential* to amount to something that is viable, interesting to read and capable of achieving a good mark. However, you must always bear in mind that whilst a supervisor may be happy to offer a certain amount of guidance and assistance in this respect, it is your responsibility to formulate appropriate research questions.

When choosing your dissertation topic, it helps to think strategically and to ask yourself the following 'what, why and how' questions:

1. **What do I want to do? What do I want to investigate? (**You are, in effect, stating the aims and objectives of your dissertation).

2. **How can I achieve my objective?** Will this require a literature research? Will it be appropriate or indeed necessary, for me to carry out empirical research? If so, what method/methodology should I adopt?

3. **Why do I want to do it?** Will this research deepen my knowledge of a particular legal issue? Will this research be of interest to prospective employers (indicating pertinent knowledge and demonstrating an eagerness to engage in a particular area of law)?

It may well be that the honest answer to the last question is, 'Because I have to'!

● Specific Suggestions for Getting You Started

You could log on to the government website (www.open.gov.uk) or a newspaper information database such as '*Guardian unlimited*' (http://www.guardian.co.uk/) for up-to-date information (including recent developments) on a particular subject area. You will need to be flexible in terms of your search requests and you will probably find this to be a very time-consuming activity. However, a few hours work manoeuvring the cursor could potentially uncover some up-to-the-minute issues and could subsequently lead to some original ideas and rewarding avenues of research.

Another strategy is to think ahead. In our experience it is advisable and advantageous for students to consider their choice of topic in a leisurely way rather than running around at the beginning of a hectic academic year hoping for a flash of inspiration. For example, in the year preceding your dissertation study, cut out interesting articles from newspapers and file them in a 'project preparation folder'. You could also jot down and file away anything that you hear on the news or any interesting issues that you come across in your lectures, seminar preparation and discussions. By doing this, with very little effort, you will have created a bank of information on potential topics. You will have focused your mind on the task ahead and will have eased yourself into the process of researching for, and writing up, your dissertation.

Once you have identified a number of possible topics, the following questions might help you to narrow the choice down.

- Do I have any prior knowledge of this subject?
- Am I genuinely interested in this subject?
- Do I have the time to carry out any necessary empirical work?
- Is my idea focused?
- Is it worthy of investigation?

Once you have decided on a specific topic, brainstorming, creating spider/wheel diagrams and 'mind mapping' are useful planning tools. Each of these activities will provide you with a diagram showing how ideas or different elements can be linked to each other so as to form a logical sequence. They are all based on a similar modus operandi – you begin by stating a central theme or key word(s) and then expand upon this by adding 'connectors' (related concepts and ideas.) An example of a spider diagram can be found at http://www.sheffield.ac.uk/learningtolearn/takingnotes_spider_espa.html.

Try this brainstorming exercise. Clear away any textbooks, lecture notes, etc. and sit down with a blank piece of paper. Write down (in note form) everything that you already know about your chosen topic (including anything that you have found interesting or controversial.) This exercise should serve a dual purpose. Firstly, you may be very surprised at the amount of knowledge you already possess and secondly, it may also help to highlight those areas where you need to do some initial or more in-depth research.

Brainstorming or mind-mapping will probably take an hour or so but you will find that it will help you to draw up a 'plan of action' (otherwise referred to as the 'research strategy').

In planning your research strategy, ask yourself the following questions:

- Has this activity highlighted uncertainties or gaps where I need to do some further research?
- How am I going to obtain this information?

Whilst the brainstorming techniques referred to above are designed to stimulate avenues of thought, they can often produce more radical consequences. For example, it may become apparent that your chosen area is too concise, vague, or has too many dimensions and would therefore lack focus. The brainstorming exercise may reveal that one particular aspect of the topic deserves to be investigated above all others. Although these effects could result in the need for a comprehensive rethink of your research proposal, it is better for this to take place at the beginning of your work rather than halfway through it.

Once you have decided upon the actual topic, you will need to focus on exactly what you are aiming to do. You can do this by stating your dissertation topic and then considering whether any of the following 'action verbs', (analyse, assess, review, evaluate, discuss, explore, compare) would indicate to your readers exactly what you are setting out to do in the dissertation. You can then incorporate the appropriate verb into your dissertation title.

A word of caution. It is a fact that there is a considerable amount of work being conducted and published into how people actually *experience* the law. This commonly goes under the heading of 'sociolegal studies'. Before you embark on a dissertation with a strong sociolegal theme, you must check with your supervisor, as to the suitability of this approach – some institutions may prefer a predominantly black-letter approach.

● Identifying the Key Issues and Marginal Issues in Your Dissertation

Once you have an idea for an interesting topic, you will need to plan your research strategy and to do this, you must have some idea at the outset as to the key (or core) and marginal issues. (Be aware that their relative importance may change, or that new issues may arise, as you progress through your research). Remember that until you have decided what you want to gather information on, it is impossible to proceed any further. In this respect, it may help to draw a diagram – similar to a spider diagram discussed above. Firstly, think about the overriding question(s) that you intend to seek the answer(s) to i.e. the key issues. Write this information down in the centre of the page. Then, give some consideration to the focus or direction of your research and how this will determine some of your initial research questions. For example, a dissertation with the title, 'Nullity of Marriage – a Redundant Concept?', would require a detailed analysis of the definition of marriage; an explanation of the law of nullity; an exploration of historical aspects; a chronological overview, and perhaps even a comparative study. These aspects would form the 'spokes' of the spider diagram and the next task would be to add a further 'layer' in the form of any related issues or difficulties that could be envisaged.

It is at this stage that students should be prepared for the unexpected. It may become apparent that marginal issues (considered as not central or important to the main research question) or incidental issues (regarded as having *some* connection with the main research question) warrant investigation. These should not be dismissed in a hurry – they may add further dimensions and depth to your propositions and arguments.

To illustrate, using our example above, a marriage is defined as voidable if at the time of the marriage, the respondent was suffering from venereal disease in a communicable form. (Matrimonial Causes Act 1973 s. 12 (e)). As the correct medical terminology is, at present, 'sexually transmitted disease' (rather than venereal disease), the question may be posed as to whether the interpretation should now encompass HIV. This marginal or incidental issue could then be developed so as to include a comparative view of the position in other jurisdictions.

As regards the identification and incorporation of core and marginal issues, think carefully about the structure of your dissertation. The key (or core) issues should be relatively easy to state, i.e. being the *what* you are attempting to prove and *how* you intend to prove it. These should be highlighted in your introduction. The main body of your text should comprise a critical evaluation or analysis of all the arguments and issues flowing from, and connected to, your core research question – the ultimate aim being to prove your point. The main body will necessarily incorporate both key and marginal issues. The conclusion should show to what extent you feel that your point has been proved, the significance of your findings and also, any further issues which may have arisen (and which were perhaps not in your contemplation when you started the research). This may therefore include references to both core and marginal issues.

● Is the Research Viable in Practice?

One of the most important things you can do is to organise yourself. We will examine this in more detail in the next chapter. At this stage, it is enough to say that you must be realistic about the amount of time you will need to devote to your research. A further issue you will need to consider is whether, from a facilities point of view, you will be able to complete the project that you have in mind. For example, is there enough literature on the subject and is it readily available? Remember that inter-library loan systems are often expensive to use and unfortunately, requests can take some time to fulfil. If you need to carry out empirical research, ask yourself whether this will involve a large number of potential respondents? If so, this will have obvious time-management implications, e.g. in relation to data analysis. Will your research project require the expenditure of money? For example, will it be necessary to provide respondents with 'incentive payments' and if so, have you located sources of funding for this? Furthermore, you will also need to give some consideration to the impact of your research upon potential respondents. This will involve ethical considerations such as the principle of informed consent (ethical considerations are expanded upon in a later chapter). You should always inform respondents of the reasons why you are doing the research and what you intend to do with the results. Depending upon the subject matter of your research, it may be necessary to preserve the anonymity of respondents and to give a guarantee of this. Finally, you will need to consider how, and to which audience(s), you will disseminate your results.

● Putting Pen to Paper

Many of our students have told us that one of the most difficult tasks they faced was actually physically writing the dissertation, i.e. putting pen to paper. Please remember that it is neither possible nor desirable to produce a perfect piece of work at the first attempt. Your final dissertation will be the product of consultations with your supervisor and the reviewing of numerous draft chapters. The advice that we offer to you in this respect is just to write, and not to be too concerned about the standard during the early stages. Your supervisor will guide you in revising your work and we examine their role in relation to this in the next chapter. There are, however, a number of self-help strategies that you can adopt when commencing the process of dissertation writing.

Firstly, attend any preparatory lectures and workshops that your institution may offer. During these you will be given institution-specific advice on how to begin your dissertation, e.g. as regards the availability of computer stations and library facilities. Secondly, it is a fact that dissertation research can be lonely. The establishment of a 'learning community' can help in this respect. Ask your supervisor if the cohort of dissertation students could be allocated a specific room for a period of time per week. You could use this to engage in collaborative learning, i.e. to discuss tactics, problems and progress with your peers.

Finally, the way in which you approach the task of writing a dissertation is key – if you begin by regarding it as a chore, then it will become just that. Instead, try to think of it as a challenge, a vehicle by which you can enhance your transferable skills and improve your job prospects. From this perspective, benefits beyond the immediate dissertation grade become apparent and the potential rewards more plentiful.

● Conclusion

This chapter has reviewed certain of the more practical elements of dissertation writing and provided exercises to assist with this. It has also clarified the meaning of research as a critical and systematic activity of defining, describing and explaining a topic, including identifying various underlying assumptions that are commonly held. This chapter has also provided some guidance concerning the crucial issue of selecting a viable dissertation topic, suggesting that students ask a series of questions concerning their interests in the operation of law. In particular, we propose that students identify issues in law about which they have a particular concern, or find especially controversial.

This chapter has also made a number of suggestions to help you overcome the problem of where to start, including the need to engage in forward planning, scanning government and quality newspaper websites, and reflecting upon the practicalities of conducting empirical or other forms of research. We have also discussed various strategies for identifying 'relevant' issues and research questions, including distinguishing between core and marginal issues, and clarifying what precisely you are attempting to argue and by what particular means. Finally, this chapter has hinted at the importance of drafting, revising and redrafting successive dissertation chapters such that each one eventually becomes an integral part of a single piece of work, rather than a series of independent essays bolted together with no common theme or sense of an unfolding argument. We will examine some of the practicalities of submitting drafts in the next chapter.

2 Getting Along with Your Supervisor

The choice of supervisor is a critical decision because your project will develop according to the supervisor's knowledge and experience. The guidance that every student receives is crucial. I chose my supervisor for two reasons. The first reason is that the subject I was planning to analyse was well known to him and, [the second was that] I was not 'afraid' of the tutor. He had a relaxed but disciplined style. His attitude towards me was exactly as I expected. He gave me straightforward guidelines in order to provide me with a good start.

● Introduction

This chapter continues the theme of addressing preliminary issues, by discussing the obligations and responsibilities of supervisors and supervisees. It also stresses the importance of setting up the supervisory relationship in a manner that best allows a student to get the most out of such guidance. (The title of this chapter may provide a subtle hint as to what can go wrong in the supervisory relationship!) We will endeavour to help you avoid, or if necessary address, problems which can often arise between students and their supervisors. Our aim is to inform and thus empower you. Finally, throughout this chapter we emphasise the correlation between mutual respect, reasonable expectations and a successful relationship. Preparation is the key – forewarned is forearmed.

Initially, we will explore issues relating to the process of *choosing* a supervisor. Many institutions view this activity as a positive aspect of the learning experience – it respects student autonomy and often results in a congenial working relationship. This chapter will then examine the development of the student – supervisor relationship. We will take a look at what you, as a student, can *reasonably* expect from your supervisor throughout the various stages of the dissertation and also (and of equal importance) what a supervisor can reasonably expect from you. We will provide you with some hints and tips on how to ensure that your relationship remains 'productive' and will highlight common problems that can beset the supervisory relationship. To summarise, the overall aim of this chapter is to help you create and maintain an environment in which you can appreciate and benefit from, your supervisor's expertise and guidance. For ease of reference, the chapter is divided into the following sections:

- Choosing your Supervisor
- When to choose
- What can you expect from your supervisor?
- The role of the dissertation supervisor
- Devise your own 'Learning Contract'

- At the beginning of your supervision
- Writing the dissertation
- Meeting your supervisor
- Reviewing draft chapters
- How much supervision?
- Making the most of constructive criticism and formative feedback
- Common problems with supervision

● Choosing Your Supervisor

If your institution allocates appropriate supervisors to its research students, then this section of the chapter will be of no *direct* assistance to you (although you may find some of the material to be of general interest). You may therefore wish to turn directly to the next section, 'What can you expect from your supervisor', which focuses on the dynamics of the supervisee – supervisor relationship and in particular, on mutual expectations and obligations.

We previously highlighted the fact that many institutions encourage their dissertation students to choose, subject to staff specialisms and research interests, their own supervisor. Given the intense nature of the supervisory relationship and the amount of one-to-one contact time (as compared to that experienced in tutorials/lectures) many of our students regarded this as a 'practical' and 'fairer' method of allocation. Furthermore, we have found that supervisory partnerships formed out of mutual agreement, rather than imposition, are more likely to be successful. However, our research did indicate that the 'self-service' process was not always perceived to be a positive experience.

Some of our students regarded the 'choose your own supervisor' procedure as an excess of autonomy. This gave rise to the dilemma of choosing the 'right' supervisor (with negative consequences if the 'wrong' decision was made) and resulted in varying amounts of stress and anxiety. Furthermore, many students would have preferred (and would have had more confidence in) a formal system of allocation organised by the Law School. For example, where a tutor with overall responsibility for research-based modules allocates appropriate supervisors to dissertation students.

In addition, devolving what is commonly regarded as an 'administrative procedure' to students has resource implications and two situations in particular can give rise to 'supply and demand' issues. Firstly, when large numbers of students elect to research popular or topical subjects for which there are a limited number of appropriate and available academic staff and secondly, when 'popular' tutors are inundated with requests to supervise.

In practice, such market forces often result in the imposition of a first-come-first-served system with disappointing consequences for the more 'relaxed' student! In the above situations, the obvious advice is that you should strive to make contact with a suitable supervisor as soon as possible. This could be at the point in time when you make a tentative decision about your research topic and we discussed related issues in Chapter 1.

Having said all this, if you are unable to secure your 'first choice' supervisor, or more worryingly, have problems in engaging a supervisor at all, be aware of the fact that if your department/faculty has registered your enrolment for a dissertation or has accepted your research proposal as a viable proposition, it is ultimately their responsibility to ensure that you receive appropriate supervision. If you encounter any problems in this respect, make contact with a member of academic staff with responsibility for research modules/programmes, as soon as possible.

The quotation at the beginning of this chapter was provided by a student who had given a fair amount of consideration to the choice of supervisor and perhaps as a result, was satisfied with the working relationship. In this context, you can give yourself a head start by setting out the criteria which will govern your choice of supervisor. You can then match this against the appropriate and available teaching staff. This may sound rather clinical and calculating but it is worth noting that our research indicated a strong correlation between the securing of a 'suitable' supervisor and the standard of, and the final grade achieved by, the completed dissertation.

When thinking about your choice of supervisor, there are a number of issues that you may wish to consider and perhaps prioritise. Clearly, your supervisor should have some connection with the subject area in which your proposal is grounded. However, in saying that, many tutors are happy to supervise a dissertation whose topic or theme is linked to their general area of specialism but which is based on an argument, question or issue that they have not necessarily researched, taught or even considered before. Indeed, many tutors find that a ground-breaking research proposal can result in an extremely interesting and stimulating supervision experience.

Detracting somewhat from the topic of choosing your own supervisor, it follows from the above that you should endeavour to be original and innovative in your preliminary ideas and proposals. Avoid topics that are 'stagnant' (with little or no development) or 'stale' (as a result of extensive reworking within academic literature.) It can be much harder for a student to write anything unique or even interesting about an over-researched topic, as compared to a topic that has received little attention within the academic literature. Giving careful consideration in your research proposal to its potential for originality and creativity will give your tutor some indication of your evaluative and analytical skills. It will also convey the degree of your commitment to the dissertation research. Furthermore, credit (in the form of marks) is often attributed to criteria such as the ability to formulate inventive and novel proposals.

When choosing your supervisor, it is important to remember that you will be relying on their skills and experience in research and in providing guidance to previous dissertation students. Further criteria you may wish to consider can include their teaching and research interests, publication record and the amount and level of their supervision experience. All of the above would seem to indicate that students should gravitate towards more established members of the academic staff. We should stress that newly appointed tutors with a limited publication or supervision record can be imaginative, committed and enthusiastic dissertation supervisors. One of the more reliable indicators of a potentially successful supervisory experience is the enthusiasm with which your prospective supervisor discusses the issues arising from your research proposal.

In our research, students placed varying amounts of emphasis on choosing the 'right' supervisor for them. This was often achieved by a process of elimination, focusing initially on identifying a person with appropriate subject expertise and knowledge, and then adding additional (and often unquantifiable subjective) criteria such as, 'one who also had a "comforting" yet "directive" manner of conducting supervision'.

Choose your supervisor carefully. It makes a huge difference (comparing my experience to that of friends doing a dissertation). I chose my supervisor because of her strength in the subject. I am sure that other students who do the same will agree that this is advantageous rather than choosing a tutor who has general knowledge of the subject but chosen because they are your favourite lecturer!

Forming a good relationship with your supervisor is the key to the successful (in terms of the grade achieved and the educational experience) completion of your dissertation.

'Compatibility', defined in terms of feeling, 'comfortable' with a supervisor's personal characteristics and qualities, was highlighted in many responses to our research. Some of our students referred to an 'affable personality' and 'good reputation' when listing criteria which governed their choice of supervisor. Various adjectives were used to describe the desirable personality traits of a potential supervisor, i.e. that they should be, 'agreeable', 'directive', 'helpful' and (interestingly) 'controlling'.

In her research, Hampson[1] asked students to *rank* factors which were 'influential' in their choice of supervisor:

- Genuine shared interest (in the research topic)   84%
- Academic expertise (specific to the research topic)   68%
- Enthusiasm   64%
- Past experience of a good working relationship   60%
- Empathy   48%
- Shared socio-political views   44%
- Interpersonal/communication skills   40%

Hampson[2] provided direct quotations from her students. Some of these are reproduced below so as to give you a further indication as to the thought processes which can direct a student's choice of a supervisor.

I think it is crucial to have had contact with a supervisor before starting a dissertation, i.e. discussion of other assignments, collaboration in seminars and probably some contact socially.

I was impressed by her ability to criticise without offending, i.e. to encourage rather than put down, i.e. confidence-building.

He shares my belief that creativity, originality and deep thinking are more important than regurgitating other people's opinions.

Personality is crucial – far more than expertise in the topic area.

I had the supervisor who was an expert on my topic and furthermore, (luckily enough) she was extremely supportive, patient and understanding.

I liked the fact that he did not try to structure it for me – I was given a lot of freedom – suggestions were only given when asked.

---

[1]L. Hampson, 'How's Your Dissertation Going?' (Unit for Innovation in Higher Education, School of Independent Studies, Lancaster University: 1994) at page 37.
[2]*Ibid.*

Given the diversity of criteria highlighted above, it is perhaps not surprising that our empirical research revealed that many students were undecided, and moreover anxious, about the range and hierarchy of criteria that they should consider when choosing a supervisor. Some of our students stated that their main concern was the ability to 'get on' with a supervisor, whereas others felt that this aspect of the relationship was secondary to the level of their supervisor's knowledge. Indeed, some students felt that personal familiarity would be counterproductive in terms of their need to adhere to a hierarchy and to 'respect' the supervisor.

Whether, or to what extent, you regard factors such as 'personality', to be relevant in your choice of supervisor, you should reflect upon two related and fundamental issues. Firstly, that in order for your work to develop, you will need to be able to communicate, exchange ideas and defend propositions, with your supervisor. Secondly, that the supervisory relationship will be more intense, particularly in terms of workload and duration, than that which you may have had with a seminar tutor or lecturer.

You should also give some consideration to the amount of contact time that your prospective supervisor will be able or prepared to offer. In this respect, it might be helpful to ask the following questions:

- Is my prospective supervisor scheduled to be away on sabbatical leave during the period in which I will be researching and writing up?
- Does my prospective supervisor have any time-consuming or complex administration responsibilities such as a Course Leadership which may limit their availability time?
- Does my prospective supervisor have extensive obligations outside of the institution, for example in legal practice?

Such responsibilities and commitments do not necessarily preclude or affect the standard of dissertation supervision, but it may be sensible to ask a tutor who may be affected by any of the above, what they regard as reasonable in terms of the frequency and duration of supervisory appointments. You will then be in a position to decide whether you consider this to be sufficient for your needs.

To sum up, in choosing your supervisor, you should give some consideration to the following factors:

- their personal qualities and reputation (these will necessarily be evaluated on a subjective basis);
- scheduled periods of time away from the institution;
- their availability time;
- their subject knowledge and teaching interests (as an indicator of expertise);
- their past and current supervision experience (as an indicator of expertise);
- their current supervisory obligations (as an indicator of available time).

● When to Choose

You need to approach a potential supervisor at the earliest possible opportunity. As regards undergraduate students, we suggest that you make contact at the end of the academic year preceding the registration of your dissertation, i.e. in June or July. As highlighted above, tutors have a range of commitments including teaching, marking, researching and administration. As a result, some tutors can offer limited amounts of time and consequently are in a position where they can efficiently supervise only a limited number of dissertations. Tutors may therefore decide to offer supervision on a first-come-first-served basis. It is also worth bearing in mind that an established tutor may have more dissertations to support than a newly appointed member of staff. The former may have more experience but less time, whereas a newer member of staff may have less experience but perhaps more time to devote to your dissertation.

At the preliminary meeting you should be prepared to discuss your proposal with commitment and enthusiasm. There is no point approaching a prospective supervisor if you are unprepared, i.e. with a vague or unfocused idea which you can only articulate in very general terms. Evaluate a provisional subject in terms of its viability and scope before you approach a tutor. Write your ideas down and be as detailed as possible, ideally providing an overview of the topic together with a logical sequence for the research process, i.e. *what* you want to examine, *why* you want to examine it and *how* you intend to examine it. Acknowledge that these ideas will be developed and may alter as you progress through the dissertation. Highlight any areas where you anticipate difficulties, e.g. in relation to any empirical research you may wish to carry out. You can then present this abstract to your potential supervisor. It is likely that they will greatly appreciate, and may be more inclined to supervise, a student who presents a well reasoned and comprehensive research proposal.

> I e-mailed several lecturers in order to find a dissertation supervisor. One lecturer advised me to do more preliminary research and to return when I had more of an idea of what I wanted to do.

● What Can You Expect from Your Supervisor?

Our research revealed a great variation in the amount of contact time offered to students and also in the degree of satisfaction with the supervision process. Many students indicated that in their opinion, the key to the successful completion of their dissertation was an 'active' form of supervision. This necessarily requires contributions from both parties on a regular basis:

> My research skills have improved tremendously as well as my writing and the ability to pick out the important information. I had weekly appointments with my supervisor and the help and guidance that I received from my supervisor in this respect was invaluable.

> This module has proved most interesting as it has made me look for a far wider range of sources than other modules. There is also a higher degree of self-discipline required than with more structured modules so this module is more challenging but also more fulfilling. The guidance, encouragement and support in the supervision have helped me to achieve this.

The amount and quality of input from your supervisor can undoubtedly help to make your experience of dissertation writing a fulfilling learning activity (as opposed to a monotonous and stressful chore!) However, in many respects, this is a two-way process and your supervisor will not want you to passively accept feedback – you will be expected to reflect upon, and if appropriate defend, your propositions. In many respects, it is *your* management and expectations of the student–supervisor relationship which are likely to be key to the success of your dissertation.

● The Role of the Dissertation Supervisor

At this stage (and in preparation for the next section), consider and then commit to paper, some initial thoughts on:

● what in your opinion is the role of a dissertation supervisor, and

● what you expect your supervisor to do for you.

We should stress that supervision is a very individual experience. Some students find that they require very little in terms of support whereas others consider weekly contact to be beneficial. You may feel confident with a minimal amount of contact and a low-key level of supervision. However, it is important to bear in mind that your supervisor will know exactly what is required in terms of meeting the assessment criteria and thus obtaining a pass/distinction. Consequently, you should ensure that your supervisor periodically receives drafts of your work so that formative feedback can be given to you on a regular basis.

Question: What are my expectations of the student – supervisor relationship?
....

Once you have focused on what you expect from the relationship with your supervisor, it is time to declare this in a more formal way, i.e. to draw up a learning contract.

● Devise Your Own 'Learning Contract'

Misunderstandings can blight a supervisory relationship. A 'learning contract' can help in this respect. Problems can be anticipated in advance and if necessary, the contract can be used as the basis for mediation. Such a document provides opportunities for both parties to clearly define their roles. In the context of a dissertation, a learning contract is quite simply a statement of mutual expectations, i.e. what you expect from your supervisor and what your supervisor expects from you. Most tutors will encourage you to take an interest, and an active role, in the way in which the supervision is to be conducted. Indeed, many tutors regard negotiation as to ground rules governing the supervision process to be an integral part of the supervision process. You may feel that such obligations are obvious to both parties and do not require clarification. However, our research suggested that a major source of discontent for some students was the perceived failure of supervisors and supervisees to meet each others' unspecified, but assumed, expectations.

A learning contract will provide both the supervisor and supervisee with a foundation on which to set out the boundaries and characteristics of their relationship. If you decide to draw up such a document you may wish to include guidance on:

- The **type of advice** that you expect your supervisor to offer. For example, relating to the topic, study skills, research skills, adoption and application of method and methodology and writing skills.
- The **extent of that advice**. For example, in-depth advice on the subject and how it is best studied and written about (methodology).
- **Expectations as to availability**. For example, as to the frequency (e.g. perhaps one meeting every two weeks) and the duration (e.g. 30 minutes per appointment) of contact.
- **Mutually convenient contact arrangements**. For example by telephone, e-mail or face to face.
- **A provisional schedule for the production of draft chapters**.
- **A provisional schedule for the return of feedback**.

It is important to remember that the supervisory relationship is not all one-way traffic. As you have expectations of your supervisor, he/she will have expectations of you. For example, you will be expected to:

- turn up to, and be prepared for, pre-arranged meetings;
- adhere to any agreed timetable for the production of drafts;
- be enthusiastic about, and committed to, your work;
- be aware of your supervisor's other commitments and not to expect advice on tap, e.g. an *immediate* reply to an e-mail;
- keep your supervisor informed as to your progress and any difficulties you may experience;
- be honest about your level of understanding and, if you require help, to ask;
- accept responsibility for the progress of your research and ultimately for your own success or failure.

Given the above, you are now in a position to construct your version of an appropriate learning contract.

Learning Contract

Title of Dissertation

Name of Student
Expectations

....
....
....

▶

Name of Supervisor
Expectations

....
....
....
....
....

You may find it helpful to take a copy of this pro-forma contract along to the first meeting with your supervisor. It can then be used as a basis for negotiating the supervision process.

● At the Beginning of Your Supervision

Our research indicated that at the beginning of their research, many students felt 'lost', i.e. they did not know where to start. Whilst you can expect some guidance in the *development* of your ideas, it is not your supervisor's role to choose the subject area, or the focus of the research, for you. In saying that, your supervisor should be able to advise you on whether your research proposal is:

● too broad or too narrow in terms of focus;

● viable, e.g. is it 'doable' in terms of time and/or research methodology;

● researchable, e.g. will it be difficult/possible to locate relevant source materials;

● interesting and whether it has the potential to establish original ideas/propositions.

During your initial meetings, your supervisor will also discuss appropriate research methodology and we will examine this topic in depth in the following chapters. Supervisors should also be able to help you to formulate and clarify your research questions, and point you in the right direction as regards initial reading materials. Our dissertation students offered the following insights into beginning dissertation research:

> After I had explained to my supervisor my aims, he said that I must change my subject because it was a massive area and that I should be very specific. The choice he offered me was to either forget all about the original topic or just narrow it down to a concrete area. I decided to follow the first option although that rendered my whole research to date useless. It was rather devastating when I realised that I must disregard everything I had in my mind until then. I was mourning for my lost work, I felt insecure in an area totally new to me and my confidence had abandoned me. This was a very counterproductive period.

> I drew up a timetable and started searching for information on the first chapter. At the beginning I was confused about what kind of structure the first chapter should have. After looking at many books, I decided to first collect all my materials, read them and then make a plan of what to write.

> I changed my plan umpteen times before starting my dissertation. I think I was just putting it off - too scared to start.

To be honest, I did not know where to start looking and the efforts I made did not seem to be useful. I tried looking on the net but maybe I wasn't looking in the right place. I had no luck so I went to see my supervisor.

At this stage, ask your supervisor for clarification as to what the department/institution requires from a dissertation, i.e. the skills and abilities that should be in evidence. These are often stated in the course handbook or the module descriptor under the heading 'marking' or 'assessment criteria'. Bear in mind that the extent to which you meet this criterion will ultimately determine the grade that you achieve. Finally, before commencing your dissertation, ask your supervisor if there is any generic research advice available. Many institutions offer introductory workshops, lectures in research methodology and research support groups. In our experience, students have found these to be extremely helpful.

● Writing the Dissertation

A fundamental point worth restating is that it is not your supervisor's role to write the dissertation for you. As the dissertation evolves, many students and indeed supervisors experience problems in this respect. Supervisors often feel that there is a fine line between giving 'advice', and students requesting 'help' which when received is then construed as material which can be legitimately copied into a dissertation in a word-for-word manner. In short, you can expect your supervisor to guide and advise you through the process of developing and revising your dissertation. However, responsibility for, and 'ownership' of, the dissertation (including researching, choosing a methodological position that is appropriate, and writing up) remains with you.

● Meeting Your Supervisor

The amount and quality of a supervisor's availability time can be a source of frustration. It is simply not realistic (nor is it fair) to expect your supervisor to be on hand whenever you encounter a crisis relating to your dissertation. Equally, when you have a pre-arranged appointment it is reasonable to expect your supervisor to earmark that time exclusively for discussing your work. The most effective way of avoiding misunderstandings and capitalising on availability time is, at your first meeting, to draw up a provisional list of times and dates for future appointments. Insert these into your diary or organiser. It will help if you can give these sessions a focus, e.g. by scheduling the targets which you hope to meet at specific times of the year. This will also serve as a source of motivation – you will have a series of meetings to attend with set goals to achieve.

Before attending an appointment with your supervisor, make a note of any problems that you have encountered since your last meeting, any issues you wish to discuss and any queries you may have. Unfortunately, once the meeting has started, it is all too easy to forget these points or become sidetracked or engrossed in another (sometimes unrelated) topic. Of course, you can always e-mail your tutor after a meeting but try not to rely on this form of communication too heavily. From the tutor's perspective, it is difficult to give *advice* via e-mail. This is because there is a limit to which this is an effective medium through which a tutor can *explain* issues and *check* your understanding. On the other hand, face-to-face meetings can be very productive, giving you the opportunity to delve further into issues, and to ask for immediate clarification if you find something to be confusing. You may find it helpful to take notes of the main points discussed at the supervision meetings and most tutors will be happy for you to do this. These notes may prove to be invaluable once you have left the meeting.

Another way of making the most of these meetings is to e-mail your supervisor a few days in advance of the appointment with a list of queries or problems you may have. This will give your supervisor the opportunity to investigate any issues that you have raised, thus saving time and resulting in a more productive meeting. However, be reasonable in your advance requests, e.g. do not expect your supervisor to do the research for you.

Always be on time! Time management was an issue that was highlighted throughout our research. This advice relates to pre-arranged appointments with your supervisor and also to the submission of draft chapters and other work. Supervisors can help you to adhere to a timetable (culminating in the 'on time' submission of your dissertation) by regularly reviewing your work. However, at this advanced stage of your academic career, your supervisor is not responsible for chasing you up if you happen to miss deadlines.

A word of warning: it is all too easy to allow deadlines to slip. This can result in a great deal of unnecessary stress and, moreover, a finished dissertation which perhaps is far from what you initially envisaged. You must factor other work commitments into your timetable, including seminar preparation and examination revision. Also, incorporate a contingency plan in case you are ill or encounter a domestic crisis, and thus find that you are unable to work for a few weeks. In other words, try to consider all eventualities and leave yourself some space in which to manoeuvre should this become necessary.

On a serious note, life is unpredictable and unfortunately you may experience difficulties which seriously affect your ability to study. Make sure that you report these to the relevant person in your department/faculty. This may be your personal tutor, pastoral care tutor or your dissertation supervisor. Tutors will respect and protect confidentiality in such situations. Most institutions have an 'extenuating circumstances' procedure and committee which considers, and responds to, the effects that such problems may have had upon your ability to complete your studies. The following quotations illustrate some of the difficulties that can arise. It should be noted that poor time management does not qualify as an 'extenuating circumstance'.

> I left my work to the last minute and was just getting it finished when I became ill, which resulted in the dissertation being three weeks late. I am very disappointed with this situation.

> I am finding it very difficult to get time for my dissertation. Having not done any in a while, it is difficult to get the enthusiasm back for it. Just realised that the deadline is in three months; I know the worst thing I could do is panic but I am starting to. The time plan I devised with my supervisor has also gone out of the window.

> I am happy with the result for the amount of time and effort that I have put in. I would have liked to have spent more time on it but couldn't since I had other courseworks to do. What I would have done differently is to allocate the amount of time I spent on my project at different times of the year; I would have liked it to be more constant rather than doing half at the start of the year and half at the other end.

● Reviewing Draft Chapters

The importance of draft chapters cannot be underestimated. They are the 'stepping stones' of your dissertation. When reviewed and amended (if and where necessary), each successive draft will bring you closer to the finished article. When we refer to a 'draft' chapter we do not mean a succession of rough notes but, rather, a piece of work which is properly referenced with appropriate authorities and citations, i.e. a chapter in its initial stages of development.

Draft chapters give your supervisor the opportunity to gauge your progress and in this respect, these pieces of work will help you to keep to a realistic work schedule. At this stage of your academic career, your supervisor can legitimately expect you to manage your workload in an efficient manner and this includes handing in draft chapters on time. If you find yourself in the situation where you are hiding furtively around corners so as to avoid your supervisor, then this should indicate to you that something is seriously amiss! Assuming that you do hand in drafts on time, the benefits are various. Once your supervisor has reviewed your work, feedback can be given which may include general study support, assistance in understanding research methodology, advice regarding presentation and specific guidance on the legal area(s) in question.

In the same context, there is absolutely no point in approaching your supervisor when you have nothing tangible to present. Engaging in stimulating conversations with your supervisor about *intentions* for your work can be enjoyable but at the end of the day, such exchanges will not contribute towards your final mark. Nor will moaning about the course, the weather, or any unforeseen and catastrophic circumstances which have prevented you from writing anything down! At the end of the day, words on paper are what count.

● How Much Supervision?

Students often ask, 'How much supervision will I need?' and, moreover, 'How much can I reasonably expect?' In answering these questions, a useful starting point will be the clarification of the term 'supervision' as used in the context of dissertation supervision. Whilst the dictionary definition provides us with a useful starting point, i.e. 'to direct or oversee the performance or operation of', this statement is somewhat vague. You need to know exactly what activities the word 'supervise' will encompass, so as to be able to quantify the amount of support you may need. Firstly, you can expect your supervisor to provide you with academic support relating to your particular subject and to your research activities. Supervisors will therefore provide advice on locating relevant sources, on legal writing and on presentation. Secondly, as stated above, supervisors will provide you with regular and constructive feedback on draft chapters. Thirdly, by requiring you to devise, and then adhere to, a realistic timetable with periodic deadlines for the submission of draft chapters, they will (albeit indirectly) motivate you.

In order to estimate the amount of contact time you will need, give some consideration to your strengths and weaknesses in respect of the activities mentioned in the previous paragraph. It may help if you write this information down, perhaps using appropriately headed columns, e.g. 'no input required', 'some input required' 'major input required'. This exercise should provide you with some indication as to the amount, and the type of, assistance you will need from your supervisor. Having done this, you should now be in a better position to answer the question posed at the beginning of this section and to make your supervisor aware of your specific needs.

We have previously highlighted the fact that supervision is a very individual experience. In our research, students reported different models and varying amounts of supervision:

> Instead of running around trying to look for my supervisor, I would have pre-booked certain dates (like seminars). I would have liked to have been given targets for my chapters so that I would have stayed motivated. This way both student and supervisor know exactly where they stand and any problems can be resolved immediately instead of trying to sort everything out at the end (which is what happened to me) and then the pressure gets too much.

> My problem was that it was difficult to get hold of my supervisor – sometimes he was ill or away from the University and there was no-one I could turn to.

> I felt very much like it was sink or swim at first. Horror stories from past students tend to reinforce how hard it will be. Issues about who will be the best tutor, which topic to choose and what is expected of you. I saw my supervisor on a few occasions but it was hard to hand work in on time. Perhaps a system could evolve whereby postgraduate students could act as mentors for a couple of months – to act as sounding boards.

Ultimately, the relationship that you develop with your supervisor will be unique. Some students will require more support and advice than others. It is therefore impossible for us to be too prescriptive in terms of quantifying an appropriate amount of supervision. In our experience, in order to achieve the optimum level of supervision, it is best to agree a timetable of regular meetings at the outset. If these turn out to be excessive, you can always cancel *ahead* of time. If, on the other hand, you find that you require assistance between meetings, then e-mail your supervisor requesting additional contact time. However, be aware that this person will have other academic commitments and may not be able to see you at *very short notice*.

● Making the Most of Constructive Criticism and Formative Feedback

Your supervisor will critically review your work. This is one of the supervisor's key functions. This activity is often referred to as the provision of 'constructive criticism' or 'formative feedback'. It is important for you to understand what these phrases actually mean.

> **Constructive** has been defined as, 'helping to improve; promoting development', and **criticism** as, 'the analysis or evaluation of a work of art or literature'.[3]

> **Formative** has been defined as, 'of or relating to formation, development or growth', and **feedback** as, 'to offer or suggest information, ideas in reaction to an enquiry'.[4]

---

[3]*Collins Softback English Dictionary*. New York: Harper Collins (1991).
[4]*Ibid.*

'Constructive criticism' and 'formative feedback' are therefore phrases that are used within academic circles to signify a critical appraisal of your work which is intended to bring about positive improvements. When on the receiving end of such comments, always try to bear in mind that your supervisor will have the benefit of substantial subject knowledge. He/she will also have experience in writing research-based materials and of supervising dissertations. Your supervisor will expect you to think about the issues raised in the feedback, to discuss them and, where appropriate, to defend your arguments and propositions. This process of consideration, reflection, evaluation and negotiation is a vital part of the learning experience and is often the impetus for the formation of new ideas and avenues of research. Indeed, the ability to reassess your own work critically is key to dissertation construction and is also a valuable professional and personal skill.

As highlighted above, your supervisor is in a position to help you develop and refine the academic content and the presentation of your dissertation. The only way in which they can achieve this is by reviewing critically the content, style and methodological assumptions of your draft chapters. Nevertheless, many students find it difficult to embrace the critical aspect of the supervisory relationship, and this is perfectly understandable. Ownership of your work can become emotionally charged. You may feel extremely possessive, and indeed protective, of your research. Consider, for example, the following quotation:

> Submitting my dissertation to the Law School office seemed like sending my child off to school for the first time.

Such emotions can lead to defensiveness in the face of perceived criticism. The worst case scenario is that such feedback can be 'taken personally'. Your supervisor may be aware of the possibility of this occurring and may therefore be prepared (having probably experienced similar feelings with respect to their own research.)

Once you have received feedback, try to handle any perceived criticism in a calm and reflective manner. An instinctive reaction is to feel hurt and uncomfortable and to retaliate in a defensive, and perhaps even (mildly) hostile, manner. Focus on the fact that the feedback is not intended as a personal attack on your academic integrity but rather, as an objective observation, provided in a professional capacity. Make sure that you have fully understood the implications of what your supervisor is saying. If you do not understand, do not agree, or do not feel that the comments are helpful, warranted or indeed valid, then get back to your supervisor for clarification. Most supervisors will be happy to engage in a debate which is based on a careful assessment of the issues, rather than having to respond to an emotional and reactive outburst. If you do feel upset then the best strategy is to give yourself some time and space to reflect upon what was said.

The feedback you receive may take various forms, e.g. a very detailed commentary, or the highlighting of a particular word, phrase or paragraph in your text. Your supervisor may be economical with comments, assuming that you will instinctively know what action to take. If you are unsure about any aspect of the feedback, ask for clarification. You may feel that the manner, format or tone in which your supervisor gives the feedback is antagonistic. This may be intentional. Supervisors often play the role of 'devil's advocate', as a way of provoking you into considering other avenues of thought or possible replies. These responses could perhaps strengthen your position by providing alternative arguments which further justify your underlying assumptions.

The degree to which you incorporate any feedback into your work is ultimately your decision. Remember that you can respond *selectively* to feedback or, indeed, not at all. Whatever you decide, your supervisor will probably welcome an opportunity to discuss the decision with you. In the same context, you should not take the comments away and include them verbatim into your work – this would amount to the supervisor rewriting the project for you and this is not the intended outcome of formative feedback or constructive criticism. The intention behind the provision of feedback is to bring about positive improvements in your work. It is extremely important for you to be able to deal with any critique and move on. Do not allow it to cloud your future work or affect the dynamics of your relationship with your supervisor. Reflect upon the comments in a considered manner and decide whether it is appropriate to incorporate the *essence* of the feedback into your work.

Students sometimes seem unsure as to the exact meaning of their supervisor's feedback and, in our experience, some comments do require translation! Here are a few examples with possible interpretations:

'Raises some very interesting and thought provoking ideas but these are not always followed through.' The draft requires more in-depth and critical analysis of the issues and perhaps further research.

'Clear evidence of research and reference to a variety of sources although over-reliance on these sources.' The student has engaged in a great deal of research, in the sense of gathering factual information. However, the work to date does not reveal any consideration or analysis of the issues raised by the research and, as a consequence, there is a lack of evaluation and little evidence of any depth of understanding.

'A good descriptive account of the legislation but lacks analytical depth.' A fair amount of reading and research has been carried out but the result is superficial and lacks depth of analysis and critical evaluation.

'Some serious problems with the use of source materials and referencing – quotations need to be clearly placed within quotation marks and referenced fully. Serious problems with the use of commas and apostrophes.' A large number of spelling and grammatical errors are present. Inadequate referencing throughout which, at best, amounts to unacceptable presentation and, at worst, a deliberate attempt to plagiarise, in the sense of claiming credit for the ideas of another.

'This lacks focus and the structure is poorly presented. It is just a long rambling piece with no clear aim. The bibliography is very thin.' The work lacks evidence of clear planning, it requires an introduction, a main body of text with arguments and a conclusion. Ideas are poorly articulated, there are no links between the paragraphs, no hypothesis, and a serious lack of evidence of thorough reading and other research.

● Common Problems with Supervision

The title of this chapter gave a hint as to the problems that students and their supervisors may encounter. Below, we have provided some of the areas of discontent that are most often raised, to which we have added some possible *constructive* responses:

Problem: A lack of supervisor's availability time, including disagreements over demands for appointments at short notice.

Solution: Agree and adhere to a timetable of appointments.

Problem: Insufficient advice and help given. Tutors often face the dilemma of encouraging autonomy and self-directed learning by giving students the space and opportunity to develop their own research in their own way. However, this can be perceived as a failure to provide support and direction.

Solution: Be honest with your supervisor about the amount and depth of advice required. Your supervisor may not agree to your requests but at least there will be no misunderstandings or resentment.

Problem: Students feeling that they have lost control of their dissertation. A situation can occur whereby a supervisor provides too much direction. At best, this can create a culture of dependency on behalf of the student and, at worst, resentment at the rigidity and volume of supervision.

Solution: As above, be honest with your supervisor.

Problem: Students getting behind with their work and expecting the supervisor to be able to sort this out.

Solution: Time management is the key to successful completion of your dissertation and of being able to submit on or before the deadline. Create a realistic work schedule with some manoeuvrability built in. Stick rigidly to that schedule.

Problem: Ineffective and inefficient use of contact time.

Solution: Keep your relationship strictly on a dissertation supervision basis. Leave other issues, such as personal problems and dissatisfaction with other elements of the course, to appropriate venues.

Problem: Feedback taking too long to obtain.

Solution: Always ensure that you give your supervisor draft chapters on time. It is unfair and unrealistic to hand in a draft chapter and expect formative feedback and advice within a few days. Agree a timetable for the return of feedback.

● Conclusion

It is vital to take active measures to make sure that your relationship with your supervisor operates in a way that is as helpful as possible. This requires both sides to respect certain basic ground rules from the start and throughout, not least with respect to the timely submission of work to an agreed schedule. The idea of developing a learning contract may prove particularly helpful in this respect. It is vital to map out the aims and purpose of the dissertation at the start, and to see how each draft chapter (and its multiple revisions) enhances, in a clear and express way, the overall argument your project is trying to make. You should always submit work that, although not perfect, is certainly presentable in terms of basic spelling and grammar, and which demonstrates that you have been able to react in a positive way to your supervisor's constructive comments and feedback generally.

To sum up we would argue that there are four main points worth bearing in mind:

1. If relevant, give careful thought to your *choice* of supervisor.
2. Negotiate your working relationship and formalise this in writing.
3. Be honest with your supervisor – concerning your level of understanding and concerning the amount of work you have done.
4. Take personal responsibility for your own success or failure.

3 Selecting Suitable Approaches to the Conduct of Dissertation Research

● Introduction

Our experience has been that undergraduate and postgraduate students need to over-come a measure of ingrained resistance to discussing *different ways* of conducting their dissertation research (i.e. academic research methodologies). Perhaps this resistance stems from the fact that, unlike most social science and humanities programmes, under-graduate law degrees rarely tackle the pros and cons of different research methodologies. However, once initial unfamiliarity and reluctance has been overcome, law students are more than able to address this important topic in an intelligent way that enhances both the quality and rigour of their work. In addition, this chapter suggests that dissertation students will inevitably have to apply *their own* interpretation of the meaning and purpose of 'research'. Student dissertations can only be improved by reflecting critically upon, and then justifying explicitly, the appropriateness of their methodologies for the disser-tation questions and topic. We raise the question of the advantages and disadvantages of deploying each of the available methodologies, as well as various possible combinations of the different approaches discussed in this book.

● Resistance to Methodological Discussion

Our experience of teaching methodology modules at both postgraduate and under-graduate levels has suggested that students are sometimes reluctant to engage in methodological discussions. A frequent response from students is that 'We have already learned sufficient about legal research methods in our first year of legal studies, and now need to expand our studies of *substantive subjects*, rather than be subjected to yet another "skills module".' However, this response confuses questions over the selection of appropriate research methodologies with technical 'legal methods' defined as com-petence in basic library skills, such as identifying relevant case and statute law, the use of electronic databases and library catalogues.

Such competences and skills are, of course, important to the task of locating and gather-ing library materials. However, other research methodologies insist that the focus of legal research, particularly at third-year-undergraduate or LLM levels, should fall upon the meaning of the subjective lived-experience of those who are most directly affected by the legal process in question. For example, an employment law dissertation written from an experiential or phenomenological perspective could address the experiences of, for example, both disabled persons and employers in relation to the theme of the perceived effectiveness of current disability discrimination measures. If a law student adopts such an experiential approach on the basis that this methodology is the only approach that is able to realise the objectives and goals of his or her dissertation, then 'research methods' will not involve providing commentary on sources located in law libraries at all. On the contrary, the required methodology will involve the researcher in arranging and conducting a series of semi-structured interviews with a sample of affected parties. Furthermore, such investigation may need to be supplemented by a period of 'participant observation'. Here, researchers immerse themselves in the subculture of the research subjects in order to be able to empathise with, and thereby better understand, their experiences of being affected, in various ways, by legal measures addressed by the dissertation. In other words, it is simply false to assume that questions of selecting an appropriate research methodology for a student dissertation are little more than a refinement of basic legal methods regarding accessing and using law library materials.

Faced with occasional and sometimes frequent resistance to methodological discussion within the internal culture of traditional law schools, it can be useful for dissertation students to reflect upon their experience of assessing the pros and cons of the particular approach or approaches which they have *previously deployed* to conduct their research for essays and projects, and the reasons why they have chosen to select *these* rather than an alternative approach. A common, but hardly sufficient, response is that: 'of course we know that there are a number of ways of doing legal research but this is not an issue that should be studied as a topic in its own right.' Instead, it is more a question of picking up research skills as one goes along, of 'learning the ropes' without any need to engage seriously in any process of systematic study and evaluation of the appropriateness of various methodologies for different types of research project.

All too frequently, however, the resistance to an open-minded comparison of the nature, strengths and limits of different approaches to the conduct of legal research, i.e. methodologies, is not based upon reasoned argument. Instead, it too often stems from an unthinking adherence to a single approach for conducting research (often but not always a black-letter approach) that has, over a period of time, become an unacknowledged but entrenched commitment, even prejudice. This may be particularly true where students have previously attained reasonable grades in earlier courseworks that deployed this approach. The resistance may, therefore, stem from students' reluctance to examine alternatives to an approach to the conduct of research that apparently is already tried and tested by its success on other earlier taught modules.

Another source of resistance to entering into a process of explicit methodological discussion can stem from the fact that the academic literature on many substantive law subjects rarely contains debate of the appropriateness, strengths and limits of different methodologies for conducting research in their specific field. This remains the case even in those subjects for which there are specialist academic journals devoted to publishing the results of legal research. For example, there are few articles in journals devoted to publishing academic research in property and environmental law that address methodological issues. This general trend, to which there are notable exceptions including both sociolegal studies, and, to a lesser extent, comparative approaches to law and contextual forms of legal history, sets the discipline of law apart from most other social sciences and natural sciences. University level courses on educational studies, sociology and psychology will nearly always include compulsory modules devoted to research methods. Here, the students' acquisition of competence in these different methods, and in debates regarding the selection of the most appropriate approach for different types of project, is often valued most highly as a learning outcome. The effect will generally mean that the supervisors of dissertations within the social sciences would themselves have had to address methodological debates during the course of their own previous (or continuing) academic studies. It is, therefore, understandable if such supervisors continue to impose this expectation upon their supervisees.

The fact that, almost uniquely amongst the social sciences, sciences and the humanities, possession of a postgraduate research degree at MPhil and PhD levels has not traditionally operated as a precondition for gaining full-time permanent lectureships in law schools has, in all likelihood, aggravated the difficulties of engaging with the serious study of research methodologies. (This point can be confirmed by checking the titles of law lecturers.) Many law students are supervised by academic staff who have not themselves successfully completed a more ambitious academic project than that which they are now supervising. In extreme cases, the supervisor may have never completed even an *undergraduate* dissertation successfully. Where this is the case, supervisors may be supervising and marking a level of academic activity that surpasses anything which they have themselves achieved.

As a result, some supervisors of law dissertations may have had little opportunity or interest in participating within academic debates regarding the comparative merits of different research methods. By act or omission, such supervisors may transmit such disinterest to their supervisees. This is unfortunate because it can result in the production of, for example, LLM dissertations that are no more sophisticated or reflective about the justification for their approach to the research topic than are most undergraduate essays, and which differ only in their word length.

● Positive Reasons for Engaging in Methodological Discussion

Given the various obstacles and sources of possible resistance, why should students preparing to undertake a legal dissertation be concerned with questions of research methodology? One answer has been provided by a postgraduate law researcher, Morag McDermott, who suggested that:

> For me a focus on theoretical and methodological perspectives at the beginning . . . is recognition that perspective determines approach and action. What sources are chosen, whether and how interviews are carried out, how statistics (your own and others) are used, and what you do with it all, is determined by the theoretical starting point. . . . the student's 'training' period . . . is an opportunity to consider alternative perspectives. Central must be the recognition that no research can be carried out free from 'bias' – good research attempts to identify what that bias is and how it affects the research process. The same can be said for methodology.[1]

During the early stages of a student's academic career, it may well be sufficient to answer problem and discussion assessment questions in a relatively straightforward way. Here, the task can involve students stating accurately, and then applying, general principles of law, largely derived from standard textbooks and a limited range of primary sources, in a conventionally legalistic manner, demonstrating that these principles have been adequately understood. Discussion of questions of research methods and methodology are somewhat limited. They may be confined to displaying the standard 'legal methods'

[1]Morag McDermott, 'A View from the Coalface', *Socio-legal Newsletter*, (1996) no.38, 5.

of source citation (showing that one knows when to use round or square brackets); and displaying a competence in how to apply traditional distinctions between points of law and points of fact; *ratio decidendi* and *obiter dicta*; and civil and criminal law (generally and in terms of differences of both terminology and the required burdens of proof).

In addition, legal-methods modules traditionally require students to master various techniques of interpretation, including those situations where it might be more appropriate to deploy literal, as distinct from purposive or golden-rule, approaches to the interpretation of statutes. Under the heading of 'legal methods', law students are also expected to demonstrate an awareness of the implications of the court hierarchy (including the European Court of Justice and European Court of Human Rights) for the traditional doctrine of precedent. In addition, students are expected to be able to:

- identify and access relevant sources of law;
- summarise cases and statutes in terms of their doctrinal significance;
- identify, classify and distinguish between different precedents in terms of their relative 'weight' and authority as guides for judges and other decision-makers in later cases;
- apply legal principles derived from factual situations to different factual situations through a process of drawing analogies and descriptive generalisation yielding a sense of which 'types' of situation and disputes evoke specific types of legal argumentation;
- manipulate the elasticity and indeterminacy of existing legal doctrine to justify rhetorically the 'legally correct result'.

In contrast to these basic skills in legal methods, traditionally emphasised on conventional English Legal System modules, law schools will often expect more with respect to the assessment of the methodological dimension of law dissertations.

On the other hand, certain recent works on the English Legal System have insisted that legal methods itself does indeed raise questions of selecting the most appropriate methodology from a range of options. For example, the authors of the course materials of the University of London LLB have argued:

> In particular we indicated that we could adopt a range of perspectives and that when we want to understand the operation of law in a legal system we inevitably face a choice as to what we include as suitable material. Do we want to take the accepted rules and principles of legal doctrine as given? (Some call this a 'black-letter approach' – 'the law is simply the law'). Or do we want to set these in context – and if so what perspective should you take, what assumptions do you use to organise the material to make sense of the diverse accounts?[2]

● Recognising the Implications of the Tension Between Different Research Methodologies

Writers have noted that legal researchers have to take into account 'the intellectual tension' and 'discernible friction' between 'black-letter academic lawyers using traditional

---

[2]See University of London external LLB programme, Chapter Two. Further details available at: www. londonexternal.ac.uk/current_students/programme_resources/laws/subject_guides/eng_legal_sys/com_law_ch2.pdf. [Accessed July 2005].

modes of legal analysis', and 'those who would classify themselves as interdisciplinary scholars using ideas and techniques borrowed from other disciplines.'[3] Within university law schools, this tension and friction between competing approaches to the conduct of research may well mean that different supervisors will have different suggestions and expectations with respect to what counts as 'suitable research'.

By selecting a supervisor who is aligned with and committed to, for instance, a black-letter approach, then a dissertation student may have to accept that he or she will also be 'buying into' the expectations, assumptions and preferred sources that form part of this particular methodological approach. Before choosing a particular supervisor, students need to be aware of the differences between the expectations associated with, say, the black-letter approach, as distinct from those of a supervisor who is aligned, for instance, to the sociolegal movement. As Vick notes, representatives of both interdisciplinary sociolegal and black-letter doctrinal approaches will often have not only a series of arguments justifying their own way of conducting research but also criticisms of the appropriateness of the various alternative methodologies:

> Many interdisciplinarians perceive doctrinalists to be intellectually rigid, inflexible, and inward looking; many doctrinalists regard [socio-legal] interdisciplinary research as amateurish dabbling with theories and methods the researchers do not fully understand.[4]

The dispute between black-letter and sociolegal approaches is often more than a purely academic controversy.[5] This dispute can become intense and heated precisely because sociolegal research is often interpreted as posing a radical challenge to the credibility, even the continued existence, of black-letter approaches. Hence, defenders of the black-letter tradition may well perceive this approach as one which needs to be resisted, not least for reasons of internal law-school politics. To many black-letter academics, sociolegal studies and other alternative approaches appear as Trojan horses threatening their type of scholarship aligned to the methods and techniques of the legal profession.[6] The interdisciplinary character and aspirations of sociolegal studies is sometimes seen as a threat. It may appear to break the boundaries of law as a distinct and self-contained academic discipline, one which possesses its own distinctive territory, methods and interpretative techniques. Worse still, sociolegal studies threatens to open up legal scholarship to colonisation by numerous rival disciplines, including the absorption of criminal law into criminology and the sociology of deviance, or contract law into the study of economic behaviour. Part of this perceived threat within law schools consists of sociolegal studies and other alternative approaches disrupting the unchallenged 'handing down' of this cultural tradition from one generation to the next.[7] As Vick notes:

---

[3]Douglas Vick, 'Interdisciplinarity and the Discipline of Law', 31 *JLS* (2004) 163 at 163–4.
[4]*Ibid.* 164.
[5]Twining suggests that law schools are necessarily fractious and conflict-ridden precisely because of the tensions between the narrow vocational training and broader liberal arts education models, which have different conceptions of law (law in books vs. law in action), the purpose of legal education, the relevance of 'lawyers' skills', the role of critical analysis (technical vs. critique of ideology and social structure), and the specific values that should inform student and academic work more generally. W. Twining, *Blackstone's Tower: The English Law School*, (London: Stevens, 1994), 80–1, 84–5.
[6]J. M. Balkan, 'Interdisciplinarity as Colonisation' (1996) 53 *Washington & Lee Law Rev.* 949, 954–6.
[7]*Ibid.*

The hostility that interdisciplinarity research has often generated is cast in a different light: the threat interdisciplinarity poses reinforces the tendency of members of a discipline to jealously guard disciplinary boundaries and marginalize those whose work strays outside those boundaries.[8]

Both sides of this controversy between black-letter and various alternative approaches to the conduct of legal research and analysis may fear that if their rivals' agenda were ever to entirely dominate their law school, then this could threaten the type of academic lawyer which they have chosen to become (or drifted into), their professional identity and possibly even their future career prospects.[9] Certainly, subscribers to sociolegal studies who actively engage in and promote empirical research into different aspects of law in action pose a challenge to more traditional library-based forms of legal scholarship. This threat consists of appearing to seek to replace more traditional black-letter forms of scholarship and learning with those ways of conducting research that are more associated with the social sciences.[10] The fact that, within ruling circles, sociology as a discipline is generally afforded less prestige than law possibly adds to the resistance that is based upon the threat posed to the perceived elevated status of more traditional legal academics.[11] The presence of sociolegal colleagues within the law school effectively challenges from within certain aspects of how those involved in the black-letter project seek to project law as a separate and independent discipline, whose methods are supposedly based on the intrinsic nature of the subject matter itself.

Students would be well-advised to recognise that the polarised, political and often heated nature of this institutional debate can, on occasions, involve both sides in the tussle between black-letter and various alternative approaches adopting distinctly hardline and even dismissive positions regarding the credibility of rival methodologies, even where it underpins the dissertation research of their students.[12] For example, the ferocious reaction of a number of black-letter legal academics to the emergence of sociolegal studies went beyond the parameters of routine academic controversy.[13] The challenges posed by the interdisciplinary approaches of sociolegal studies to the black-letter view of legal studies as a single, autonomous and self-contained discipline appears, to many of its critics, as an all-out attack on the distinct identity and viability of an entire

---

[8]Douglas Vick, 'Interdisciplinarity and the Discipline of Law' (2004) 31 *JLS*, n.86, 173.

[9]Vick maintains that such polarisation is based on an exaggerated view of the vulnerability of law as a distinct academic discipline and an underestimation of the continuing resilience of doctrinal black-letter approaches that stems from the affiliation with the legal profession, *ibid.*, 166, 186. Certain legal academics continue to define themselves proudly as 'black-letter lawyers' see Malcolm Clarke, 'A Black Letter Lawyer Looks at Bolero' (1999) *I.T.L.Q.*, 2 (May), 69-78.

[10]Alan Bradshaw, 'Sense and Sensibility: Debates and Developments in Socio-Legal Research Methods' in Philip Thomas (ed.), *Socio-Legal Studies*, (Aldershot: Ashgate-Dartmouth, 1997), 107.

[11]*Ibid.*

[12]The polarisation has on occasions even threatened to destroy certain law schools. E. Clark and M. Tsamenyi, 'Legal Education in the Twenty-First Century: A Time of Challenge' in Peter Birks (ed.), *Pressing Problems in the Law: What are Law Schools for?* (Oxford: Oxford University Press, 1996), 17 at 23.

[13]For examples of powerful and sometimes personalised attacks on sociolegal work by doctrinalists, see the content and tone of reviews of the first edition of Hugh Collins' *Introduction to the Law of Contract* (1984) by Tony Weir, (1986) 45 *Cambridge Law Journal* 503 and - to a lesser extent - 'The critique of Wheeler and Shaw's *Contract Law*' by Tettenborn in 54 *Cambridge Law Journal* (1995) 212, which attacked the approach, rather than the author personally. See D. Campbell, 'Socio-Legal Analysis of Contract' in P. Thomas, 1997 *op. cit.*, 271.

way of life and tradition of black-letter practices within law schools.[14] Seen in these terms, it is not surprising that these challenges have often evoked a sustained and uncompromising counter-attack from traditionalists. Pioneers of sociolegal studies were subject to the charge that their work, and even perhaps that of their student supervisees, was substandard, superficial and ill-informed, and pursued to promote the claimed 'sophistication' of the writers. Furthermore, the social theory wing of sociolegal studies was, at times, accused of resorting to unintelligible and pretentious theoretical jargon that made no contribution to the proper role of practical legal scholarship and the production of communicable teaching materials.[15] Lee also recalls that 'from the earliest days, this attracted criticism from those who accused sociolegal scholars of eclecticism and almost intellectual burglary.'[16]

Such negative reactions may not always be expressed so forcefully now that aspects of sociolegal studies have forced themselves into legal scholarship without really providing an effective challenge and displacement of the core of the legal curriculum (as distinct from some supplementary background contextual material).[17] However, it would perhaps be a mistake for students to assume that their adoption of sociolegal or other non-traditional types of research methodology, such as critical legal studies or law and economics, will be universally welcomed by all supervisors in every British law faculty. Hence, even at the level of the internal politics of law schools, dissertation students need to be aware of the potential ramifications of adopting the particular methodology they have selected, particularly where this is likely to be perceived as controversial by their supervisors, second-markers and external examiners.

As the next chapter will discuss in greater detail, there are some defensible intellectual criticisms made by traditionalists. However, students need to be aware that much of the counter-attack is not strictly cognitive at all, or located within the parameters of 'normal' academic disputes over the claims of different and rival approaches. Instead, much of the heat and fervour of the traditionalist reaction has stemmed from a perceived need to repel the alien invaders from planet sociolegal, and thereby reclaim once more the territorial integrity of the discipline of law understood as a homeland for black-letter research and analysis. There is a material dimension to this defensive reaction because any 'across the board' triumph of sociolegal studies could lead to the assimilation, or dispersal, of members of still independent law schools into social-science departments or faculties that have little use for their traditional skills and expertise regarding legal doctrine.[18] The strength

---

[14]Murphy and Roberts, 'Introduction' (1987) 50 *MLR* 677, at 680; Wilson, 'English Legal Scholarship' (1987) 50 *MLR* 818, at 824.

[15]G. Jones, ' "Traditional" Legal Scholarship: A Personal View' in Birks, 1996 *op. cit.*, 14; Vick, 2004 *op. cit.*, 186. See also B. Leiter, 'Intellectual Voyeurism in Legal Scholarship' (1992) 4 *Yale J. of Law and Humanities* 79; C. W. Collier, 'The Use and Abuse of Humanistic Theory in Law: Re-examining the Assumptions of Interdisciplinary Legal Scholarship' (1991) 41 *Duke Law J.* 191; J. S. Kaye, 'One Judge's View of Academic Law Review Writing' (1989) *J. of Legal Education* 313; K. Lasson, 'Scholarship Amok: Excesses in Pursuit of Truth and Tenure' (1990) 103 *Harvard Law Rev.* 926; G. C. Lilly, 'Law Schools Without Lawyers? Winds of Change in Legal Education' (1995) 81 *Virginia Law Rev.* 1421.

[16]Robert Lee, 'Socio-Legal Research – What's the Use?' in Thomas, 1997 *op. cit.*, 84. See also I. Willock, 'Getting On With Sociologists' and C. Campbell, 'Legal Thought and Juristic Values' both in 1 *British Jnl. of Law and Society* (1974) 3 and 13 respectively.

[17]Twining noted that, within English law schools, the black-letter tradition still remains dominant despite the growth in sociolegal and other alternative methodologies and approaches: 1994 *op. cit.*, 112.

[18]Vick, 2004, *op. cit.*, 187; Twining, 1994, *op. cit.*, 28 – noting 'law's credentials as a proper academic subject were questioned by colleagues in science, social science and the humanities'.

of the reaction against sociolegal studies, which in some cases has even included demands for the dismissal of academics who have published work whose findings were critical of the work of the legal profession,[19] is instructive. Indeed, it may reflect lack of confidence regarding the place of the discipline of law within modern universities, particularly where this subject is merely a department within a wider social science or business studies faculty. In such contexts, academic law departments may become subject to the sovereignty of deans who are non-lawyers, and have difficulties accepting that law could ever be an autonomous discipline and academic subject in its own right.[20]

Students weighing up the merits of adopting different methodologies with respect to the conduct of their dissertation research should, perhaps, bear in mind that there can also be a distinctly *ideological dimension* to the controversy between black-letter and alternative approaches. Certainly interdisciplinary research within the law in context or critical legal studies tradition is often rejected by black-letter legal academics for being rooted, implicitly or explicitly, in socialist ideology. On the other hand, the rejection of law and economics programmes may be influenced by their connection, in many cases, to radical free-market and new-right ideological agendas. It is arguable that any approach to legal research which is obviously rooted in ideological agendas would have to be rejected by subscribers to the black-letter approach in order to keep faith with its commitment to the political neutrality of strict legal analysis. We shall later discuss the extent to which the uncompromising rejection of politically charged agendas of any kind is a common characteristic of black-letter approaches to legal research more generally.[21]

For present purposes, the key point is that, at the outset, students need to understand, at least in a broad and general way, the nature and differences between the competing methodologies in order to appreciate the possible implications of signing up to any specific approach. Otherwise students risk selecting a supervisor whose approach and expectations regarding 'acceptable' forms of legal research are fundamentally at odds with the type of dissertation project they actually wish to carry out, the particular manner in which they want to undertake their research, and the type of sources they intend to examine. Many supervisors who identify with, and contribute to, sociolegal studies may have defined themselves as 'rebels' against the earlier dominance of more traditional black-letter approaches.[22] Hence, it is unlikely that they would be particularly impressed with a dissertation project that explicitly or implicitly rejects (without argument) the basic assumptions that inform their own approach and indeed professional identity.

Certainly dissertation students would be wise to avoid being caught in any 'crossfire' between rival camps in their law school, particularly if these frictions have become so

---

[19]For example, Baldwin and McConville, *Negotiated Justice: Pressures to Plead Guilty* (London: Martin Robertson, 1977) – a work that created enormous controversy because it exposed the existence of extensive plea-bargaining and undue pressure on defendants to plead guilty, which contradicted existing reassurances that such practices were rare in Britain. See V. Jupp, *Methods of Criminological Research* (London: Routledge, 1989) for a detailed discussion of this negative reaction, which is also summarised by the foreword by the Vice Chancellor of Birmingham University, and Baldwin and McConville, 'Introductory Note', 1977 *op. cit.*

[20]Baldwin and McConville, 1977, *op. cit.*

[21]Vick, 2004 *op. cit.*, 186.

[22]*Ibid.*, 165 – noting that 'dissatisfaction with the restraints of disciplinarity' has been a 'driving force' behind the efforts of sociolegalists to create an alternative interdisciplinary approach to the conduct of legal research and analysis, and that were this to be fully realised it would 'threaten the power structures within existing disciplines'.

intense and polarised that they could influence both the supervision, marking and second-marking processes. Such conflict will not always be present, however. Even those academics who are unusually open-minded with respect to different arguments that arise *within* their preferred agenda, may become dogmatic, closed-minded and dismissive when confronted with legal research that embodies an entirely different methodological agenda, particularly one that supposedly threatens the credibility of the approach that defines their professional identity.

There are other reasons for dissertation students becoming well informed about methodological issues. One part of the enhanced expectations of third-year-undergraduate and postgraduate students relates to the conscious assessment and selection of a particular methodology from a range of possibilities, which then requires students to justify their approach to the conduct of legal research. It is reasonable for supervisors and examiners to expect dissertation students to demonstrate, in a clear and express way, that the particular approach they have adopted is the most appropriate to how they are defining the issues addressed by their proposed project.

Experienced legal researchers have testified that there is no possibility of conducting research other than through the application of a particular frame of reference which determines how the dissertation is created, formulated and pursued. Such frameworks (also termed 'paradigms' or 'methodologies'):

> set the direction of our research, inform what we regard as a legitimate and interesting topic of research and involve epistemological assumptions [about what counts as reliable knowledge]. They mould our ways of seeing the world, our ways of studying the world (including the questions we ask) and our ways of making sense of the world.[23]

● Avoiding the Pitfalls of Selecting an Inappropriate Methodology

Since any dissertation will inevitably be guided by methodological principles of some kind, it is important that the process of selection is made in a deliberate and conscious fashion. The assessment regimes of law schools are entitled to expect that students completing dissertations will avoid selecting an approach that could, from the start, have been predicted to prove inadequate to the task. An exasperated examiner may, for example, comment that the method chosen by a student is no more related to the realisation of the specific objectives of the research than architecture is to singing! In other words, one of the pitfalls awaiting students undertaking a dissertation is the risk of selecting a methodology that is clearly out of step with the requirements of their topic or with the objectives of their specific project; or, in the worst case scenario, incompatible with both.

One possible pitfall would be for a dissertation student to adopt a traditional black-letter approach to a dissertation project that claims to be addressing issues, such as the comparative 'effectiveness' of the operation of a legislative scheme in the light of its claimed objectives. The goals of such a dissertation project can only be adequately realised through

---

[23]Hutter and Lloyd-Bostock, in Keith Hawkins, *The Human Face of Law: Essays in Honour of Donald Harris,* (Oxford: OUP, 1997), 25. All extracts from Hawkins, K. (1997) are reproduced by permission of Oxford University Press.

the adoption of a sociolegal approach to the conduct of research that is specifically designed to address policy aspects of the law-in-context. This attempt to make a black-letter methodology do the work of a sociolegal approach would be as problematic as deploying sociolegal methods to the goals of a dissertation that aims to clarify the position of current legal doctrine on a topic. In both these cases, students would be selecting the wrong 'tool for the job' because there would be a basic conflict between the particular methodological tools selected, and the specific requirements of the task in hand.

Another possible difficulty for students who refuse to address methodological issues arises whenever they select unfortunate *combinations* of approach that, in the context of their particular project, are not especially compatible (at least not without creative and possibly disastrous adaptation creating a Heath Robinson-like mixture of random and discrepant parts).

The discussion above suffices to make two points:

1. Examiners of undergraduate and postgraduate dissertations are likely to expect that students avoid the pitfalls identified above, particularly if these projects are to merit above average grades.
2. In order to avoid such pitfalls, it is necessary for students to address, in an express manner, the suitability of different possible approaches to conducting research into their specific dissertation topics.

Having discussed the relative pros and cons of different possible methodologies, probably within the introduction of the undergraduate dissertation or in a short initial section within a LLM dissertation or thesis, students should provide good reasons justifying the selection of their particular approach to the conduct of research. They should be able to explain why the chosen approach provides the best, or 'the least inappropriate', approach, or a combination of complementary approaches, to their particular dissertation topic. This insistence on the unavoidability of having to make and justify a choice between different possible methodological options, some of which are associated with distinctly ideological and other normative agendas linked to specific value judgements, has been expressed clearly by legal academics presenting materials to London University's external students:

> In particular . . . we could adopt a range of perspectives when we want to understand the operation of law . . . Note the difference between the internal and the external, between the participant and the 'observer' – the difference between: accepting law as a normative phenomenon, where normative precepts or ideals – statements of oughts – are appropriate language and the world of facts, where statements of is are the proper expression. There are others who appear to see law in negative terms, as required only by the failings of human society (anarchists, Marxists). They associate law and the operations of the legal system closely with coercive governmental structures which compel humans into artificial associations, where law distributes a structure of unearned benefits and enforces unjust relationships. Others, rejecting the coercive image of law see it as an expression of societal ideals, as articulating principles and standards of human worth (human rights etc.), and the legal system as providing an array of protective devices for citizens to use.[24]

---

[24]www.londonexternal.ac.uk/current_students/programme_resources/laws/subject_guides/eng_legal_sy/com_law_ch2.pdf. [Accessed July 2005].

Students have, in one sense, already made a decision regarding the most appropriate manner of studying law with respect to their choice of law schools (assuming one's grades and circumstances allowed a practical choice from a range of alternatives). Although we are aware of no systematic research on this point within the UK, it appears that the law schools of Lancaster, Sheffield, Hull, Kent, Bristol, Birbeck College (University of London), Leeds, Warwick, Central Lancashire, Keele, Sussex, Westminster, Sheffield and, to an increasing extent, Manchester University, have specifically sought to develop alternatives to traditional black-letter forms of legal education and research. Apparently, this factor of choice from a diversity of institutional approaches is also a feature of legal education in Australia.[25]

What is arguably worse than dissertations that lack any methodological discussion whatever, are those where the treatment of issues relating to the choice and justification of approach to the conduct of research are treated in an entirely token fashion without making any clear linkage to the approach taken and applied in practice. We would suggest that the inclusion of such 'undigested' material derived from methodological discussions within the academic literature could be counterproductive. It only draws attention to the fact that students have not considered the relationship between their research activity and the specific challenges raised by their dissertation topic. Furthermore, such dissertations inevitably convey the unfortunate impression that the student has made little attempt to engage in reasoned justification regarding the link between the goals of the research and the selection of an appropriate methodological means to realise these goals. Hence, those marking the dissertation may well form the impression that the discussion of limited methodology represents little more than a reluctant token effort, which is merely 'bolted on', and, relative to the remainder of the dissertation, remains 'undigested'.

What is ironic with respect to this frequent lack of systematic methodological self-reflection within mainstream legal studies is that most practising lawyers will readily affirm that the same facts and area of legal doctrine can, with equal merit, be interpreted in at least two different ways depending on which party they are representing. Hence, the meaning of these materials depends ultimately upon how they are interpreted. In other words, the same points of law and fact that have been interpreted in a certain way by one side to a legal dispute are frequently susceptible to diametrically opposite interpretations of no lesser plausibility by lawyers representing the other party. It follows that the significance of many legal issues, including even technical questions involving the identification of the legal position in such and such a situation, varies depending upon how the issues are identified, defined and analysed relative to the 'methodology' (i.e. the interests, orientation and concerns) guiding the interpreter's analysis. The significance of the issues addressed by law dissertations will inevitably vary depending upon whether they are defined and then approached from, say, a black-letter as distinct from either a sociolegal or an historical perspective. Hence, there is every reason for law students to want to gain a measure of clarity about the relative merits of these different approaches

---

[25]One recent guide to Australian legal education notes: 'The legal education you would receive in these law schools is varied. Some, for example, place particular emphasis on developing practical skills as well as knowledge and understanding of the law. Others ensure that their students develop a critical perspective on the law, setting it in economic, political, historical or philosophical contexts. Others, still, have a more "black-letter law" approach.' The Law: Legal Education: http://www.intstudy.com/articles/law.htm. [Accessed July 2005].

prior to adopting any single methodology or combination of methodologies. This is, perhaps, the clearest reason why law students beginning their dissertation projects should take methodological discussions far more seriously than is often the case.

The main aim of the methodology part of this book is to provide resources that, with appropriate supplementation, should help students to meet the requirements of a viable dissertation, particularly with respect to their justification of the approach to the conduct of research. Our aim is to provide a clear but not simplistic introduction to the nature, strengths and limits of a number of different approaches to the conduct of legal research. When finalising the present book, we discovered that aspects of the approach to the study of methodology we are suggesting appears to be endorsed by the research methods course offered to law students at the University of Glasgow. For example, this module devotes a workshop to the question of the nature and limits of black-letter law, which addresses the questions:

> What is 'black letter' law and what is the 'black letter' approach to legal analysis? Does it provide a way of understanding law and legal questions that is not encompassed by other approaches? Why do so many alternative approaches seek to discredit 'black letter' law? These questions are addressed in this session through an examination of the law relating to unfair contract terms.[26]

In fact, the readings offered to students undertaking the Glasgow module also relate to black-letter analysis in the sense of a series of rules of precedent and statutory interpretation relating to how law, itself understood as an autonomous system of rules, should be interpreted.[27] This rule-based approach is illustrated and assessed with respect to both mainstream and more critical approaches to contract law.[28] This methodological module also addresses various alternative approaches to the black-letter way of conducting legal research including, for example, both sociolegal studies and law and economics.[29] Both alternatives are presented not as *simply different* from the black-letter methodology but as distinctive alternatives that could replace it altogether.[30]

Our account of the different methodologies is, of course, a selective and partial interpretation. Specialists and partisan advocates of any of these approaches could, no doubt, take issue in whole or in part with our interpretation. We are aware also that each section could, if every aspect was fully developed, be expanded into a full-length book,

---

[26]http://www.lib.gla.ac.uk/courses/law/MacNeil2.shtml [Accessed July 2005].

[27]Citing White and Willock, *The Scottish Legal System*, 187–214 (Statutory Interpretation) and ch. 6 (Precedent); *Walker and Walker's English Legal System* 8th edition, (London: Butterworths, 1998), ch. 2 (Legislation) and ch. 3 (Law Reports and Precedents).

[28]Citing Woolman and Lake, *Contract*, 3rd edn (London, ch. 8 (Interpretation); Adams and Brownsword, *Key Issues in Contract* (London, Lexis Law Publishing, 1994), ch. 8 (Unfair Contract Terms).

[29] This is characterised as: 'A critical approach to, and evaluation of, law by way of the application of economic tools came to prominence in the early 1960s, centred primarily around the University of Chicago. The seminal piece of work in this line was an article by Richard Coase which considers the extent to which legal mechanisms may simply be a substitute for economic bargaining. Many commentators, both lawyers and economists, have expanded this work to most areas of law, ranging from legal processes, to private law of obligations, to criminal law. . . . How, if at all, might a better understanding of the area in which you are engaged in research be affected by an application of economic principles? Most of the core work in this area that is still reproduced, even in modern anthologies, is still relatively old. Why might this be the case, and is the approach advocated by these writers still valid? What values do those working in this area bring to the subject?' http://www.lib.gla.ac.uk/courses/law/MacNeil2.shtml [Accessed July 2005].

[30]*Ibid.*

and our account can only represent a relatively brief summary painted in broad-brush strokes that necessarily presents bold generalisations regarding the characteristics of each approach. Within the present book, it is neither possible nor desirable to do justice to the diversity of different types of, for example, sociolegal studies, or to the ways in which black-letter modes of analysis have been mixed with certain others, often in the same project. This introductory book aims to stimulate further reading on methodological issues within legal research, rather than provide an alternative to such further explorations of the vast literature. For those readers who want to follow up any of the approaches discussed in this book, we have included hundreds of citations to the works of other authors that illustrate aspects of these internal variants and controversies in far greater detail.

● Conclusion

We have discussed the source of the ingrained resistance to explicit methodological discussion and the reasons why this needs to be challenged. In practice, law students are as capable of addressing this important topic in an intelligent way as those on social science and humanities degrees for which research methods are an integral part of their syllabi. Providing a methodological section can enhance both the quality and rigour of a law dissertation by not only explaining aspects of the topic but also justifying the appropriateness of the student's own approach to this topic. We have suggested that it is not possible to avoid questions of methodology because all researchers inevitably bring to their tasks a certain interpretation of the meaning and purpose of 'research'. What one discovers through research will always be determined, to some extent, by how one initially sets up the dissertation project, the type of questions students raise and their choice of materials to be studied. It is, therefore, important to reflect critically upon and justify with good reasons that can withstand scrutiny, the appropriateness of methodologies to the dissertation topic. What is more, if students are biased in favour of quantitative methodologies, then this will predetermine some of the questions and issues their dissertations address (How much X is there?). By contrast, if students are biased in favour of qualitative methodologies, then this too will influence the type of questions they address in their dissertations (What is the meaning of the topic and how is this being interpreted differently by various groups including the judges and legal academics?). It is important for dissertation students to exercise caution if they are planning to use multiple methodologies. This is because a single dissertation may not be able to combine effectively two different approaches to the same topic. Students also need to reflect upon the limitations of each of the possible methodologies through which they are planning to conduct their dissertation research. Such critical reflection should enable students to avoid the danger of attempting to raise and answer questions that their chosen approach is incapable of successfully addressing. For example, research into the current state of legal doctrine can hardly be pursued through the methods of sociolegal studies, whilst the strictly doctrinal approach of the black-letter methodology is incapable of analysing policy and moral questions effectively.

The next chapter discusses the most traditional approach to legal research: the black-letter approach. This is followed by a summary of a quite different, and indeed in some respects diametrically opposed, method of conducting legal research: that adopted by the sociolegal studies movement.

Black-Letter Approaches to Doctrinal Research

● Introduction

Law students would be well advised to at least consider the reasons for and against adopting a 'black-letter' approach to conducting dissertation research.[1] The following chapter will discuss this methodology's defining characteristics, and its analytical techniques, assumptions and limitations. The central point to recognise at the outset is that the black-letter approach is a particular way of interpreting what is deemed to count as legal research, including which materials are considered relevant. In other words, the black-letter methodology is not simply a perspective upon, or even a style of articulating, the substantial nature of a dissertation topic: instead, it is an interpretative scheme whose overall framework of categories, assumptions and concerns operate to both set up and demarcate the very meaning, scope and purpose of your dissertation topic and project. If students adopt an alternative research methodology, such as that of sociolegal studies, then their dissertations would be operating with very different definitions of the appropriate range and scope of relevant source materials, as well as with different expectations as to the type of questions that are appropriate for legal researchers to ask.

This fairly long chapter tackles a broad range of issues concerning the definition, characteristics and practical operation of the black-letter approach, which is perhaps most completely exemplified within classic student law textbooks that amount to detailed descriptions of formal legal rules and principles. One element of the operation of this approach is to seek to insulate your analysis of the dissertation topic from supposedly 'non-legal factors' regarding, for example, policy and ideological issues as if these were somehow 'external' to, and independent of, strictly legal research. Having sought to insulate the topic, the black-letter approach then poses a particular type of questioning that usually takes the form of: what is the legal meaning of X (e.g. the definition of marriage) as defined by cases and statutes, and that of X in relation to Y and Z (e.g. parental responsibility and the division of assets on relationship breakdown).

A central goal of black-letter analysis is to reveal the presence of a series of rules based upon a smaller number of general legal principles defining, for instance, the difference between valid, voidable and void marriages. The central assumption is that the detailed rules give effect to, and specify, certain underlying and more general legal principles, such that law can be interpreted as a more or less rational and coherent system of rules. For example, one principle is that a legally valid marriage has to be based upon valid consent (involving, for example, the absence of duress). This is elucidated by more detailed

---

[1] The phrase 'black-letter' refers to the black or Gothic type that was traditionally used in formal statements of legal principles or rules at the start of a section, which was typically followed by a descriptive exposition or commentary.

and specific legal rules that spell out what, for instance, is to count as valid consent concerning the age, gender, soundness of mind and identity of the parties to the marriage. Black-letter analysis involves students *cross-referencing* these specific rules to more general underlying principles as if together they formed a single, mutually reinforcing and rational system of regulation. The presence within legal doctrine of various contradictions, gaps, ambiguities and irrationalities, including those stemming from 'external' policy and political factors, must be treated as deviant and exceptional. Legal categories, such as marriage, possess a stable meaning for which it is possible in principle to give a single correct definition that captures its essence.

Like all methodologies, black-letter analysis reflects a certain standpoint, typically that of a lawyer advising clients as to the legal implications of their situation. Hence, a student dissertation is supposed to interpret disputes in a strictly legalistic manner, not from the perspective of lay persons but rather in terms of their significance for lawyers within the legal process. Hence, a dissertation addressing aspects of the legal regulation of family relationships must respect the idea that law is a separate and independent academic discipline. It follows that it is not necessary for dissertation students to have regard to the research sociologists who, for instance, study the changing role and functions of the family in modern society. Contrary to a social science approach, the black-letter methodology requires students to rigorously exclude supposedly 'external' factors, such as policy, ideological and moral issues regarding same-sex relationships, forced marriages and property ownership within cohabitation.

Classic forms of black-letter analysis deploy a distinctly *deductive* form of legal reasoning from legal principles. Hence, it is supposed to be possible for students to deduce by thought alone the necessity for specific rules as if these represented logical implications of a general principle. For example, the detailed legal rules regarding what is to count as consent to a valid marriage can be deduced by pure logic from the basic axioms of contract law that govern legally enforceable agreements in general.

Students who adopt the black-letter approach are not prevented from making criticisms of legal doctrine, although such permissible criticisms are limited in nature and scope to the exposure of ambiguities and gaps within existing law (defined narrowly as legal doctrine). However, students are not expected to engage in fundamental criticisms of the nature and operation of basic social institutions, such as marriage, and how law continues to prioritise this institution over cohabitation.

● Towards a Provisional Working Definition: Black-Letter Law as Legal Formalism

For reasons already discussed, it is important for students to be able to spell out their approach to the conduct of dissertation research. Indeed, this can be studied as a topic in its own right. This has been recognised by, for example, an academic module seeking to help Master's students at Norwich Law School to undertake a law dissertation:

> This unit is intended for students wishing to undertake a significant piece of research, as part of a taught Master's programme. The unit has two components. The aim of the first component is to give students a broad overview of the different approaches, techniques and research skills involved in the planning, researching and writing of a dissertation in the field of law. The course will incorporate the conduct of 'black-

letter' or doctrinal legal research, as well as normative evaluation of laws and legal regimes, and empirical socio-legal research in both single country and comparative research designs. The aim of the second component is to expose students to legal research through the actual writing of a dissertation on a topic to be approved and supervised by the school.[2]

It follows that if, after weighing up the pros and cons for your particular topic and dissertation title, you decide to adopt a black-letter methodology, then your research will be participating in a framework of interpretation. This framework will determine in advance what is to count as the substantial content and basic materials of your dissertation topic. Hence, the black-letter approach to legal research is more than a particular way of analysing the legal materials that you need to gather and analyse to complete your dissertation. It is also a framework of interpretation for both determining and setting up what falls within the scope of 'relevant' source material. This methodology provides a way of asking a certain range of questions and subjecting legal material to an 'appropriate' type of analysis.

Dissertation supervisors and examiners are entitled to expect that law students should be able to apply, discuss and evaluate the perceived appropriateness of this (or any alternative) methodology for different types of law dissertation. This expectation requires students to identify examples of how previous publications have, to a greater or lesser extent, applied the black-letter approach to their field of research. It also means that student dissertations should discuss the nature, strengths and limits of this particular methodology. This discussion would need to evaluate the appropriateness of any chosen methodology for both the general area of law in question, and for students' own particular dissertation topics. Before this process of assessment, selection and justification can even start, however, we first need to clarify the general outlines of the black-letter approach. We need to provide an initial working definition of this methodology, the bare bones of which will need to be fleshed out and developed more fully in later subsections.

For interesting reasons, discussed later in this chapter, those students and academics who adopt a black-letter approach to legal research rarely offer an express definition or engage in discussions that openly debate its possible advantages and disadvantages in an explicit or systematic way. Consequently, it is mainly the critics of this approach, rather than those who deploy it as their preferred approach, who have discussed its nature.[3] Furthermore, critics use a variety of other terms to refer to the black-letter approach, including 'classical legal thought' and the 'expository orthodoxy.'[4] Students need to bear in mind this element of potential bias and confusion as to terminology when reading such discussions. They may need to study actual examples of black-letter analysis within traditional textbooks and associated scholarship to satisfy themselves that the critics of this approach have indeed characterised it in a fair and accurate way.[5]

---

[2]Lindsay Stirton, Researching and Writing a Dissertation in the Field of Law. http://www.uea.ac.uk/menu/acad_depts/law/prospective_students/research.htm.

[3]P. Aldridge, 'What is Wrong With The Traditional Criminal Law Course', (1990) 10 *LS* 38.

[4]W. Twining, *Blackstone's Tower: The English Law School*, (London: Stevens, 1994), 141.

[5]For the criticism of the 'stereotypical pattern' of traditional black-letter textbooks, see W. Twining, 'Reflections on Law in Context' in Cane and Stapleton, *Essays for Patrick Atiyah*, (Oxford: Clarendon, 1991), 1–30.

At the outset, it is necessary to provide a caveat: whilst for purposes of analysis it is helpful to refer to *the* black-letter approach, it is equally important to recognise that there can be a variety of different ways of conducting legal research that, to a greater or lesser extent, share one or more of the characteristics that we can identify as distinctly 'black letter'. It is more precise, therefore, to refer in a shorthand manner to certain *tendencies* within legal research that can be usefully identified and labelled as 'black letter'. However, it is necessary to immediately qualify this claim by recognising that, in practice, there may be few examples of 'pure' black-letter analysis that not only fully embody every one of these tendencies but also contain no other elements. Thus, it is necessary for readers to bear these nuances and qualifications in mind when we refer to '*the* black-letter approach'.

In order to highlight the distinctive features of this approach, our focus will be on a type of research that most fully realises these tendencies (i.e. an 'ideal type') located towards one end of the spectrum, which, in practice, cannot be entirely representative of every example. Students may well find that, within their law department or law school, both the critics of, and subscribers to, the black-letter approach have a rather one-sided and selective interpretation of the nature and justification of this particular methodology. For example, certain dissertation supervisors who adopt, to a greater or lesser extent, a black-letter approach may identify only with those features they regard as positive, such as systematic rigour and detailed technical analysis based on a thorough, careful and close reading of the meaning and scope of primary sources. However, such supervisors may resist other defining characteristics of this approach that appear to challenge, or even undermine, their own approach to scholarship.

Indeed, and for reasons discussed below, students may have to deal with an understandable and deep-seated defensiveness and personal sensitivity concerning this topic. In some cases, this may stem from a measure of status anxiety that many legal academics feel. This can arise from their ambiguous position located uneasily between legal practitioners (self-defined as 'proper lawyers') and fully-fledged and accredited academic social scientists, often without being fully accepted by either group.[6] Becher has summarised a common view within academic circles:

> The predominant notion of academic lawyers is that they are not really academic ... their scholarly activities are thought to be unexciting and uncreative, comprising of a series of intellectual puzzles scattered among large 'areas of description'.[7]

Students need to recall that, for the bulk of the history of the legal profession, legal education was not defined as an academic enterprise. Barristers studied non-law subjects, such as classics and history, before attending craft schools to sit professional exams; whilst solicitors were rarely university graduates at all.[8]

---

[6]*Ibid.*, 23–5, 27–8, 30, 33, 52. W. Twining, 'Some Jobs for Jurisprudence', (1974) *Brit Jnl of Law and Society*, 149, 161–4; Elizabeth Mensch, 'A History of Mainstream Legal Thought' in David Kearys (ed.), *The Politics of Law: A Progressive Critique* (NY: Pantheon Press, 1982). Twining notes how law schools are typically caught in a 'tug of war' between academic respectability and being a service institution for a legal profession which is itself caught between noble ideals, lucrative service of powerful interests and unromantic cleaning up of society's messes. On the long-standing tradition of lack of respect for legal academics within academia more generally, see Abel-Smith and Stevens, *Lawyers and the Courts*: *A Sociological Study of the English Legal System 1750–1965*, (London: Heinemann, 1967), 375.
[7]Tony Becher, *Academic Tribes and Territories* (Buckingham: Open University Press, 1989), 30.
[8]Twining, 1994 *op. cit.*, 30; Abel-Smith and Stevens, *op. cit.*, ch.13.

It is also necessary at the outset to warn students against misleading interpretations of the black-letter approach that are sometimes found in the academic literature. Such methodologies are sometimes equated with 'doctrinalism', a type of study that focuses exclusively on the cases, rules and principles comprising the substantive content of legal doctrine. This equation is at least questionable for a number of reasons. Even apparently 'non-doctrinal' subjects, such as legal history, comparative law and jurisprudence, often remain linked with, and at least partially subordinated to, the implicit legal positivism that underpins black-letter modes of analysis.[9] For present purposes, such positivism can be defined as a descriptive focus on whatever is laid down and given as rules of law by state officials, a strictly objective focus on 'what is' the law (or legal position with respect to X), which therefore aspires to become free of all moral and political value judgements regarding how law 'ought to be'.[10] Webb argues that: 'Adopting a frequently implicit, sometimes crude, objectivist epistemology . . . black-letter law often pays scant regard to either grand theory or practice, though in its choice of tools it remains closer to the analytical framework of practice than to the more reflective methodologies of the social and human sciences.'[11] For example, legal history is often considered to involve a historical reconstruction of the evolutionary processes through which judges and Parliament developed current rules and principles, thereby deriving its definition of 'law' from a distinctly state-centred positivism of the black-letter definition.[12] To the lament of many, even jurisprudence (the philosophy of law) can be studied as if it consisted of a series of factual statements about different large-scale legal concepts and the relationship between concepts, for example, statements concerning the connection between law and morality, law and justice, law and a system of rules, etc., as developed by different schools of thought. What should be clear from these examples is that dissertation students should not equate a black-letter approach with the study of legal doctrine as such. This is because various *other areas* of the legal curriculum, which are not generally regarded as substantive law subjects, are taught and researched using this approach.

Another reason why you should not confuse the black-letter approach to the analysis of legal doctrine with doctrinal analysis in general is because there are no legal sources, not even cases and statutes, which are, *in themselves*, inherently 'black letter' materials that automatically require researchers to adopt an exclusively black-letter approach to their analysis. In fact, this particular approach to the conduct of dissertation research represents only one amongst many other methodologies that legal researchers have applied to the study of legal doctrine.[13] Whilst cases and statutes are clearly susceptible *to being*

---

[9]Twining, 1994 *op. cit.*, 136, 155 – who warns us not to exaggerate this domination.

[10]Twining, *ibid.*, identifies Hans Kelsen's positivism as providing the best available theoretical support for black-letter analysis.

[11]Julian Webb, 'Extending the Theory–Practice Spiral: Action Research as a Mechanism for Crossing the Academic/Professional Divide' [1995] 2 *Web JCLI. http://webjcli.ncl.ac.uk/articles2/webb2.html*; J. Macfarlane 'Look Before You Leap: Knowledge and Learning in Legal Skills Education' (1992) 19 *Journal of Law & Society* 293, 298-301.

[12]Douglas Vick, 'Interdisciplinarity and the Discipline of Law' (2004) 31 *JLS*, n.86 at 77–8. For a criticism of the nature and limits of black-letter approaches to the history of land and equity and trusts, which contrasts markedly with the far more convincing historians' histories, see Doupe and Salter, 'Concealing the Past?: Questioning Textbook Interpretations of the History of Equity and Trusts', 2-3 (2000) *Liverpool Law Review* 253; Doupe and Salter, 'The Cheshire World-view', 11(1) *Kings College Law Journal*, (2000) 49.

[13]Twining, 1994 *op. cit.*, 96, 109 – noting that the exploitation of primary sources by other disciplines deserves to be more fully addressed by scholars of other disciplines, and noting that the arrangement of the law library and the idea that law is a separate and autonomous discipline have frustrated this.

interpreted according to the protocols of the black-letter approach, these materials can also be studied and analysed, possibly with equal merit, by alternative approaches. Over the last three decades, these alternative approaches have included sociolegal studies, sociology of law, feminism, law and economics, semiotics and Marxism.

Student dissertations should recognise that a number of these alternative methodologies have superimposed upon the analysis of cases and statutes a series of moral, gender and political issues, which members of the black-letter tradition typically reject as entirely inappropriate to a 'strictly legal' mode of analysis. Legal academics, criminologists, feminists and others within the social sciences have produced critical studies of, for example, judicial rhetoric, metaphors, imagery, concealed gender and other ideological assumptions, which fall well outside the scope of black-letter analysis.[14] Although such research has included studies of legal doctrine in an intensive and rigorous fashion, the researchers have made no attempt to conform to the black-letter perspective. On the contrary, they have more often defined their objectives in sharp opposition to this perspective.[15]

In short, students undertaking dissertations whose objectives can only be realised by a close analysis of legal doctrine need to take seriously the possibility of adopting a black-letter approach, whilst also recognising that it represents only one of a number of possible candidates. After weighing up the alternatives and the various arguments for and against each approach to the conduct of legal research, students may perhaps decide that the black-letter approach is the most appropriate for their particular topic. However, it would be a mistake to endorse this particular methodology on the basis of the mistaken belief that such endorsement is demanded by the 'inherent nature' of either the legal doctrine or the dissertation topic.

Having highlighted certain sources of possible confusion, it may now be useful to clarify some defining characteristics of the black-letter methodology. We can neither expect too much from any formal definitions of the 'essence' of the black-letter approach, nor expect to avoid defining key terms, at least provisionally, at the outset. This approach takes its name from the tendency of legalistic approaches to concentrate exclusively on the 'letter of the law', on the black-letters printed on dark gothic script on white paper. Black-letter modes of dissertation research aim to reduce the study of law to an essentially descriptive exposition of the meaning for lawyers of a large number of technical and coordinated legal rules contained in 'primary sources' (mainly cases and statutes). We suggest that the typical black-letter approach is best defined, albeit in a provisional way, as a research methodology that concentrates on seeking to provide a detailed and highly technical commentary upon, and systematic exposition of, the content of legal doctrine. This doctrine is interpreted as if it is a separate, independent and coherent 'system of rules'. The priority is to gather, organise and describe legal rules, and offer commentary upon the emergence and significance of the authoritative legal sources that contain these rules, especially cases. Here, students need to recall that the fact that a series of judicial decisions, of varying degrees of consistency in individual cases, are recorded in law reports does not, in itself, constitute a 'system' of legal rules and principles at all. To identify an underlying system requires mastering a *particular way of*

---

[14]See for example Alison Diduck, 'Ideologies of Motherhood, 2 *Social and Legal Studies*, (1993) 461; Culley and Salter, 'Why Study Legal Metaphors?' (2004) 15 *Kings College Law Review*, 347.

[15]The next chapter will discuss these broadly social scientific approaches in extensive detail.

interpreting these cases. This involves researchers undertaking a process of generalisation, in order to detect the alleged presence of such 'rules' as the reasons that explain the various decisions. Hofheinz claims:

> What is black letter law? It is simply the rules applicable to a particular area of the law, stated (often in outline form), without application to the particular facts and circumstances of a hypothetical or real legal problem, plus the pattern of questions necessary to apply those rules in a logical manner.[16]

These processes of generalisation require students undertaking dissertation research to reject the idea that the law reports contain a series of one-off decisions, 'a wilderness of single instances'. Instead, each case must be interpreted as if it formed part of a system of rules which are internally connected and related to each other in distinct clusters and groups. This is because they 'bear directly on a single precise point of law or . . . represent a historical sequence, a story of legal development'.[17] Black-letter analysis works on the assumption that individual cases 'feed off, build on, confirm, extend, erode, displace or overturn other cases.'[18] Once identified, such rules need to be further generalised as binding or 'normative' for future disputes that fall under their scope, so that each takes its place in a coherent and seamless web. If students interpret cases and rules in this way, it will lead to the insight that the dissertation's source materials will contain inter-related points of law, which 'taken together, form the basis of a systematic account of a topic or field of law.'[19]

How then can we put more flesh on the bones of our earlier definition? Black-letter analysis rarely, if ever, starts 'from scratch', as it were. Instead, it both participates within, and contributes to, an ongoing project of providing additional doctrinal commentaries that are superimposed upon the prior contributions of other researchers, and which, in turn, may be adapted and modified by others perhaps in the near future. The black-letter approach is thus a way of reinterpreting cases and statutes through the resources of a well-established traditional framework, even where it is typically applied in law schools many of which have only existed for less than fifty years.[20] The application of this approach generates a type of research project that accumulates and integrates the results of analysing many hundreds of prior cases. These are treated as an archive of raw material from which it is possible for researchers to elucidate and clarify both the meaning and scope of legal rules and principles supposedly contained within them.

Law students adopting the black-letter approach for their dissertations will seek to study the primary sources contained in the law library in order to answer the question: what is the meaning and scope of the relevant legal provisions? This approach to research aims to offer an authoritative exposition, fully supported by relevant citations, that describes how the specific rights and obligations of substantive legal doctrine have been assigned through judicial interpretations and reinterpretations of the meaning, scope and

---

[16]W. Hofheinz, (1997) 'Legal Analysis': http://www.hofheinzlaw.com/LANLSYS.php#anchor47300 (accessed August 2005).

[17]Twining, 1994 *op. cit.*, 104.

[18]*Ibid*.

[19]*Ibid*.

[20]In 1994 Twining noted that, relative to most other academic subjects, the 'emergence of university-based law schools is a quite recent phenomenon.' 1994 *op. cit.*, 2.

WRITING LAW DISSERTATIONS

requirements of 'given' legal categories, general principles and specific rules. Black-letter analysis will describe, often in intricate technical detail, the technical meaning of the relevant rules and principles. This emphasis on providing a description and exposition, as distinct from an explanation or critique of the origins, policy values or social impact of the law in action, is considered a goal in itself.[21]

Black-letter analysis is a law-centred and legalistic approach, which includes a specific orientation or 'state of mind'.[22] Such analysis is concerned to establish and define a relationship between individual cases and prior legal rules (and vice-versa), and, at the next level up, between specific rules to both principles and axioms.[23] This process of cross-referencing cases, rules, principles and axioms can be found on virtually every page of the traditional black-letter textbooks on law, apart from the brief historical introductions.[24] Such cross-referencing operates to reaffirm the underlying belief that each part or level (cases are located at the lowest level with basic axioms located at the highest level of the pyramid) forms part of a mutually defining system of legal doctrine, in which a largely harmonious relationship exists between the cases, rules, principles and basic axioms.

Commentators in both North America and Britain have characterised these interpretative activities as 'formalist', and labelled black-letter analysis as a type of legal formalism in a number of senses of this term. The ascendancy of formalism in the second half of the nineteenth century coincided with the decline of the traditional mode of judicial decision-making associated, for example, with equity. The latter had long emphasised the importance of judges exercising discretionary remedies according to substantive, if often vague, standards of fairness, justice, 'good faith' and 'good conscience', in which the moral qualities of the motivations and actions of the parties were often decisive factors.[25] Atiyah notes that the emergence of formalism within legal reasoning and analysis coincided with the rise of liberalism and associated free-market principles and practices within the economy.[26] The emergence of formalism was never uncontested, even within those law schools where its main advocates were employed. In other words, it would be fair to conclude that the authors of even the most formalistic examples of legal scholarship, the classic law textbook or treatise, were entirely and exclusively committed to this approach to legal scholarship.[27]

Furthermore, by the start of the twentieth century in North America, formalism was rapidly losing its grip upon legal education, partly in response to the influential work of

---

[21]On the idea that there is frequently a 'gap' between the 'paper rules' systematised in law books and law in action, see D. Nelken, 'The "Gap Problem" in the Sociology of Law: A Theoretical Review' (1981) 1 *Windsor Yearbook of Access to Justice*, 35.

[22]P. S. Atiyah, *The Rise and Fall of Freedom of Contract*, (Oxford: Clarendon, 1979), 388.

[23]Twining, 1994 *op. cit.*, 107.

[24]Robert Goff, 'The Search for Principle', 69, *Procs Brit Acad* 169, and 'Judge, Jurist and Legislator', [1987] *Denning Law J* 70. Connaghan and Mansell notes that: 'The common impression of the *form* of negligence is as an essentially "black-letter" discipline with perhaps more woolly edges than most and a more explicit if nevertheless limited role for political considerations in the determination of results. This is certainly the impression created by classical tort texts such as Winfield & Jolowicz, and Street.' Joanne Connaghan and Wade Mansell, 'Tort Law', in I. Grigg-Spall and P. Ireland, *Critical Lawyers Handbook*, Vol.1, (Oxford: Pluto Press, 1992), 83.

[25]Atiyah, 1979 *op. cit.*, 393.

[26]*Ibid.*, 389.

[27]P. Carrington, 'Aftermath' in Cane and Stapleton, *Essays for Patrick Atiyah*, (Oxford: Clarendon, 1991), 144-5.

legal realists but mainly because of wider cultural and social changes.[28] The result was that doctrinal rules were taken to operate in a looser way as guidelines, rather than hard-and-fast rules.[29] In England and Wales, by contrast, the formalist emphasis on law as hard-and-fast rules continued to be influential in legal scholarship and legal argumentation before appeal courts, and has declined in influence and prestige only from the late 1960s onwards.[30] Twining has shown how many of the key features of the black-letter tradition, in particular its preferred way of conducting legal analysis, are embodied in the genre of the standard legal textbook oriented towards LLB students. He identifies these features as follows:

> The emphasis upon the autonomy of law as an independent discipline or science; the centrality of doctrine (rules and principles) to the concept of 'law'; the clear differentiation of law as it is from law as it ought to be; exposition and 'neutral' analysis usually given pride of place over criticism and suggestion for reform; and a reluctance to discuss questions of policy in detail.[31]

Each of these points merits more detailed discussion, and we will undertake such discussion in the remainder of this chapter.

Following on from, but also supplementing, Twining's list, we would suggest that the distinct but related senses in which black-letter analysis can be defined as formalist, include the following:[32]

- The common law has its own self-contained existence and integrity, derived from essential principles endorsed by custom.[33]

- Influenced by the type of legal positivism espoused by Austin, Kelsen and Hart, legal formalism views law as a system of rules enacted and applied by the state;[34] it rejects the claims of 'legal pluralism' that law should be more widely defined to include cultural and institutional rules of conduct not underpinned by state sanctions for non-compliance.[35]

- Hence, all such rules appear imperative and willed by the ruling powers acting as an external and impersonal force governing the rest of society. The legal realm is a distinctive and independent area of social activity emerging from courts and related state institutions, which stand over and above other aspects of social organisation regulating society 'from on high', as it were.[36]

- There are other constitutional aspects of legal formalism. Subject only to limitations that are enshrined in constitutional measures, law is supposed to have unrestricted sovereignty and is an expression of the absolute power of the law-makers to make, interpret, revise and enforce rules.

---

[28]*Ibid.*

[29]Atiyah and Summers, *Form and Substance in Anglo-American Law* (Oxford: Clarendon, 1987)

[30]*Ibid.*, both generally and 88-9.

[31]Twining, in Cane and Stapleton, 1991 *op. cit.*, 4.

[32]See F. Schauer, 'Formalism', (1988) 97 *Yale Law Jnl*, 509-48.

[33]Tamanaha, *Realistic Socio-legal Theory*, (Oxford: Clarendon, 1997), 236; Atiyah and Summers, 1987 *op. cit.*, 250.

[34]Twining, 1994 *op. cit.*, 155.

[35]*Ibid.*, 17-18, 171-2.

[36]*Ibid.*

- However, the potential tyranny and arbitrariness inherent in uncontrolled state power are, it is claimed, limited by principles of the rule of law, the separation of powers between Parliament, the judiciary and government, and conventions of democratic accountability. Other limitations include legal controls over the political executive, formal universal rules equally applicable to all citizens, and the ostensible neutrality of the legal system itself.[37]

- Legal formalism is strongly committed to the nineteenth-century liberal doctrine of the separation of powers, particularly the independence of formal legal reasoning from deliberations of ideology and policy factors relevant to law-makers in Parliament.[38]

- Such formalism insists that legitimate forms of legal reasoning must respect the distinction between political law-making and the non-political application of law within individual cases, and gains its claimed objectivity, and by implication superior status, from such detachment and neutrality.

- The separation of powers and commitment to democracy restricts the role of all categories of lawyers. It is not the role of judges or lawyers more generally (including legal researchers and academics) to move beyond the role of identifying, interpreting and applying relevant legal rules and principles.[39] They exceed their remit if they attempt to create new law or engage in reform-oriented movements that seek to modify either the principles or the operation of law, or if they allow their subjective values and beliefs to influence the decision-making process.[40]

- Legal analysis, reasoning and research do not need to, and should not, look behind the rules to identify the purpose and function underpinning any particular doctrinal requirement.[41] Formalism in property law, for instance, has resulted in the refusal of judges to respond to calls for judicial reform even where these would amount to little more than the acceptance and endorsement of already settled professional (and judicial) practice, and where this refusal would necessitate legislative intervention.[42]

- Despite the commitment to the political neutrality of law, formalism endorses the validity of a series of highly individualistic values and assumptions associated with

---

[37]Atiyah and Summers, 1987 *op. cit.*, 25 – emphasising that formalistic emphasis upon rules and rule-based reasoning is important to the liberal model of the rule of law and orderly and accountable government.

[38]Atiyah, 1979 *op. cit.*, 660–61. Of course, even the most formalistic form of legal reasoning may be influenced by policy factors. The point is that formalism requires the prohibition of the 'intrusion' into legal reasoning of overt policy and other political and moral factors. The question of whether this demand can always be met even by the most formalistic of adherents to the black-letter tradition is another question altogether.

[39]Tamanaha, 1997 *op. cit.*, 35.

[40]Atiyah, 1979 *op. cit.*, 664 – citing Lord Jowitt's firm statement of this belief in 1951. See also Lord Evershed, 'The Judicial Process in Twentieth Century England', (1961) 61 *Columbia Law Rev*. 761, n.1.

[41]J. Bell, 'Conceptions of Public Policy', in Cane and Stapleton, 1991 *op. cit.*, 88–9, 105.

[42]For example in *Chapman v Chapman* [1954] AC 429, both the Court of Appeal and the House of Lords refused, because of the absence of any precedent 'authorising' this practice, to recognise any inherent power of the Chancery Court to vary a trust, even where it was clearly desirable in the interests of infant beneficiaries that this be done. As a result, Parliament was obliged to pass the Variation of Trusts Act 1958. This is one result of the formalists' argument that, even where the law is plainly unjust, it is simply improper for judges to alter established private property rights. See R. Megarry (1952) 68 *LQR* 379. See also the House of Lords' decision in *Pettitt v Pettitt* [1970] AC 904 regarding the improper judicial creation of the 'deserted wife's equity', which was itself promptly reversed by the 1970 Matrimonial Proceedings and Property Act.

classical liberalism and liberal political theory. It endorses those distinctly 'modern' (dominant nineteenth century) values relating to individual civil and political liberty and equal treatment within the constitutional sphere, and laissez-faire and freedom of contract within the economic realm.[43]

● Such commitments are enshrined within, and operate through, a series of basic axioms, legal principles and judicial practices. These include the insistence that, providing individuals comply with formal requirements for creating private law devices, the actual terms and conditions must be decided upon by the parties themselves.[44]

● Individual freedom includes the right to make a foolish bargain under which one party is exploited by another. It is the role of law to facilitate and enforce all types of contractual bargains between adults, without attempting to exercise paternalistic oversight to protect competent adults from the consequences of their own actions.[45]

● Questions of validity in legal analysis are determined not by the substantive content of legal doctrine and decisions (whether either the legal rules or how they are applied appear fair and just in terms of their substantive or distributive outcomes). Instead, such questions focus on strictly formal issues regarding whether a decision is legitimate in the sense of being consistent with prior precedent, whether the rule itself was properly created (questions of 'pedigree' in fact), and whether its judicial or quasi-judicial application fully complied with technical standards of 'due process' and other formal procedural standards.

● In a purely technical sense, it is possible to distinguish correct and incorrect applications of a precedent or a procedural requirement of the legal system, without resort to moral or political value judgements.[46]

● Legal formalism has a distinct definition of justice. It focuses not on political and moral issues of substantive or social justice, but rather on technical standards of 'procedural justice' (the avoidance of any appearance of bias and discrimination) and 'corrective justice' (individual remedies for specific violations of individual rights).[47] For example, formalism maintains that it is not the role of judges to refuse to enforce a private law device, such as a contract or a trust or other property disposition, simply because the effect would be to create a possible injustice to one of the parties or to third parties.

● Because the application of law within courts and tribunals is clearly distinct and independent from other areas of society, legal analysis needs to reflect this autonomy by operating as an objective and formal science of legal principles. Legal analysis and reasoning, the characteristic way of thinking like a lawyer is, and should remain, unique and distinctive. As such, it needs to be isolated as far as possible from the outside influences of political, social and ethical/moral discourses.

● Judges are expected to preserve public confidence in the integrity of the legal system and the coherence of legal doctrine by giving an objective and neutral interpretation

---

[43]Karl Llewellyn quoted in Twining, 1994 *op. cit.*, 99 – noting that the principle that like cases should be treated in a like manner which underpins the doctrine of precedent has a distinctly *moral* dimension linked to liberal conceptions of justice.

[44]*Ibid.*, 666.

[45]*Ibid.*, 389.

[46]*Ibid.*, 664; Twining, in Cane and Stapleton, 1991 *op. cit.*, 5.

[47]Baldwin, 1995 *op. cit.*, 38.

of existing doctrine in a manner that supports key liberal values of the rule of law. These values include consistency, certainty and predictability in the sense of settled doctrine, which allows individuals to plan their lives in a more rational way. These traditional and indeed conservative values are typically treated as paramount, particularly by black-letter textbooks.[48]

- Legal discourse is expected to be an *explicitly rational* type of discourse in keeping with the secular enlightenment imperatives of science, in which all knowledge is supported by objective evidence validated by supposedly rigorous and scientific methods.

- Hence, legal formalism conceives of legal doctrine as ideally a seamless, logical and internally coherent system of intelligible and broadly reasonable rules and principles, whose specific meaning can be precisely and clearly stated in advance of its application to any specific case.[49]

- The existence of this generally coherent and seamless system, combined with the requirement that judges will strictly follow the clear meaning and implications of the established rules, allows the judiciary to make 'legally correct' decisions on a regular basis. This is made possible by judges logically deducing the implications of rules and principles for the relevant facts of a specific case.[50]

- Rigorous and objective legal reasoning by judges, as well as by academic researchers, is always capable of arriving at the single correct answer to any legal problem by properly analysing the implications of prior legal doctrine for the material facts of any dispute or issue. Because law consists of a 'set of abstract rational concepts and principles with rationally governed internal and external relations', it is possible to apply an almost 'mechanical process' of legal reasoning to generate 'specific answers to particular cases.'[51]

- Strict legal reasoning is a deductive science of principles, whose formal nature (i.e. its independence from the observation of factual events or states of affairs) is broadly analogous to the sciences of mathematics or geometry.[52]

- The different strands of formalism, including the commitment to liberal political and free-market values, means that rights contained in legal doctrine are typically defined in absolute terms, as universal entitlements of the one who has the right. For instance, if individuals have a clear legal right to enjoy their private property as they see fit, then there is no question of the court qualifying this right to merely balance the interests of neighbours or the wider community's need for a site for a new hospital.

- Legislation, and legal doctrine more generally, should be interpreted in terms of criteria that are strictly 'internal' to the legal doctrine, as distinct from the 'external' political purpose or policy goal.[53]

---

[48]J. Bell, in Cane and Stapleton, 1991 *op. cit.*, 111–12; Twining, in Cane and Stapleton, 1991 *op. cit.*, 5.

[49]This idea of law as a deductive science from rational axioms and established principles was one of the main elements of legal formalism criticised by O. Holmes, 'The Path of the Law', (1897) 10 *Harv. LR* 451, 460–61.

[50]Tamanaha, 1997 *op. cit.*, 35.

[51]*Ibid.*

[52]Atiyah, 1979 *op. cit.*, 660.

[53]For a dramatic counter-example where the courts rejected formalism by restricting and qualifying the literal meaning of legal rules by reference to an entirely novel ground of public policy, See *R v Registrar General, ex. p. Smith*, [1990] 2 All ER 170.

- Types of reasoning stemming from the assignment of rights and obligations to private individuals in their exchanges with other such individuals, which are characteristic of private law, provide the general framework and blueprint for legal analysis and reasoning more generally. This remains the case even with public law subjects, such as criminal, constitutional and family law.[54]

- Taken as an overall package, formalist dimensions of black-letter analysis require researchers to study the relevant case law in order to reveal the 'essence' of both the rules followed by judges, and the underlying principles that are supposed to both underpin and authorise the rule. As Peritz notes:

  > As law professors . . . , we demand of our students first and foremost that they read and learn from textbooks filled with judicial opinions. The traditional process of reading a case opinion concludes with a statement of its holding, a formulation of the rule that grounds the decision. The traditional process of reading common law concludes with a more general statement of legal doctrine, a formulation of grounds to bind the individual rules together to discover a coherent body of law. This traditional pedagogy is formalist in the strong sense that it is founded in the belief that there are general principles governing common law development and the corresponding belief that these principles, along with other principles derived from them, constitute the elements of legal knowledge. This traditional process, still the standard fare in most American law schools despite the Legal Realist-flavored education of most law professors, is known as teaching 'black letter law'.[55]

Hence, the formalism of the black-letter approach includes the idea that to conduct dissertation research into law, students are required to display their acquired analytical competence in the techniques of 'problem-solving' through the application of supposedly clear, pertinent and precise rules, and legal justification by reference to the clear implications of these rules. Dissertation students must acquire and apply an in-depth knowledge of a distinct set of rules, techniques and procedures which amount to a closely guarded canon of argument and inference.[56]

Subsequent subsections will consider key elements of these strands more fully after a brief discussion of the changing, and arguably increasingly contested, status of the black-letter approach.

● Other Features of the Black-Letter Approach

Our earlier broad-brush definition characterised black-letter law as an approach that aims to produce and renew doctrinal commentaries upon law understood as an internally coherent system of rules, principles and basic axioms. Although useful as an initial and provisional clarification of the black-letter approach, as it stands this definition raises as many issues as it resolves. For example, how does this approach interpret the defining characteristics of technical rules of law that distinguish them from more general legal

---

[54]Baldwin, 1995 *op. cit.*, 29.

[55]R. J. Peritz, 'Exploring the Limits of Formalism: AI and Legal Pedagogy', (1999) *Law Technology Journal*, Vol.1, No.1: http://www.law.warwick.ac.uk/ltj/1-1f.html.

[56]R. Unger, *Law and Modern Society*, (NY: Free Press 1983), 1, 6ff.

principles and basic axioms?[57] Does the black-letter methodology focus exclusively on the semantics of written rules alone (their meaning and scope), or does it also embrace their meaning and scope in the context of their practical full, selective or partial enforcement? Students are, perhaps, entitled to expect a more extended discussion of this methodology's various explicit and implicit features, underlying assumptions and beliefs: in short, a more fleshed out and better-illustrated clarification of the nature of the black-letter approach to legal research.

This approach focuses on a limited range of questions and issues deemed to be 'strictly legal' in nature. This does not, of course, preclude students from conducting research into the possible application of established rules to new areas of social life, such as new technology or internet auctions. What it does preclude is an imaginative reconstruction of how law could, in principle, be substantially different from how it currently is and operates. Those questions that cannot be 'answered' in a precise and objective way by reference to what is already contained in specific cases and statutes will, typically, be deemed to fall outside the scope of black-letter forms of legal reasoning, research and analysis. Dissertation students adopting a black-letter approach will be expected to recognise and comply with this distinction.

To meet the requirements of a black-letter methodology, dissertation students and other legal researchers must also learn to emulate how specific types of lawyers, particularly senior barristers and judges, conduct legal arguments. Through their own writings, students must demonstrate that they have acquired the ability to 'think like a lawyer'. This is supposed to involve successfully imitating these distinctive techniques of linguistic argumentation and 'reasoning', of making and justifying specific claims about rights and responsibilities with reference to existing legal rules embodied fully, or at least by implication and analogy, in a system of precedents.[58] This taught skill is difficult to obtain without researchers first engaging in a period of sustained and disciplined instruction into the appropriate argumentative and linguistic techniques. Students must endure such 'drilling' to the point where these newly-acquired and, in one sense, 'artificial' interpretative skills finally become 'second nature'. Part of the difficulty lies in the fact that, even after students have bracketed out and excluded wider moral and political questions regarding human values and moral worth, doctrinal categories remain complicated and abstruse, 'learned only at the expense of great personal effort'.[59] Subscribers to the black-letter tradition insist that overcoming these initial difficulties forms a necessary part of the law students' acquisition of the rigorous analysis and acute interpretative skills of the trained legal mind, which are characteristic of law as a distinctive academic discipline. The successful law student's ability to ultimately acquire, cultivate and fluently display such analytical and interpretative skills is, to those who form part of the black-letter tradition, a valuable end in itself.

---

[57]Few black-letter works actually define what they mean by legal rules, let alone rules in general. However, Twining and Miers correct this by defining a rule as 'a general norm mandating or guiding conduct or action in a given type of situation'. *How to Do Things with Rules*, 3rd edition, (London: Weidenfeld and Nicolson, 1991), 131. Whilst Roscoe Pound defined a legal rule as 'a legal precept attaching a definite detailed legal consequence to a definite detailed state of fact.' *Jurisprudence*, 5 vols. (St. Paul, MN: West Publishing, 1959), ii, 124. See also F. Schauer, *Playing by the Rules* (Oxford: Clarendon Press, 1991) ch.1.

[58]T. Murphy, 'Reference without Reality' (1990) 1 *Law and Critique*, 74.

[59]Anthony Bradney, 'Law as a Parasitic Discipline', (1998) 25 *JLS* 71 at 78.

● The Centrality of Classic Textbooks

It is not possible to discuss the operation of the black-letter tradition without also examining the type of legal scholarship that most perfectly embodies this approach: the traditional student textbooks, which themselves imitated earlier practitioner-oriented texts and manuals. Indeed, for some purposes, the idea of the textbook tradition could also be used as a synonym for the black-letter approach. In the preface to his book on contract law, Hugh Collins claims:

> Perhaps no other subject in the standard canon of legal education can claim such an august tradition, such rigour of analysis, and such sublime irrelevance, as the law of contract. The multitude of textbooks repeat an interpretation of the subject which has remained unaltered for a century or more in its categorisation and organisation of the legal materials . . . this fidelity to nineteenth century *laissez-faire* ideals, which is unmatched in other fields of legal studies, often remains concealed behind a presentation of the law which emphasise the formal, technical, and ahistorical qualities of legal reasoning. The result of this fidelity to tradition is that students learn in their early years a misleading and almost entirely irrelevant set of rules.[60]

He further argues that:

> As long as students continue to receive the implicit message from traditional texts that legal reasoning comprises the formal application of rules gleaned from ancient precedents which embrace *laissez-faire* values, their legal education commences on the wrong foot and never recovers.[61]

A formalistic orientation has even been reflected in the style of presentation and organisation of legal materials with early student textbooks consisting of numbered paragraphs, or as codes subdivided into numbered rules.

Certainly there is a close linkage between textbooks and the traditional legal curriculum, which organises law under formal, doctrinal headings, such as criminal, land and contract law, rather than according to substantive social categories and the particular areas of social life that are regulated and affected by law.[62] Classic student textbooks on contract, tort and equity 'lump together a wide variety of disparate social situations and categories', which could not survive in this form if the field was reinterpreted by placing law in its wider contexts in which this institution performs a variety of different social functions (discussed below).[63] It is noticeable that many (but not all) of those law in context works that explicitly reject the black-letter approach also refuse to accept the idea of

---

[60]Hugh Collins, *The Law of Contract*, 3rd ed, (London: Butterworths, 1997), preface, v.

[61]*Ibid.*

[62]Twining, in Cane and Stapleton, 1991 *op. cit.*; see, for example, Moffat and Chesterman, *Trusts Law: Text and Material*: (London: Weidenfeld, 1988), in which, instead of the standard listing, of statutes and cases, we are treated to a series of articles and other materials from a wide range of economic, fiscal, governmental and sociological sources drawn from both the UK and America. To the student bogged down in a mass of standard and insular legal materials, this may seem a long-overdue reform in the treatment of the subject. As a result of their adoption of a law in context approach, Moffat and Chesterman divide the book up in a four-part way which is quite different from that of black-letter texts. These parts study trusts in the 'context' of the preservation of family wealth, family breakdown, commerce and 'non-profit activity'. *Ibid.*, 6-7.

[63]*Ibid.*, 7.

discrete fields of law and prefer more fact-based classifications. Hence, 'compensation for accidents' can be substituted for tort law, 'public control of land' for real property, and 'information in litigation' for the law of evidence.[64]

Twining has argued that the centrality of the textbook is closely linked to institutional, rather than strictly intellectual, factors in legal education:

> The textbook is still the most used form of students' books. This is largely due to the style of examinations that law students have to undergo; the professional examinations have traditionally been little more than tests of memory . . . the information content of university law exams has tended to be significantly more than in most other subjects. This is to be explained by the influence of the profession both direct and indirect . . . it is not surprising that the majority of candidates for law examinations . . . rely heavily upon the textbook and its satellite, the nutshell.'[65]

Traditionally, there has also been a vicious circle in which academics' attempts to publish books, which are oriented towards students but which depart from the style of a traditional student textbook, have been rejected by mainstream law publishers. They have been rejected because the subject discussed by these proposed works is not, or not yet, studied as a separate topic in law degrees. At the same time, attempts to introduce such new topics into legal education have often been opposed by traditionalists because of the lack of a specialist textbook in this field around which the proposed law module/course could operate.[66] Although casebooks have become increasingly used in legal education to remove pressure from library sources, unlike in North America, this has not displaced traditional textbooks.[67] This may be because the systematic classification provided by such works is particularly highly valued by academics who subscribe to a black-letter methodology.

Unlike members of other academic disciplines, dissertation students working within the parameters of the black-letter tradition are not expected to generate new data through empirical research or experimentation in the way that scientific researchers are expected to produce new scientific findings. Instead, their roles have largely been confined to the task of systematising existing and emerging case law and legislative developments. Such material must be reinterpreted so that it becomes fully integrated into apparently coherent bodies of doctrine organised in encyclopaedia of rules, principles and axioms, and related doctrinal commentaries.[68] These textbook and related works of doctrinal exposition and commentary resemble a chemistry book in the way in which they are 'divided up into a number of elements or rules, traced back to their origins through strings of cases.'[69] They embody the narrow and technical values associated with traditional, standard reference books, including accuracy, internal coherence and authoritativeness. These 'law books' differ markedly from those research monographs whose focus is on 'law in action', and where originality of approach, systematic criticism and imaginative speculation regarding the future direction of law are highly valued. Indeed,

---

[64]*Ibid.*, 23.

[65]*Ibid.*, 6.

[66]*Ibid.*

[67]*Ibid.*

[68]Twining, 1994 *op. cit.*, 135–7.

[69]A. Harding, *A Social History of English Law*, (Harmondsworth: Penguin, 1966); Twining, in Cane and Stapleton, 1991 *op. cit.*, 4.

many textbooks advertise themselves as useful for legal practitioners as well as law students, and gloss over the obvious difficulties of satisfying the requirements and demands of these very different types of readership.[70] The task of updating these standard works to ensure that they appear to remain a current and authoritative statement of law is a vital part of the black-letter agenda that contributes to its replication from one generation of scholars to the next.

Twining claims that 'at least until recently, the expository textbook has been the dominant form of educational work in England at both degree and professional levels'.[71] Within land law, for example, Simpson goes as far as to refer to the historical standing of Cheshire's classic *Modern Law of Real Property* as 'the Bible', and notes how the original classification and organisation of land law, which at the time represented a highly original and contestable interpretation, became accepted by the authors of later textbooks, including Megarry and Megarry and Wade.[72] For example, most later textbooks have followed Cheshire's original (and by no means necessary) classification of equitable interests into 'family' and 'commercial' sub-categories.[73] Clark *et al.* are surely right when they note: 'The orthodoxy of the "Cheshire world view" of land law and legal education continues to retain a firm grip on mainstream property law teaching'.[74] Cheshire's black-letter agenda concerning legal research and analysis in land law has not only been widely used by generations of law students and teachers, but it has also filtered down as a 'book of authority', constituting a blueprint for subsequent textbooks. It has also entered into the substantive case law that such works seek to interpret, order and classify. For example, in *Re Ellenborough Park*,[75] Sir Raymond Evershed MR uses Cheshire's formula for understanding, and then analysing, the essential characteristics of an easement. He even goes so far as to consider it unnecessary to review prior cases, because Cheshire itself is taken as a primary source of the law, one, moreover, which is unaffected by alternative views expressed in the case law.[76]

Indeed, although law degree modules are routinely centred around textbooks that embody the black-letter agenda, Twining notes that many academics, even those who teach such modules, may not entirely endorse the particular 'intellectual attitudes' and 'educational values' embodied in such works. In particular, even traditionally-minded legal academics may in part disassociate themselves from how such rule books simplify complex issues by providing students a diet of predigested generalisations, expressed in a dogmatic and authoritarian manner. Such works invite students to memorise, in parrot fashion, masses of technical and intricate detail as a precondition for passing end-of-year exams (initially at Universities and later within professional training courses), and, as such, hardly endorse any more elevated role for university level education.[77]

---

[70]Twining, in Cane and Stapleton, 1991 *op. cit.*, 6.

[71]Twining, 1994 *op. cit.*, 137.

[72]A. W. Simpson, 'Book Review', (1993) 56 *MLR* 608.

[73]Cheshire's approach was largely followed by Megarry and Megarry and Wade; see A. W. Simpson: 'The tradition established by Cheshire was maintained by R. E. Megarry in his "Manual", and by him and his collaborator W. Wade in their major systematising treatise on the subject.' 1993 *op. cit.*, 608.

[74]Twining, 1994 *op. cit.*, 91.

[75][1955] 3 All ER 667.

[76]*Ibid.*, at 673–82: At 677 he notes: 'We think it unnecessary to review the authorities in which the principle has been applied for the effect of the decisions is stated with accuracy in Dr Cheshire's book.'

[77]Twining, in Cane and Stapleton, 1991 *op. cit.*, 4.

The dominant approach to the teaching of law can be characterised as 'black-letter'. This approach takes law to be a system of rules to be learned, and it was considered to be the ideal preparation for the aspiring lawyer. The old-style Law Society Finals were archetypal 'black-letter' in this respect. The approach can be described by the rather bald statement 'R + F = C' or 'Rule plus Fact yields Conclusion'.[78]

Many legal academics consider that university level education requires students and researchers to engage in systematic reflection (and critical self-reflection) upon the adequacy and assumptions behind existing legal categories and institutional practices. Where a supervisor takes this view, then the type of educational practices endorsed by the standard black-letter textbook will rarely, if ever, entirely fulfil such expectations.[79] In particular, supervisors may be critical of the tendency of such textbooks to produce rather bland descriptions of what was held in particular cases that gloss over the difficulties and issues of interpretation, which are clear from a close reading of the cases themselves.

Twining suggests that the typical black-letter textbook rarely shows any appreciation of the existence of such interpretative issues, and will typically maintain an 'attitude of indifference to their own methodological assumptions.'[80] Recognition, in full or part, of such limitations may explain why many supervisors often insist that students also move beyond the textbooks by studying the primary sources because this alone will allow a better appreciation of more complex issues of interpretation, the analysis of precedent and legal reasoning more generally.

Certainly, traditional textbooks exemplify rigorous technicality almost for its own sake, and positively invite students to use their chapters as substitutes for a close analysis of primary sources. Insofar as this is the case, then those academics who subscribe to the black-letter agenda may often retain an ambiguous attitude to these works. Some supervisors will endorse the necessity of referring dissertation and other students to such works of synthesis and classification as, for instance, particularly useful for undergraduate students new to the topic who need to rapidly obtain a general overview. However, they may also expect students to recognise that, although perhaps accurate, the textbook accounts will rarely exhaust the intellectual possibilities of each topic covered.[81] Hence, referring dissertation students to the relevant chapters of classic textbooks may appear to supervisors to be a necessary first step that makes it possible for students to engage in more serious and detailed research into a particular area of legal doctrine. This may be thought to be possible through a close reading of original primary sources and academic articles, in which textbooks play a role akin to that of the overview provided by large-scale maps for those exploring a new region.[82] Even legal academics who have reservations about particular aspects of standard textbooks, or the overall genre itself, may still welcome the fact that traditional textbooks provide such a general map which enables students to initially 'find their feet', as it were. Such works means that

---

[78]'What is Jurisprudence?': Ilex course document: http://www.ilex-tutorial.ac.uk/uploads/4253B0A8_4.pdf
[79]Twining, in Cane and Stapleton, 1991 *op. cit.*, 10.
[80]*Ibid.*, 5.
[81]*Ibid.*, 4–5.
[82]*Ibid.*, 4, 6.

dissertation (and other) law students do not have to 'reinvent the wheel' by super-imposing their own system of classification and order upon the previous wilderness of case law and statutory provisions, a possibility which would make the task of supervision a far harder, and perhaps less rewarding, task.

Dissertation supervisors who subscribe to the black-letter tradition may also value some of the technical and analytical rigour demonstrated in such texts. These include the detailed focus on legalistic questions regarding the nature and scope of doctrinal mean-ing, such as 'what constitutes the nature of contractual acceptance?', and the close link-age of abstract concepts, such as ownership and property, to general principles, specific rules and individual cases. Such supervisors may also require the strict exclusion of supposedly 'non-legal' factors, such as how the policy embodied in a particular legal measure gives effect to a specific political ideology or aspect of public policy more generally.[83] Supervisors may also endorse the general attempt of such works to provide authoritative and confident statements of 'what the law' itself says on any particular topic in a lucid and well-structured manner, and which are apparently free of speculation or gratuitous value judgements superimposed by the subjectivity of the authors and/or editors. This tendency harmonises with the ideals of objectivity and neutrality endorsed by legal formalism more generally. In short, many traditional law textbooks provide an almost perfect embodiment of the nature and assumptions of the black-letter approach to legal research and analysis.

● Insulating the Dissertation Topic from 'External' Factors

Wherever dissertation students adopt the black-letter approach, this will require under-taking two related operations: a narrowing down of scope, and a bracketing out of certain types of material deemed irrelevant to a strictly legal type of analysis. The first operation involves identifying, and then zooming in on, those aspects of the topic that are supposed to be distinctly and uniquely 'legal' in the sense that they fall within the range of technical and legalistic questions that a lawyer could raise before an appeal court regarding points of law.[84] These would include questions regarding the meaning and scope of substantive legal categories (including procedural and evidential rules). Students are expected to engage in a very close, careful and rigorous analysis of 'every phrase, word or punctuation mark' of relevant cases and statutes.[85]

For students adopting a strictly black-letter approach, the second type of operation is the requirement, stemming from its commitment to a formalistic mode of analysis, to strictly exclude from the scope of the dissertation all political, moral and economic factors that are deemed to be 'extrinsic' to the distinctly legal aspects. In other words, the subscribers to the black-letter approach either expressly claim, or simply assume, that, in order to engage in legal research and analysis, it is necessary to strictly exclude moral and ethical values. This requirement explains why morality or ethics are rarely considered explicitly.[86]

---

[83]*Ibid.*, 5.

[84]Twining, 1994 *op. cit.*, 100, 155.

[85]*Ibid.*, 92.

[86]See A. Hutchinson, 'Beyond Black-letterism: Ethics in Law and Legal Education', (1999) 33 *Law Teacher*, 301-9; D. Sugarman, 'A Hatred of Disorder: Legal Science, Liberalism and Imperialism', in P. Fitzpatrick, *Dangerous Supplements*, (London: Pluto, 1991), 34.

For example, if students adopt a strictly black-letter approach to plea-bargaining within either national or international criminal justice systems, then they are likely to exclude the following questions from consideration:

- Are the principles that guide legal decision-making with respect to plea-bargaining morally justifiable?

- How should legal systems define and regulate the practice of plea-bargaining to avoid morally unacceptable results?

- Should criminal justice systems allow plea-bargaining, either only under specific conditions or more generally?

- The requirement to strictly exclude moral and ethical considerations as irrelevant for, and indeed as an impediment to, strict legal analysis of the meaning and implications of legal provisions is supported by one of the key assumptions of legal formalism: that is, the belief that questions of values are essentially subjective and partial, whereas strictly legal analysis is rigorously objective.

By contrast, sociolegal studies tends to address 'law in action', that is, law's social origins and impact upon different groups in society. This approach will often require interviews to be conducted with lawyers' clients and other parties affected by legal processes. As a result, researchers will inevitably have to confront and respond to a series of *ethical questions* related to the conduct of their research. On the other hand, because black-letter analysis restricts itself to analysing law in books, it can in one sense afford to exclude discussion of ethical values and their implications.[87] This is because all the sources used by legal researchers will be public documents contained in the law library. Hence, no particular individuals are being discussed with respect to previously confidential aspects of their personal lives, except insofar as they may have already become involved in a legally important case in which such details have already been revealed.

● Setting and Answering the Question: What is the Legal Position on X?

As part of the wider imperative to ensure the continued renewal of the tradition of doctrinal commentary, what other requirements does the black-letter methodology present to those students and other researchers who adopt it for their research? Researchers are expected to provide a definitive and precise statement and commentary that answers the question: 'What is the legal position on X?' More sophisticated versions of this methodology, which involve an element of historical reconstruction, may rephrase this question as: 'How has legal doctrine come to develop the current position on X?'[88] In both cases, students will be expected to provide answers that are fully supported by references to, and short apt quotations from, a wide range of relevant and current cases and statutes, against which the accuracy of these statements of the nature and scope of points of law can be assessed. In such situations, more 'hardline' black-letter lecturers sometimes disapprove of student-oriented publications in the tradition of 'cases and materials'. They are seen as representing unacceptable shortcuts to the process of students

---

[87]Twining, 1994 *op. cit.*, 16, 91 – noting that traditionally, 'most learning about law centres on books and the centre of the law school is the library'.

[88]See, for example, Maudsley and Burn, *Trust and Trustees: Cases and Materials*, (London: 1990) preface.

building up for themselves extracts of relevant cases and statutes, as a way of demonstrating that they have acquired the ability to identify and analyse relevant material.

Students whose dissertation research embodies the black-letter tradition will generally be expected to present their work as if it has been built, from the bottom up, as it were, from their own close analysis of a full range of primary sources. Such students are expected to give particular attention to the implications of the most recent appeal judgments, particularly those of the Court of Appeal, the House of Lords or the European Court of Justice.[89] Hence, student dissertations that mainly or only cite secondary sources, particularly student textbooks, will be considered to have bypassed a necessary stage of the research process, even where the textbook account does not amount to an undue simplification.

The scientific disciplines expect researchers who present their findings to show that these stem directly from their own experiments. In a similar way, the black-letter approach expects legal researchers to demonstrate that they have immersed themselves within the primary sources to the point where they eventually become familiar with the meaning, scope, trajectory and implications of doctrinal rules, principles and categories. This expectation, that they will recognise the authority of primary sources, typically remains in force where students, and perhaps even their supervisors, are aware that, in practice, various 'shortcuts' are likely to be made. These shortcuts can include the use of nutshells, borrowed lecture notes, and casebooks containing extracts and summary paraphrases of the most 'relevant' parts of the primary sources.[90]

In short, one of the key requirements of successfully completing black-letter analysis is that researchers will be able to interpret cases and statutes in such a way as to provide an apparently definitive answer to the question: 'What is the law on X?' Such an answer must be fully grounded in, and supported by, citations to so-called 'primary sources': that is, cases and statutes and authoritative commentaries on their legal significance.

● The Requirement to Reveal a System of Underlying Principles Ordering Legal Rules

As already noted, the focus of black-letter analysis falls upon providing a descriptive commentary on points of law within legal doctrine in a way that is abstracted from the more mundane standpoints of everyday life.[91] It follows that students adopting this approach to their dissertation research are expected to focus on the precise and technical wording of the relevant statutes and on providing a close, and largely 'literal' analysis of judicial reasoning in a series of cases. Researchers are required to adopt and maintain this narrow but intensive focus in order to carry out a vital aspect of formalist legal reasoning, relating a certain claim as to what was decided in the reported judgments to prior legal rules, and then relating these cases and rules to more general legal principles and basic axioms that are considered to underpin both. Viewed in this way, legal principles are treated as though they both justified, and were clearly contained within, each aspect of the field of law in question.

---

[89]Twining, 1994 *op. cit.*, 105, 155 – noting that disputed points of fact largely dominate lower-level court and tribunal hearings, and that points of law prioritised by the black-letter tradition are mainly found in superior courts.

[90]Twining, in Cane and Stapleton, 1991 *op. cit.*, 6.

[91]Murphy, 1990 *op. cit.*, 77, Roger Cotterrell, *Law's Community*, (Oxford: OUP, 1995), ch.1.

In order to illustrate one aspect of the emergence of this tendency, it is helpful to review certain developments within the field of equity. Traditionally, decision-making in equity had emphasised judges 'doing justice' as between the individual parties, even at the expense of consistency and adherence to precedent. By contrast, later and more forma-listic modes of judging insisted that the identification and adherence to the implications of enduring legal principles was far more important.[92] As Atiyah notes: 'Principles were what mattered; if the right principles were selected they had to be applied in the belief that their general tendency would be to produce justice overall, even though in the case in hand the decision might seem harsh.'[93] The expectation that legal researchers will undertake a search for rational principles governing the application and development of legal doctrine is a general tendency of the black-letter tradition. If either students or their lecturers do not present law in terms of what is seemed to represent the 'appro-priate method', then this can be defined as representing a failing of legal skills. In teach-ing property law, for instance, it can easily be assumed that, if the lecturer presents a series of case-law decisions as though they were lacking any systematic coherence, any internally consistent logic, then this is deemed to reflect the illogical approach of the lecturer to this subject. This expectation is also apparent amongst reviewers of academic publications who are typically very quick to criticise any private law textbooks that fail to conform to the belief that there exists a set of guiding principles underpinning the case law. For example, Thompson's review article 'The Textbook Approach to Modern Land Law'[94] strongly attacks parts of Riddall's *Introduction to Land Law*[95] because this work does not give priority to the search for general principles underlying various case-law decisions. Thompson claims:

> All too often the reader is presented with lists of cases, some decided one way some decided another . . . with no attempt made to extract any principles from them . . . It is hard to see the point of this. . . . One should be able to analyse the underlying principles.[96]

The point of this example is not to endorse this criticism; it is rather to illustrate the extent to which subscribers to the black-letter tradition are committed to the view that any viable type of legal research and analysis must cross-reference individual reported cases to underlying principles either directly (case X illustrates and clarifies the meaning and scope of principle Y) or, more frequently, through the intermediary of specific tech-nical rules. This can involve an element of both synthesis and generalisation, leading to a precise sense of what questions are relevant for analysis. As Hofheinz notes:

> Understanding black letter law has two parts: first, identification and synthesis of rules and principles; second, construction of a question set. In the first part of this step you identify the rules and principles (whether judicial, legislative, or constitu-tional) which governed the resolution of prior problems. This is the process neces-sary for basic case analysis and briefing. You must identify the holding of each case dealing with a similar problem, and each black letter rule or principle relied upon by the court in reaching the holding. Synthesis into general statements reflecting

---

[92]Atiyah, 1979 *op. cit.*, 671ff.
[93]*Ibid.*, 1979 *op. cit.*, 394.
[94]*Conv*. (1989) 268.
[95]2nd edn, (London: Butterworths, 1988).
[96]Thompson, 1989 *op. cit.*, 277.

the decisions follows, and is commonly organized into a topical outline of such statements. In the second part of this step you must create a question set which requires each fact relevant to evaluation of the outcome (called 'material facts'), logically structured to allow efficient analysis of a new problem presenting new facts.[97]

Take, for example, the specific case on the resale of a fraudulently obtained car where a judge has to decide whether either an innocent seller or ultimate buyer should stand the total loss when a fraudster (who used a false name and address and whose cheque was later dishonoured) is not traceable. A black-letter analysis will need to identify and then relate the relevant cases to prior rules in the contract law doctrine of 'mistake' regarding the effect of mistaken identity as to the contracting parties and their attributes. The expectation of black-letter analysis is that a student dissertation on this topic will be able to interpret specific cases insofar, but only insofar, as they appear to contain and illustrate the operation of aspects of prior legal doctrine, doctrinal categories, rules and principles. Only those aspects of a law report that relate to the identification or exemplification of prior legal doctrine, or which illustrate or clarify its operation in a novel area of application, are deemed relevant materials for legal analysis.

One key idea that dissertation students who adopt a black-letter methodology will be required to reject is the apparently superficial contention that legal decision-making is a relatively arbitrary and unpredictable process, which is dependent not only upon the unique circumstances of each case but also the subjectivity of the decision-maker. The appearance of arbitrariness and subjectivity is supposed to be deceptive because, once students have acquired an adequate depth of understanding of legal skills and analytical competence, they will soon be able to appreciate the role of 'rational principles' governing the workings of the system. For example, the black-letter methodology claims that, underlying the apparent flux of 'like cases' being decided in different ways by different decision-makers, or decided the same way but for very different reasons, an underlying system of rules, principles and basic axioms is supposed to govern all acts of interpreting and applying law to facts.

Apparently, if one knows where and how to look, the presence and operation of general principles means that, according to the black-letter approach, there really is a logical method behind the merely apparent chaos and random madness of case law! Beneath the chaotic flux of case law lies the 'true nature' of certain legal categories that can be discovered and characterised through the rigorous application of formal legal methods. As Vick notes:

> By applying a distinctive mode of analysis to these authoritative texts, not only can the principles and rules of a legal system be discovered, but the texts themselves can be scrutinised to determine the extent to which they comply with the internal conventions of legal decision-making.[98]

More recently, Atiyah's comprehensive review of the emergence of formalism within contract law recognises 'the tendency to search for fixed principles which would govern large numbers of cases without too close an enquiry into the facts, and with the danger,

---

[97]Hofheinz, 1997 *op. cit.*
[98]Vick, 2004 *op. cit.*, 178.

therefore, that the individual decision might be (or anyhow might seem) hard and perhaps even unjust.'[99]

As far as the black-letter approach is concerned, the role of legal research is to identify and give an authoritative exposition and clarification of underlying principles of law. This task requires researchers to reimpose a supposedly native order and system, to 'rationalise' a large body of case law into a manageable shape. They are expected to accomplish this task by interpreting each individual reported decision as if it represented the exemplification of rules, and to interpret the rules themselves as if they were informed by a small number of underlying principles that govern the process of legal decision-making.[100] Hence, from the perspective of the black-letter methodology, dissertation research can and should engage in an exclusively 'doctrinal' type of analysis. Within this narrowly defined zone, legal researchers are required to apply a formal and logical 'analysis' to doctrinal materials. Such analysis must map out and classify, in a systematic manner, the precise relationship between cases, specific rules, general principles and underlying basic axioms.[101] Dicey summed up this commitment when he noted that 'by adequate study and careful thought whole departments of law can . . . be reduced to order and exhibited under the form of a few principles which sum up the effect of a hundred cases.'[102] In short, if dissertation students adopt the black-letter approach, then this would involve them focusing on, and then carefully describing the meaning and illustrating the ramifications of, a potentially large number of detailed and complex rules governed by the implications of a small number of general principles.

Furthermore, the belief in the general coherence of legal doctrine stemming from its governance by legal principles, and the harmonious relationships between individual cases, rules, general principles and basic axioms, also encompasses another contention: namely, that the values and beliefs that underscore the doctrine, particularly its basic axioms, are self-evidently valid. These values are treated as given, as both non-political and uncontentious. For example, with respect to black-letter approaches to the study of tort law, Connaghan and Mansell note that:

> The common impression of the form of negligence is as an essentially 'black-letter' discipline with perhaps more woolly edges than most and a more explicit if nevertheless limited role for political considerations in the determination of results. This is certainly the impression created by classical tort texts such as Winfield & Jolowicz, and Street.[103]

In sum, one of the goals of the black-letter approach is to distil, from the apparent chaotic and often inconsistent flux of particular law reports, a seamless web of rules. These must be analysed as if they were coordinated by principles that are universally applicable within their particular field. The task for researchers is to discover for themselves and then carefully reconstruct the existence, significance and implications of these underlying legal principles. Dissertation students are required to apply their interpretation

---

[99]Atiyah, 1979 op. cit., 392.

[100]See R. Goff, 'The Search for Principle' (1983) 69 Procs Brit Acad 169 at 171; 'Judge, Jurist and Legislator', 87 Denning Law J 70, at 92.

[101]Sugarman, 1991 op. cit., 34.

[102]A. Dicey, Can English Law be Taught at the Universities? (London: 1883), 20.

[103]Connaghan and Mansell, 'Tort Law' in Grigg-Spall and Ireland, 1992, 85.

of these principles to classify and rationalise a large body of apparently chaotic case-law decisions into a manageable shape. This involves students interpreting these decisions as if they exemplified rules which in turn are informed and governed by a small number of such underlying principles.[104]

● Searching for Coherence and Systematic Order

If, as our last section claims, the black-letter approach requires the search for principles governing and explaining the application of rules to facts in a body of case-law decisions, then this implies that this form of governance results in cases, rules and principles forming a system, akin to the components of a clock. Hence, one of the basic claims or assumptions of the black-letter tradition is that legal doctrine possesses logical coherence. This stems largely from the fact that the principles, which mediate between rules and basic axioms, are mutually reinforcing parts of a single coherent order. For example, Warrington has drawn attention to formalist tendencies, even within Equity, which emphasise, possibly even exaggerate, the 'quality and coherence' of legal doctrine.[105] This was first asserted by legal academics concerned to establish law as a distinct and even scientific discipline within the universities.[106] It is this assumption of coherence and systematic order which explains why the deployment of traditional textbooks provides a blueprint for the black-letter project of distilling 'the vast acreage of the law library into a set of principles, which it is assumed, can be coherently stated.'[107] A classic statement is Lawson's view of Land Law:

> The law is intensely abstract and has become a calculus remarkably similar to mathematics. . . . Logical and orderly, its concepts are perfectly defined and they stand in well recognised relations to one another . . . The various concepts . . . seem to move among themselves according to the rules of a game which exists for its own purpose. So extreme are these various characteristics that they make of this part of the law something more logical and more abstract than anything that to my knowledge can be found in any other law in the world.[108]

As already noted, this tradition regards the initial appearance of arbitrariness and subjectivity within court judgments published in law reports as deceptive. This impression is deemed to be false because, once researchers have acquired an adequate depth of understanding of legal skills and analytical competences, they will appreciate the *underlying coherence* of the workings of the system of specific technical rules governed, in a logical manner, by general principles.

Thus, one vital task for students conducting dissertation research from a black-letter approach is to carefully disclose the existence and operation of this underlying systematic order, which both integrates and 'makes sense of' the otherwise unwieldy mass of case-law decisions. Lord Goff summed up this systematising and rationalising aspect of

---

[104]See R. Goff, 'The Search for Principle' (1983) 69 *Procs Brit Acad* 169 at 171.

[105]R. Warrington, 'Land Law and Legal Education: Is There Any Justice or Morality in Blackacre?', [1984] *The Law Teacher*, 77–94, at 93.

[106]See Stuart Anderson, 'The 1925 Property Legislation: Setting Contexts' in Susan Bright and John Dewar (eds), *Land Law: Themes and Perspectives*, (Oxford: OUP, 1998), 126, n. 61.

[107]Warrington, 1984 *op. cit.*, 68.

[108]F. Lawson, *The Rational Strength of English Law*, (London: Stevens and Sons, 1952), 79.

black-letter analysis when he stated: 'The prime task of the jurist [legal researcher] is to take the cases and statutes which provide the raw material of the law on any particular topic; and . . . to build up a systematic statement of the law on the relevant topic in a coherent form'.[109]

An initial requirement for dissertation students searching for a coherent system and order is to focus on the relevance of the meaning and scope of a series of interrelated and often highly technical and intricate rules. Thus, one aspect of the assumption that law needs to be analysed as a coherent system of doctrine is the idea that legal subjects are founded upon a limited number of core 'general principles' rooted in a far smaller number of basic axioms. Whilst undertaking their dissertation research, students must be able to show that they can assess the requirements of 'the law' in their chosen area by reconstructing the relationship between different elements and levels of legal doctrine relevant to their specific topic. This means analysing past and present cases to identify how judges have clarified the meaning, scope and doctrinal implications of relevant rules, principles and basic axioms as applied to a range of given facts. Hofheinz has even argued that black-letter analysis, focusing on the identification of relevant legal rules and principles to specific facts, involves students applying a type of algorithm:

> The second part of understanding the black letter law is creating a structured set of questions, each of which require only one material fact to answer, which allow the efficient analysis of a particular problem. This type of structured process of asking questions is called an algorithm. The optimal algorithm will at each step ask the question which if negative eliminates the most remaining possibilities, and which step by step asks for each material fact necessary to support the legal conclusion that a particular black letter rule or principle applies or does not apply to the problem presented. It is helpful to be aware of the difference between material and relevant facts. Material facts being those dispositive of the outcome under current law. Relevant facts are those contextual facts which might be useful to consider if the result indicated by the material facts is not preferred, or if the case is one of first impression and policy analysis is appropriate. Thus if the black letter rule for the substantive area applicable to the problem states that if A, B, and C are true, Y is the result, and if A, D, and E are true Z is the result, the algorithm developed might be the following (note that by convention yes answers move analysis in one level of detail, no answers drop analysis down to the next question at the same level of detail): Is A present in the fact pattern? If yes, is B present in the fact pattern? If yes, is C present in the fact pattern? Then Y is the result. If yes, is D present in the fact pattern? If yes, is E present in the fact pattern? Then Z is the result. If no, then the black letter rule does not apply.[110]

In other words, black-letter analysis systematically applies a series of tests (if this, then that) derived from supposedly clearly defined rules to distinguish between factual contexts which, as matter of strict legal logic, give rise to, for example, a trust as distinct from a contract. Another example of the logical coherence of legal doctrine is the belief that the majority of land law derives from the basic axiom that land needs to be treated as a commodity to be bought and sold without restriction on the free market, regulated

---

[109]Lord Goff, 'Judge, Jurist and Legislature' [1987] *Denning Law J.* 79 at 92.
[110]Hofheinz, 1997 *op. cit*.

as far as possible only by the terms and conditions that buyers and sellers have negotiated and agreed between themselves. Many of the 'general principles' of land law (and key parts of trust law regarding real property) can be rationalised as giving effect to different aspects of this basic axiom, which serves as their premise. In turn, the mass of technical rules of land law can be treated as elements of a coherent system of doctrine because they are explicable as the logical implication of general principles, whose existence is logically necessary to give effect to these principles. Finally, the even greater number of law reports studied within land law are capable of being treated as concrete applications of these technical rules, rules which provide the *ratio decidendi* of the decisions in the cases. In short, individual cases form part of a coherent system because judges deciding cases essentially apply these rules to the particular facts of the case.

Whilst this process of analysis may generally duplicate the work of traditional textbooks, the expectation is that researchers will address the latest cases that have yet to be integrated into legal doctrine by such textbooks. In one sense, 'the proof of the pudding', as far as the expectations of the black-letter project are concerned, will be the student's ability to subject these recent cases to the same type of doctrinal exposition, involving the cross-referencing of cases, rules, principles and axioms, as has already taken place with respect to longer-standing cases. Thus, one major question in the assessment of student dissertations is whether they have analysed recent case and statute law in a manner that succeeds in supplementing and further developing existing knowledge of the relevant doctrinal cases, rules, principles and axioms, or their applicability to new factual contexts. The established textbooks provide extensive examples of the application of the standard formulae with respect to earlier materials. However, the expectation that students will analyse the most recent cases and statutes in a way that successfully applies these formulae to new materials is taken as proof that they have fully understood the meaning and logical operation of the relevant doctrine.

Certainly, the black-letter approach assumes that legal doctrine must be analysed on the assumption that it is broadly coherent. What, however, are the practical implications of this assumption for the conduct of dissertation research? The coherence of the system is supposed to stem from the fact that judges do not apply legal rules in a random way. Instead, they make decisions in a fashion that, from the start and throughout, are governed by the requirements and implications of the general principles of law from which the more detailed rules are logically derived. In other words, detailed and specific rules of law need to be analysed in terms of their logical structure and relations with other rules, principles and cases. This is because they are, as already noted, supposed to both embody, and be logically derived from, a wider and underlying 'principle' of legal doctrine. Hence, students will be expected to demonstrate that judges' application of even the most specific and technical of rules *also* involves the application of a wider and more general principle that is, in part at least, allegedly embodied in the rule itself. At the same time, a small number of basic legal axioms are themselves supposed to be embodied in a range of general principles.

By contrast, a student whose dissertation paraphrases the textbook analysis of the topic but, with respect to recent materials, fails to apply the standard analytical techniques of cross-referencing cases to rules and rules to both principles and axioms in order to bring out the general coherence and internal consistency of law, will typically be deemed to have failed to have demonstrated the required analytical technique. One such example would be a student dissertation that interprets recent materials as if the new cases were decided on their unique facts, and thus do not exemplify the application of a prior rule. Another would be an analysis suggesting that the rules themselves lack intelligible or consistent meaning, and have no necessary connection to the so-called general principles from which they are supposed to be logically derived. Hence, students who adopt this methodology must not analyse the topic in a way that contradicts its basic tenets. For example, dissertations should not discuss the cases independently of the rules (or points of law), or interpret the applicable rules as if they were entirely disconnected from those general principles that supposedly govern their application. Nor should student dissertations discuss the meaning and scope of general principles in a way that fails to identify how these are logically derived from basic axioms.

Researchers can assume that the overall doctrine will remain coherent providing certain conditions are met. These include: first, the requirement that legal principles (such as the ability of contracting parties to negotiate their own terms and conditions) are logically derived from the implications of the underlying axioms (such as freedom of contract). Secondly, that the rules of legal doctrine, for example those spelling out the criteria for a valid contractual acceptance) are themselves logically derived directly from the principles, and stem indirectly from the basic axioms, such as freedom of contract. In other words, legal doctrine will remain coherent providing it is possible to interpret the relationship between case decisions, legal rules, principles and axioms as enjoying a largely harmonious relationship. It follows that students are expected to interpret their dissertation topic as forming part of a system of doctrinal rules. This system in turn is coherent in the specific sense of having no major or permanent gaps, or internal conflicts, or qualities stemming from the impact of supposedly 'irrelevant' outside factors. These may include political ideology, or economic interests, or other factors stemming from the subjectivities of judges. In short, legal doctrine is believed to be largely coherent because all, or virtually all, its rules and principles directly or indirectly derive from basic axioms, whilst individual cases are governed by these rules and principles.

It follows that students are required to explain cases by reference to the internal logic of a system of legal doctrine. In other words, they must account for the fact that one party to litigation won their legal dispute by reference to the fact that this was logically required and determined by the judges' objective understanding and impartial application of the meaning of technical rules. A student's dissertation should analyse relevant case law on their topic on the assumption that it participates in the internal logic of legal doctrine: in other words, on the basis of the belief that such rules embody and specify the logical implications of a smaller number of uncontentious general principles of law governing the legal regulation of the dissertation topic, which in turn develop the logical implications of basic axioms. With respect to black-letter approaches to the study of tort law, Connaghan and Mansell note:

> Students are encouraged to see negligence law as rule-based. The task for the student is to discover the rules and also to discover which 'rules' are uncertain or unresolved. They are provided with a framework within which the rules fit and the implication is that rules which do not readily fit the framework are the 'hard cases' of particular interest to examiners. Underlying such a presentation of negligence is a belief that it is, to some extent at least, coherent, logical, rational and deducible from previous cases and fundamental principle. The subject of tort is one of the

most beguiling to students whose conception of legal study is that it is about discrete subjects apparently clearly defined and governed by a satisfying intermingling of statute and case law. If the textbooks are to be believed, tort appears to consist of a number of general principles (in most cases strongly corresponding with common sense) exemplified by case applications which seem, if the premises of tort are accepted, logical, coherent and essentially just.... Conventional texts, such as Winfield & Jolowicz, proceed on the basis that tort law consists of a basically uncontentious and apolitical body of principles.[111]

A dissertation that follows the demands of the black-letter approach should, it is believed, uncover and bring to the surface the underlying coherence of a system of doctrine, which underpins individual cases, and which less sophisticated interpretations would miss. If the dissertation is to succeed in revealing this element of a coherent system of doctrine, it must also explain away possible discrepancies within the case law, for example between specific rules, principles and axioms. Students are required to interpret these 'merely apparent' contradictions as either comparatively insignificant 'exceptions' to a rule or principle, or as evidence of another more specific rule confined to a narrow range of circumstances that was found in the original facts of the case, or from a cluster of like cases. Both interpretations effectively redeem and reinstate the starting assumption of coherence. The underlying tendency is to automatically exclude or marginalise the significance of those interpretations that challenge such rationalisations by disclosing the presence of factors other than strict and objective adherence to rule-following within the decision-making process.

By contrast, a layperson will typically interpret a law report through the lens of an everyday understanding and frame of reference. He or she will probably focus on the facts of the case, the source of the dispute, or the practical impact of the ultimate decision upon the parties, often seen as representatives of different groups in society. The assumption here, which is clear from introductory legal-methods textbooks, is that a layperson's way of interpreting the law will never be able to uncover the existence of the underlying order. This is because laypersons supposedly lack the specialist frame of reference possessed by those who have acquired the art of 'thinking like a lawyer'. Such 'ignorance' would remain even if he or she spent an entire lifetime reading every law report and statute in the law library. This is because the presence of the underlying rational order will remain a closed book for anyone who, through lack of training in formalistic legal methods endorsed by the black-letter model, does not possess the necessary analytical skills necessary to interpret the primary sources in *strictly doctrinal terms*, such as the renewal of earlier precedents, the extension or narrowing down of earlier authorities and so forth.

Students adopting the black-letter approach will be required to disregard any interpretations of legal decision-making that suggest that case decisions only make sense once subjective judicial prejudices linked to the elite social background, hidden ideological commitments and gender of most senior judges is taken into account.[112] This type of account deviates from the expectation that all proper legal analysis favours

---

[111]Connaghan and Mansell, in Grigg-Spall and Ireland, 1992 *op. cit.*, 87.
[112]J. Griffiths, *The Politics of The Judiciary*, 4th edn, (London: Fontana, 1991), 'introduction' – a work whose first edition generated enormous controversy for violating these basic tenets of the black-letter viewpoint.

interpretations of law that reveal the underlying coherence and hidden logical connection. Such expectations are maintained by explaining away, (or 'rationalising'), apparent contradictions, uncertainties or ambiguities as if they were 'mere exceptions', whose status as such confirms the general coherence of the system of rules, principles and basic axioms. The practical implication of this aspect of the black-letter approach, which seeks to reaffirm the coherence of legal doctrine, is that students should attempt to relate the materials of their dissertation to a coherent doctrinal system embodying, in a clear and express manner, the logical relationship between cases, rules, principles and basic axioms. For example, within contract law, this could require student dissertations to reconstruct the relationship between a group of cases tackling, for example, the issue of mistaken identity/attributes insofar as it is possible to interpret these cases as a group, which taken together, clarify the nature of a doctrinal rule regarding the legal significance of such a mistake. Researchers would be expected to give a clear exposition of the meaning and scope of the rule or rules that specify the legal effect of significant mistakes as to the existence of the subject matter of the contract, or either the qualities or the identity of the contracting parties.[113]

Once students have realised this goal, their next task would be to show how the given rules are logically derived from one of the practical implications of the more general principle that legally recognised contracts are based on the acceptance of the terms of a prior contractual offer. Whilst this general principle clearly governs many other areas in addition to disputes over mistaken identity and attributes, within the specific area in question this rule is logically necessary to give effect to this principle. The black-letter project will also expect students to recognise that this principle of contract law is not a random, free-floating or arbitrary dictat, or linked to specific ideological projects. Instead, it is derived, in a strictly logical manner, from the basic legal axiom that, as a core branch of private law, contract law aims, wherever possible, to give effect to the clear intentions of the parties.

Through this process of bringing out the logical relations between individual cases, rules, principles and basic axioms, students will be reaffirming a central tenet of the black-letter enterprise: that legal doctrine is a logically coherent, self-sufficient and mutually reinforcing system in which each element fulfils its allocated function. In other words, students are expected to interpret cases as specific instances of the application of the logical implications of underlying rules, whilst analysing the rules themselves as devices of a doctrinal system that gives effect to the logical implications of both underlying general principles of law, and, at one stage removed, basic axioms.

In short, for students engaged in dissertation projects deploying a black-letter methodology, it is important to conduct research on the assumption that, beneath the seemingly apparently chaotic flux of often ad hoc, inconsistent, contradictory and ambiguous case-law decisions, it is possible for strict legal analysis to reveal an underlying rational order embodied in meaningful 'principles' of wider applicability.[114]

This discovery requires the demonstration of the student's specialist interpretative skills and legal methods. These can be shown by providing a detailed analysis that reconstructs, in a precise way, how relevant legal rules governing the dissertation topic belong

---

[113]Bradney, 1998 *op. cit.*, 72.
[114]Murphy, 1990 *op. cit.*, 70.

to a wider system of which they are an integral part. Furthermore, the dissertation should analyse in detail how these rules mediate between a series of individual cases on one side, and general principles and axioms on the other. A competent black-letter analysis will be able to both uncover and describe in a precise way these mediating relationships and linkages. For example, it must show how rules X, Y and Z both embody, and give practical effect to, a general principle of law. The dissertation must also demonstrate how the principle operates at an intermediary level that mediates between specific rules (and then, indirectly, cases) on one side, and a small number of basic axioms on the other side. Hence, students are required to reinterpret primary materials in a way that demonstrates how even a specific case, which is located at the bottom of a pyramid-style structure of the doctrinal system, is, through many different intermediary levels, connected to those basic axioms located at the top of this hierarchical structure.

The black-letter methodology operates on the basis of the assumption that, because each part takes its allotted role in the overall system, like the various components of a watch, its meaning can be deduced from the functions it plays within the overall doctrinal system. A full analysis of the strictly legal significance of the dissertation topic will, therefore, require students to provide a careful exposition of the meaning and nature of each one of the direct and indirect relationships linking cases to rules, rules to principles and principles to axioms. A dissertation will be expected to interpret decisions contained in law reports as if they *can only* be properly interpreted as the straightforward application by judges of prior rules and underlying precedents. To interpret such primary sources in any other way, as connected to various 'non-legal' factors, would be to depart from the requirements of a 'strictly legal' type of analysis and reasoning by trespassing, for example, into the territory of sociology or some other discipline. Once researchers have learned how to interpret primary sources in terms of their place within a system of doctrine guided by a system of underlying principles, that is, in terms of the required formulae, law can then be analysed as a distinct and proper academic subject, that is, as 'an essentially principled discipline, amenable to systematic study and able to transcend a purely *ad hoc* . . . approach to problem-solving.'[115] In short, dissertation students need to rigorously apply appropriate legal methods to an archive of primary sources to uncover and reveal the underlying logical order of an internal coherent system of cases, rules, principles and basic axioms which, it is assumed, 'are doing their best, sometimes against the odds, to fight their way through to the light of day.'[116]

Given that a black-letter analysis attempts to show how the rules relevant to the dissertation topic relate not only to individual cases (and clusters of related cases) but also to prior legal principles, how should students analyse these principles themselves? A dissertation would be expected to demonstrate how general principles of law both organise and express themselves through the internally coherent and unified body of technical rules which regulate the topic. Their analysis would be an important perhaps even central part of the dissertation because, without their organising and intermediary role connecting rules to basic axioms, there could be *no system* of doctrine regulating the

---

[115]M. H. Hoeflich, 'The Americanisation of British Legal Education in the Nineteenth Century', (1987) 8 *J. of Legal History*, 244 at 245.

[116]Murphy, 1990 *op. cit.*, 69. For an example, see Look Chan Ho's review of Roy Goode's, *Legal Problems Of Credit And Security* (2003) 18 *Journal of International Banking Law and Regulation* 468–9 - noting that the author has succeeded in a key task of black-letter analysis, explaining and remedying inconsistencies in case decisions and formal rules in terms of a clarification of 'first principles'.

topic at all – only a random collection of rules operating without rhyme or reason. Students would be expected to appreciate that, in the absence of applicable principles of law, the legal rules relevant to the topic would risk appearing as arbitrary dictates of an irrational sovereign power. Furthermore, the basic axioms of relevant legal doctrine would be relegated to mere ideals, lacking any institutional roots or other means of consistent and predictable implementation in practice. If students adopt a black-letter approach, their dissertation research will not merely assume the existence of an underlying rational order of rules, principles and axioms, it will constantly act on this assumption to reaffirm the belief that the topic in question is being regulated by a doctrine possessing a high measure of coherence and unity.

The attractiveness of the black-letter approach to many students and academics is clear. It creates the impression that, by adopting this approach, researchers are participating within a system of authority, of being engaged with a distinctive type of analysis of a high-prestige institution and the elite of an associated profession (judges and senior barristers). The process of justifying black-letter assumptions clearly resorts to a circular form of reasoning (it assumes what first needs to be established). However, this technique is still highly effective in sustaining its authority and credibility amongst adherents, particularly newcomers to legal education. A legal topic is reinterpreted to adjust to the demands of the black-letter approach, which then appears the only methodology that is capable to analysing it in a strictly legal fashion. This approach retains its own authority by constantly generating interpretations of legal decision-making as though these were activities strictly governed by prior rules (of precedent, statutory interpretation and constitutional separation of law-legislative from judicial powers), and involving the application of rules based on principles to given facts. By so doing, the black-letter methodology continuously produces expositions of different aspects of legal doctrine within, for example, each new edition of classic law textbooks.

Such expositions appear to reinforce, confirm and give the impression of validity to the deeply seated assumptions of the black-letter enterprise. In particular, students may be convinced that, by using this methodology, their dissertation will be able to produce a series of definitive statements of the law, in which a range of case-law decisions reaffirm and illustrate the meaning and scope of specific rules, which in turn reaffirm the governance of rules by underlying principles and prior axioms. In the face of new case and statute law, students adopting a black-letter model of analysis will aim, wherever possible, to successfully reorganise and rationalise these underlying principles applicable to their dissertation in the most systematic manner possible – that is, in a way that preserves the appearance of a coherent system in which rules, principles and axioms harmonise together as different parts of an integrated and rational whole. In its own terms, the black-letter project appears to routinely succeed in this quest.

● Legal Principles and Rules are Largely Determinate

We have noted that the black-letter approach to legal research aims to provide a clear, precise and certain characterisation of legal categories embedded, it is claimed, within primary sources. This approach requires students to work on the premise that the source materials possess a core of already 'determinate', and thus 'objective', meaning. If interpreted correctly, legal categories are supposed to be determinate in the sense of exhibiting a largely clear, precise and certain meaning. Such meaning is contained, quite literally, within the 'letter of the law'. In other words, subscribers to the black-letter methodology generally assume not only that cases typically possess a determinate core of ascertainable meaning (or meanings), but also that the relationship of individual cases to a cluster of prior precedents, a group of interrelated cases on the same point of law, is also determinate. Furthermore, the relationships between the rule and the underlying principle, and, at the next level up, between the principle and the basic axiom to which this principle gives effect, are equally determinate in this sense of the term. In short, one goal of dissertation research based on the black-letter methodology is to show not only that individual legal categories relevant to the topic possess a core of determinate meaning but also that the relationship between the various categories, operating at different levels within the hierarchical system of cases, rules, principles and axiom, is equally determinate to a greater or lesser extent.

It then becomes the task of legal researchers to both determine and articulate this strictly legal meaning, and to do so as though it were possible to identify a single and comparatively straightforward or 'proper' meaning. This would represent the proverbial 'right answer' to a legal problem arrived at through the rigorous application of the correct legal method of interpretation. Dissertation students are expected to accept that this method of analysis can, in principle, provide a definitive solution to any conflicts of interpretation drawn from within the strict meaning of the doctrine itself.

The very fact that the black-letter methodology requires its users to interpret less determinate cases and rules as exceptional makes the assumption that their comparatively 'abnormal' status proves that the overwhelming majority of cases, rules, principles and axioms are determinate – that is, they form part of a coherent system of rules, which, when grasped in the context of the overall system of doctrine, are generally determinate. In contrast to vague and open-ended standards, such as 'justice and good conscience' and 'good faith', which are typically applied in a highly discretionary way after the fact, strictly legal categories exhibit an objective core of stable meaning. Through the application of traditional legal methods, this meaning can be identified and articulated in a clear way with a high degree of precision by removing ambiguities, multiple meanings and other sources of uncertainty within legal doctrine.

Hence, those who subscribe to this way of conducting research must accept the underlying assumption that, a student's first impressions that the dissertation topic is governed by a disorienting flux of uncertain and obscure judicial decisions, is in fact misleading. Instead, the true nature of the case must be that the area of legal doctrine addressed by the dissertation possesses a core of already determinate, and thus 'objective', meaning, which is simply awaiting discovery and careful exposition. A competent dissertation will succeed in analysing the topic in a manner that cuts through this apparently superficial first impression, and peels away the surface layer in order to reveal this core of established meanings forming part of an internal and largely coherent doctrinal system.

Once legal researchers have revealed this core of largely determinate meanings regarding the nature and scope of a given topic through the application of formalistic legal methods, it then becomes possible to articulate, in a systematic way, both the meaning and scope of these rules, principles and basic axioms as though they could, in principle, possess one straightforward, or 'proper', meaning. In other words, if students opt for a black-letter approach to their dissertation research, they must necessarily assume that, if they devote an appropriate amount of time, effort and skill in interpreting precedents and other primary sources, it will be possible to establish a high level of determinacy with respect to the nature of their topic. For example, they should be able to precisely define and richly illustrate what, for example, plea-bargaining has come to mean, the precise circumstances in which different types of plea-bargaining are legally permitted, required and prohibited, and highlight any areas of remaining partial indeterminacy awaiting future clarification, possibly by Parliament or the judiciary. Although a rule taken in isolation from both cases and general principles of law may initially appear vague, uncertain and imprecise, legal researchers both can and should resolve such apparent indeterminacy by carefully analysing the precise way in which the rule is mediated by, and gives effect to, a legal principle. In this way, such researchers can come to appreciate more fully their topic's core of settled meaning, whose definition thereby becomes increasingly clear and fleshed-out. In turn, by treating the general legal principle which mediates the relevant rules as an expression of one or more basic axioms (such as the need for the criminal justice system to comply with the rule of law), the settled meaning and scope of the principle itself can be grasped in a more complete and adequate manner. The presumption is that, when approached in this formalistic way, students can show that individual cases applicable to their topic possess a clear and determined legal meaning precisely because judges decided them on the basis of the impartial application of given doctrinal rules governed by general principles and axioms.

It is important not to exaggerate the emphasis this approach places upon the determinacy of legal meaning. Determinacy is not presumed to be total and it is generally taken to be a question of degree, that is, a matter of relatively clear, unambiguous and precise legal meanings. By focusing on exceptional areas where there still remains a residual measure of indeterminacy, and hence scope for debate between different researchers over the precise meaning, implication and scope of a doctrinal rule, legal interpreters can display their ability to exploit supposedly exceptional gaps, ambiguities and discrepancies. As Kennedy notes, students

> learn to retain large numbers of rules organised into categorical systems (requisites for a contract, rules about breach, etc.). They learn 'issue spotting', which means identifying the ways in which the rules are ambiguous, in conflict, or have a gap when applied to a particular fact situation. They learn elementary case analysis, meaning the art of generating broad holdings for cases so they will apply beyond their intuitive scope, and narrow holdings for cases so they won't apply where it at first seemed they would.[117]

To be more precise, the black-letter approach does not claim that no element of legal doctrine has or could ever contain the slightest trace of ambiguity, doubt, imprecision or inconsistency. To make this claim would be to invite ridicule even from first-year law students preparing cases for their first ever tutorial or seminar. On the contrary, this approach claims, first, that existing doctrine must be analysed by researchers as if, to a greater or lesser extent, it was largely determinate; and, secondly, that the impartial and rigorous application of appropriate legal methods by lawyers and judges over time will mean that the legal system has an inbuilt tendency to both minimise and correct any sources of actual or potential indeterminacy, such as ambiguities or lack of precision in the definition of categories.

---

[117]Duncan Kennedy, 'The Structure of Blackstone's Commentaries' (1979) 28 *Buffalo L. Rev.* 205.

The assumption underpinning the black-letter approach that the legal system, particularly the judicial application of legal doctrine governed by precedent to specific facts, possesses an inherent tendency to correct itself has specific implications. A judicial application of legal rules with a settled meaning to new circumstances is believed to merit particular emphasis insofar as this case clarifies and resolves a possible source of doubt, at least in terms of the scope of the rule and its range of applicability. The range of circumstances covered by this rule have already largely been established by prior case law. However, a new case resolves a source of possible doubt and uncertainty by establishing that the rule has now been held to cover these new circumstances. Hence, one of the key goals of a dissertation that adopts this methodology is to show that not only the meaning but also *the scope* of legal doctrine is generally becoming evermore coherent, precise and certain, not least through the efforts of fellow researchers who also apply the same approach. It assumes that sources of uncertainty, doubt and ambiguity within legal doctrine are always in the process of being ironed out through the self-development of legal doctrine. The optimistic view of progress, which is shared with many natural scientific disciplines, believes that academic analysis is a collaborative task in which a body of knowledge is tested, revised and improved in a step-by-step fashion, with problems, gaps and contradictions being ironed out over time as the discipline moves 'onwards and upwards'.

Legal researchers can of course acknowledge the existence of difficult and inconsistent precedents. However, these are not generally attributed to the unrealistic nature of the basic assumption of the black-letter approach that legal doctrine must be analysed as if it represented a coherent system of rules, principles and axioms. Instead, these elements are taken as mere exceptions destined, over time, to be resolved. They can be remedied not only by academic analysis but also through a judicial process of distinguishing, not following, implied judicial abolition or outright legislative repeal.

The historical sections of black-letter textbooks offer a particularly clear example of this 'progressive' view of historical development which assumes that legal developments have an inbuilt trajectory to achieve a certain goal of ever-greater determinacy. Such introductory sections will typically concoct stories of the historical development of legal doctrine from indeterminate principles of the medieval era to evermore precise, clear and determinate rules, principles and axioms of the present day. The modernisation of legal doctrine is assumed to be the equivalent of step-by-step refinement and improvement from the less rational to the more rational state that prevails today.[118] From this assumption radiates the belief that future doctrinal developments will continue this process of organic and step-by-step refinement. Hence, the deeply entrenched assumption is that legal researchers are not required to consider any need for fundamental social reforms.

Subscribers to the black-letter approach can seek to explain and even justify their commitment to the determinacy of relevant legal doctrine largely on pragmatic grounds. The consistent governance over time of rules and cases by settled legal principles allows lawyers to make reasonably accurate predictions. Legal advisers can predict, with a reasonable degree of certainty, how a court would react to different future actions if a

---

[118]This aspect is covered with respect to textbook analysis of legal history within land and equity texts by Doupe and Salter, 2000(a) *op. cit.*; Doupe and Salter, 2000(b) *op. cit.*

client's affairs were ever to be subjected to litigation. Such ostensible consistency and predictability of doctrine allows clients to rationally calculate and plan ahead with a clear view as to the likely effects and implications of different possible alternatives. For example, insofar as property law doctrine confers 'exclusive possession' on the bearer of private property rights, then all that which falls within the scope of the owner's rights can be identified and defined in a precise way, and with a high degree of certainty, as belonging fully to that owner alone; whilst all that falls outside the scope of the right can be obtained only through purchase or trade. Such determinacy creates not only certainty and consistency but also a highly desirable measure of security for the owner who, as a result, is encouraged to plan, invest and trade.

In short, it is precisely this 'determinacy' of legal categories that makes it possible for legal researchers to identify, demarcate and describe in exhaustive detail various clear-cut rules that can be clearly specified. Once clarified in this way, judges and other lawyers can apply such determinate and precise rules, for the benefit of all, with a high degree of consistency not only from one context of application to another, but also across differently constituted courts and tribunals.[119]

● The Standpoint of Black-Letter Analysis

All methodologies enable research to be carried out, but only from the necessarily limited and partial field of vision made possible from a particular standpoint. All research will inevitably analyse law in terms of some presumed aim, and assume the standpoint of one of the various participants in the legal process, or at least that of a party who is affected by legal decisions. For example, questions of the rationale behind different types of sentencing practice vary markedly if one analyses these from the point of view of the judge or that of Parliament, or the accused in the criminal court.[120] If dissertation students, who are addressing the same topic, adopt different standpoints, then their dissertations will inevitably identify and highlight different aspects of the source material as important and relevant: indeed, they may even differ as to what counts as source material in the first place.[121] No vantage point can provide a complete and comprehensive overview. Each allows law to be understood from a certain angle and through the lens of specific assumptions and blind spots that limit what can be grasped. The implicit standpoint students must adopt to carry out black-letter analysis is that of a judge or barrister engaging in conflicts of interpretation regarding the meaning and scope of points of law contained in reported law cases, particularly those stemming from the senior courts.[122] Such analysis of doctrinal categories and distinctions tends to disregard the standpoint of both lower courts engaged in more mundane fact-finding and fact-disputing activities where elaborate points of law are rarely central, and the activities of solicitors advising clients and attempting to navigate the complex requirements of different procedures of court and law-enforcement bureaucracies.[123] In short, black-letter analysis is geared, from the start, to a certain largely unacknowledged standpoint upon law and the

---

[119]This view has been disputed by Murphy and Rawlings, 'After the Ancient Regime' (1981) 44 *MLR* 617.

[120]Twining, in Cane and Stapleton, 1991 *op. cit.*, 16–17.

[121]*Ibid.*, 15, noting that: 'differences of standpoint produce different criteria of relevance and importance'.

[122]Twining, in Cane and Stapleton, 1991 op. *cit.*, 16.

[123]*Ibid.*

experience of law: that of a barrister presenting formal arguments before an appeal court regarding the precise meaning and scope of contested points of law.[124] This may seem paradoxical given the self-image of black-letter law as a detached academic science and discipline, yet the focus on pure points of law provides a common ground.[125] Students deploying this approach will, therefore, be expected to show that they can provide authoritative and well-supported expositions of the principles of legal doctrine, and produce formal arguments about their scope and implications for any particular dispute. This standpoint harmonises with both the self-image of law as an academic discipline, and the work of barristers appearing before appeal courts.

● Wider Strategies of Selective Exclusion

The focus of the black-letter approach upon the purely doctrinal significance of primary sources to the exclusion of a wide range of other potentially relevant factors cannot be overestimated.[126] Students conducting dissertations through the application of this approach must learn and practise the rigours of this argumentative technique, must learn to focus consistently and exclusively on points of law, on the subtleties of doctrinal distinctions and even distinctions within distinctions, on distinguishing rules from exceptions and even 'exceptions to exceptions'. Bell, for examples, notes that the application of narrowly focused black-letter forms of reasoning necessarily involves decision-makers to appear to accept the idea of law as a largely or totally 'closed system requiring only limited external justification'. This in turn requires 'excluding a whole range of substantive arguments from debate' that might otherwise be considered relevant to deciding the merits of particular cases. In this way, 'decisions are justified often by reference to precise legal standards, rather than by reference to the reasons justifying them'.[127] Black-letter analysis is, thereby, linked to rigorous and sustained 'discipline' in every sense of that term, including drilling the mind to automatically focus on doctrinal questions understood as rules embodying underlying principles, to the exclusion of all other factors.

The range of legal materials are narrowly defined, with case law prioritised massively over statute law, partly because of the more obvious linkage between most social legislation and both policy and ideological factors whose analysis would violate the exclusion of political factors from strict legal analysis.[128] It is also widely assumed that legal reasoning should, in principle, be severed from any external criterion or the instrumentalism of 'purposive reasoning' used to evaluate social behaviour in terms of its effectiveness in achieving policy goals.[129] A hardline black-letter approach may even exclude books within a law in context or law and society series on the basis that their wider focus on policy contexts and political values means that they are not really law books at all.[130] Consider, for instance, Hofheinz's frank statement to his students:

---

[124]Twining, 1994 *op. cit.*, 155; Twining, in Cane and Stapleton, 1991 *op. cit.*, 15.

[125]Twining, in Cane and Stapleton, 1991 *op. cit.*, 16.

[126]Twining, 1994 *op. cit.*, 106-7.

[127]J. Bell, 'Conceptions of Public Policy' in Cane and Stapleton, 1991 *op. cit.*, 88-9.

[128]*Ibid.*; Twining, in Cane and Stapleton, 1991 *op. cit.*, 13.

[129]Atiyah, 1979 *op. cit.*, 390.

[130]Twining, 1994 *op. cit.*, 112.

For the purpose of this course, the materials available to determine black-letter law are limited to the text and supplemental materials provided. This is 'Textbook Jurisdiction.' We arbitrarily limit our consideration to these materials to make possible a specific definition of the substantive domain of this course. While I do not forbid the use of supplemental materials, I strongly discourage their use since they add substantial complexity and possible confusion to your task with little or no benefit.[131]

There is a long tradition of defining 'law books' as expository commentaries written for legal practitioners by current or former legal practitioners, which largely take the form of reference works rather than academic texts.[132] Whereas sociology or psychology students will mainly treat published research by academic sociologists and psychologists as primary texts, it is different for law students. It is practitioners who select and edit law reports for publication, whilst statutes are of course 'written' by parliament and parliamentary counsel. Legal research feeds mainly off these primary sources, not the writings of other legal academics.[133] Critics, such as Twining, interpret this publishing tradition as a 'self-renewing straightjacket' that, until recently, has restricted publishing outlets for less traditional types of legal scholarship.[134]

If a legal dispute is covered by a subsection of a particular statute, then the resolution of that dispute must concentrate primarily on determining the 'true meaning' of that subsection, and then applying this interpretation to the issues of the particular case. Judges must not, therefore, go beyond the 'four corners' of the applicable statute or law report by admitting considerations that are not contained within the existing system of rules and established principles. Proper legal analysis must pay close and exclusive attention to the contents of authoritative legal texts, and reject the idea that anything outside these texts could ever be relevant to strict legal analysis.[135] One requirement of this narrowly focused, 'heads down' approach to the precise meaning and scope of existing doctrinal categories, and distinctions between categories, is a close and intensive reading of 'primary sources' (assumed to be cases and statutes). What must be excluded is any broader 'heads up' focus upon the part legal decisions play in the definition of wider social issues. In short, the insistence on preserving closure, the idea that the legal system is a closed series of rules, 'a mindset about law as a closed language and discipline',[136] leads to a series of other exclusions and prohibitions on legal reasoning and analysis.

Furthermore, the black-letter approach treats individual rights as paramount, if not always as absolute. Hence, in a case at which the prerogative right of contracting parties to insist upon enforcing any one of the terms of a legally binding agreement (such as a loan to a debtor) is at issue, the black-letter analysis will exclude as irrelevant a variety of evidence, including the human-interest dimension. For example, it will expel as irrelevant any evidence that explains the claimant's decision to endorse the contract as

---

[131]Hofheinz, 1997 *op. cit.*

[132]*Ibid.*, 114.

[133]*Ibid.*, 191.

[134]*Ibid.*, 114-15.

[135]Bradney, 1998 *op. cit.*, 77.

[136]Jo Shaw, 'Socio-Legal Studies and the European Union', in Philip Thomas (ed.), *Socio-Legal Studies*, (Aldershot: Ashgate-Dartmouth, 1997), 310.

'reasonable in all the circumstances', or which justifies his or her underlying motivations.[137] Other questions have also been deemed largely irrelevant (unless forced upon the agenda by the doctrine itself), including the issue of whether the defendant's non-payment was deliberate, or forced by lack of resources, or whether the punitive terms of an original bargain stemmed from the exploitation of gross imbalances stemming from structural inequalities between different social groups and classes.[138] As Twining notes, the black-letter approach, enshrined in law reports, generally involves a highly selective processing of the material facts and the framing of legal issues 'for a quite narrow and specific purpose' from which a variety of contextual factors are excluded. Indeed, through the routine application of this process of exclusion, black-letter analysis only has to address those factors *that a judge* is obliged to consider as legally relevant: namely, the rules and principles of legal doctrine deduced from earlier binding precedents and other primary sources.[139] Only those 'facts' that are relevant in the light of the tests required by doctrinal rules, that is, 'institutional facts', as distinct from brute facts as experienced by laypersons including the original parties, should be considered.[140]

The restricted and literal type of analysis required by the black-letter approach interprets the judicial process in remarkably non-political terms: that is, as involving taking the words of a statute according to their 'proper' construction, and then considering whether, on the facts proved, the case in question falls within them.[141] This narrow and technical focus necessarily brackets out and expels a range of interpretative possibilities. It precludes other ways of interpreting the wording of contracts and other private-law devices, where the presumed, imputed or actual 'intentions' of the parties are supposed to provide the decisive criteria to resolve, in a definitive way, any possible conflicts of interpretation. Such interpretations require the exclusion of all other types of evidence. Indeed, the court is only entitled to supplement such (imputed) 'intentions' where this is strictly necessary to prevent the overall device from becoming unworkable in practice.[142] In short, within the black-letter enterprise, interpreters are generally expected, as far as possible, to seek out the plain or literal meaning of cases and statutes and other sources in order to incorporate these into established legal doctrine. If this is in doubt with respect to statutes, then there can be an appeal to the 'original intentions' of Parliament, considered as if this institution possessed a collective 'mind'.[143] Only if it is not possible to identify a plain or literal meaning with respect to case decisions, are interpreters permitted to consider the underlying purpose or policy behind a specific doctrine, and then only if this can be defined in a largely non-political manner.

As already noted, the black-letter tradition defines individual legal rights in absolute terms, as unqualified and universally applicable. Hence, it necessarily insists that there can be no question of judges or other legal interpreters having to 'balance' the enforcement of such rights with factors stemming from the perceived social and economic needs of others, even where these are particularly acute. Whilst the balancing-out of

---

[137]Twining, 1994 *op. cit.*, 106-7.
[138]Atiyah, 1979 *op. cit.*, 392.
[139]*Ibid.*
[140]Vick, 2004 *op. cit.*, 179; Hart, *The Concept of Law*, (Oxford: Clarendon, 1961), 123.
[141]Atiyah, 1979 *op. cit.*, 665.
[142]*Ibid.*, 389.
[143]Bell, in Cane and Stapleton, 1991 *op. cit.*, 95-7.

needs, rights and interests may be necessary for civil servants and administrators, such considerations must be excluded as clearly falling outside the decision-making role of legal officials.[144] The black-letter enterprise reinterprets the complex dilemmas contained in the facts of many legal disputes and relevant points of law strictly in terms of whether they support only one of two possible options. As Twining notes, they are interpreted 'in an artificially rigid, all or nothing, winner-takes-all dichotomy: guilty/not guilty, liable/not liable.'[145] Twining could have extended his examples to include the either/or dichotomy of actionable / no cause of action shown, standing / no standing, justiciable/non-justiciable. The methodology's superimposition of this all-or-nothing dichotomy rules out in advance any consideration of alternative possible legal responses to disputes, particularly once these have entered into the trial process.

According to the black-letter approach to the conduct of legal research, including student dissertations, proper legal reasoning is still able to perform its role despite excluding a wide range of 'external' factors because it both can and should rely exclusively upon strictly formal criteria derived from internal sources and standards, such as consistency with precedent (directly or by analogy) and due process. The choices facing judges and other legal decision-makers can be deduced sufficiently from the meaning of prior doctrinal rules and/or principles without any need to venture beyond these strictly legal sources. Hofheinz has noted that this deductive element can be combined with more inductive types of reasoning, including reasoning by analogy:

> Understanding black letter law serves several functions. First, it allows one to determine which set of legal rules and principles should be applied in determining likely outcomes to a problem, what facts are *material* to the application of those rules and principles, and when there is no applicable rule directly and unambiguously determining the likely outcome. This group of functions involve deductive reasoning. Second, it provides a substantive context which may be applied by analogy to the particular facts and circumstances of the problem under analysis. This function involves analogic and inductive reasoning.[146]

Hence, disregarding the 'external' question of impact upon the well-being of the immediate parties to a dispute makes it possible to focus entirely on the impact of any particular judicial interpretation as a future precedent within the ongoing processes of legal reasoning.[147] Indeed, the exclusion of the former is vital if strict legal reasoning is to maintain the integrity of legal doctrine understood as a coherent system of rules to which all legal interpreters owe a particular obligation.

The predominantly descriptive focus of the black-letter enterprise is, as already noted, related to the idea that the positive law, as already laid-down rules, provides the starting point for legal analysis. For present purposes, the most important implication of this commitment is that it is equally inappropriate for legal researchers to investigate the possible economic, political, ethical or other reasons that could perhaps *explain* the

---

[144]Atiyah, 1979 *op. cit.*, 389.

[145]Twining, 1994 *op. cit.*, 106.

[146]Hofheinz, 1997 *op. cit.*

[147]Baldwin, 1995 *op. cit.*, 44; Atiyah, 1979 *op. cit.*, 392 – emphasising the commitment of formalism to the perceived need to subordinate the dispute settling role of courts to priorities stemming from the longer-term precedential value of decisions and the need to reaffirm doctrinal certainty and consistency so that commercially important expectations of rational calculability are more fully met.

principles and rules of legal doctrine. In other words, this approach, at its purest, requires researchers to exclude, in a rigorous manner, all references to historical, political, social or cultural factors as forces shaping the operation of law as a social phenomenon. A classic example is found in the embarrassment caused to authors of black-letter text-books in equity by the linguistic and institutional link between equity and conceptions of justice and good conscience. For example, in Pettit's work the concept of justice lying in the heart of equity causes certain difficulties. As early as the first sentence we are told, significantly via a mere footnote, that:

> This begs the real question, what is justice? which is, however, outside the scope of this book, being a question for jurisprudence and philosophy. Of course, in prac-tice, many matters that justice would demand are not enforced in the courts for various reasons, many being unsuitable for judicial enforcement, and some of the rules enforced fail to achieve justice either generally or in a particular case.[148]

More generally, the black-letter tradition prohibits any reference to potentially explana-tory factors, which aim to illustrate, contextualise and explain different aspects of the legal process. It is also necessary to exclude any assessment of the operation of the com-peting interests of different groups, and not to identify the wider social and economic implications of judges deciding this type of case in one way rather than another. Hence, the project of sustaining the integrity of this formalistic approach requires legal researchers to systematically exclude a wide range of materials and issues, ranging from policy issues to economic factors, which *other methodologies* would otherwise consider particu-larly relevant to explaining how law operates in practice and its real social roles and functions, and their impact upon different sectors of society. Instead, legal researchers are expected to endorse the idea that the true explanation of why any particular reported case was decided the way it was, lies in the judges' faithful adherence to, and application of, the meaning and implications of established legal doctrine.

Hence, student dissertations adopting a black-letter approach are required to engage in an exclusively doctrinal type of reasoning to settle conflicts of interpretation between parties to disputes. This in turn requires the student to avoid any explicit discussion of the *policy arguments* for and against the practical implications of any particular deci-sion.[149] Of course, this creates problems for the researcher whenever decisions within, for example, nervous shock cases, are explicitly developed in terms of policy implications of various possible alternatives. Hence, supposedly extraneous moral standards, ethical behaviour and, crucially, questions of justice must be considered irrelevant to strict legal reasoning.[150] As Atiyah notes with respect to the presence of formalism within the tradi-tion of contract law: 'the justice of a contract, the fairness of a bargain, was, indeed, not a matter which concerned the court at all.'[151] The black-letter methodology in its purest form thus requires that obligations towards the ideal of objectivity mean that it is not the function of the judge or legal researcher to 'invoke policy considerations, or even arguments about the relative justice of the parties' claims'.[152] In short, for strict legal

---

[148]P. Pettit, *Equity and the Law of Trusts*, (London: Butterworths, 1989), 1.

[149]Atiyah, 1979 *op. cit.*, 660. Cf. *R v Registrar General, ex. p. Smith*, [1990] 2 All ER 170.

[150]Baldwin, 1995 *op. cit.*, 29.

[151]Atiyah, 1979 *op. cit.*, 389.

[152]*Ibid.*, 388.

analysis, such questions, which may relate to the critical assessment and evaluation of the worth of particular institutional arrangements and policy goals within the law, or the moral or political legitimacy of law's institutional response to the perceived social, economic and welfare 'needs' and claims of particular parties, are considered largely or entirely irrelevant to the demanding 'logic' of doctrinal analysis.[153]

In addition to buying into the specialist frame of reference of a legalistic agenda, students adopting a black-letter approach would also be expected to strictly discard ways of identifying and interpreting the issues that would be characteristic of the so-called 'common sense' of laypersons. Even in areas where the issues in question, such as making contracts, are a familiar and routine activity within everyday life, the lawyers' categories and tests contained in legal doctrine remain aloof from, and unaccountable to, the frame of reference of laypersons.[154] Students are expected to acquire the ability to apply legal methods of identifying, stating and applying principles to speak and write 'like a lawyer'.[155] This acquisition yields a magic key that supposedly opens a previously sealed door to the world of black-letter analysis and reasoning. This world is a realm of its own making, and one of its main features is a formalist analysis involving the 'wilful … abstraction from the close texture and fine tissue of processes of life'.[156] Such abstraction distinguishes black-letter analysis of legal doctrine from the work of sociolegal studies and many other alternative methodologies.

Most legal disputes involve numerous different types of persons and institutions with various and competing individual and group interests and perspectives. Within everyday life, the combination of a series of perspectives within legal processes will typically result in the nature and implications of the dispute becoming defined in noticeably different ways. Students adopting a black-letter approach would also be expected to strictly discard ways of identifying and interpreting the issues that would be characteristic of the so-called 'common sense' of laypersons who are blissfully ignorant of strict 'legal methods'. The black-letter approach considers that many facts relevant to understanding the actions, motivations and goals of the parties to a dispute, and the latter's different economic underlying interests, need to be excluded from the scope of strict legal analysis because they are not deemed 'institutional facts' directly relevant to arguable 'points of law'.[157] Here it is worth re-emphasising our earlier point that, for those who adopt the black-letter methodology, it is necessary to avoid being 'distracted' by such 'diversions' arising from irrelevant, external factors. To achieve this it is necessary to focus on the precise meaning and scope of the categories and distinctions within prevailing legal doctrine as revealed by a close and precise reading of relevant cases and statutes.[158]

For instance, unlike the manner in which an economic or other social scientific analysis would consider the same dispute, the black-letter approach places off the agenda the actual 'facts' of specific cases. It also removes consideration of the impact in practice of different actual and possible decisions upon the interests and well-being of the parties. The resulting case analysis is, therefore, highly selective, and the ability to be able to

---

[153]Bradney, 1998 *op. cit.*, 76.

[154]Atiyah, 1979 *op. cit.*, 391.

[155]Twining, 1994 *op. cit.*, 165.

[156]*Ibid.*, 67.

[157]Atiyah, 1979 *op. cit.*, 391; Grant Gilmore, *The Death of Contract* (Columus, Ohio: 1974), 99.

[158]Cf. O. Kahn-Freund, 'Reflections on Legal Education' (1966) 29 *MLR* 121, at 129.

identify (initially with a highlighter pen in practice!) only those aspects of a reported case that are 'relevant' to the task of providing an authoritative statement of the nature of the applicable legal rules and principles is deemed a necessary skill. Thus, for example, formalistic modes of legal reasoning will stress the importance of the general principle or axiom which asserts that 'promises intended to be relied upon should be carried out', even in cases where, as a matter of fact, the promise was not actually relied upon.[159] As far as formalistic types of legal reasoning are concerned, the correct question is, for example, not whether, as a matter of fact, two parties agreed to create what *they regarded* as a binding trust – instead, the appropriate question for black-letter legal analysis is whether the facts about their actions, as legally interpreted, conformed to the requirements of the trust device as defined and regulated by the objective meaning of prior legal rules and principles.

A final aspect of the selective deployment of strategies of exclusion relates to a point already noted above but which merits repeating here: the marginalisation of those examples of academic research (and even researchers) that fail to fulfil the expectation that legal education takes the form of transmitting a model of law as a singular and autonomous discipline. The emergence of alternative approaches was, as already noted, subjected to considerable defensive reactions by leading members of the black-letter tradition, who, in their more extreme expressions, argued for the expulsion of non-conformists from law faculties.[160] This represents the more extreme expression of the idea that black-letter approaches have, through the force of convention, become hardened into orthodoxy.[161]

By contrast, law students who adopt a sociolegal approach to the conduct of research, which entails conducting field research and interviews with parties affected by, say, legal proceedings, are far more likely to be confronted with a series of ethical issues. This is especially the case if the active and informed cooperation of research subjects is required. Furthermore, because black-letter research focuses largely on *the content* of current legal doctrine, including its development, trends and trajectory, this type of research only requires access to a law library, or internet access to various electronic databases. As a result, some of the ethical issues that can arise with respect to, for example, drug or biotechnology companies funding medical research cannot arise. In other words, no outside funding body has any special authority over legal researchers who adopt this approach. In short, library-based black-letter research can apparently avoid any requirement to confront, discuss and resolve difficult moral and ethical issues regarding the conduct of research, such as the obligation to respect confidentiality and to ensure that funding bodies do not directly or indirectly interfere with the objectivity of the research.

In other respects as well, the requirement to engage in a strictly legal type of reasoning and analysis necessitates the exclusion of alternative ways of making sense of legal materials and the facts of disputes, which might otherwise appear sensible to adopt. For

---

[159]Atiyah, 1979 *op. cit.*, 393.

[160]Twining, 1994 *op. cit.*, 140; Dean Paul Carrington, 'Of Law and the River' (1984) *Jo Leg Educ.* 437; Harry Edwards, 'The Growing Disjunction Between Legal Education and the Legal Profession', (1992) 91 *Michigan Law. Rev*, 8.

[161]R. Posner, 'Conventionalism: The Key to Law as an Autonomous Discipline', (1988) 38 *University of Toronto Law Jo*, 333; Twining, 1994 *op. cit.*, 173.

example, one result of applying the black-letter perspective is that students interpret their legal dissertation projects as if they formed part of an essentially *technical* subject governed by specialist forms and protocols of interpretation. Hence, a black-letter dissertation on the legal regulation of plea-bargaining would attempt to duplicate the specialist ways of identifying, defining and applying questions of interpretation that are supposed to distinguish the analysis of lawyers from that of both laypersons and other professionals. The student would be expected to simulate the semantic games played by advocates with respect to identifying relevant questions of interpretation ('issue spotting'), distinguishing 'relevant' from 'irrelevant' precedents and other sources both in terms of the material facts and the points of law.

Students adopting the black-letter approach would also be expected to show an awareness of, and an ability to, manipulate arguments regarding 'relevant' law and 'material facts' from both sides of the case. For present purposes, however, the most important question is not what is selectively included within the scope of legal interpretation – on the contrary, what is vital is to appreciate the nature and impact of the strategies of exclusion deployed by the black-letter enterprise that narrow down the range of issues by expelling all other factors which the original parties regard as central to their dispute. Those facts to a dispute that fall inside the realm of admissible materials, for example events deemed to be relevant to be discussed as 'material facts' within the law reports, are, as Twining notes, the results of a highly selective process of interpretation. Such a process constructs and packages their significance 'in ways that often take them a long way from the original events and that "the facts" are often homogenised or distorted or translated into lawyers' categories that may make them almost unrecognisable to the original parties.'[162]

Other supposedly unique 'legal methods' required for black-letter analysis include an awareness of the operation of rules of statutory interpretation. For example, students could be rewarded for arguing that, if a strictly literal approach is taken to the interpretation of statutory provision X, then the likely effect upon the scope of permissible plea-bargaining would be . . . ; whereas if judges could be convinced by legal advocacy that a broader purposive approach to their task was more appropriate, then the effect of this, by contrast, would be. . . . The adoption of a literal approach to the interpretation of statutes involves a severe narrowing down of focus and the exclusion of broader questions regarding the purpose behind the measure, or the 'mischief' towards which the measure was, on policy grounds, directed as a legislative remedy. Take for example the interpretation of Section 24 of the Social Security Act 1975, which provided that, if a woman was under pensionable age when her husband died and had made sufficient national insurance payments, then she was entitled to receive a widow's allowance. On a strictly literal, black-letter interpretation, any widow who meets the two requirements is legally entitled irrespective of any countervailing policy or moral considerations. However, in the case of *R v National Insurance Commr., ex. P. Connor*, the tribunal had to decide whether a women who fully met this criteria but who had been convicted of killing her husband, should be allowed to receive widow's allowance. The tribunal rejected the black-letter preference for literal modes of interpretation, which focuses exclusively on the meaning and scope of the 'letter of the law', in favour of taking into account wider 'extra-legal' policy considerations that restricted the automatic application of paper

---

[162]Twining, 1994 *op. cit.*, 103. Twining also notes that the rich description of facts are highly truncated and thus 'conceal and omit as well as inform' (at 106).

rules, particularly the principle that criminals should not be allowed to materially benefit from their crimes. As a result, the tribunal members rejected the widow's claim despite the clear meaning of the requirements and lack of any doubts as to her own eligibility.[163] By contrast, *Fisher v Bell*[164] was an extreme example of a judge refusing to deviate from the literalism of the black-letter approach, insisting that the language of Parliament, in this case the meaning of the term 'offer for sale', had to be interpreted, not as it was intended as a policy measure to stop the sale of flick knives. Instead, this judge focused on the precise technical meaning of 'offer for sale' as it had traditionally been defined and used within contract law doctrine. The effect of this strictly literal judicial inter- pretation of the statute that such 'offers' constituted 'invitations to treat', meant that sellers could no longer be prosecuted. This was because, within contract law doctrine, 'offer' is deemed to have a precise technical meaning. This case shows how formalism is more concerned to stick rigidly to interpretative practices that reaffirm and reinforce established doctrinal categories, than it is to apply the clear policy goals underpinning a statute.

The dissertation might also be expected to display competences with respect to the operation, and, equally importantly, the strategic manipulability of, the doctrine of prece- dent. Once again, the narrowing down of focus is purchased at the price of expelling a range of other ways of interpreting the issues of fact and law contained in the law reports. For example, a particularly impressive example of black-letter analysis may be able to show how earlier precedents relating to the rules (and so-called exceptions to these rules) have been creatively adapted over the previous decades, and to identify the likely effects if judges and other lawyers were to continue trends of doctrinal develop- ment into the immediate future. A student's dissertation would, therefore, be expected to illustrate in considerable detail, and with ample direct quotation of relevant extracts from the law reports, noteworthy aspects of how the doctrine of precedent appears to be operating within a specific area.

Such an approach attempts to integrate and systematise the materials in hand. It gives effect to the positivist assumption that the doctrine of precedent (as well as judicial interpretation of statutes) involves the rule-governed (and hence objectively controlled) application of doctrinal rules to established facts. Adopting this focus rules out any attempt to consider a range of different factors that could, perhaps with equal merit, explain the process of decision-making in terms other than adherence to rules of pre- cedent or statutory interpretation. In other words, it excludes from the agenda of legal research any attempt to identify factors other than adherence to rules in the judicial application of formal rules. The American realist school of legal thought, by contrast, emphasised the importance of recognising the impact of judicial values, background ideologies and particular understandings of the nature of the 'public interest'.

There is a *distinctly linguistic* element to this process of exclusion and specialisation. The black-letter methodology insists that students display technical competence and fluency in the lawyer's vocabulary of specialist terms of art and jargon, including aspects of its

---

[163][1981] 1 All ER 770. There are of course numerous other similar examples. See *R v Registrar General, ex. p. Smith*, [1990] 2 All ER 170 where a mental patient convicted of manslaughter of a cell mate he mistook for his foster mother was refused a record of his birth that could allow him to identify and possibly inflict violence upon his actual mother.

[164][1961] 1 QB 394, [1960] 3 All ER 731.

requisite Latin-related phraseology. Not only must the interpretative customs of every-day life be set to one side, so too must the lay understanding of certain familiar terms.[165] Hence, it is the technical legal meaning of a 'contract' or 'contractual offer' as defined and revised *by judges* and other senior lawyers that is central to the task of doctrinal exposition. This remains the case even where this specialist expression is unheard of within everyday life, or is inconsistent with how the phrase in question is used within everyday life (e.g. the difference between 'trust' in the sense of trust law and 'trust' as defined and understood within everyday life).

Fisher v Bell represents only an extreme example of the more general tendency of the black-letter approach to insist that legalistic expressions prevail at the expense of the language of everyday life, even in contexts where it is the transactions of everyday life that form the substance of the legal dispute in question. It is arguable that, from the perspective of the layperson, the legal question of whether or not a defendant who has assaulted two children, resulting in their deaths, should be held guilty of 'murder' or 'manslaughter' is entirely irrelevant as a purely technical issue relevant only to the lawyers. Hence, if such an individual is ultimately convicted and imprisoned for commit-ting manslaughter, they will still be widely categorised as 'murderers' simply because the distinction between murder and manslaughter belongs only to the specialist vocabulary and subculture of law. Hence, the black-letter approach transforms a situation that is typically defined in terms of the multiple subcultures and perspectives of the parties and laypersons more generally, by translating it into the terminology and linguistic distinc-tions that form a distinctive part of the subculture of *lawyers' law*.[166]

In short, one strict requirement of the black-letter approach is that it is necessary to identify, and then expel, all styles of interpretation and frames of reference that differ from the orientation, and both the analytical and rhetorical devices routinely applied by the legal profession during legal advocacy when addressing disputable points of law. In other words, the decision to adopt this approach to dissertation research carries with it the requirement to exclude all perspectives, methods and rhetorical skills except those that are distinctive to the specialist orientations of competent practising lawyers argu-ing about the technical meaning of points of law, and the applicability of legal rules and requirements to the material facts of an individual case.

● The Focus on Law in Books

It is widely recognised that pure forms of the black-letter approach focus exclusively on substantive legal doctrine contained in primary written sources. Hence, this approach shares with theology the idea that true statements can be ascertained through a close and rigorous elucidation of the meaning and implications of primary texts, which are deemed to be authoritative for events and actions in the world beyond the law library, even where the legal interpretation differs markedly from their 'common-sense' mean-ing within everyday life.[167]

---

[165]Twining, 1994 *op. cit.*, 10. (Although Twining challenges the view that lay experience should be treated as irrelevant to legal studies, claiming our 'legal education begins at birth').

[166]Twining, 1994 *op. cit.*, noting that: 'Undoubtedly lawyers use unfamiliar terms and familiar terms in un-familiar ways' (at 95). The tendency of legal culture to deploy its own distinctive and exclusionary vocabu-lary was noted by Bentham's *Rationale of Judicial Evidence* (1827) Book V111, Chap. XVII.

[167]Murphy and Roberts, 'Introduction' (1987) 50 *MLR* 677 at 681.

Bradney and Cownie, for example, recognise that: 'Black-letter courses . . . are based on the student's use of statutes and cases as a primary source. Traditionally this has meant teaching the students how to find, update and read the paper-based versions of these materials.'[168] As Vick notes, this focus upon law in books (as distinct from studies of the behaviour of legal officials or the perceived impact of the application of different legal measures upon different groups in society) narrows down the range of materials to be studied considerably:

> In its purest form, 'black letter' research aims to understand the law from no more than a thorough examination of a finite and relatively fixed universe of authoritative texts consisting of cases, statutes, and other primary sources, the relative importance of which depends upon the legal tradition and system within which the legal researcher operates.[169]

It remains true that written sources containing legal doctrine can be studied by a number of different methodologies. However, it is inconceivable that black-letter analysis could be applied to *sources other than texts of this kind*. Such analysis cannot address law as part of the lived experience of those who encounter and subjectively interpret various aspects of the legal system, such as the behaviour of safety inspectors and other regulators, within their working lives. For example, a dissertation project on plea-bargaining that intends to include a series of interviews with judges, prosecutors, lawyers and defendants who have first-hand experience of this practice, could not use the black-letter methodology. On the contrary, the researcher would necessarily have to adopt social-science research methods of observation and interviewing that go well beyond the remit of the black-letter agenda. In other words, such a project could not confine itself to a purely black-letter approach.

Hence, students seeking to apply black-letter types of analysis need to acquire and deploy the key legal skill of translating disputes originally expressed within the 'native' terminology of everyday life, into instances of specifically 'legal issues' (including doctrinal points of law) identified as such through deploying distinctly legal categories. Ideally, once legal interpreters have succeeded in this process of abstraction, the results can be translated back in the language of everyday life in such a way that the parties to the dispute would be able to broadly understand at least *the implications* of their different legal options. In short, the black-letter approach remains firmly attached to the analysis of legal texts contained in the law library, particularly legal doctrine contained in cases and statutes which are themselves defined as 'primary sources'.

● Deductive Methods of Reasoning From First Principles

Barristers appearing before appeal courts had, for most of the twentieth century, grown accustomed to constructing arguments that assumed law was an autonomous body of scientific principles from which the single correct answer could be inferred through an almost mechanical and formal process of deduction.[170] The simulation of scientific

---

[168]'Teaching Legal Methods', 1999, *op. cit.*

[169]Vick, 2004 *op. cit.*, 178.

[170]B. Abel-Smith and R. Stevens, *Lawyers and the Courts* (London: Heinemann, 1967) 124; Twining, in Cane and Stapleton, 1991 *op. cit.*, 5.

method by formalism is found in the systematic and rigorous quality of its classification, division and verbal analysis of legal concepts and rules. Black-letter analysis adopts distinctly legalistic methods of deduction from certain abstract axioms. Thus, in the case of land law, it is possible for researchers, through the use of deductive legal reasoning, to fully explain the rule against perpetuities as a logical consequence and implication flowing from the basic axiom that property must be essentially alienable. These types of deductions of rules and principles from basic axioms treat the axiom itself as a premise of an argument from which legal analysis can draw logical inferences from its meaning. Researchers can successfully employ such deductive reasoning without ever importing any social policy and ideological considerations into legal analysis concerning, for example, the workings of the free market in property. This deductive method is supposed to allow the judiciary to test out the implications of competing legal claims before reaching a conclusion. For example, if a question of whether a broad or narrow interpretation of the rights of a beneficiary is raised, then it would be possible to decide the issue in terms of what the logical implications are of the proper definition of the legal concepts of 'beneficial ownership, or even of 'ownership per se'.[171]

Black-letter forms of legal reasoning may, therefore, aspire to be formal exercises in deductive logic and formal argumentation with basic axioms serving as first principles. For example, the basic axiom that contractual and private property rights should be legally recognised and enforced as unqualified entitlements clearly stems from liberal beliefs and principles of political theory. However, doctrinal principles and rules that give effect to this axiom are considered by the black-letter approach as 'strictly legal' in nature, that is, 'inexorable deductions drawn from neutral principles'.[172]

Such reasoning will often deploy formalistic methods of deduction from basic axioms treated as the premises for a logical claim. The classic example is the premise that it is true that all bachelors are unmarried, and if we know that Socrates is a bachelor then it follows that we can 'infer' that he is not married, and reject all alternative interpretations of his marital status as illogical. Such deductive inferences from basic premises are sometimes referred to as 'syllogistic' reasoning. This type of reasoning is formalistic because it does not require any factual investigations of the type practised by social sciences. For example, if the premise is that private property rights are based on the principle of exclusive possession, then the process of deducing a logical inference from this principle for a particular dispute between a landlord and tenant can be settled by reference to whichever interpretation can best be shown to be consistent with the logical implications of applying this principle to the facts of this case. Legal reasoning remains strictly formal because it focuses exclusively on the meaning, scope and implications of the principle itself, not the factual origins of the dispute, or the likely factual impact of any decision.

Peritz notes that deductive forms of legal reasoning dominated the research and analysis of nineteenth-century law schools not only in Britain but also in North America:

> [F]or most of the 19th Century, members of the American legal community experienced legal reasoning as a deductive process. Treatise writers and proponents of

---

[171]See, for example, *Gartside v IRC* [1968] 1 All ER 121.
[172]Atiyah, 1979 *op. cit.*, 389. See also M. Horwitz, 'The Rise of Legal Formalism', (1975) 19 *American J. of Legal Hist.* 251, 256-7.

codification proceeded from the prevailing view that legal science involved the derivation of inferences from a set of first principles, ground norms, enunciated by the sovereign, whether (super)natural or political. Judges applied first principles, or their corollaries, to all particular cases in these coherent and complete systems of laws. The common law was understood teleologically – that is, as evolving or progressing toward a coherent set of general principles or goals. Teaching students to 'think like a lawyer' meant reading cases to learn their governing rules, the general principles of the common law. Once mastered, these general rules (and their corollaries) would govern all particular cases. Good legal argument meant rehearsing these general rules and citing the cases that instantiated them.[173]

In other words, the black-letter approach claims that legal researchers (and those involved in legal interpretation) can justify their conclusions through the proper application of 'pure' legal reasoning to logical principles, axioms and rules. In the same way that the idea of a perfect triangle has an objective reality governed by formal rules that can be objectively described and analysed, the meaning of legal categories has an objective existence capable of being subject to an equally rigorous analysis.[174] Awareness of the meaning of principles and how these govern the application of rules and principles is the main characteristic of legal knowledge. Such knowledge of law (enshrined in 'law books' which focus on legal doctrine defined as what the law says) is different in kind from the empirical type of *knowledge about* law possessed by, say, probation officers or criminologists or developed through the writings of sociolegal studies.[175] There is little overlap between the various books about law sold by general bookshops, which are intended to be read cover to cover, and the more narrowly defined 'law books' contained in law libraries, which are primarily reference works.[176]

Legal doctrine is governed by its own internal logic. This is because legal principles are determined by the logical implications of underlying axioms, whilst the rules are created and governed by the requirements of such principles. Hence, a judicial decision can be explained and justified logically by reference to correct interpretation of the meaning and scope of a specific rule, whilst the rule itself is explicable as a logical requirement of a more general principle. Hence, black-letter analysis is justified in relating individual cases to the internal logic of this closed system of legal doctrine. A decision is valid if it can be explained as strictly and exclusively determined by the logical implications of a prior specific rule, whilst the rule is valid insofar as it clearly embodies, and gives effect to, a prior general principle. Formalism includes the belief that the one 'true' answer to legal questions can be found by a strictly logical process. Formalism thus firmly rejects any suggestion that legal reasoning has more in common with rhetoric than logic, oriented as it is to reinterpreting facts and prior law in terms most likely either to win a case for a client, or, in the case of judicial reasoning, to forestall a successful appeal to a higher court.

It would be inaccurate to claim that deductive reasoning is the only type of reasoning that is consistent with the black-letter approach. For many subscribers to this approach, legal reasoning includes, but is not confined to, a process of deduction from first principles treated as a basic premise, such as freedom of contract. As Vick notes: 'The science of

---

[173]Peritz, 1999 *op. cit.*

[174]*Ibid.*

[175]R. Abel, 'Law Books and Books about Law' (1974) 26 *Stanford L. Rev.* 175.

[176]Twining, 1994 *op. cit.*, 92–4.

law combined inductive inquiry and systematic analogical reasoning of the sort associated with the works of Francis Bacon with the deductive methods of analysing law associated with Leibnitz, Pufendorf, and Christian Wolf.'[177] In other words, in some situations judges will not be able to deduce a correct legal answer from first principles, so that they may have to resort to arguments based on analogy, such as a present case being sufficiently similar in kind to another binding rule or precedent that it should be decided in the same way.

According to the black-letter tradition, deductive forms of legal reasoning are necessary in order to safeguard and reinforce other aspects of this tradition, particularly the claim that law is a closed and independent system of rules. Legal reasoning that draws exclusively upon the axioms, principles and rules of legal doctrine allows legal analysis and ultimately decision-making, to take place in a way that remains uncontaminated by external, and hence 'non-legal', factors, such as moral values or policy factors. The simulation of deductive logic supports the idea that legal reasoning can be scientific in the following sense: where a decision can be supported in more than one way, then interpreters must select whichever interpretation would be generally accepted as most consistent with the logical implications of an underlying legal principle. Hence, providing interpreters have properly understood the true meaning of the underlying legal principle, its objective meaning, it is possible to use a process of inference to arrive at the single right answer to the question of interpretation. Hence, legal analysis should aspire, as far as possible, to become a 'deductive and autonomous science that is self-contained in the sense that particular decisions follow from the application of legal principles, precedents and rules of procedure without regard to values, social goals, or political or economic context.'[178] Valid forms of legal reasoning will demonstrate that if one accepts the truth of a legal principle treated as a premise, then its logical application to the situation in question will provide the means to distinguish true from false interpretations of the implications of this premise. The formalism of the black-letter approach accepts the idea that it is possible to identify and apply a 'deductive or quasi-deductive method capable of giving determinate solutions to particular problems of legal choice.'[179]

It is possible to illustrate this by an example drawn from property law: the claim that the axiom stating that the legal category of 'property' must be essentially private, and that this requires a type of ownership characterised by 'exclusive possession' together with the ability to buy and sell this asset, makes it possible for legal interpreters to deduce the validity of various legal principles and rules in a direct way.[180] Such rules and principles make sense as exemplifications of this underlying axiom, treated as a basic premise. This deductive method is typically claimed to allow both the judiciary and legal researchers to 'test out' the implications of competing legal claims before reaching a conclusion. For example, if a particular question concerning the disputed property rights of a party is raised, then, according to this approach, it should prove possible to solve the problem by establishing through logical deduction which of the available interpretations

---

[177]Vick, 2004 *op. cit.*, 180.

[178]See L. Schwartz, 'With Gun and Camera through Darkest CLS-land' (1984) 36 *Stanf L. Rev.* 413 at 431.

[179]R. Unger, 'The Critical Legal Studies Movement' (1983) 96 *Harv L Rev* 563, at 564.

[180]The idea that underlying the right to property was the basic axiom of 'exclusive possession', 'the sole and despotic dominion . . . in total exclusion of the right of any other individual in the universe' is found, with some qualification, in William Blackstone, *Commentaries on the Law of England*, facsimile reprint 1979 of 1765–69 editions, 2.

represents the best realisation of the implications of an underlying legal axiom, category or principle. If the decision of an individual case can be shown to be derived directly through a process of logical deduction from the meaning of the applicable rule, and if the rule itself is logically required to give effect to the objective meaning of an underlying principle, then deductive reasoning helps reinforce the belief that legal doctrine is a coherent, autonomous and self-contained system. In other words, this logical process of deduction respects another feature of the black-letter approach: the requirement that legal doctrine be treated as if it represented a *closed* system of rules. Insofar as legal reasoning can rely upon a deductive logic that remains within the realm of law, there is no need to 'import' any social policy and ideological considerations concerning, for example, the workings of the free market in property. Hence the belief that the system of rules is closed also implies that it is 'autonomous' in the sense of being capable of playing its role without having to draw upon the resources of any other fields or academic disciplines.

● Law as a Distinct and Unique Discipline

Even where the grand claim that the application of the black-letter methodology represents a scientific activity is no longer made, subscribers to this approach will typically act on the assumption that their subject has, since the late nineteenth century, been a specific, autonomous and singular academic discipline. Law has become a cohesive discipline with a well-defined and stable core-subject matter, combined with a series of practices related to a distinct body of materials.[181] In terms of the analytical posture, black-letter analysis most closely resembles the empirical philosophy of language, which also focuses on how the meaning of words depends on the context of usage, e.g. what a contractual offer means depends upon how judges typically use this expression in the context of settling disputes.[182] However, only within the relatively marginal sub-discipline of jurisprudence is this linkage developed to any extent. In most other areas of legal research within the black-letter tradition, the potential contributions of other disciplines to the discussion of the topic in question is simply excluded (or marginalised) as legally irrelevant. Even within areas of legal theory, only those forms of jurisprudence, such as legal positivism, which broadly endorse the key assumptions of legal formalism, have found a receptive audience wherever the black-letter tradition has been dominant. Legal positivism, of course, reinforces the idea of law as a separate area of social activity whose study requires a singular and rigorous academic discipline that is uncontaminated by, for example, the interdisciplinary aspirations of many of the social sciences.[183]

As Twining notes with respect to the 'prevailing orthodoxy':

> At some point in the history of the Anglo-American tradition, law as an academic discipline could have been described as cohesive and centripedal: the object of

---

[181]Reza Banakar, 'Reflections on the Methodological Issues of the Sociology of Law', (2000) 27(2) *J. Law & Soc.* 273-95, 280. Twining by contrast dates the isolation of law as a development stemming from the late nineteenth century and reflecting the 'peculiar history and culture of the institutional study of law' within the law school which, from the 1970's onwards, has begun to decline.

[182]Twining, in Cane and Stapleton, 1991 *op. cit.,* 5.

[183]This closure and advocacy of pure legal science, which focuses only upon the most general and abstract problems of legal form, e.g., the concept of property as such and of rules as such, is clearest in the work of Hans Kelsen.

study was legal rules and the role of the jurist was to systematise, to rationalise and to expound legal doctrine.[184]

The idea of law as a distinct and autonomous 'discipline', with a distinct core and defining range of activities, does not mean that it is organised within universities to produce new discoveries akin to scientific breakthroughs in which new truths are consciously generated.[185] Instead, what it means is that distinctly and strictly legal modes of analysis and methods of interpretation of sources and application of precedents must be taught and practised in universities as a major device for initiating students into the subculture of the legal world, akin to the way university science degrees are meant to introduce students into the practices, expertise and way of life of institutional science as a specific type of social activity.[186] The distinct and singular character of law as a separate discipline, which has been in decline since the 1970's,[187] contrasts markedly with the commitment of more recent approaches, such as sociolegal studies, to interdisciplinary research.[188]

As a discipline, law possesses its own unique vocabulary, cultural practices, institutional conventions and interpretative methods for carrying out legal analysis. These methods are designed to carry out a type of doctrinal exposition and commentary that is capable of providing authoritative statements of the meaning and scope of applicable substantive legal tests and requirements on various topics.[189] The results of such exposition and commentary provide the basis for assessing the validity and limits of various claims regarding the nature and scope of rights and obligations arising from a range of actual and possible contexts of application. As Vick notes, at the core of the identity of law as an academic discipline for the last century has been 'a doctrinal approach involving the use of particularly interpretative tools and critical techniques in order to systematize and evaluate legal rules.'[190]

The claim that law is a distinct and independent discipline includes the belief that legal research must conform to certain long-established and accepted internal protocols regarding not only the selection, analysis and presentation of research data, but also the specific values that are characteristic of the knowledge and skills of a distinct community of authoritative experts.[191] As an academic discipline, law is a distinctive *style* of thinking, acting and generating an understanding of 'relevant' topics in the surrounding world through the lens of a specific interpretative framework. The style is highly technical and legalistic. The framework is itself a simplified mental model for the formation, recognition and resolution of specific questions and problems, which are rooted in specific institutional and linguistic conventions.[192]

---

[184]Twining, 1994 *op. cit.*, 153.

[185]Cf Becher, 1989 *op. cit.* 5.

[186]R. Posner, 1988 *op. cit.*

[187]R. Posner, 'The Decline of Law as an Autonomous Discipline: 1962–1987', (1987) 100 *Harv. L. Rev* 761.

[188]Vick, 2004 *op. cit.*, 166–8.

[189]Vick, 2004 *op. cit.*, 174. For a historical reconstruction of how legal studies separated from modern empirical social sciences as the latter developed quantitative and explanatory approaches, see W. T. Murphy, 'The Oldest Social Science? The Epistemic Properties of the Common Law Tradition' (1991) 54 *MLR* 182, at 185–91.

[190]Vick, 2004 *op. cit.*, 165.

[191]Vick, 2004 *op. cit.*, 166; C. Tomlins, 'Framing the Field of Law's Disciplinary Encounters: A Historical Narrative' (2000) 34 *Law and Society Rev.* 911 at 912.

[192]J. M. Balkan, 'Interdisciplinarity as Colonisation' (1996) 53 *Washington & Lee Law Rev.* 949, at 956.

One justification for interpreting legal studies as a distinct and independent academic discipline is that only this interpretation is adequate to the intrinsic nature of law as an institutional practice in the world outside academia. In other words, the academic study of law needs to conform to the special nature of law as a distinctive and independent institutional and professional activity within society. Those disputing this will claim that academic disciplines are relatively arbitrary divisions shaped by a range of other historical, economic and political factors, including the ideological need for the legal profession to claim that it has independently accredited expertise in legal knowledge.[193]

The black-letter view of law as a distinct and unique academic discipline endorses the self-image of the legal profession, particularly senior judges. It reinforces this group's sense of its own identity as a profession that possesses expertise understood primarily as insight into the operation of a formal body of rules and underlying principles. The profession's knowledge and objective application of these rules allows lawyers to under-stand and advise on the rights and duties of individuals.[194] Thus, the discipline of law is perceived as a rigorous analytical activity that both generates and revises a distinct body of knowledge, which itself possesses a range of practical applications for a genuinely 'learned' profession.

This assertion ignored the fact that, for most of the extended history of the British legal profession, law has been treated as a craft trade that needs to be learned 'on the job' through an apprenticeship system. However, law has more recently been reclassified as a distinctly expert body of learning and specialist substantive knowledge that needs to be taught at universities where it represents a distinctive discipline with its own unique methods of analysis and distinctive range of materials. As a specialist academic dis-cipline akin to botany and other classifying sciences, legal knowledge stands over and above the interpretation and experience of laypersons. Hence, the acquisition of such knowledge requires law students to develop a considerable range of new interpretative skills through their successful completion of a sustained and intensive period of aca-demic study.[195] Such study is needed not only to inculcate knowledge of the principles and rules of legal doctrine, but also the various ways judges react to how advocates selectively interpret and apply these points of law during the trial process.

Students who claim to have acquired the required skills of law as a distinct discipline need to demonstrate their ability to extract general propositions regarding the current legal doctrine from the reading of specific cases and statutes. They also must be able to relate new case law and statutory developments to the body of previously established doctrine, if need be reassessing the status of earlier cases and statutes. As Banakar recognises, understood as a specialist legal knowledge: 'Law becomes essentially concerned with interpretation of acts and case readings, expounding legal doctrine, and constitutes itself through textual manifestations of legal decisions, judgements and opinions.'[196]

The doctrinal analysis of Blackstone's *Commentaries*, which appears to have 'systemat-ised the unsystematic' and provided a 'comprehensive map' of the law, serves as a blue-print for the ideal type of strictly and uniquely legal analysis required by the discipline

---

[193]Vick, 2004 *op. cit.*, 167.

[194]Banakar, 2000 *op. cit.*, 281

[195]Twining, 1994 *op. cit.*, 219.

[196]Banakar, 2000 *op. cit.*, 13.

of law. Indeed, mentors of newly appointed academic staff have even been known to recommend a close study of this venerable work as an exemplary role model for a distinctive way of engaging in legal analysis.[197] The authors of a series of classical textbooks and studies, particularly Anson (on contract), Dicey (on public and administrative law), Maitland (on equity), Pollock (on torts) and Kenny (on criminal law), extended Blackstone's general approach.[198] These textbook writers continued to develop Blackstone's systematic and largely uncritical type of exposition and commentary upon basic legal principles and categories of particular branches of law.[199] It is also worth noting in this context that critics of the black-letter tradition, ranging from Jeremy Bentham to those contributing to the critical legal studies movement, still take the *Commentaries* as a main target. These critics claim that the tradition, originating with Blackstone, provides an unacceptably abstract and formal nature of analysis that disconnects law in books from law in action.[200]

The claims that law constitutes a separate and singular discipline, which has a distinct identity, have been further reinforced and justified by reference to the close relationship and division of labour between legal studies and the legal profession. The latter claims to be a 'learned' profession that possesses a valuable and distinctive type of expert knowledge to unlock the otherwise mysterious workings of law. Traditionally, university law schools have uneasily spanned two roles: firstly, they have served the training needs of the legal profession through inculcating successive generations of practitioners into 'core' legal subjects policed by the legal professions. Secondly, law schools have also needed to claim respectability as custodians of a *bona fide* academic subject serviced by properly accredited and qualified academics applying a scientific approach by, for example, generalising and harmonising legal materials into a systematic body of knowledge.[201] Indeed, it is arguable that the current tendency to define law as a distinct academic discipline with its own positivist scientific methods of analysis, whose application generates encyclopaedic doctrinal commentaries, was originally linked to a specific vested interest of early generations of legal academics. That is, they needed to carve out a distinctive niche for themselves, which was both different from, but also useful to, that of legal practitioners, whilst also conforming to currently prevailing understandings of 'science' within nineteenth-century universities.[202] Twining notes that: 'The pioneers of English academic law in the late nineteenth century had to establish their professional legitimacy in the eyes of sceptical universities and a largely hostile profession by claiming a special body of expertise of which they had a monopoly. The jurist could systematise the chaotic common law through scientific exposition and analysis.'[203] Murphy and Roberts note that, in this period, such doctrinal commentary became 'the unmistakable, unchallenged province of academic law'.[204]

---

[197]Twining, 1994 *op. cit.*, xix, 1.

[198]Vick, 2004 *op. cit.*, 174; Twining, 1994 *op. cit.*, 113, 135–6; A.W. Simpson, 'The Rise and Fall of the Legal Treatise: Legal Principles and Forms of Legal Literature' (1981) 48 *University of Chicago Law Rev.* 632. Pollock's classic work on the *Principles of Contract* first appeared in 1876.

[199]Twining, 1994 *op. cit.*, 135.

[200]Twining, 1994 *op. cit.*, 1, 2, 131–2; Kennedy, 1979 *op. cit.*; Atiyah, 1979 *op. cit.*, 391–2.

[201]Richard Collier, 'The Changing University and the (Legal) Academic Career – Rethinking the Relationship between Women, Men and the "Private Life" of the Law School' (2002) 22 *Legal Studies* 1, at 5.

[202]Vick, 2004 *op. cit.*, 180.

[203]Twining, 1994 *op. cit.*, 134.

[204]Murphy and Roberts, 'Introduction' (1987) 50 *MLR* 677 at 677.

Only in the last three decades have legal academics developed forms of social science research that have become free of the pull of vocational training and of servicing the demands of the legal profession. Inevitably, these developments have often challenged the traditional conception of law as a self-sufficient discipline dominated by traditional black-letter methods of doctrinal analysis. Indeed, it is arguable that, if law schools entirely broke their relationship with the legal profession, and developed the same relationship of distance that most criminologists have with criminals, then they would cut themselves adrift from this subject's traditional foundations as an academic discipline. Law could lose its identity as a distinctive academic subject.[205] Certainly, if the linkage between law as a distinct academic subject and the legal profession were broken, the risk would be that a pluralistic and interdisciplinary conception of legal studies could emerge. This would no longer focus exclusively on state-centred rules, legislation and court judgments, but include 'living law' of informal definitions and handling of disputes by different social groups and subcultures. The study of such normative and challenging forms of regulation is, to a great extent, excluded from the discipline of law because they generally bypass the interventions of the legal profession, and knowledge of such activities could have little relevance to vocational legal training.[206]

As apprentices of a unique and singular discipline, students need to take into account the fact that, from a black-letter perspective, law has clearly defined and jealously guarded its academic borders since it became an academic subject. These territorial borders prevent, for example, international law being subsumed into international relations or contract law being collapsed into a subset within economic analysis, or legal history being assimilated in the discipline of history (that is historians' history). Insofar as a dissertation loses its specifically 'legal' focus through such slippages, it risks addressing issues and using sources and methods that subscribers to the black-letter approach may deem 'irrelevant'. Twining has argued that the law schools, particularly those which have attained the status of separate faculties, have been allowed to retain a self-perpetuating understanding of their subject as a unique discipline only by virtue of the rigidity and insularity of academic institutional traditions.[207] In addition, over many decades, academic lawyers have established their own distinctive customs, ways of communication, vocabulary and interpretative styles. Through sheer force of routine and convention, these have become self-perpetuating.[208] Students need to be aware of some of the restraints under which their supervisors may be operating. The black-letter approach is in one sense a distinctive cultural tradition that has become firmly rooted in the organisational structure of most but not all law schools. This tradition is sustained in part through the impact of a system of esteem, promotion and other rewards, which are also reinforced through sanctions for those individuals who fail to conform.[209] Vick suggests that, as an academic discipline, law is largely 'concerned with authority, exercised often unconsciously through the penalties and rewards of academic life'. He argues that:

---

[205]Peter Birks, 'Introduction', in Birks, 1996 *op. cit.*, ix; Murphy and Roberts, 1987 *op. cit.*, 680.

[206]The Joint Qualifying Statement permits no more than one-third of 'non-law' subjects to be included as part of a qualifying legal degree providing that all the core or foundation subjects are taught as well.

[207]Twining, 1994 *op. cit.*, 64.

[208]Vick, 2004 *op. cit.*, 167.

[209]*Ibid.*, 168–9.

Conformity with the ways of the disciplinary tribe is ensured through the marks and degree classifications awarded at University; peer review of book proposals, academic articles, and research grant applications; the marginalisation of non-conforming work; and the natural desire of members of a discipline to obtain the approval of others in the tribe, especially the tribe leaders.[210]

The problem facing dissertation students is that many of the customary expectations applicable to their work are largely implicit. This makes it difficult for students to know what precisely is expected of the criteria that, for example, really distinguish a dissertation which attracts a mid 2.1 mark from one which receives a 2.2 grade. Standard criteria, such as 'depth of analysis', 'demonstrating adequate research skills', 'coherent organisation and structure' and 'citation of relevant material', are rarely definable in any clear and precise way that applies consistently across the board, and which would allow a student to mount an effective challenge to any specific grade. As a result, such formal criteria conceal as much as they reveal about the real expectations of students' work, and permit all manner of highly subjective variations of actual criteria to take place, particularly if the works are not blind second-marked. Legal developments and the facts of cases, which cannot easily be assimilated into the expectations of the discipline's matrix, will typically be rejected as 'irrelevant'. Such rejection further reinforces the grip this discipline exerts upon its members.[211] By conforming fluently to these customs, both students and legal academics display their badges of accredited membership of the discipline. Once acquired, this identity and related disciplinary integrity may be defended against supposedly external threats to its integrity.[212]

By contrast, a subject such as criminology, which clearly relates to aspects of the criminal justice system, lacks such clear disciplinary boundaries and methods. Hence, this subject remains at risk of assimilation into, for example, sociological approaches to deviance, or applied behavioural sciences (including psychology and psychiatry) or social administration or penology.[213] Supporters of the black-letter approach within law schools can argue that no particular way of conducting research and analysis within criminology has traditionally enjoyed the status traditionally afforded to their own discipline. Indeed, research within subjects such as criminology almost invites a multi-disciplinary approach and the multiplication of often-incompatible qualitative and quantitative research methods that accompanies this. Law schools, by contrast, resolved this potential confusion many decades ago by devising and refining black-letter methods that are typically claimed by subscribers to be uniquely appropriate to the analysis of the positive content of legal doctrine.

● The Restricted Character of Black-Letter Forms of Criticism of Law

As already noted, the primary aim of black-letter analysis is to provide an accurate and authoritative description of legal doctrine, which can be fully checked and verified

---

[210]*Ibid.*, 169. See also Balkan, 1996 *op. cit.*, 954.

[211]Regarding the 'rules of relationship' governing relations between members of the legal discipline, see Peter Goodrich, 'Of Blackstone's Tower: Metaphors of Distance and Histories of the English Law School' in Birks, 1996 *op. cit.*, 68.

[212]*Ibid.*, 168-9.

[213]On the idea of colonisation of vulnerable disciplines, see Balkan, 1996 *op. cit.*

against the cited case and statute law, as an end in itself. However, contrary to many common stereotypes, such analysis does permit, even require, a certain form of criticism, and even calls for significant reform of substantive and procedural aspects of law. Such criticism can be justified wherever existing doctrine can be shown to be falling short of the formalist ideal of internal coherence. This can occur whenever apparent inconsistencies emerge in the relationship between individual cases, established rules, more general legal principles and underlying basic axioms.

Students should not, perhaps, underestimate the extent to which black-letter legal academics are intensely concerned with the prevailing state of 'their area' of expertise (to whose study they may have devoted decades of teaching and research), and the desire of academics to have judicial and legislative practice conform strictly to traditional ideals of doctrinal coherence. A researcher's commitment to the black-letter approach is, therefore, entirely consistent with varying degrees of scepticism regarding the validity of certain 'deviant' judicial decisions, and even statutory innovations (particularly where these give effect to welfare-state schemes that exhibit different priorities and values). Indeed, in some instances, such scepticism and calls for reform, or the reversal of recent statutory interventions, may be *positively required* of those academic lawyers who are fully committed to the internal standards and expectations of the black-letter tradition. In short, black-letter analysis should not be classified as purely descriptive, and hence as necessarily uncritical of the form and substance of legal doctrine. This is particularly so because the pioneering works of the textbook tradition actually invented a new discipline founded upon an orderly science of general legal principles through a process of creative selection of sources, organising categories and divisions, and through an ingenious and novel way of defining, classifying and narrating legal sources.[214]

Students adopting a black-letter methodology may even be expected to conclude their dissertations with a call for reforms to substantive doctrine or procedural aspects of the legal system. This may be required because, for example, the dissertation has revealed the existence of discrepancies, inconsistencies or ambiguities stemming from questionable judicial decisions or ill-drafted legislative interventions. Its findings may also indicate that existing doctrine has yet to fully adapt to challenges created by new technical or social developments, for which traditional legal tests, originally designed to deal with circumstances that no longer exist, have clearly become inadequate. A dissertation's failure to identify such internal difficulties, or its display of indifference to 'ironing out' of inconsistencies by future reforms, are unlikely to impress those internal or external examiners who subscribe to the black-letter perspective. Indeed, such examiners may even argue that such a dissertation needs to be marked down because it is 'too descriptive' and 'lacks critical analysis'.

On the other hand, it is important not to exaggerate the critical dimension to black-letter analysis because, on balance, such analysis tends towards conservatism rather than radicalism. For example, the formalistic dimensions of black-letter approaches tend to assume that once legal problems are reinterpreted as disputes between discrete individuals, a judge can apply a legal rule to 'solve' the legal problem in question by granting of a specific remedy in favour of one or other of the individual parties. This belief further assumes that, whatever the nature of the problem, the law could, perhaps with

---

[214]Cf. Becher, 1989 *op. cit.*, 8; Twining, 1994 *op. cit.*, 138.

slight adaptations, provide both a reasonable and practical answer to many conflicts and disputes. The conservative effect stems, in part, from the belief that existing or reformed law can always form part of the *solution* for disputes and conflicts, as distinct from being one part of the problem. It would be difficult for committed 'Thatcherite' students to deploy a black-letter analysis to argue in favour of widespread deregulation of commercial activity, including the complete abolition of regulatory schemes and related legislation. Students whose dissertations are shaped by their commitment to anarchism would presumably have a similar difficulty.

For interesting reasons, which are rarely acknowledged, black-letter legal analysis requires an endorsement of particular *substantive values* that operate as the yardstick for making critical assessments in legal research. Recognition of the worth of these liberal values and expectations is typically expected of more ambitious forms of black-letter analysis, even though this is rarely explicitly stated of, for example, law dissertations.[215] However, in practice, these values supply the ideals that underpin the standards used within this type of legal research to criticise existing law for falling short of the mark. Amongst the most important values endorsed is the traditional liberal commitment to the ideals of individualism, the civil and political rights of private individuals, and Dicey's model of the rule of law more generally. The commitment to individualism means that law is interpreted in terms of the neutral application of objectively given rules to particular disputes between discrete individuals. As a result, the *social* character of conflicts between groups is largely disregarded as attention focuses instead on, for example, the formal legal duties and rights of this particular landlord and that particular tenant. Thus, the interpretation and application of legal doctrine by judges and other lawyers may be presented as if it essentially involved the working out of the technical details of the legal rights and duties of the parties as individuals, as distinct from representatives of broader social groups with competing and perhaps incompatible collective interests. The practical result of this individualistic tendency for present purposes is that students undertaking dissertation research from the black-letter perspective are spared the formidable task of relating case law to various sociological and economic data regarding the operation of conflicts between groups, classes and other collective entities within society.

The pervasiveness of legalistic values of liberal constitutionalism that underpin the criteria assessment deployed by black-letter methodologies also includes respect for the values of formal equality (legal procedures treating all individuals as if they were equal), corrective or remedial justice (attaching remedies to breaches of specific individual rights) and due process norms (right to be heard within an independent and fair procedure). Hence, legal researchers who aim to apply the black-letter approach in a consistent way will need to show their clear appreciation of a series of other claimed 'virtues'. These are closely related to classic liberal values and ideals associated with Dicey's concept of the rule of law. Such values demand a preference for strict adherence to political neutrality, and for decision-makers to adopt a stance of reflective detachment in deciding individual cases. A second related preference is for decision-making according to rules, as distinct from administrative discretion. In other words, liberal values are also associated with the tendency of black-letter analysis to analyse society in legalistic terms, that is, as essentially governable by rules. Indeed, this forms part of a more general

---

[215]Twining, 1994 *op. cit.*, 138.

tendency to set up issues of government regulation as a simple choice between clear and previously announced rules versus administrative discretion. In addition to setting up this issue as requiring an either/or choice between stark alternatives, black-letter analysis approaches this 'choice' with a definite preference for clear and previously announced rules as a virtuous device for exercising vital control over administrative discretion.[216] The commitment of black-letter analysis to liberal standards assumes that the ever-greater regulation of society by rules, and the subsequent reduction in the scope for uncontrolled discretion by public officials, including civil servants, the police and even courts, will necessarily result in greater liberty and justice for private individual citizens.[217] This is typically justified as a means of exploiting accumulated experience stored in earlier precedents. It leads naturally to the familiar 'rules versus discretion' approach to a wide range of topics addressed by legal researchers in the public law areas.[218]

Hence, consideration of alternative and 'non-lawyerly' criteria for interpreting and evaluating state processes of the kind discussed by political scientists will rarely, if ever, be expected of black-letter projects. These alternatives may include ways of promoting *greater* use of administrative discretion and a *reduction* of legalistic procedures to realise the goals of 'sound government', both of which are heretical to the liberal agenda.[219]

The black-letter methodology's endorsement of the values of individualism is clear from its focus upon private individuals, as distinct from collective entities such as either entire classes of the population, or an area of the economy. Hence, it suggests that dissertation research should focus not only on legally significant decisions made by private individuals but also the impact upon such individuals of administrative discretion. Liberalism endorses respect for individual personal liberty and civil and political liberties, particularly those modelled on private property rights.[220] For example, in an employment-law dissertation addressing trade union involvement in the workplace, the focus would fall upon the alleged denial of individual freedom associated with the 'closed shop', and not the 'right' of workers to insist that all those employees who gain real benefits from gains made through trade union collective bargaining should also be obliged to join the union. Instead, the commitment to individualistic values will ensure that the issue will be reinterpreted to focus on the right of each employee, as a private individual, not to have to become a member of any organisation they do not wish to join. It is an affront to civil and political rights to deny private individuals their absolute right to exercise free choice with respect to 'freedom of association'.

The individualistic values endorsed by the black-letter approach are also linked with a series of alleged virtues associated with liberalism more generally. In particular, they are associated with the importance of Dicey's conception of the rule of law as a protection against lawless executive power and discretion.[221] In this way, the black-letter tradition, whilst claiming to be politically neutral, positively affirms certain liberal values. These

---

[216]*Ibid.*, 16.

[217]Baldwin, 1995 *op. cit.*, 23.

[218]*Ibid.*, 19, 21.

[219]*Ibid.*, 19; C. J. Edley, *Administrative Law: Rethinking Judicial Control of Bureaucracy* (New Haven, CT: 1990), 217.

[220]R. Stewart, 'The Reformation of American Administrative Law' (1975) 88 *Harv. L.R* 1667.

[221]K. Davis, *Discretionary Justice* (Chicago, IL: 1971); P. Craig, 'Dicey: Unitary, Self-Correcting Democracy and Public Law' (1990) 106 *LQR* 105; Baldwin, 1995 *op. cit.*, 34.

values include those promoting the legal accountability of public sector power to law, and forms of decision-making that accord with 'due process' standards', such as the right to be heard by an independent adjudicator and to be given reasons for all legal decisions. Hence, dissertation students may be expected to show their appreciation of the alleged benefits of an essentially formal model of justice and legal procedures deemed to be based on 'fairness to individuals', and the exercise of executive power according to clear, precise and transparent rules subject to judicial review by an independent non-political judiciary.

Despite the countervailing positivistic assumptions of this tradition, it still incorporates these liberal values and ideals into the criteria and expectations that its subscribers deploy to make criticisms of existing law, even though the values themselves are neither purely internal to legal doctrine, nor independent from broader political morality.[222] Although such values and ideals are clearly derived from classic liberal political theories, their endorsement by research that is guided by the black-letter approach is typically passed over in silence. Where this deployment of value judgements is acknowledged, it is typically treated as providing an essentially non-political and largely self-evident standard for critical assessment.

The endorsement of individualistic values results in questions of justice being taken to relate mainly, if not exclusively, to the demands that private individuals make upon public sector organisations, including courts and tribunals, such as expectations of equal treatment, openness and respect for precedent. Amongst the alleged virtues of rule-based decision-making is the claim that it leads to greater 'justice' for private individuals involved in the legal process. The black-letter approach interprets the meaning of justice in a formal and procedural way. This focuses on respect for clear precedents leading to consistent decision-making with respect to comparable cases over extended periods of time. It also insists not only upon formal equality of treatment of 'like cases' across a range of different situations but also the possibility of appeal before an independent panel or court to check that decision-makers have properly applied the relevant legal rules.

Black-letter analysis will focus mainly on elaborating, refining and extending rights of private individuals against government and public sector bodies, even in a context where the welfare state has already established collective agencies to hear the grievances of individuals and groups.[223] The priority given to classic private sector values of individual choice, operating through an unregulated marketplace, takes place at the expense of wider issues relating to efficiency in the furtherance of the public interest, such as the delivery of core public services relating to the regulation of environmental pollution and health and safety at work.[224] As a result, black-letter methodology implicitly rejects traditional public sector values in policy-making, which relate to wider collective issues and state-defined 'social needs'.[225] (Of course, during periods where the public sector is itself subjected to liberal, free-market reforms, such as market-testing and contracting out of services as has taken place over the last two decades, then this distinction between private and public sector orientations and values becomes far less clear).

---

[222]D. Galligan, *Discretionary Powers* (Oxford. OUP, 1986) 4.

[223]P. McAuslan, 'Administrative Law, Collective Consumption and Judicial Policy' (1983) *MLR* 1.

[224]Baldwin, 1995 *op. cit.*, 21.

[225]*Ibid.*

The black-letter approach insists that the category of justice used by subscribers as a criterion for evaluating the research topic in question must be confined to corrective and formal justice of the liberal model, as distinct from the model of substantive 'social justice'. The latter raises prohibited political questions regarding the distribution of wealth, power and life chances, and also focuses on how policy-makers could combat social injustices through engaging in substantive social, economic and institutional changes.[226]

The ideals of liberalism that inform black-letter types of evaluation also operate on the premise that rule-based decision-making not only ensures continuity of policy application, but also minimises the influence of irrelevant or inappropriate factors (such as undue influence from powerful or influential individuals, or institutions with a vested interest in the decision). Student dissertations will be expected to appreciate that rule-based decision-making is an important virtue because it not only reduces the possibility of mistakes, but also removes any requirement for policies to be justified and reinvestigated every time a fresh decision has to be made.[227] Furthermore, rule-based decision-making is also deemed more efficient because valid decisions can be clearly justified by reference to the technical meaning and scope of the rule in a way that should minimise unwarranted appeals and challenges.

The commitment to these individualistic values is very strong and deeply entrenched. This explains why the results of empirical studies of law in action remain incapable of denting such commitment to formalistic rule-based decision-making.[228] This commitment has not been questioned even where such empirical studies demonstrate that rules often fail, or become counter-productive in practice (as where more detailed rules governing tax legislation actually *increases* the scope for official discretion). These law-in-action studies have also revealed not only that rules can be used defensively by bureaucracies to thwart the rights and interests of private individuals, but also that, contrary to the liberal premise, discretion does not always lead to arbitrary decision-making. The entrenched nature of this commitment to liberal values is clear from the fact that no amount of empirical evidence to the contrary is capable of displacing it. This is possibly because subscribers to the black-letter enterprise do not generally view empirical studies of law in action conducted by members of the sociolegal studies movement as important contributions to legal knowledge at all.

The values deployed as normative standards for critical assessment, which stem from the classic liberal political theories of Mill and Dicey, continue to provide the underlying criteria for the type of criticisms that supervisors and examiners are likely to expect to see applied, with suitable prudence and caution, within at least the conclusion of a black-letter dissertation. Thus, insofar as dissertations are expected to consider possibilities for reform, they must be reform proposals of a *standard type* stemming from, and giving further effect to, the liberal values of legalism and Dicey's interpretation of the rule of law. Lacey notes that the pervasiveness of liberal values influences not only the very definition of what the 'problems' are within the existing law but also the measures deemed capable of resolving these problems:

> Problems are typically seen as arising from 'gaps' in the rules, calling for clearer interpretation or further legislative or quasi-legislative action. Disputes are seen as

---

[226]*Ibid.*, 21.

[227]*Ibid.*, 13.

[228]*Ibid.*, 23.

calling for resolution on the basis of the given rules and according to standards of due process. The approach is closely associated with the ideal of the rule of law and hence with liberalism as a doctrine of political morality.[229]

Baldwin also notes that 'lawyerly critiques . . . tend to produce calls for more rules, more trial type processes – in short more of the trimmings of formal justice.'[230] Student dissertations that criticise the existing law will therefore be expected to focus their criticisms only on those areas where a case can be made for yet further rule-based reforms. If student work includes a call for law reform, then this must be of a type that is most likely to harmonise with the remainder of the black-letter agenda – for instance, by suggesting purely legalistic changes centred around the courts, which aim to provide enhanced protection for private individuals' procedural rights.[231] A student dissertation may conclude on a critical note by questioning whether current forms of plea-bargaining are compatible with those liberal principles that are supposed to confer legitimacy upon the legal system, such as strict compliance with the rule of law and the minimisation of administrative discretion by prosecutors and other state officials. In short, the individualistic values that underpin and inform the black-letter approach provide a predisposition to criticise problems and gaps in the nature and scope of existing legal measures on the premise that all areas of social activity and every type of dispute can, if need be, be regulated by the adoption of this legalistic, rule-centred approach.[232]

The endorsement of individualistic liberal values also rules out from the start reform proposals that are *collectivist in nature*, such as responding to disputes between landlords and tenants through policies of mass nationalisation and redistribution of private property rights.[233] Indeed, students should recognise that the type of criticisms that are consistent with a black-letter methodology are of a strictly limited type. They must focus not on the substantive outcomes of legal and social reforms (such as reducing real inequalities of wealth, power and life opportunities), but rather on improving formal legal procedures. This requires any dissertation that makes proposals for law reform to operate within an agenda that is already committed to liberal values of 'openness, rationality, generality and predictability', which stem from a commitment to a classic law-centred interpretation of the rule of law.[234]

Rarely will criticism (or, more precisely, self-criticism) be directed at uncovering the underlying assumptions, working methods and ideals of black-letter analysis itself. Nor, generally, will it be acceptable for this type of analysis to address critically the social, economic or political factors that may explain why certain types of dispute arise in the way that they currently do. As already noted, such criticism, which trespasses into the forbidden zone of policy analysis, would be deemed inappropriate because it falls outside the 'strictly legal' remit of black-letter analysis entirely. If student dissertations contain criticisms of the law, they must be of a certain predetermined type. Such criticism must not involve a sustained discussion of policy issues based on factual evidence of where

---

[229]N. Lacey, 'The Jurisprudence of Discretion: Escaping the Legal Paradigm' in K. Hawkins (ed.), 'The Use of Discretion' (Oxford: OUP, 1992), 362.

[230]Baldwin, 1995 *op. cit.*, 19.

[231]*Ibid.*, 18.

[232]Baldwin, 1995 *op. cit.*, 18.

[233]J. W. McAuslan, 'Administrative Law, Collective Consumption and Judicial Policy' (1983) 46 *MLR* 1.

[234]Lacey, 1992, *op. cit.*, 369.

the public interest actually lies. They must not for example, address such issues as government efficiency in serving the public interest, drawing upon materials contained in the social science section of the university library. This will be deemed inappropriate because it would involve the dissertation trespassing upon questions of substantive values, ideology and politics, and upon sources other than cases, statutes and doctrinal commentaries. All of these clearly fall outside the remit of strict legal analysis as defined within black-letter methodology as a single and self-contained discipline isolated from both the social sciences and the humanities.[235]

Students attempting to apply the black-letter approach in a coherent way need to respect the *restricted nature* of the criticisms that can be advanced within this agenda. They should, in particularly, avoid the temptation to make wider criticisms that highlight alleged fundamental failings in state provision, and government strategy more generally, or which criticise organisational frameworks and institutional goals.[236] Hence, whenever Parliament or Judges reform legal doctrine, black-letter texts will typically incorporate these developments into the settled body of legal doctrine, sometimes with positive comments. However, if one turns to earlier editions of the same works, it is rarely possible to discover any criticism of the previous law. Even where the new reforms are welcomed positively in newer editions of standard black-letter textbooks, they will rarely comment upon *their own* earlier failure to identify such defects in the doctrine. As a result, a key element of the rationale of the new law remains incapable of analysis, i.e. the way in which previous aspects of the law were believed to be failing to meet their purpose and modern social needs. For example, if we compare editions of *Megarry's Manual*,[237] the recent edition welcomes positively the repeal of section 40 of the Law of Property Act 1925 as removing 'three centuries of a luxuriant but not very elevating jurisprudence'.[238] However, earlier editions of this textbook had previously provided no more than a simple exposition of the details of s. 40 and its subsequent case-law interpretation without including a single critical comment of a purely technical kind. Hence, students who adopt the black-letter perspective will typically not be expected to give priority to what is arguably a central dynamic element in legal doctrine, that is, its constant evolution and change according to criticisms made of its perceived defects by practitioners, academics and judges.

The black-letter methodology tends to assume that legal doctrine reflects, embodies and secures a *broad social consensus* as to core values and beliefs, that it articulates both the 'common sense' and 'reasonableness' of all right-thinking persons. Subscribers to this approach act as if their preferred method embodies, understands and in one sense gives effect to the shared value system of a presumed social consensus, whilst, at the same time, also remaining essentially neutral and detached from the political dimension of that value system. Judicial and other subscribers to this approach may insist that legal doctrine must adapt, in a flexible and responsive way, to new social needs, practices, attitudes and expectations, e.g. in relation to the legal regulation of the property rights of cohabitees.[239] What is taken for granted here is the idea that there really is a shared

---

[235]Baldwin, 1995 *op. cit.*, 18; Twining, 1994 *op. cit.*, xix.
[236]Baldwin, 1995 *op. cit.*, 18.
[237]*Ibid.*
[238]*Ibid.*, preface v.
[239]See the judgment of May LJ in *Burns v Burns* (1984) 1 All ER 244 at 255.

system of core interests and values that is *valid across society as a whole*. In other words, the main issue facing legal doctrine is one of adapting the scope and application of traditional doctrines to changes within a broad consensus about basic social values, needs and perceptions of the public good and public interest. Hence, students who adopt the black-letter approach to their dissertation projects will rarely if ever be expected to differentiate between the often very different value systems associated with particular social groups, ethnic traditions, generations, gender differences or social classes.[240] On the contrary, those who subscribe to this approach can continue to simply assume that the effort to make such a differentiation is unnecessary, precisely because there is a broad consensus of interests shared by, for instance, tenants as well as landlords, landowners as well as both ramblers and squatters, divorcing wives as well as their husbands.[241]

This presupposition of a value consensus restricts the type of criticism towards the law and the supposed core social values which it embodies. Unger notes that this consensual aspect includes:

> The belief that the authoritative legal materials – the system of statutes, cases and accepted legal ideas – embody and sustain a defensible scheme of human association. They display . . . an intelligible moral order . . . The laws are not merely the outcome of contingent power struggles or practical pressures lacking in rightful authority.[242]

A number of the black-letter textbooks on property provide clear illustrations of this aspect. For example, Megarry's most recent 'Manual'[243] exhibits a clear tendency to simply presuppose, as distinct from establishing by means of critical argument, that a social consensus as to basic values and the desirable future direction of society exists. In relation to the Settled Land Act 1882, this work rationalises those values in terms of the presumed need to secure 'the well-being of settled land'.[244] This assumes that this 'need' can be understood in abstraction of any consideration of social and historical conflicts over land ownership, usage and distribution. In this example, the belief that a social consensus exists as to key values explains why there are rarely any attempts within black-letter analysis to address conflicts regarding conceptual issues, contests concerning the definition of the subject matter,[245] and, more broadly, the character of the various ideological values contained in the specific commitments of the law.

The black-letter approach typically regards critical analysis of the ideological values that underpin the policy element of legal doctrine as inappropriate because such analysis cannot be developed in a way that avoids contradicting fundamental tenets and premises of this methodology. Indeed, if a dissertation concludes by calling for such wider reforms, then this may be perceived by examiners as evidence that the student has either not really appreciated the nature of 'proper' black-letter analysis in the first place, or that they have realised this but are not willing to respect the implications of choosing to apply this methodology through to the end in a consistent and coherent way.

---

[240]A. Bottomley, 'Self and Subjectivities: Languages of Claim in Property Law', (1993) 20 *JLS*, 56ff.

[241]For studies that question whether the ideal of political neutrality has been achieved with respect to private property rights see J. Griffiths, *The Politics of The Judiciary*, 4th edn (London: Fontana, 1991), 114–16; P. Harris, *Introduction To Law*, 3rd edn, (London: Weidenfeld and Nicolson, 1988), 42–4.

[242]See R. Unger, *The Critical Legal Studies Movement*, (Cambridge, MA: Harvard University Press, 1983), 2.

[243]*Megarry's Manual of The Law Of Real Property*, 7th edn, (London: Maxwell, 1993).

[244]*Ibid.*, 218.

[245]*Ibid.*, preface v.

In short, it would be a mistake to conclude that, because the black-letter approach endorses specific individualistic and liberal values, which serve as a benchmark for assessing and making criticisms of legal topics, that this methodology can engage in criticism in any wider sense of the term, e.g. a systematic critique of ideology or social structure. Calls for reforms are likely to be confined to appeals for lawyers' law to be further rationalised in a set direction, and to aim to conserve intact the main rules, principles and axioms, indeed to re-establish a coherent relationship between them.

The restricted aim of any criticism will be to propose that the ideal of doctrine as an independent system of rules without gaps, contradictions or ambiguities, and which operates according to Dicey's model of the rule of law, is either restored or at least better approximated.[246] This narrowly focused type of criticism should not be confused with 'critique' in the traditional social science sense of this term – for example, a critique of how society is structured and justified by reference to distorting ideologies (including those contained in Dicey's liberal model of the rule of law), and the impact this structure of inequality continues to exert upon the life chances of members of disadvantaged and marginalised groups. Students should not, therefore, claim that because their conclusion contains criticisms of the kind discussed above, they have somehow combined black-letter analysis with, for example, that of critical legal studies or critical social theories. On the contrary, if this were the case, then the activity of criticism would extend to the credibility and social impact of the underlying liberal values that underpin the black-letter orientation in general, particularly its 'view of the world through legalistic eyes'.[247] If students opted for this more thoroughgoing and 'radical' type of critique, then their dissertations would appear to many to be fundamentally inconsistent with, and indeed even subversive of, the very foundations of the black-letter approach.

● Questions of Evaluation: The Advantages and Problems of Black-Letter Analysis

It is now possible to examine in more depth those defining features of this approach, which have attracted both uncritical support and often heated polemical attack from opponents. By so doing, the aim is to put some more flesh on the skeleton of our earlier provisional and working definition sketched out above. It is one thing to appreciate that part of the significance of adopting a black-letter approach to a dissertation project is to participate in a traditional custom hardened over time into an orthodoxy, it is quite another to use this characteristic as a ground for either accepting or rejecting this methodology. From the perspective of a law student seeking to identify the best possible approach to the conduct of dissertation research, what are the implications of the fact that, until comparatively recently, the black-letter approach achieved the status of an entrenched orthodoxy? We would suggest that it does not follow that this provides evidence either of this methodology's intrinsic worth, or, on the contrary, that the black-letter approach must necessarily lack any possible justification outside of habitual obedience to custom and tradition. It would be perfectly reasonable for students to accept that the black-letter approach has taken on the characteristics of orthodoxy without

---

[246]With respect to black-letter analysis of criminal law doctrine, see Lacey and Wells *Reconstructing Criminal Law* (London: Butterworths, 1998) 1–90.
[247]Baldwin, 1995 *op. cit.*, 19.

relying upon this characteristic to justify either its automatic adoption or rejection as a methodology for their particular projects.

Those students who are by inclination conservative in orientation may be more attracted to this methodology precisely because of its status as a long-standing and established traditional approach, but such subjective preferences hardly amount to a convincing methodological argument. Equally, other students who like to define themselves as 'radical' or 'free thinking' may want to reject any long-established traditional approach *precisely because* it has hardened into orthodoxy – as if more recently developed approaches must necessarily be superior to earlier more traditional ones. This ground for rejection upon the basis of subjective inclinations is no more impressive than the conservative 'case' for acceptance. In other words, the fact that a methodology has, over many decades, attained an authoritative status signals neither that this tradition must necessarily deserve this status, nor, following a process of critical scrutiny, that its main claims to offer the best possible way of conducting legal research must be incapable of justification.

Instead, what dissertation students need to appreciate is that, irrespective of the current status of any particular methodology, it remains the responsibility of legal researchers to decide for themselves, and upon the basis of clear and explicit arguments, whether or not this approach provides the best available methodology to realise the goals of their particular research project. Providing a sensible and well-informed answer to this question clearly requires students to undertake a close examination of the characteristics of the black-letter approach. It is necessary to identify the approaches' perceived advantages and disadvantages relative to *different types* of research project with diverse goals. Claims that this approach has become an orthodoxy, a traditional and dominant methodology within mainstream law schools, may have some bearing on one aspect of this process of assessment. However, it is arguable that the question of whether or not this, or the various sociolegal approaches examined in the next chapter, currently enjoy high status should not be treated by legal researchers as a decisive factor. The sad fact is that many research agendas that once enjoyed fashionable status within the academy, including the idea that habitual criminals have identifiable physical characteristics, have been discredited, and are now looked back on with considerable puzzlement by later generations of researchers.

The remainder of this section summarises the main points that have been argued for and against the adoption of the black-letter approach to the conduct of research. The arguments for its adoption by researchers include at least the following:

1. It continues to be popular with many law students, as witnessed by the sale of student textbooks which, despite recent competition from works using alternative methodologies, continue to sell well.

2. By emulating the interpretative techniques deployed by senior lawyers when contesting disputed points of law, this approach helps law students to learn to 'think like a lawyer'.

3. The black-letter methodology provides a degree of continuity and coherence across a student's experience of different elements of their degree programme, particularly at undergraduate level. This is because each course taught from this perspective connects with others taught from the same standpoint.

4. Only the black-letter approach operates on the basis that law is a singular and independent academic discipline with its own unique methods linked through a viable division of labour with the work of the legal profession.

5. Students within law schools where the black-letter methodology predominates acquire a clear and distinct idea of what it means to engage in recognised forms of legal analysis and reasoning. This facilitates communication between lawyers, and bridges the divide between university studies and legal practice.

6. The necessary materials for black-letter analysis are public texts readily available in both hard copy and electronically. This, together with increasingly helpful finding and search aids, makes it possible for even comprehensive research projects to be completed in a timely fashion. This minimises the chances of black-letter methods generating a mass of irrelevant data with little pertinent material data.

7. Because the primary sources studied by black-letter methods are public documents, the gathering of relevant extracts of primary sources does not raise the ethical difficulties associated with empirical fieldwork conducted according to alternative social scientific approaches to law in action.

8. Insofar as this methodology is consistently applied over a number of courses on the LLB or LLM degrees, law students can improve their level of technical skills by applying this methodology to different areas of law, so that skills and competences gained in one area of study can positively reinforce their ability to succeed in others, even where the level of expectation is higher. By contrast, alternative approaches require dissertation students (and their supervisors) to acquire, adopt and master a range of unfamiliar social science methodologies, which may prove difficult for a variety of reasons.[248]

9. The black-letter approach focuses on an important range of primary materials and issues that professional lawyers need to become familiar with during the course of their professional work. It interprets these materials through the lens of the practical application to a range of different fact situations. Only the black-letter approach teaches legal knowledge in a way that harmonises with 'lawyers' law.'

10. The black-letter approach, with its clear preference for problem questions as a common mode of student assessment within both exams and seminars, has greater direct and indirect relevance for students wishing to enter into the legal profession.

11. This approach ensures that would-be lawyers leave universities equipped with a common core of subject knowledge taught and assessed in a broadly similar fashion, which later permits communication to take place on a degree of common ground, shared vocabulary and similar conceptions of the nature of the legal enterprise.

12. Through rigorously excluding factors that fall outside the remit of strict legal analysis, students are enabled to develop a strictly and exclusively legal approach to a clearly defined and limited range of primary sources. This narrowing down of the research agenda is necessary to allow students to gain a greater depth of understanding and to make possible disciplined and rigorous analysis of the meaning and scope of legal categories.

13. Only the black-letter approach respects the practical need to recognise the closed and self-sufficient nature of the rules, principles and basic axioms that comprise the

---

[248]Twining, in Cane and Stapleton, 1991 *op. cit.*, 9.

legal system. This is vital to ensuring the continuity and purity of law as a distinct area of social activity that remains capable of governing society from above according to the principle of the rule of law.

14. Adopting a black-letter form of analysis reduces the aims, scope and the range of materials to be studied by the dissertation project to manageable proportions with a clear sense of direction.

15. The insistence upon providing an objective description of primary sources and their analysis according to established legal methods found, for example, in law reports is vital. It successfully insulates legal analysis from irresolvable, and ultimately subjective, issues related to the validity of moral and political value judgements.

16. This narrowing down of aims, scope and range of materials also makes it possible for students to appreciate the complex and changing meanings of key legal categories (the meaning of trusts, land, contract, negligence, etc.), and the various system of doctrinal rules and principles that have been developed to govern their application to facts. This appreciation is vital because it alone provides the foundations for students to acquire an adequate understanding of legal doctrine.

17. The practical result of adopting a restrictive view of subject matter and analytical methods compares favourably with the failure of alternative law in context approaches to establish clear boundaries within which any research project can operate. Indeed, attempts to broaden the scope of legal analysis by incorporating social scientific methods and sources other than statutes and case law, in respect to the argument that legal analysis cannot be confined to the study of legal rules, open a Pandora's Box in which virtually anything can count as 'legal analysis'. This, in turn, dissolves the unity of law as a distinct discipline by fragmenting both the sources and methodology of legal analysis.[249] Few of the so-called alternatives to black-letter analysis have succeeded in striking a coherent and sustainable balance between theoretical, empirical and methodological analysis.[250]

18. The skills of cross-referencing 'relevant' legal categories, rules and principles with 'relevant' material facts of a hypothetic problem scenario are uniquely developed and tested by black-letter analysis. Such skills are not only valuable in training an acute legal mind, but also have a practical relevance in terms of acquiring a competence in various problem-solving.

19. There is little doubt that certain dissertation projects formulated by law students almost certainly require the adoption of the black-letter approach. For example, if a law student proposed a dissertation title such as, 'What are the relevant legal rules and principles governing plea-bargaining in cases of mass murder?', then this individual would be well advised to adopt an exclusively black-letter approach to this project. It is even arguable that many fields of law, such as contract law, are not susceptible to any approach other than that of the black-letter tradition.[251]

20. The emphasis on relating changing case law to a system of stable general principles, with an objective core of settled and determinate meaning, provides stable

[249]Twining, *Rethinking Evidence*, (Oxford: Blackwell, 1990), 24-7.

[250]Twining, 1994 *op. cit.*, 173; K. Hawkins, General Editor's Introduction to B. Tamanaha, *Realistic Socio-Legal Theory*, (Oxford: Clarendon, 1997).

[251]D. Lloyd, *Introduction to Jurisprudence*, 2nd edn. (London: 1965) 262 (modified in later editions).

foundations to legal education which harmonises with the staid and gradual pace of the common law's evolution.[252]

On the other hand, there is large body of literature that is both explicitly and implicitly critical of the black-letter methodology. An appreciation of the implications of these and other criticisms as summarised below is vital. It is important not only for those dissertation students who become convinced that the black-letter approach is inappropriate for their chosen project but also for those who decide to adopt it as their own methodology. Ideally, students who choose to adopt the black-letter approach should provide justifications that show either that the general criticisms are misplaced, or that, whilst these criticisms may be relevant to certain applications of the black-letter approach, they are inapplicable to their specific dissertation. Equally, dissertation students who reject a black-letter approach in favour of, say, the methods of sociolegal studies (discussed in our next chapter) need to provide some credible reasons justifying this decision both generally and with respect to their specific project.

For example, a student could propose a dissertation project that seeks to answer the question: 'Is permitting plea-bargaining in cases of mass murder perceived as an affront to the families of victims and their representatives?' Realising the aims of this dissertation would necessarily involve reviewing written materials and submissions produced by victim groups, media reportage, and perhaps even conducting telephone interviews with a sample of surviving victims. This project will have to clarify the nature, purpose and implications of plea-bargaining in such cases, which entails a degree of doctrinal analysis of cases and statutes. Yet the main part of the research will need to adopt methods that differ from, and indeed violate the protocols of, the black-letter approach. Part of the rationale justifying the conduct of such research must be that the project requires the deployment of sociolegal methods as a viable alternative to the black-letter approach, the latter being clearly inappropriate for a number of identifiable reasons. In short, students who accept, reject or remain undecided regarding the adequacy of the black-letter approach ought to appreciate the implications of the criticisms. The critics of black-letter methodologies have raised the following main objections:

1. Vick argues that 'law's traditional preoccupation with doctrine . . . has attracted the harshest criticism from many legal scholars. Doctrinalism has been accused of being rigid, dogmatic, formalistic, and close-minded.'[253] Twining notes that 'the central charge was that English academic law has been dominated by a monolithic orthodoxy which was narrow, conservative, illiberal, unrealistic and boring.'[254]

2. Traditional black-letter textbooks have, in pursuit of both breadth of coverage and intricate detail, oversimplified the complexities of both legal doctrine and the process of its judicial interpretation, application and revision.

3. As a result, this tradition underestimates the potential intellectual abilities of well-qualified law students to tackle more sophisticated issues at a greater depth of analysis and from a broader perspective. Instead, students are presented with pre-digested summary statements 'on a plate', as it were, and without any real need to puzzle out, analyse and evaluate the complexities of law for themselves, that is, to

---

[252]Cf. Twining, in Cane and Stapleton, 1991 *op. cit.*, 13.

[253]Vick, 2004 *op. cit.*, 181.

[254]Twining, 1994 *op. cit.*, 141.

respond to questions regarding the how and why of law, not merely the issue of 'what constitutes the doctrinal meaning of X?'[255]

4. The view that law is an independent, objective and coherent system of state-sanctioned rules hardly captures the complexity of law in action within modern society as a form of administrative governance and device for exercising political power.

5. This view ignores the role played by acts of subjective interpretation in the creation, identification, articulation and application of rules, and also in their practical implementation and justification.[256]

6. Black-letter analysis lacks the resources to accomplish the vital task of relating law in books to law in action. For instance, it is unable to relate contract law doctrine to what actually happens in practice, including questions relating to what those who deploy or avoid legal agreements actually do with respect to mediation, or how factors relating to insurance affect their choice of options in practice.

7. In addition, this approach to contract law cannot analyse whether the requirement for consideration has any practical relevance to those who make contracts.[257]

8. Equally, for decades, traditional black-letter textbooks on tort notoriously fail to address seriously insurance aspects of personal injuries, despite their obvious relevance in practice.[258]

9. Law is never simply 'positive' law that is 'just there' to be studied as a certain type of object. Instead, it is a continuing, dynamic and largely institutional process of re-interpretation not only of doctrine but also of procedural requirements, analytical and rhetorical techniques, specialist craft skills and fact-finding.

10. The formalistic emphasis upon objective systems of rules, treated as a determinant and guide to legal decision-making, as the explanation of why judges decide cases the way they do ignores a number of equally important factors. These include the use of rules as a way of rationalising actions decided upon for other reasons but which can be departed from or manipulated by exploiting ambiguities as to their scope and/or meaning whenever they prove inconvenient – again for other reasons.

11. It is the *selective interpretation* of rules, rather than the objective meaning inherent in the rules themselves, that needs to be studied closely by legal researchers, that is, the essentially interpretative activities of identifying, making sense and applying the rules.

12. The rise of realist and, more recently, interpretative and deconstructionist approaches to legal studies have shown that, in many cases, it is judicial behaviour in relation to rules, and the specific judicial values and ideologies which motivate such behaviour, which actually explains rules, not the other way round.

13. These more recent theories suggest that rules themselves lack the objectivity, neutrality and determinacy that the black-letter tradition ascribes to them.[259] For example, Hofheinz notes that: 'You will find that understanding the black letter law

---

[255]Twining, in Cane and Stapleton, 1991 *op. cit.*, 12.

[256]Twining, in Cane and Stapleton, 1994 *op. cit.*, 175.

[257]Twining, in Cane and Stapleton, 1991 *op. cit.*, 11.

[258]For example, it was not until the 14th edition of Salmond's *The Law of Torts* (London: 1965) that the editors even referred to the insurance dimensions.

[259]Tamanaha, 1997 *op. cit.*, 196–8.

is a necessary but not sufficient predicate to the analysis of each legal problem with which you are presented. Only rarely will there be a rule that directly and unambiguously determines the outcome of the problem presented. Seldom will the applicable black-letter rule (precedent) have been determined in a case with identical facts and circumstances and near in time ("on all fours") to the problem under consideration. Seldom will legislation or regulations unambiguously determine the outcome of problems which arise.'[260] Others have maintained even more forcefully that: 'There is no "black-letter law". Everything is subject to interpretation by the courts.... Lawyers specializing this field still need to research, and cannot guarantee what the law is, simply because it is so vast and changing, subject to your judge's interpretations and the facts of your case as the judge believes.'[261]

14. The impact of the constitutional separation of powers between law-making activities by Parliament and law application by judges is exaggerated by legal formalism, and thereby ignores the extent to which judges are, through acts of interpretation and reinterpretation of the meaning and scope of points of law, actively engaged in the making and revising of law according to their intuitions of what the public interest is and the requirements of public policy.[262]

15. Black-letter approaches are reluctant to admit that judicial conceptions of policy, including a framework of conventional goals and objectives for both society in general and the legal system, influence legal decision-making. However, there are so many clear examples of this in practice, not least within the case law on negligence, that the denial of the role of policy is unrealistic.[263]

16. Judges have a far more difficult, sophisticated and less mechanical task than formalism suggests. In many cases, their role is to integrate specific technical rules with broad statements of social values and policy goals, and to decide in specific cases when it is appropriate to allow the latter to qualify the former.[264]

17. The black-letter approach, which excludes moral considerations from strictly legal research, analysis and reasoning, is inconsistent with a well-established tendency of the common law to qualify the strict application of paper rules where this is deemed to promote 'immorality' by, for example, subverting family values and the institution of marriage.[265]

---

[260]Hofheinz, 1997 *op. cit.*

[261]Anon, 'Legal research': http://www.caltenantlaw.com/Laws.htm

[262]J. Bell, in Cane and Stapleton, 1991 *op. cit.*, 89, 104–5 noting with respect to the judicial role that: 'When public policy is a criterion for the interpretation of statutes, the role of delegated legislator is more appropriate as a description.' (at 105).

[263]P. Atiyah, 'Judges and Policy' (1980) 15 *Israel LR* 346; J. Bell, in Cane and Stapleton, 1991 *op. cit.*, 89; Joel Grossman, 'Social Backgrounds and Judicial Decision-Making' (1966) 79 *Harvard Law Review*, 1551–64.

[264]J. Bell, in Cane and Stapleton, 1991 *op. cit.*, 111.

[265]For example, contracts relating to the supply of goods to brothels where the law would in effect be used as a device to facilitate activities that are deemed immoral: *Taylor v Chester* (1869) LR 4 QB 309, or regarding gambling 'contracts'. On the endorsement of the moral importance of safeguarding the traditional family structures as a policy factor restricting the automatic application of legal rules, see *Humphreys v Polak* [1901] 2 KB 385, and (with respect to contracts relating to extra-marital sexual relationship) *Frances v Bolton*, (1797) 3 Ves. 368. Many of the doctrines and maxims of equity rely directly or indirectly on moral principles relating to the 'justice and good conscience' and Christian standards of reciprocity (do unto others . . .). On the other hand, some judges still insist on reaffirming the prohibition on legal arguments based on moral values: see *Re an Adoption Application (Surrogacy)* [1987] 2 All ER 826, per Latey, J.

18. The very activity of debating the meaning and scope of a point of law generates a measure of indeterminacy. Such debates mean that judges need to exercise choice between two competing interpretations in a context free of any objective criteria for proclaiming that either is the single correct answer to the problem or question posed by the case.[266]

19. The restrictions upon choice stem from cultural, linguistic, values, conventions, habits and ideological factors that cannot be analysed using the resources of the black-letter approach.[267]

20. The black-letter approach disguises the operation of judicial discretion and judicial law-making, and thereby allows this form of power to operate in a manner that is unaccountable to law, and hence violates the rule of law which this approach otherwise endorses.[268]

21. The liberal free-market assumptions and values that underpin black-letter methodologies have, with the emergence of collectivist welfare-state institutions and new models of public sector regulation within a context of rapid social and technological change, become increasingly outdated.

22. Changes in the educational context (including the flood of younger, more socially aware, academics who entered academia in the 1970s and 80s) and developments within the related areas of law publishing (including the paperback revolution of the 1970s onwards), have also meant black-letter approaches have become increasingly defined as outmoded.[269] Indeed, one of the 'fatal weaknesses' of the black-letter tradition lies in 'its inability to cope with rapidly changing situations'.[270]

23. The close relationship between black-letter analysis and legal positivism, particularly their common assumption that legal analysis requires the separation of questions of 'what is the law' from moral and political value judgements regarding how it 'ought to be', is questionable. This dichotomy is especially dubious, given the liberal moral values that underpin its own approach and the fact that the very identification of a legal topic is never value-free but rather requires making a moral judgement.

24. The attempt to justify, at a theoretical level, the assumptions that the black-letter approach shares with the legal positivism of, for example, Hans Kelsen breaks down in practice. In particular, the formalistic attempt to safeguard the 'purity' of legal analysis from 'contamination' by not only non-legal factors (morality and political values) but also the substantive *contents* of legal doctrine (such as interaction of points of law with material facts in individual cases) cannot account for the realities of real-life examples within academic analysis of law.

25. Whatever the other merits of legal positivism at the theoretical level, including its view that law can represent an autonomous science of the formal structure of legal norms (the categories of contract, property, etc. considered purely as such), any close examination of what actually takes place in real examples of black-letter analysis leads to conclusions that contradict the basic claims of this theory. Hence, black-letter analysis cannot sustain the theoretical assumptions it continues to rely upon.[271]

---

[266] Atiyah, 1980 *op. cit.*; Twining, in Cane and Stapleton, 1991 *op. cit.*, 5.

[267] S. Fish, *Doing What Comes Naturally*, (Durham, NC: Duke University Press, 1989), 127, 138–9.

[268] Bell, in Cane and Stapleton, 1991 *op. cit.*, 105.

[269] Twining, in Cane and Stapleton, 1991 *op. cit.*, 8, 13–14.

[270] *Ibid.*, 13.

[271] Twining, 1994 *op. cit.*, 157–8, 171.

26. Black-letter analysis makes a series of other assumptions regarding the nature of law, legal reasoning and the relationship between society that cannot be discussed, established or denied for as long as legal researchers continue to rely exclusively upon the analytical tools of the black-letter approach.

27. The unduly narrow focus of this approach, which downplays a range of important subjects ranging from legal history through to criminology and labour law, separates law from precisely those social, economic, political and cultural contexts of emergence and application that explain how law operates in practice. The analytical techniques and range of questions typically deployed are also unduly narrow.[272]

28. An appropriate understanding of the complexity of most legal issues and topics requires the supplementation of doctrinal analysis with methods and approaches drawn from other social sciences, including economics and sociology. Law cannot be considered a single independent discipline any more than law itself can be viewed as entirely separate from the remainder of society.[273]

29. The black-letter approach ignores the fact that most legislation is made for a particular purpose and therefore needs to be critically assessed not merely in terms of its supplementation of prior doctrinal sources but also in the light of its relative success or failure in realising specific policy goals.[274] Because law is essentially a purposeful enterprise, it is entirely proper that legal analysis includes a discussion of issues relating to these purposes and how best they should be realised in the context of deciding individual cases.[275] This is particularly true where there is a choice between one interpretation of law, whose impact would be to give effect to policy goals, and another that, although equally valid in a formalistic sense, would obstruct their realisation in practice.[276]

30. Despite its claims to provide non-political and strictly objective analyses of law, the black-letter approach remains implicitly committed to a series of values and interests shared with liberalism and free-market ideologies more generally.

31. This approach stifles any systematic and substantive type of critique of law in action, or law's alleged complicity with various institutional, political and social forms of injustice and systematic inequalities. It fails not only to emphasise the policies that underpin existing case and statute law, but also to evaluate these policies in terms of what the law ought to be.[277] Instead, the positivism of the black-letter tradition treats the status quo, the positive rules as laid down, as a given starting point for an essentially uncritical type of analysis, and this takes place at the expense of any analysis of factors that could potentially change the status quo.[278]

32. The assumption that legal doctrine is broadly determinate and intelligible understates the extent to which subjective, contextual and political factors shape conflicts of interpretation leading to large measures of indeterminacy.[279] Indeed, the level of

---

[272]*Ibid.*, 142; Twining, in Cane and Stapleton, 1991 *op. cit.*, 5.

[273]Twining, 1994 *op. cit.*, 20,174 – making the point that legal records are directly relevant to the concerns of historians and sociologists, and that legal analysis cannot be isolated from supposedly 'external' factors.

[274]Twining, in Cane and Stapleton, 1991 *op. cit.*, 11.

[275]*Ibid.*

[276]P. Atiyah, *Pragmatism and Theory in English Law*, (London: 1987), 144.

[277]Twining, in Cane and Stapleton, 1991 *op. cit.*, 11.

[278]Atiyah, 1987 *op. cit.*, 142.

[279]For a discussion of unavoidable levels of indeterminacy see J. Singer, 'The Player and the Cards: Nihilism and Legal Theory' (1984) *Yale Law Jnl* 1-70.

indeterminacy, and hence the increased extent to which decisions are not entirely controlled by prior doctrine or indisputable facts, increases in cases before the higher appeal courts, which is precisely the focus of black-letter analysis.[280] In practice, there will always remain discrepancies between individual cases and specific legal rules, rules and general principles, and between basic axioms on the one hand, and principles, rules and cases on the other.

33. Black-letter analysis is out of touch with the realities of solicitors' legal practice, which have generally been dominated more by procedural issues than sophisticated disputes over the precise meaning and scope of points of law.[281]

34. Such analysis relies too heavily on the uncritical memorising of a mass of technical and highly intricate rules and exceptions to rules (and exceptions to exceptions to rules), lacks intellectual depth or merit as a contribution to broad, liberal-arts based educational and theoretical sophistication.[282]

35. Many of the puzzles given priority by black-letter analysis are, from the point of view of social policy, essentially trivial and socially unrepresentative, focusing on, for example, property disputes regarding country estates rather than upon questions of urban homelessness.[283]

36. Despite numerous attempts to delimit the field of legal studies, efforts to identify a single essential core of law as a distinct discipline, which distinguishes this approach from the analytical activities of other disciplines, has not succeeded. Many of the activities undertaken by both legal practitioners and legal academics overlaps with those of non-lawyers (such as accountants), and many, if not all, of those which could be claimed to be distinctive (a close examination of the meaning and scope of rules relating to legal categories) provide a fragile basis for the claim that law is a singular and autonomous discipline.[284]

37. Black-letter analysis that remains fixated mainly on points of law as contested in appeal courts remains excessively abstract and distant from how law is actually used in society as a matter of empirical fact, and how it is experienced differently by members of various social groups.[285] Law cannot be understood adequately when it is viewed only from the standpoint of a barrister arguing over the meaning and scope of points of law. On the contrary, it must be studied from the perspective of those whose actions and life chances are most likely to be affected by legal decision-making, for whom predictions as to what is the likely reaction of a court or tribunal to a proposed act or omission constitutes 'law' for all practical purposes.[286]

38. The black-letter tradition is largely authoritarian and dogmatic, not least because it assumes that it can, from its own resources, provide a single correct answer to any legal issue. This tradition can only replicate its way of life as an orthodoxy through the power of custom and conformity to questionable assumptions regarding the nature of law, the methodological requirements of justifiable forms of legal research and the insulation

---

[280]Tamanaha, 1997 *op. cit.*, 202-3.

[281]R. Dworkin, 'The Model of Rules', (1987) 35 *University of Chicago L. Rev.* 14.

[282]Twining, 1994 *op. cit.*, 142.

[283]*Ibid.*

[284]*Ibid.*, 174, 192-3.

[285]W. Twining, *Karl Llewellyn and the Realist Movement*, (London: 1985), 32; W. Twining, 1990 *op. cit.*, ch.2.

[286]O. Holmes, 'The Path of the Law', (1897) 10 *Harv. LR* 451, 460-61.

of legal issues and analysis from the contemporary world of affairs that is found in traditional textbook analysis and the related supplementary works of scholarship, such as the case note or 'recent developments' case and statute analysis.[287]

39. This approach has neither the analytical resources nor the apparent commitment to examine critically the theoretical, methodological and political assumptions that underpin legal processes or its own interpretative practices, including the choice of organising categories and divisions.[288]

40. The dogmatism and lack of critical self-awareness of black-letter analysis results in the replication of a self-justifying circle. For example, one consequence of formalistic analysis is that law is understood in terms of legal doctrine, an interpretation that is supposed to be dictated by the very nature of the subject matter.

41. Because law is presented as a number of autonomous doctrinal rules and principles embodied, for the most part, in a series of distinct legal materials, then it can appear 'obvious' that a completely distinct set of legal methods is demanded by the very nature of the subject matter. The application of such legal methods, in turn, reinforces the initial assumption that law is, in essence, a systematic set of autonomous doctrinal rules. In this respect, the application of the premises of black-letter analysis creates the spurious impression that these premises are themselves justified, a strategy of closure shared with all manner of religious fundamentalisms.

42. The view that legal doctrine contained in primary sources is both the source and explanation of legal decision-making, understood as the application of rules, is simply wrong. On the contrary, it would be better if we defined interpretations of law as 'hopefully informed guesses', based on insight into judicial habits, values and ideologies, as to how the courts will react to various disputes. The continued publication of law reports containing elaborate formalistic legal arguments on points of law only serve to obscure the true basis of judicial decision-making, and should, therefore, carry a health warning.[289]

● Conclusion

Black-letter analysis is one amongst many other possible ways of conducting dissertation research according to a certain 'recipe'. This requires the adoption of a strictly legalistic approach excluding all supposedly external factors and modes of social science analysis. Law is defined as an autonomous system of rules (answers to what-type questions) underpinned by a smaller number of more general legal principles which give coherence to these rules. Black-letter analysis remains internal to legal doctrine, and focuses primarily on cases and statutes and, to a lesser extent, academic commentaries on these sources. Black-letter law focuses on law in books rather than law in action to the point where social science accounts of the enforcement of legal rules, or the politics of law reform, remain at most marginal topics. Hence, a series of supposedly non-legal factors and arguments based on moral and political values must always be marginal to the dissertation, other than perhaps the conclusion.

---

[287]Twining, in Cane and Stapleton, 1991 *op. cit.*, 5, 11.

[288]*Ibid.*, 11.

[289]J. Bingham, 'What is the law?' (1912) 11 *Mich. LR*; E. Purcell, 'American Jurisprudence Between the Wars: Legal Realism and the Crisis of Democratic Theory' (1969) 75 *Am Hist. Rev.* 424.

Sociolegal Approaches to the Conduct of Dissertation Research

● Introduction

This chapter will, as far as possible, define the meaning and scope of sociolegal studies as a distinct methodology for the conduct of legal research. Students should appreciate that there are many types of sociolegal research applied to a broad range of topics that do not coincide with traditional legal divisions between, for example, private and public law. The previous chapter emphasised that black-letter analysis addresses legal sources narrowly defined as cases and statutes and academic commentaries on these. By contrast, the approach of sociolegal studies reinstates the centrality of social scientific approaches, using both qualitative and quantitative research methods, to investigate the impact of law in action, and the key role played by ideological factors, including public policy. As with the previous chapter, we suggest that it is important for students to appreciate the strengths and weaknesses of the sociolegal approach. Students must also recognise a range of ethical issues that can arise during the conduct of research in this tradition.

● Defining Sociolegal Studies

Students considering alternatives to the adoption of a purely black-letter approach to the conduct of dissertation research might want to the explore the implications of Professor Roger Cotterrell's claim that:

> All the centuries of purely doctrinal writing on law has produced less valuable knowledge about what law is, as a social phenomena, and what it does than the relatively few decades of work in sophisticated modern empirical socio-legal studies . . . Socio-legal scholarship in the broadest sense is the most important scholarship presently being undertaken in the legal world. Its importance is not only in what it has achieved, which is considerable, but also in what it promises.[1]

A similar point applies to Professor Nicola Lacey's statement that, within little more than two decades, sociolegal studies has effectively transformed the nature of legal education, at least within academically respectable law departments.[2]

However, it is reasonable for students to expect answers to the following questions before they decide to adopt a sociolegal approach to their dissertation research:

● What are its nature and goals?

● In what ways is a sociolegal methodology distinctive from other approaches, particularly traditional doctrinal research? In other words, what difference would it make

---

[1] Roger Cotterrell, *Law's Community*, (Oxford: OUP, 1995), 296, 314.

[2] Socio-legal Newsletter 12 (1994) 2 – also quoted in Philip Thomas, 'Socio-Legal Studies: The Case of Disappearing Fleas and Bustards', in Philip Thomas (ed.), *Socio-Legal Studies*, (Aldershot: Ashgate-Dartmouth, 1997), 4.

with respect to my conduct of dissertation research if I decide to adopt a sociolegal, rather than, say, a black-letter approach?

● Which new research methods and skills, if any, might I be expected to learn and apply?

● What kinds of issues and factors that are excluded by black-letter approaches are positively required by a sociolegal methodology?

● In what specific areas of legal research, if any, is there evidence that this methodology has proved itself successful in earlier studies, which could therefore provide a helpful precedent for framing my own research questions and practices?

● What are the main arguments for and against adopting this approach both generally, and with respect to my own particular dissertation topic?

In common with the other chapters of this book, we have designed and structured this chapter to provide detailed answers to these legitimate questions. One of our aims is to assess whether or not dissertation students face a stark either/or choice between black-letter and sociolegal approaches because these represent two mutually incompatible ways of realising the objectives of their dissertations. Alternatively, is it feasible for at least certain types of legal dissertation to combine aspects of both black-letter and sociolegal approaches?

The first point to make is that students looking to examine methodological aspects of sociolegal studies can draw upon an existing literature containing many explicit discussions of the nature, strengths and limitations of different available methodologies.[3] There are even sections within annual sociolegal studies conferences regularly devoted to methodological discussions and evaluations. Equally, many published findings of empirical types of sociolegal research include discussion of, and attempted justification for, the strategy used with respect to, for example, research samples or interview technique.[4] Such conscious reflection upon the methodological dimensions can, on occasions, generate considerable follow-up discussion and debate within the academic literature.[5]

---

[3]See, for example, Mavis Maclean and Hazel Genn, *Methodological Issues in Social Surveys*, (Atlantic Highlands, NJ: Humanities Press, 1979; Austin Sarat, *et al.*, *Crossing Boundaries: Traditions And Transformations in Law And Society Research*, (Evanston, IL: Northwestern University Press, 1998), Part One.

[4]Ute Gerhard, 'Women's Experiences of Injustice: Some Methodological Problems and Empirical Findings of Legal Research.' *Social & Legal Studies* 1993, 2(3), 303-21 (with reference to research in equal opportunities in employment); Maureen Cain, 'Realism, Feminism, Methodology, and the Law' *Int. J. Soc. L.* 1986, 14 (3-4), 255-67; Ruth Lewis, 'Making Justice Work: Effective Legal Interventions for Domestic Violence' *Brit. J. Criminol.* 2004, 44(2), 204-24 (with reference to researching restorative justice in the UK); Adrian Grounds and Ruth Jamieson, 'No Sense of an Ending: Researching the Experience of Imprisonment and Release Among Republican ex Prisoners', *Theo. Crim.* 2003, 7(3), 347-62 (re studying the effects of long-term imprisonment on 18 Republican prisoners and their families, and associated psychological coping strategies, employment, social integration and family relationships, through interviews and other methods); Reza Banakar, 'Reflections on the Methodological Issues of the Sociology of Law', (2000) 27(2) *J. Law & Soc.* 273-95; Trevor Bennett, 'What's New in Evaluation Research? A Note on the Pawson and Tilley Article' (1996) 36(4) *Brit. J. Criminol.* 567-73 (defending the appropriateness of quasi-experimental design research methods in criminal justice studies and criminology); John Paterson and Gunther Teubner, 'Changing Maps: Empirical Legal Autopoiesis' (1998) 7(4) *Social & Legal Studies*, 451-86 (discussion of the deployment of the theory of self-organisation ('autopoiesis') for empirical sociolegal research 'cognitive mapping' to issues raised by the health-and-safety regulation of offshore industry.

[5]Michael Faure, 'The Future of Social Legal Research with Respect to Environmental Problems', (1995) 22(1) *J. Law & Soc.* 127-32; Anita Kalunta-Crumpton, 'Claims Making and the Prosecution of Black Defendants in Drug Trafficking Trials: The Influence of Deprivation,' (1998) 3(1), *International Journal of Discrimination and the Law*, 29-49.

Such methodological awareness and self-criticism contrasts markedly with legal research carried out using black-letter methodologies, where, as already noted, discussion remains generally focused on technical 'legal methods'. Rarely are the nature, limits and possible future directions of black-letter methods of analysis addressed as specific topics in their own right. On the other hand, the fact that sociolegal studies remain dominated by legal academics whose own undergraduate and postgraduate degrees in law generally contained little coverage of empirical research methods has still limited the range and quantity of methodological debate within sociolegal studies compared with other social sciences.

By contrast, it is arguable that more sophisticated forms of sociolegal research include a high level of methodological awareness and an appreciation of the need to justify, with convincing reasons, why the researchers have chosen their particular methodological strategies. It would be possible, and in many cases, advisable for dissertation students to seek to emulate this level of justification, even if this was only undertaken in a relatively modest way. For example, students could follow the lead set in Nazroo's study of crimes of domestic violence. This includes a self-critical account of the limits of its chosen methodology (a mixture of semi-structured open-ended interviewing with quantitative data-gathering), and an appreciation of the difficulties that can stem from the various methodologies underpinning earlier studies by other researchers. These difficulties have included drawing general inferences from the deployment of a small sample of subjects selected for in-depth interviewing, or from using larger-scale survey methods whose questionnaires remain insensitive to differences in how the key terms are likely to be variously interpreted by respondents.[6]

Before we can make any further progress with assessing the potential relevance and limits of sociolegal studies as a way of conducting dissertation research, it is necessary to define the nature, or at least clarify, some key features of this particular approach.

Many writers within sociolegal studies have recognised that attempts to provide a single and fixed definition of the essence of sociolegal studies are frustrated by the existence of many different and incompatible interpretations of the nature and scope of this approach to the conduct of research.[7] Cotterrell argues that current sociolegal studies contain a 'rich, almost anarchic heterogeneity and . . . consistent openness to many different aims, outlooks, and disciplinary backgrounds'.[8] Other writers have noted the difficulties this diversity creates for those seeking to define the nature of sociolegal research because 'many incompatible views could be found on what constitutes socio-legal studies, and many different activities are now pursued under its rubric.'[9] Although certain sociolegal writers have attempted to establish a fixed identity for this approach with clear boundaries, these efforts have, for the most part, proved to be instructive

---

[6]Nazroo, 'Uncovering Gender Differences in the Use of Marital Violence: The Effect of Methodology', (1995) 29 *Sociology*, 475.

[7]For an attempted definition and characterisation see 'Review of Sociolegal Studies' (Swindon: ESRC, 1994), ch. 1

[8]Roger Cotterrell, 'Subverting Orthodoxy, Making Law Central: A View of Sociolegal Studies, (2002) 29 *JLS*, 632-44, 632. See also Thomas, 1997 *op. cit.*, 2-3; F. Levine, Presidential Address, (1990) *Law and Society Review*, 1-25 at 9ff.

[9]Bridget Hutter and Sally Lloyd-Bostock, 'Law's Relationship with Social Science: The Interdependence of Theory, Empirical Work and Social Relevance in Socio-legal Studies' in Keith Hawkins, *The Human Face of Law: Essays in Honour of Donald Harris*, (Oxford: OUP, 1997a), 20.

failures.[10] There is even debate whether the expression 'sociolegal studies' should be treated as singular or plural, hyphenated, or, as a result of the claimed fusion of law and social sciences, one word (as is common in American literature), an option selected by the present writers.[11] It is not possible to build a definition of the nature of sociolegal studies from the bottom up, as it were. This is because the problems of arriving at a viable definition affect even specific sub-branches of sociolegal studies. For example, even long-standing contributors to various multidisciplinary combinations, which are firmly rooted within sociolegal studies, such as law and economics, recognise 'there are problems defining what is "law and economics" and classifying the work.'[12]

Hence, the present authors will not attempt to rush in where angels fear to tread by trying to offer a fixed and unambiguous definition of the essential nature of sociolegal studies, which finally resolves these debates.[13] Instead, it may be wise to recognise that the source of this difficulty, of providing a single correct definition, is potentially instructive. It shows us that the meaning of sociolegal studies cannot be decided upon once and for all. This is because it largely depends upon types of activity carried out by those who identify themselves as contributors to this movement, and whose work is published in book series and academic journals that specialise and promote its application to different areas of law.

Although issues raised by successive attempts to define sociolegal studies will be studied later, at this point a provisional definition may be helpful, particularly one that is linked to the rationale for adopting this methodology. Phil Thomas has summed up a key belief that underpins the commitment to sociolegal studies as a fully-fledged law in context approach when he claims that: 'Empirically, law is a component part of the wider social and political structure, is inextricably related to it in an infinite variety of ways, and can therefore only be properly understood if studied in that context.'[14]

The promotion of the sociolegal approach is supported by the Socio-Legal Studies Association (SLSA), which states that it 'is dedicated to improving the quality of and facilities for sociolegal research'.[15] This raises the question of how this association answers the question of 'What is sociolegal research?' They note that there are at least three recognisable strands to current sociolegal work, each of which are broadly interdisciplinary in nature. These strands include higher-level social theories of law

---

[10]Thomas, 1997 *op. cit.*; Peter Fitzpatrick, 'Being Social in Socio-legal Studies', in D. J. Galligan (ed.), *Socio-legal Studies in Context*, The Oxford Centre Past and Future, (Oxford: Blackwell, 1995), 105.

[11]Some writers hyphenate the expression sociolegal studies, whilst others note that the approach has become sufficiently established that the hyphen, which suggests a problematic and *ad hoc* linking of different approaches, has become redundant. Paddy Hillyard, 'Invoking Indignation: Reflections on the Future Directions of Socio-legal Studies', (2002) 29 *JLS* 645-56.

[12]Anthony Ogus, 'Law and Economics in the UK: Past, Present, and Future' (1995) 22 *J. Law and Society*, 28.

[13]Hazel Gann and Martin Partington, unpublished paper presented to an ESRC conference in 1993: quoted in Philip Thomas, 1997 *op. cit.*, 2.

[14]Philip Thomas, 'Curriculum Development in Legal Studies' (1986) 20 *Law Teacher* 110 at 112.

[15]The organisation itself claims: 'The SLSA is a forum for socio-legal scholars in the UK and elsewhere to come together and share interests and exchange ideas. We do this in a number of ways including the following: Through the Annual Conference. . . . we publish a Directory of members . . . maintain an email network and website. (http://www.ukc.ac.uk/slsa/index.htm). We publish and distribute a Newsletter . . . support postgraduate/student events and hold conferences for postgraduates/students, as well as provide bursaries for SLSA student members. We host a series of one-day conferences/workshops on particular topics. We respond to consultation exercises on behalf of our members.' http://www.kent.ac.uk/slsa/download/response3.rtf.

disconnected from empirical studies;[16] theories developed in the middle-range that are 'grounded' in the findings of empirical research (and which, in turn, aim to prompt further empirical studies to test the validity of their theoretical claims);[17] and, thirdly, policy-driven projects that are entirely empirical and have little explicit relationship with prior or current theoretical reflections:[18]

> This is not easy to define and embraces many areas of work. What follows is a definition used in a past RAE document [document relating to the Research Assessment Exercise to which university departments are subject]: 'The socio-legal community represents a "broad church" and this is an aspect of the association which we have always cherished. Our members undertake library based theoretical work, empirical work which leads to the development of grounded theory, as well as more policy orientated studies which feeds directly into the policy making process. What binds the socio-legal community is an approach to the study of legal phenomena which is multi or inter-disciplinary in its approach. Our theoretical perspectives and methodologies are informed by research undertaken in many other disciplines. Traditionally socio-legal scholars have bridged the divide between law and sociology, social policy, and economics. But there is increasing interest in law and disciplines within the field of humanities.'[19]

This definition is useful in that it recognises that sociolegal studies are best understood as that which legal researchers who are recognised members of this tradition actually do in practice, and that this encompasses a diversity of interdisciplinary and multidisciplinary contextual approaches within current research. The existence of such diversity is also evident from literature produced on behalf of the Law and Society Association, an organisation that, despite its largely American base, provides a wider international focus for sociolegal research:

> Although they share a common commitment to developing theoretical and empirical understandings of law, interests of the members range widely. Some colleagues are concerned with the place of law in relation to other social institutions and consider law in the context of broad social theories. Others seek to understand legal decision-making by individuals and groups. Still others systematically study the impact of specific reforms, compliance with tax laws, the criminal justice system, dispute processing, the functioning of juries, globalization of law, and the many roles played by various types of lawyers. Some seek to describe legal systems and identify and explain patterns of behaviour. Others use the operations of law as a perspective for understanding ideology, culture, identity, and social life. Whatever the issue, there is an openness in the Association to exploring the contours of law through a variety of research methods and modes of analysis.[20]

---

[16]The systems theory work of Luhmann, Teubner, and abstract theoretical writings of Marxists influenced by Althusser have been clear examples.

[17]Hutter and Lloyd-Bostock, 1997 *op. cit.*, 23.

[18]These will typically be both funded and shaped by policy-makers who simply commission projects to assess the effectiveness of current policies in the light of official policy goals, and often insist that researchers deploy less expensive survey methods to generate apparently more 'objective' quantitative results palatable to senior civil servants.

[19]Http://www.kent.ac.uk/slsa/Accessed August 2005.

[20]Http://www.lawandsociety.org/Accessed August 2005.

The nature of both the work and the parameters recognised by publishing outlets has been subject to constant change and contestation, even over the comparatively brief duration of the last thirty years. Furthermore, the topics addressed by sociolegal studies, from which so much of the identity of this movement depends, are themselves subject to constant change and redefinition. The result has been that this approach to legal research necessarily remains exploratory, prone to unpredictable reinterpretations and open-ended in nature.[21] Hillyard, for example, recognises the 'huge diversity ... in terms of subject areas, theoretical orientations, and methodologies'.[22] He also notes that participants' interpretation and reinterpretation of the meaning, scope and implications of the two elements of the hybrid term 'sociolegal studies' has shown remarkable elasticity:

> There are continuing debates about the meaning and extent of the two elements – the 'socio' and 'legal' – which make up the subject. It has been both fascinating and exciting to observe as a member of the editorial board for ten years of one of the key journals for the paradigm, how elastic the notions of both the 'social' and 'legal' can be.[23]

Thomas, editor of the *Journal of Law and Society*, has also recognised that the diversity of content, approach, motivations, and style of research conducted under the broad banner of sociolegal studies means that this collective body of work could be categorised in numerous possible ways. For example, it could be classified as constituting: 'a new discipline, a sub-discipline and if so of what? an approach, a methodology, a political position or paradigm'.[24] Different contributors to this movement also disagree regarding the meaning, scope and purpose of sociolegal studies. A significant proportion of those who identify themselves as participants within sociolegal studies would criticise each one of these different possible characterisations and definitions as, perhaps, either unduly restrictive (e.g. if it excludes social theory and theoretical strands of the sociology of law), or too wide-ranging (e.g. if it incorporates criminologists' studies of aspects of the criminal justice and penal systems).

Given this diversity, the most dissertation students can hope for, as a substitute for a precise and conclusive definition, is a provisional clarification of a number of the overlapping features and commitments of sociolegal studies. Such clarification cannot, however, be expected to identify any particular feature, or combination, which is somehow definitive or essential.

The absence of a clear, once-and-for-all definition and fixed boundaries for sociolegal studies has not, however, noticeably impeded the establishment and growth of work within this tradition over past decades. Arguably, the diversity of different types of sociolegal studies does not necessarily prevent law students from completing dissertations that are recognisably sociolegal in nature. After all, it is clearly possible to work with

---

[21]Hutter and Lloyd-Bostock, 'The Interdependence of Theory, Empirical Work and Social Relevance in Socio-legal Studies', in K. Hawkins (ed.), *The Human Face of Law: Essays in Honour of Donald Harris* (Oxford: Oxford University Press, 1997), 29.

[22]Paddy Hillyard, 'Invoking Indignation: Reflections on the Future Directions of Socio-legal Studies', (2002) 29 *JLS* 645–56, at 645.

[23]*Ibid*.

[24]Thomas, 1997 *op. cit.*, 3.

and mend many electrical devices without really knowing what electricity is, particularly if one takes seriously the practices and pragmatic know-how of surviving electricians.

Indeed, it remains instructive to draw upon the know-how and working knowledge of contributors to sociolegal studies. Jolly, for example, has interpreted sociolegal studies as possessing one negative and one positive feature: it is a type of research that, he claims, investigates law in action, and thereby transcends exclusively doctrinal analysis of supposedly authoritative legal texts.[25] By implication, this requires a close study of the actions (and omissions?) of legal officials. Jolly argues that it is often possible to identify a significant difference between the *legal form* of a particular measure and its actual effect and practical force. That is, a tension between the meaning or 'paper rights', and the options individuals have, in practice, within different circumstances. Indeed, certain supposedly extra-legal measures, such as administrative circulars may, in practice, exert greater 'legal force' on the topic under examination than, for example, specific examples of delegated or even primary legislation. Furthermore, on occasions, the courts may themselves have to take into account the legal implications of discrepancies created by this 'gap'. This occurs, for example, when judges have to consider violations of health-and-safety measures, or when litigation is directed against regulatory bodies engaging in non-enforcement or selective enforcement or self-exemption from rules.[26] As Baldwin notes: 'The legal form of a rule is only of limited help as an indication of its legal effect or government role.'[27]

The existence of this 'gap' between 'law in books' and 'law in action' means that a legal dissertation that aims to provide a complete coverage of its topic in a fulsome way must address both these dimensions. In addition, more ambitious levels of sociolegal research may seek to explain the reasons for the existence of this gap and discrepancy. For example, Baldwin insists that no account of legal rules is complete which is not based on an empirical grasp of how they are selectively used in practice, ideally through a series of detailed case studies, including as the enforcement practices of occupational health-and-safety officials.[28] Such case studies provide ample evidence that many areas of social life are, in practice, not governed by legal or any other type of rule. For example, even where legal rules do apply in principle, they are, in practice, often either bypassed or only selectively enforced. Alternatively, the goals of legal regulatory schemes can be implemented by other less formal means, such as advice and negotiation, supported only indirectly by the threat of initiating a prosecution culminating in legal sanctions.[29]

With respect to their chosen topic, student dissertations that adopt a sociolegal methodology may, for example, ask the following questions: what difference does Parliament enacting relevant legislation actually make? What is the relationship between state-sanctioned rules and other less formal, operating norms and standards? How do those individuals and groups whose actions are being regulated react to law enforcement?[30] Furthermore, students should recognise that legal rules are used for a variety of different functions. These include the provision of guidance or clarification of the meaning of

---

[25]Simon Jolly, 'Family Law', in Thomas, 1997 *op. cit.*, 343.

[26]Robert Baldwin, *Rules and Government*, (Oxford: Clarendon, 1995), 9, ch. 4.

[27]*Ibid.*, 9.

[28]*Ibid.*, particularly Part 2.

[29]*Ibid.*, 3 and ch. 3.

[30]Hawkins, 1997 *op. cit.*, prologue, 5.

earlier statutory measures, public education, the promotion of the governing party's political values and ideology. According to Baldwin, other functions can include providing instructions for officials, and allowing extra-statutory concessions and exemptions from legal enforcement (regarding taxation, for example).[31] Hence, for a dissertation to focus only on the promulgation, semantics and design of legal rules is to provide an incomplete, and therefore one-sided and potentially misleading, account of any topic. Such an approach ignores vital questions regarding how, and to what extent and in what circumstances, legal rules are implemented in practice, and the various way in which individuals, groups and institutions use them as means to achieve specific ends.[32]

If you decide to adopt the law-in-action focus of sociolegal studies, then your dissertation may produce empirical results that question key tenets of the black-letter tradition's emphasis upon formal rules as vital devices for minimising unbridled executive and administrative discretion. This is because the creation of rules can, in some contexts, actually widen the real scope for such discretion.[33] Furthermore, law-in-action studies can investigate issues that, although vital to any informed assessment of a specific legal measure, are simply beyond the abilities of doctrinal analysis. For instance, dissertations could seek to explain the reasons why certain types of legal regulation can be predicted to fail to consistently achieve their stated objectives in specific contexts, including pan-European forms of legal regulation through the implementation of directives.[34] In this respect, sociolegal studies are thus 'driven by a desire to investigate the workings of the law, and the behaviour of legal actors'. For Cotterrell, sociolegal studies contribute 'systematic behaviour studies'. However, he immediately widens the focus of sociolegal research on legal behaviour by regarding the many localised reinterpretations of the multiple meanings and implications of such behaviour by non-lawyers as falling within its scope: 'what law as institutionalised doctrine means in the varied local contexts of social life is where its ultimate value and significance must be judged.'[35]

Cotterrell's broader interpretation of the meaning and scope of sociolegal studies is largely supported by a statement of 'ethical practice' in the Socio-Legal Studies Association's 1995 *Directory of Members*. This maintains that sociolegal studies needs to be given a far wider definition than a focus on the actual behaviour of legal officials, even where this is broadly defined to cover police, mediators, bailiffs, etc. Instead, this document suggests a definition in terms of 'the social effects of the law, legal processes, institutions and services'. By concentrating on the social effects and impact of law, this definition broadens the scope to include non-lawyers' interpretation of their experiences of law in action, ranging presumably from lawyers' clients to defendants and trial witnesses. Hillyard and Sim define sociolegal studies in even broader terms that, in addition to the elements we have already noted, also embrace the emergence and organisation of law and legal processes: 'research which takes all forms of law and legal institutions, broadly defined, and attempts to further our understanding of how they are constructed, organised and operate in their social, cultural, political and economic contexts.'[36]

---

[31]*Ibid.*, 9.

[32]*Ibid.*, 5.

[33]*Ibid.*, 3 and chs 3–6.

[34]*Ibid.*, ch. 8.

[35]Cotterrell, 1995 *op. cit.*, 296.

[36]Hillyard and Sim, 'The Political Economy of Socio-Legal Research', in Thomas, 1997 *op. cit.*, 45.

Before leaving the working interpretations of the nature(s) of sociolegal studies expressed by contributors to this approach, it is worth emphasising that, for many, the main focus is not the clarification of sociolegal studies in general. On the contrary, their attention is directed towards working through the practical implications and ramifications of a range of issues within a specific field of legal studies, such that the main reference point is, for example, carrying forward positive developments within sociolegal approaches to contract. For example, Campbell's summary of core elements of the sociolegal approach to the study of contract suggests that, in addition to the features already noted, this approach requires taking a decidedly critical orientation towards the viability of more traditional doctrinal approaches: 'a stress on the empirical reality of business relationships as the fundamental subject of contract; a stress on the problematic relationship of the classical law of contract expressed in legal texts to those business relationships, and a consequent stress on the shortcomings of the law of contract expressed in legal texts.'[37] Campbell's clarification is useful. It suggests that providing a credible and effective critique of traditional black-letter (or 'classical') approaches to doctrine, primarily by exploiting discrepancies between law in books and law in action, remains central to the task of establishing and consolidating the viability of sociolegal studies itself.

Researchers who exploit identifiable gaps between legal rhetoric contained in formal principles and empirical realities of law in action are not confined to contract or even civil law. Indeed, such discrepancies were clearly identified and highlighted by Baldwin and McConville's controversial research on plea-bargaining in British Courts. This study highlighted the yawning gap between the official position that all defendants retain an absolute right to plead innocent, and thereby have the prosecution's case against them assessed by an independent judge and jury, and the actual operation of plea-bargaining in daily pre-trial practices. Their findings indicated that this aspect of criminal 'law in action' often contradicted, and even practically nullified, the supposed 'rights' of defendants. Despite considering themselves innocent, a proportion of defendants gave in to various pressures to plead guilty, including that exerted by their own lawyers, in the hope of attracting a reduced sentence.[38] Contrary to Campbell's definition, however, this form of sociolegal project does not direct its criticism at the adequacy of a legal doctrine which, for example, maintains that defendants have a basic right to be presumed innocent until proven otherwise: a claim that is of course asserted as an inviolable truth by criminal law and constitutional law textbooks. On the contrary, within Baldwin and McConvilles' approach to sociolegal studies, the critical focus falls upon the complicity of lawyers and others in their routine and casual disregard of the practical recognition of such doctrinal 'rights.' Here, the validity of those formal rights is not treated as disproved because of their limited recognition in practice. Instead, in this research they are treated as broadly valid expectations that continue to be legitimate despite their routine violation within the criminal justice system. Indeed, it might be possible for you to reassess the findings of existing research on plea-bargaining by means of a small-scale study at a local criminal court, including observations and a series of interviews with the relevant participants.

Insofar as sociolegal studies involves conducting research that exposes discrepancies between law in books and law in action, that is, between official accounts and practical

---

[37]David Campbell, 'Socio-Legal Analysis of Contract' in Thomas, 1997 *op. cit.*, 252.

[38]Baldwin and McConville, *Negotiated Justice: Pressures to Plead Guilty* (London: Martin Robertson, 1977).

realities as experienced by those most closely affected by legal procedures, it will continue to be potentially controversial. If students adopt this approach, their findings might support an empirically-grounded criticism of legal doctrine understood not as given truths within a self-contained realm to be assimilated by students and applied by lawyers, but rather as specific and questionable ideological claims. Examples of this type of research may, perhaps, reveal that such claims *selectively misrepresent* the reality of what is actually taking place in practice. Therefore, and for interesting sociological reasons, such claims can perpetrate a deception upon the public at large, at least insofar as they accept official rhetoric regarding how law recognises and enforces their basic civil rights.[39]

Although helpful, generalisations defining sociolegal studies as entailing a switch from the traditional focus exclusively upon 'law in books', traditionally associated with black-letter approaches to legal research, to empirical studies of 'law in action' are not sufficient to capture every strand of this movement. In particular, this generalisation glosses over other non-empirical aspects of sociolegal studies, particularly the continuing publication of studies of the relationship between law, ideology and the state, which stem from sociological theory.[40] As the hybrid term suggests, there must remain a 'socio', as well as a 'legal', dimension to sociolegal studies, however these ambiguous terms are interpreted and redefined differently in multiple contexts. It would, therefore, be entirely misleading to define sociolegal studies as nothing other than empirical studies of law in action, and thus as 'applied' legal studies, and to contrast this with theoretical work on law's various functions within society and society's multiple roles within the legal sphere.

As Jolly recognises, it is not possible to justify a hard-and-fast division between empirical and theoretical variants of sociolegal studies. This is because many empirical studies of 'law in action' are grounded in, and derive their key categories from, various competing social theories, including those classic theories of Marx, Weber and Durkheim. Hence, dissertation students interested in legal and social theory should take note that the sociolegal studies movement reflects a shared interest in accounting for the social dimensions of law, of law as a social phenomenon, partly at least by drawing, knowingly or otherwise, upon the implications of different theories. Jolly notes: 'the main strength of socio-legal studies has been the wide range of methodological approaches, deriving from many (often opposing) theoretical bases, which can be drawn upon in order to critically consider the relationship between law and society. . . . socio-legal studies is less a shared perspective than a common interest'.[41]

Shaw, for example, argues that Cotterrell's focus upon the study of the behaviour of legal officials as essential to the nature of sociolegal studies needs to be extended. It should include new types of understanding of topics that have arisen as a result of the application of self-consciously developed *interdisciplinary methods* drawn largely from

[39]See V. Jupp, *Methods of Criminological Research* (London: Unwin Hyman, 1989) for a detailed discussion of the controversy created by *Negotiated Justice*, which is also summarised by the 'forward' by the Vice Chancellor of Birmingham University and the author's 'Introductory Note', *ibid*.

[40]Roger Cotterrell's writings over the last two decades on the importance of different sociological theories are widely included and cited within current sociolegal publications even though they are not based on his own empirical studies of law in action. A similar point applies broadly to the theoretical writings of Alan Hunt, Gunther Teubner and Thomas Luhmann and David Nelken.

[41]S. Jolly, in Thomas 1997 *op. cit.*, 343.

the social sciences.[42] In other words, in addition to studying the behaviour of legal officials, any adequate working definition of sociolegal studies needs to address not only the systematic study of the implications of earlier research within this tradition, but also the commitment to carry forward a *distinctly interdisciplinary agenda* within legal studies. This can include collaboration on a shared topic by regulation specialists from a number of disciplines, including, for example, sociology, social administration, social psychology, economics and history.[43]

In a pragmatic vein, Eekelaar and Maclean suggest that any definition of sociolegal studies must be based on the self-definitions of those in the field: 'socio-legal study imposes the unifying discipline of observing the way in which law works through those who believe themselves to be acting out the law.'[44] For similar, entirely pragmatic reasons then, we can define sociolegal studies in a loose and formal way as: whatever practices are being conducted and widely accepted *as* contributions to the ongoing tradition of sociolegal studies by researchers, funding councils, editorial boards of relevant academic journals and book publishers.[45]

On the other hand, there are certain core commitments that could, for the time being at least, be taken as defining the distinctive nature of sociolegal research. One defining feature of sociolegal studies, which students could usefully take note of and possibly adapt to their own dissertations, is the shared belief that the assumptions of black-letter agenda provide a totally inadequate, or at least an insufficient, basis for conducting a viable form of legal research. This is because its focus upon describing doctrinal rules and principles 'out of context' ignores the derivation, practical operation and social impact of specific legal measures. In a similar vein, the ESRC review stated:

> Socio-legal studies is an umbrella for what is now an exciting, wide-ranging and varied area of research activity. In all its forms, the approach to socio-legal scholars to the contextual study of law and legal processes are very different from the pure doctrinal research which had been the staple of traditional legal scholarship.[46]

Bradney and Cownie note that law students adopting a sociolegal approach must be prepared to use a *far wider* range of sources in both paper and electronic formats than would be the case for a black-letter project:

> Socio-legal courses will look to the policy behind the legal rule as much as to the rule itself. An ever-increasing amount of government material is now available via the Web. Thus, for example, the Lord Chancellor's Department now has a home page (http://www.open.gov.uk/lcd/lcdhome.htm) which will lead the reader to a range of material from reports on legal aid to the texts of speeches given by leading members of the judiciary. Parliament has its own home page (http://www. Parliament.uk/) with links to both the House of Commons and the House of Lords. Nor is this kind of material limited to official sources. The Law Society, for example, also has its own home page giving access to a wide range of Law Society

---

[42]Shaw, in Thomas, 1997 *op. cit.*, 311-12.

[43]*Ibid.*

[44]Eekelaar and Maclean (eds), *A Reader in Family Law* (Oxford: OUP, 1994) 2.

[45]See Paddy Hillyard, 'What is Socio-legal Studies?' ESRC Review of Socio-Legal Studies, (Swindon: ESRC, 1994).

[46]ESRC, 1994 *op. cit.*, 1.

documentation (http://www.Lawsociety.org.uk/home.html). Many of the leading newspapers are available either via the Web or as CD-ROMs. Hansard is available as a CD-ROM.[47]

Most sociolegal scholars would agree that law, as defined by the black-letter tradition, as a singular and self-contained discipline focused on 'law in books' needs to be either replaced with, or at least supplemented by, a different type of research deploying methodologies drawn largely from the social sciences.[48] As Bradshaw notes, sociolegal research 'takes legal study outside the legal "office" [it] . . . considers the law and the process of law (law-making, legal procedure) beyond legal texts'.[49] This can include addressing 'the socio-politic-economic considerations that surround and inform the enactment of laws, the operation of procedure, and the results of the passage and enforcement of laws'.[50] The empirical and contextual focus of sociolegal research on law in action, on laws in their social contexts, is required to provide: 'A wholly necessary complement to descriptions and analyses of the positive law'.[51] Whilst if students adopted a black-letter approach to their dissertations they would focus on the content of legal rules, the choice of a sociolegal methodology would mean focusing on the social nature, functions and implications of these rules. In this way, the dissertation would seek to understand law in one or more of its various contexts of emergence and operation.[52] Adopting a sociolegal approach requires researchers to be willing to cast their net wider than law reports, statutes and Hansard, and academic commentaries upon doctrinal sources. Instead, it requires researchers to gather 'data wherever appropriate to the problem' by using whatever methods are most likely to generate such data.[53] In short, a sociolegal dissertation will differ from a black-letter one both in the definition of the issues that comprise the themes, and the locations that researchers will look for relevant information.

Another key part of sociolegal studies includes research projects that investigate and assess the *practical impact* of law in action. This would cover dissertations addressing the effects of enacting specific measures upon the interests and conduct of different groups and institutions in society, which requires researchers to identify winners and losers.[54] Such research includes one classic study, using individual and group interviews, which addressed how a sample of long-term high-security prisoners adopted different strategies for coping with the different effects of continuing imprisonment.[55] Other studies have

---

[47]'Teaching Legal System,' 1999, *op. cit.*

[48]The resort to social scientific methods as a supplement to and corrective for the formalism of the black-letter tradition was clear in the American Realist movement of the 1930s. See C. Tomlins, 'Framing the Field of Law's Disciplinary Encounters: A Historical Narrative' (2000) 34 *Law and Society Rev*. 911, at 934. Anthony Ogus, maintains that sociolegal studies is 'a necessary complement to doctrinal analysis of law and as a major input into policymaking.' 'Exemplary Damages and Economic Analysis', in Hawkins 1997 *op. cit.*, 85. One of the pioneers of sociolegal studies, Donald Harris, continued to edit two distinctly doctrinal works: *Chitty on Contracts* and *Benjamin's Sale of Goods*.

[49]Alan Bradshaw, 'Sense and Sensibility: Debates and Developments in Socio-Legal Research Methods' in Thomas, 1997 *op. cit.*, 99.

[50]*Ibid*.

[51]Shaw, 1997 *op. cit.*, 312.

[52]*Ibid.*; Passas and Nelken, 'The Thin Line Between Legitimate and Criminal Enterprises: Subsidy Frauds in the EC' (1993) 18 *Crime, Law and Social Change*, 223.

[53]Bradshaw, 1997 *op. cit.*, 99.

[54]Shaw, 1997 *op. cit.*, 312.

[55]Cohen and Taylor, *Psychological Survival*: *The Experience of Long Term Imprisonment*, (London: Penguin, 1972).

assessed the impact upon proposed and emerging laws of specific political and economic pressures, including those exerted by ideological agendas, concerns and interests.[56]

Another common theme of sociolegal methodologies are their focus upon precisely those functional aspects of law in relation to the realisation of public policy that are excluded by the black-letter tradition. Dissertations using this approach would need to address the relationship between legal developments and wider changes within public policy, relating the function played by the former to the goals of the latter. For instance, pioneering work on the social functions played by contract law claimed that contractual regulation during earlier free-market conditions helped secure freedom of movement, provided insurance against calculated economic risks, secured individual freedom, and ensured relative equality between the parties.[57] Yet, the emergence of the modern welfare state largely from 1948 generated an increasing gap between these former roles and how individuals and groups really used contracts in practice.[58]

Members of the sociolegal movement often present their commitment to *interdisciplinary* types of legal research as lying at the core of this movement. Sociolegal projects frequently draw upon the methods and techniques of other social scientists, including quantified sample surveys conducted via questionnaires or interviews, or more qualitative types of fieldwork based on observation and questioning, such as 'ethnography'.[59] For example, Sally Wheeler, who has made a sustained contribution in relation to the development of sociolegal approaches to corporate issues, defines this approach formally to designate research that deploys ideas and techniques 'from other disciplines primarily but not exclusively from within the social sciences and humanities fields'.[60] She has argued that any emerging sociolegal model of corporate structure will find it necessary to build upon 'pump-priming work that has been undertaken ... in disciplines complementary to law ... but which of itself does not engage with legal doctrine or structures in a way that can be considered sociolegal'.[61] Wheeler cites literature from both sociology and management studies on 'conceptions of organisations and power' as key ingredients for future sociolegal accounts of corporate governance.

In short, students need to recognise that dissertations that contribute to sociolegal studies will differ markedly from doctrinal approaches by studying law in action, including possibly the impact of specific legal measures, and this will require drawing upon the methods and methodologies of one or more of the social sciences. Any more precise, fixed and substantive definition is likely to be contested by different strands within this diverse movement, a number of which would reject any definition that excludes or downplays their own distinctive type of research. As Don Harris, former Director of the Oxford Centre for Socio-Legal Studies, recognises:

> There is no agreed definition of socio-legal studies: some use the term broadly to cover the study of law in its social context, but I prefer to use it to refer to the study

---

[56]*Ibid.*; C. Harlow, 'A Community of Interests: Making the Most of European Law' (1992) 55 *MLR* 331.

[57]W. Friedmann, *Law in a Changing Society* (London: Stevens, 1959) 93ff (cf. Campbell, 1997 *op. cit.*, 240-2).

[58]*Ibid.*

[59]Bradshaw, 1997 *op. cit.*, 107.

[60]Sally Wheeler, 'Company Law' in Thomas, 1997 *op. cit.*, n.8/285.

[61]*Ibid.*, 286.

of the law and legal institutions from the perspective of the social sciences. . . . It is arguable that the attempt to impose rigid boundaries is likely to inhibit the development of the field . . . we feel that the term 'socio-legal studies' should be given the broadest possible definition, as it is in other countries.[62]

A broad definition will include much criminological research and purely theoretical studies within the sociology of law and law and economics.[63] A narrower definition, which is sometimes adopted in practice for pragmatic reasons, may exclude criminology and social theory.[64] Whilst it is interesting for those interested in using a sociolegal approach for their dissertations to recognise the existence and claims of both broad and narrow definitions of sociolegal studies, it is equally important to take into account the fact that the various 'boundary disputes' that generate controversy within this movement change over time, sometimes even within a single decade, and thus rapidly 'become stale'.

For entirely pragmatic reasons, law students considering applying this approach, and thus faced with their supervisors' expectation that a definition must be provided, would be best advised to characterise it as follows: sociolegal studies are a branch of legal studies that are distinguished from doctrinal research through the deployment of one or more research methodologies drawn largely but not exclusively from the social sciences. These methodologies are applied to a wider range of materials that provide evidence of the underlying public policy dimension underpinning doctrinal law, including interview data, records of direct observations, government reports and policy documents.

If students decide to select a sociolegal methodology, a further question arises concerning the relationship between this type of legal research and existing disciplines and sub-disciplines. It is probably not helpful to try to claim that work taking place under the banner of sociolegal studies is contributing to a separate discipline in its own right, or even to a distinct 'sub-discipline' of either law or the social sciences. Instead, this approach is better viewed as a device that can operate as a tool for breaking open disciplinary boundaries and creating novel combinations of methodologies and approaches to dissertation topics within law interpreted in a suitably broad manner.[65] For example, much sociolegal research in the field of the legal regulation of the family and divorce has brought together the policy concerns of academics studying social administration with those concerned with family law. Such research has identified a continuing tension between different policy agendas, such as a welfare-state oriented 'best interests of the child' approach, and an individual rights-based approach.[66] Another example is David Cowan's critical evaluation of UK housing law and policy, which analyses developments in both economic and official policy aspects of housing to suggest that there is a

---

[62]Don Harris, 'The Development of Socio-Legal Studies in the United Kingdom', (1983) 2 *Legal Studies*, 315.

[63]Bradshaw, 1997 *op. cit.*, 99–100.

[64]For example, the Oxford Centre for Socio-Legal Studies confined itself to civil justice issues so as not to compete or overlap with the efforts of existing criminological centres, whilst the Sheffield Centre was originally named 'Socio-legal and Criminological Studies' – again suggesting that the former element did not necessarily cover criminology.

[65]Roger Cotterrell, 'Subverting Orthodoxy, Making Law Central: A View of Sociolegal Studies, (2002) 29 *JLS*, 632–44, 635.

[66]See J. Roche and C. Piper, in S. Day-Sclater and C. Piper (eds), *Undercurrents of Divorce* (Aldershot: Ashgate Publishing Ltd, 1999); H. Hendrick, *Children, Childhood and English Society*, (Cambridge: Cambridge University Press, 1990), at 97–9; and K. Marshall, *Children's Rights in the Balance: The Participation–Protection Debate* (London: The Stationery Office, 1997).

growing regulatory crisis affecting different types of housing tenure, access to housing, and individual housing rights. These difficulties have, he suggests, stemmed from a policy and ideological shift from 1979 onwards towards greater emphasis upon 'individual responsibility' and reliance upon market forces to meet citizens' need for housing.[67] Research of this kind cannot be treated as belonging fully to any single discipline precisely because it brings together the themes and methods of at least two disciplines.

It would not be possible for your dissertation to define sociolegal studies in an adequate way without mentioning the importance of interdisciplinarity and multidisciplinarity. Interdisciplinarity involves researchers studying law through a combination of the theories, methods and research techniques of sociological, economic, social policy and cultural studies that are integrated and synthesised.[68] Multidisciplinary legal research, by contrast, entails researchers bringing together a distinctly 'legal' analysis of, say, housing with an economic approach, or relating courtroom criteria of responsibility with those of contemporary psychology without necessarily attempting to synthesise or fuse these approaches into a single coherent perspective.[69]

Interdisciplinary dissertations involve research in which the techniques and methods of law and at least one other discipline engage with each other and interact to produce a type of analysis that would not otherwise be possible from the application of either discipline in isolation.[70] We have already noted that early studies by Harris and the Oxford Centre for Socio-Legal Studies involved, as a matter of principle, close collaboration between legal academics and statisticians, economists, social historians, sociologists and others.[71] Twining has applauded the multidisciplinary subculture of the early phase of the Oxford Centre 'that views almost everything through the multiple lenses of several disciplines'.[72] This Centre itself was deliberately structured in a way to remove the departmental barriers that often impede effective research collaboration between legal academics and members of other social science departments, and to thereby allow the complementary skills to be pooled within interdisciplinary projects.[73] Some contributors to the sociolegal studies movement believe that gaining the respect of social scientific audience for sociolegal work is at least as important as recognition from other legal academics.[74]

---

[67]David Cownie, *Housing Law and Policy*, (London: Palgrave Macmillan 1999). For an early sociolegal study, see Tom Hadden, *Compulsory Repair and Improvement*: *A Study of the Operation of the Housing Acts 1957–1974* (Oxford: Centre for Socio-Legal Studies, 1978).

[68]For a useful overview see Douglas Vick, 'Interdisciplinarity and the Discipline of Law' (2004) 31 *JLS*, 163–93, and more generally, J. Moran, *The New Critical Idiom*: *Interdisciplinarity*, (London: Routledge, 2001); William Twining, 'Law and Anthropology: A Case-study of Interdisciplinary Collaboration' (1973) 7 *Law & Society Review* 561; B. Garth and J. Sterling, 'From Legal Realism to Law and Society: Reshaping Law for the Last Stages of the Social Activist State' (1988) 32 *Law and Society Review* 409.

[69]Vick, 2004 *op. cit.*, n.9/165; Farrington *et al.*, (eds), *Psychology, Law and Legal Processes*, (London: Macmillan, 1979); C. Kemp, 'The Uses of Abstraction; Remarks on the Interdisciplinary Efforts in Law and Philosophy' (1997) 74 *Denver University Law Rev*. 877. Levine notes with respect to the early days of the Law and Society Association: 'Interdisciplinary outreach across law and social science was always contemplated.', 1990 *op. cit.*, 11.

[70]Vick, 2004 *op. cit.*, 164–5; J. Weinstein, 'Coming of Age: Recognising the Importance of Interdisciplinary Education in Law Practice' (1999) 74 *Washington Law Rev*. 319 at 353.

[71]Hawkins, 1997 *op. cit.*, prologue, 4. Vick considers such collaboration to be desirable in future interdisciplinary research projects to avoid basic mistakes in research design, data collection and data analysis, 2004 *op. cit.*, 192–3.

[72]William Twining, 'Remembering 1972' in D. J. Galligan, 1995 *op. cit.*, 43.

[73]Hawkins, 1997 *op. cit.*, prologue, 8.

[74]*Ibid.*, 4.

Multidisciplinary forms of sociolegal studies cannot be classified as law plus any single social science.[75] In both multi- and interdisciplinary research the aim is to 'transcend disciplinary boundaries by taking as the focus the subject area of law in society'.[76] For example, a recent sociolegal study on the social and legal definition and regulation of human bodies and body parts consisted of a diverse collection of essays stemming from multidisciplinary and interdisciplinary seminars held in 2000 by the Cambridge Socio-Legal Group. The contributors address a variety of issues relating to this topic through the application of a series of disciplinary perspectives. These include criminology, legal doctrine relating to court-ordered Caesareans, medicine, sociolegal analyses of the body in the context of familial relationships, midwifery, philosophy, psychology and sociology.[77] Another recent multidisciplinary study on environmental law and policy included contributions from representatives of academic disciplines as diverse as management studies, policy studies and sociology, applied to a broadly defined range of materials and issues, including the relationship of the law and science, the impact of regulation, and alternative methods of environmental regulation.[78] A third example is a collection of essays entitled *What is a Parent? A Socio-Legal Analysis*, which explores the question 'What is a parent?' from the disciplinary orientations of law, sociology, psychology, biology, history and criminology.[79]

As already discussed, sociolegal research in both Britain and North America tends to rely generally upon a shared belief in interdisciplinarity. For example, Shaw identifies sociolegal research in the European area as 'work of an interdisciplinary nature specifically focused on integration processes which addresses the "legal dimension"'.[80] She notes that 'lawyers are beginning to work fruitfully with political scientists and economists in particular to build up a more complete picture of institutional interactions.'[81] Arguably the law-in-context branch of sociolegal studies falls outside the scope of this strand of our working definition. This is because it provides a broader frame of reference for the study of legal doctrine that is largely drawn from within the discipline of law itself to the exclusion of other social scientific disciplines.[82]

The choice facing dissertation students is not necessarily that of having to decide between either a single disciplinary approach of a purely black-letter analysis, or an

---

[75]Harris, 1983 *op. cit.*, 316. For example, George P. Smith's *Legal and Healthcare Ethics for the Elderly*, (London: Taylor & Francis, 1996) is an example of a multidisciplinary study of the complex sociolegal, medico-ethical and political dimensions of gerontology, including topics such as financing healthcare, considerations of quality of life, informed consent to medical treatment, elder abuse and 'death with dignity'. This study could not really be classified under the category of 'law and medicine' without considerable falsification of its breadth and range of issues.

[76]Editorial, *BJLS* 1 (1974) 1.

[77]Andrew Bainham, Shelley Day Sclater, Martin Richards (eds), *Body Lore and Laws*, (Oxford: Hart Publishing, 2002).

[78]Bridget Hutter (ed.) *A Reader in Environmental Law*, Oxford Readings in Socio Legal Studies, (Oxford: Oxford University Press), 1999.

[79]Edited by Andrew Bainham, Shelley Day Sclater and Martin Richards, (Oxford: Hart Publishing, 1999).

[80]Shaw, in Thomas 1997 *op. cit.*, 313.

[81]*Ibid.* – citing K. Armstrong, 'Regulating the Free-Market of Goods, Institutions and Institutional Change' in Shaw and G. More (eds), *New Legal Dynamics of European Union*, (Oxford: OUP, 1996) 166.

[82]Wheeler, 1997 *op. cit.*, 285; Campbell 1997 *op. cit.* 246–7, places P. Atiyah's, *Introduction to the Law of Contract* 2nd edition, 1971, and *The Rise and Fall of Freedom of Contract* (Oxford: Clarendon, 1979) in this tradition of law in context that, whilst contextualising legal doctrine and its functions, does not seriously integrate the findings of other disciplines, such as sociological accounts of the structures of capitalist economy and society.

entirely interdisciplinary/multidisciplinary orientation. This is because there are numerous degrees of interdisciplinarity and multidisciplinarity within a broad spectrum of possibilities.[83] At the relatively modest end of the spectrum, a postgraduate law student with a background in, say, business studies and economics, may decide to include a dissertation chapter on a review of evidence relating to the economic impact of recent legal developments. This could be useful for counterbalancing an otherwise doctrinal account of the topic. Postgraduate students who have previously studied aspects of British social history could decide to devote the first half of their dissertation to a discussion of the implications of recent historical research by both historians and legal academics for our understanding of the factors that may explain the emergence and development of their dissertation topic over the past fifty years. Undergraduate students who have previously undertaken a course on sociology could exploit this by discussing a selection of academic literature addressing the specifically sociological aspects of their dissertation topic.

At the more ambitious end of the spectrum would be students attempting to bring three or more disciplinary orientations together. This would be particularly ingenious, if perhaps risky, where this combination has not previously been attempted, and where the disciplines themselves are particularly dissimilar, such as qualitative forms of sociology with quantitative types of 'law and economics'.[84] At the extreme point of the spectrum of interdisciplinarity would be an attempt to create an entirely new sub-discipline, linking for example, the approach to war-crimes trials adopted by international criminal lawyers with that type of analysis which is characteristic of military historians.

Dissertations located between these extremes could limit themselves to applying the methods or concepts of another discipline to familiar legal issues and primary source materials. The goal could be to ascertain whether this reinterpretation could yield insights that usefully supplement purely doctrinal accounts of these materials. Another possibility would be for a dissertation to identify an area of doctrinal analysis where a legal topic, such as plea-bargaining within international criminal law, has traditionally been analysed in isolation from social, institutional or political issues that are related to, or affected by, the application of law. This could address the involvement of diplomats, politicians and intelligence officials in brokering immunities for certain types of war criminals. Here, the aim of the dissertation would be to analyse critically and partially 'correct' the abstract quality of more traditional doctrinal analysis of questions of immunity by reconnecting the dissertation topic to the findings of social science or historical research relating to the context in which this process takes place in practice.[85]

Even experienced academics might be cautious before undertaking more ambitious types of interdisciplinary projects, unless they are working as part of an experienced and compatible team comprising specialists in each of the disciplines being brought together, allowing a high degree of integration in practice. There certainly remains a risk of dissertation students adopting interdisciplinary projects that their supervisors and other more experienced researchers would reject as overly ambitious.

---

[83]Vick, 2004 *op. cit.*, 184.

[84]Law and economics includes the application of economic theory and methods to the general body of legal institutions and legal principles, and largely stems from Coase's ground-breaking article on social costs. Ogus, 1995 *op. cit.*, 27.

[85]Vick, 2004 *op. cit.*, 184–5. For criticisms of its approach to corporate issues, see Wheeler, in Thomas 1997 *op. cit.*, 288.

Given that interdisciplinarity represents one of the distinctive and core elements of sociolegal research (arguably a defining quality), it is not surprising that the SLSA has strongly affirmed its commitment to the production of interdisciplinary analyses of law as a social phenomenon. Indeed, the SLSA exists in part to encourage the study of legal phenomena which is distinctly multi- or interdisciplinary in its approach.[86] The Economic and Social Research Council (ESRC), one of the main sources for funding sociolegal research, including university modules designed to enhance students' research methods, also note the effort to synthesise and integrate previously separate disciplines:

> Socio-legal Studies and Criminology are multi-disciplinary in that they draw on basic theories and methods developed in the social science disciplines. Socio-legal studies may make more use of traditional legal research skills, but this is not neces-sarily so. Students in each area are likely to be recruited from a wide variety of disciplines in the arts, humanities and social sciences, though students also come from the natural sciences and, increasingly, from the environmental and medical sciences who show an interest in the application of research in social and/or legal areas. Socio-legalists looking at civil justice processes and procedures are often drawn from Economics or Sociology rather than Law. Students who are likely to do best within Socio-legal Studies will be those who have either demonstrated or shown strong potential to think independently, to deal with abstract concepts and analysis, and be able to communicate effectively in writing. Students in both areas need to have the ability to draw together ideas from different disciplines and to be able to synthesise them into an integrated output.[87]

This agency has also sought to encourage greater multidisciplinary collaboration between legal researchers and both economists and psychologists,[88] a goal partly met by the work of the Oxford Centre where legal themes have been analysed from both economic and psychological approaches.[89]

The statements of other sociolegal researchers committed to interdisciplinarity and multidisciplinarity are found in the descriptions of various sociolegal oriented research centres. These include the 'AHRC Centre for Law, Gender and Sexuality' at Kent University, whose publicity claims: 'Intellectually, the centre will adopt a critical interdisciplinary and cross-national perspective to the field of gender, law and sexuality, focusing in particu-lar on developing new work in the areas of governance and regulation, cultural studies and healthcare, and bioethics.'[90] The commitment to multidisciplinary methodologies is apparent from the statement of Donald Harris, a former Director of the Centre for Socio-Legal Studies at Oxford University:[91]

> We regard the law as a complex phenomenon, which is not likely to be adequately explained by reference to a single macro-theory. We believe that in the immediate future, progress in socio-legal studies will best be made by building up a number of

---

[86]http://www.kent.ac.uk/slsa/home_links/aboutslsa.htm

[87]Http://www.esrc.ac.uk/esrccontent/postgradfunding/2000_Guidelines_f15.asp

[88]Martin Partington, 'Socio-Legal research in Britain: Shaping the Funding Environment', in Thomas, 1997 *op. cit.*, 23-44.

[89]Hawkins, 1997 *op. cit.*, vii.

[90]Http://www.kent.ac.uk/slsa/research/centres.htm: accessed August 2005.

[91]For more details on the pioneering Oxford Centre, see Galligan, 1995 *op. cit.*

detailed studies of particular topics in the law, using as many relevant perspectives as our resources permit. If we bring together the insights of sociology, economics, psychology and history upon a particular problem area in society, we hope that the cumulative effect will be a deeper understanding than could be gained from any one discipline, given the all-pervasive nature of law in its social context.[92]

More recent descriptions of the membership of this centre emphasise that research staff are drawn from the disciplines of Law, Sociology, Anthropology and Political Science.[93] The following description of a number of the projects undertaken helps clarify the broad range of themes and interdisciplinary methods encompassed by sociolegal research:

Socio-legal research involves interdisciplinary research drawing on law and social science methodologies and perspectives, and taking empirical and/or theoretical approaches. . . . The Centre's research is currently focused on a number of research programmes. Among them are studies of public law and public administration in Central and Eastern Europe; legal regulation of government and administration; the nature and effectiveness of internal administrative governance in Central and Eastern Europe; lawyers' transaction work, including the role of legal work in a global economy; the contribution of lawyers to Government and how business and other interests interact with government agencies when writing and implementing regulations; lawyers in British central government; courts and the internet; human rights in social context; making human rights effective; financial reporting regulation and corporate responsibility; regulation and compliance; tax avoidance and tax policy; lawyers and transnational transactions; legal culture in post-Soviet Societies; evaluating health care reform; law and informal practices in post-communist societies; international law and society including the globalisation of resources and ideas, the movement of people, human rights and the link between local governance and international norms; international environmental law; the impact of non-state agencies on human rights; and the relationship between the academy and the practice of international law and international relations.[94]

Students completing dissertations may be particularly interested in the difference made to legal research by any decision they make to adopt a sociolegal approach. This difference is clear from a module offered at the University of New South Wales, which focuses on forms of legal regulation. The module begins with materials designed to allow students to demonstrate their awareness of the nature of traditional regulation theories, to evaluate critically how they analyse different types of legal regulation, and whether 'they can provide meaningful insights into the function of public law'. After appreciating the limits of traditional approaches, students are expected to:

Design [their] own socio-legal model of regulation: students should be able to re-fashion traditional regulation theory into a more functional model, by incorporating contextual factors that will ensure a more meaningful engagement with different legal systems and political structures.[95]

---

[92]Harris, 1983 *op. cit.*, 319.

[93]Http://www.csls.ox.ac.uk/, accessed August 2005.

[94]Http://www.admin.ox.ac.uk/gsp/courses/socialsciences/socleg.shtml.

[95]www.law.unsw.edu.au/Course/course_guide/LAWS4128.doc. The module takes Japanese regulation as a running example but the approach and skills are clearly far wider than this and more generally applicable.

The idea is that, having designed their own model, 'students should be able to apply their own sociolegal model of regulation to . . . regulatory issues'. This goal is supplemented by an exploration of 'the critical contextual factors that influence the development and operation of law'.

The distinctive type of skills that this innovative module aims to develop are worth citing in full. This is because a number of these are directly relevant to the expectations of examiners of law dissertations whose chosen methodology is that of sociolegal studies:

1. To identify the contextual factors especially, political but also theoretical, systemic, and cultural, which impact on the function of public law and public legal institutions.

2. To critically weigh their relative impact and importance.

3. To predict how current developments (e.g. deregulation and post-bubble depression) will impact on these factors and, accordingly, map out the future shape and direction of public law and regulation law.

4. To identify additional factors and weigh up for themselves how these influence the nature of public law and its operation.

5. To strike a balance when assessing whether law is universal in nature or inextricably linked to its political context.

6. To self-reflect on what academic skills and practices in non-law disciplines (i.e., political science) they lack and develop strategies to acquaint themselves with the necessary contours of this discourse to aid them in their holistic analysis.

7. To apply their own sociolegal model of regulation to examine, research and report on new [legal] developments.

8. To adapt their legal research strategies to incorporate 'contextual research variables' (especially political variables) in order to find, analyse and make informed judgments on contemporary legal developments.

9. To exercise critical, reflective and creative thinking skills to place . . . public law in its context, evaluate the implications this has on . . . the broader global community and independently fashion convincing policy solutions.[96]

In short, sociolegal studies includes an interdisciplinary approach focusing on a variety of contextual factors shaping law in action, as well as different theoretical perspectives on the operation of law in society which seek to explain the different functions of law as a social phenomenon. It is clear that adopting a sociolegal methodology will, therefore, make a real difference to how the issues addressed by a dissertation will be defined, the type and range of sources gathered, and the specific ways in which they are analysed.

● The Diversity of Topics and Themes Addressed by Sociolegal Studies

Sociolegal studies have been successful in creating an extensive body of literature in most but not all of the core areas of the legal curriculum. There has been less development within property, company and, until recently, European law.[97] The wide range of

---

[96]*Ibid.*

[97]Jo Shaw, 'Socio-Legal Studies and the European Union' in Thomas, 1997 *op. cit.*, 310 – noting the reputation as narrowly focused and unreflective doctrinal specialists commonly attributed to specialists in EC law within sociolegal circles.

topics addressed by sociolegal studies are commonly interpreted under different categories from traditional black-letter legal classifications, such as private/public law. The ESRC recognises the wide range of topics covered by current sociolegal research, including some 'subjects' typically excluded from black-letter types of research:

> Socio-legal studies covers a range of disciplinary contexts within the social sciences and law, and relates the legal to the sociological, political and economic dimensions of human activity. Whereas Criminology is a substantive concept, Socio-legal Studies is more about approach, making it difficult to describe specific domains of expertise. The essence of Socio-legal research might be described as an appreciation of interdisciplinary relationships and an application of such a perspective to problems. Some Socio-legal Studies students are likely to be interested in evaluating normative approaches within one or more social scientific contexts; typically, for instance, probing how political or economic processes and social, cultural or scientific phenomena affect the development and application of law. Other students may be interested in civil justice or the legal professions with a focus on civil justice processes and their relation to procedure and views of the state, funding, consumer views or tribunal services, etc.[98]

The diversity and range of topics addressed through the application of sociolegal methodologies is also clear from the workshops held at the 2004 SLSA conference. These have included streams on: access to justice, affirmative action for minority groups; corporate governance;[99] children and the law; education law and policy; family law and policy; freedom of expression; miscarriages of justices; research methodology; law and cyberspace; globalisation; regulation, sex offending; administrative justice; law and social/sociological theory;[100] law and history, and law and popular culture. This breadth is also clear if students examine the topics of a selection of conference papers presented at recent sociolegal studies conferences within the UK. These have included: 'The Rights of Minorities and the Right to Democracy: Are they Compatible?' (1996); 'Police Powers, The Rule of Law and Quasi-Legislation' (1998); 'Family law in South Asian Context' (1997); 'The Treatment of Muslim Law in the Courts of England and Wales' (1992); 'Children, Young People and Identity Formation within the European Union' (1999);[101]

---

[98]Http://www.esrc.ac.uk/esrccontent/postgradfunding/2000_Guidelines_f15.asp

[99]On sociolegal approaches to company law issues, see, for example, Sally Wheeler, 'The Business Enterprise: A Socio-Legal Introduction' in Sally Wheeler (ed.), *A Reader on the Law of the Business Enterprise: Selected Essays* (Oxford: OUP, 1995); George P. Gilligan, 'The Potential of Socio-legal Approaches in the Development of Company Law' (2000) 21 *Company Lawyer* 127; Mahmut Yavasi, 2001: a study which: 'by examining changing relationship between the economy, politics and moral values which have been the main factors of the development of the law, to show the problems of corporate governance and the weaknesses of proposed solutions.' *Ibid*.

[100]More generally, see the essays on the relationship between legal analysis and different sociological traditions in Reza Banakar and Max Travers (eds), *An Introduction to Law and Social Theory*, (Oxford: Hart Publishing, 2002). *The Journal of Law and Society* regularly publishes collections of articles on social theory or the application of social theories to legal themes. See for example *JLS* 11(4) 2002 and 12(1) 2003.

[101]For other broadly socio-studies in the field of EC law see, Slaughter, Stone Sweet and Weiler (eds), *The European Court and National Courts: Legal Change in its Social Context* (Oxford: Hart Press, 1998); C. Harlow, 'Towards a Theory of Access for the European Court of Justice' (1992) 12 *Y.E.L.* 213; C. Harding, 'Who goes to Court in Europe. An analysis of Litigation Against the European Community' (1992) 17 *E.L.Rev.* 103; T. de la Mare, 'Article 177 EC in Social and Political Context: Perspective on the Key Procedure for EC Legal Integration' in Craig and De Búrca (eds), *The Evolution of EU Law* (Oxford: OUP, 1999), and H. Schepel and E. Blankenburg, 'Mobilising the European Court of Justice' in De Búrca and Weiler (eds), *The European Court of Justice* (Oxford: OUP, 2001).

'Risk and Gender in the Context of Immigration and Refugee Determination in Canada.' (2002).

These conference streams thus address a variety of topics relating to law in action that defy the terms of black-letter classification.[102] Clear examples drawn from the annual conferences 2003 and 2004 include: education law and policy, family law and policy,[103] regulation,[104] law and literature, globalisation, legal profession and ethics, law and social theory, gender, different forms of commercial and environmental regulation and sex offending.[105] Themes relating to the impact of law upon women, the role of women within legal institutions and feminist themes relating to the gendered operation of law more generally, now appear more frequently in sociolegal research than was the case in the early days of sociolegal studies in Britain and North America when this field was dominated by men.[106] Any overview of themes will inevitably be selective and become overtaken by events rapidly, not least because sociolegal studies has an inherent dynamism that aims to address and apply new themes and approaches.[107]

The movement from doctrinal legal analysis to law in action has meant, in many cases, that the focus of empirical sociolegal research has shifted to actions and processes taking place in the world outside the courtroom.[108] However, there have been a number of sociolegal projects that have remained focused upon the judiciary, their ideological orientations and social background. Indeed, an early theme of sociolegal research within the UK was empirical studies of judges and lawyers, often based on extensive periods of fieldwork involving observation of day-to-day practices of the courts,[109] or interviews with legal officials ranging from Law Lords and Divorce Registrars through to barristers' clerks and solicitors specialising in family law proceedings.[110] As Jolly notes:

> Much of this work is carried out by academic lawyers who have often fostered close links with local judges/solicitors. Access is thus easier to obtain, and research can often by conducted on the basis of the existence of shared assumptions and

---

[102]Hillyard, however, complains that too many still retain doctrinal classifications, such as family law (2002 *op. cit.*, 652).

[103]Mediation has been a prominent theme in sociolegal research. See G. Bevan *et al.*, 'Piloting a Quasi-Market for Family Mediation Amongst Clients Eligible for Legal Aid' (1999) 18 *Civil Justice Quarterly* 239; Davis *et al.*, 'Mediation and Legal Services – The Client Speaks' (2001) *Fam Law* 110; G. Bevan *et al.*, 'Can Mediation Reduce Expenditure on Lawyers?' (2001) *Fam Law* 186; G. Davis *et al.*, 'Family Mediation – Where Do We Go From Here?' (2001) *Fam Law* 265; and R. Dingwell and D. Greatbatch, 'Family Mediators – What are They Doing?' (2001) *Fam Law* 378.

[104]On the role of state regulation and of competition policy, see S. Deakin, T. Goodwin, and A. Hughes, 'Co-operation and Trust in Inter-Firm Relations: Beyond Competition Policy?' and S. Anderman, 'Commercial Co-operation, International Competitiveness, and EC Competition Policy' both in Deakin and Michie (eds), *Contracts, Co-operation, and Competition* (Oxford: OUP, 1997).

[105]Http://www.law.gla.ac.uk/slsa2004/; 2003 Conference announcement *Socio-Legal Newsletter*, No.38 (2002) 13.

[106]Levine, 1990 *op. cit.*, 28.

[107]*Ibid.*, 28–9.

[108]Robert Stevens, 'Judges, Politics, Politicians and the Confusing Role of the Judiciary,' in Hawkins, 1997 *op. cit.*, 245–90.

[109]Pat Carlen, 1976 *op. cit.*; McBarnet, 1981 *op. cit.*; Whelan and McBarnet, 'Lawyers in the Market: Delivering Legal Services in Europe' (1992) 19 *J. Law and Society* 49.

[110]A. Paterson, *The Law Lords: How Britain's Top Judges See their Role*, (London: Macmillan, 1982); John Flood, *Barristers' Clerks: The Law's Middle-men*, (Manchester: Manchester University Press 1983); John Flood, 'Doing Business: The Management of Uncertainty in Lawyers' Work', (1991) 25 *Law and Society Review*, 41.

knowledge between interviewer and interviewee. Studying lawyers is also a more efficient way of gathering large amounts of information about law's works, since lawyers are obviously the archetypical 'repeat players' within the legal system, which additionally makes longitudinal, follow-up studies possible.[111]

Studies of the actions and orientations of lawyers continue to form an important element of current sociolegal research in the UK.[112] Meanwhile, American research has studied the practical operation of standards of procedural justice within different sectors of the legal system.[113] This strand of research focuses not only on lawyers' law or law from a lawyers' perspective, but rather on the social, economic and political role played by different categories of lawyer.[114]

For example, much American sociolegal work on client's perceptions of their lawyers indicates that, in relation to the profession's responsiveness to the clients' needs, they are 'thought to be inattentive, unresponsive, insensitive, non-empathetic, uncooperative, and arrogant'.[115] Lawyers are widely perceived to fail to treat clients' needs with respect, fail to recognise the importance of interpersonal aspects of lawyer–client interaction (particularly accessibility, communicative skills and responsiveness) and are motivated more by financial returns than professional values.[116] Such features need to be invest-igated in terms of their 'structural origins . . . rooted in the training and socialisation of lawyers and in the structure, organisation, and economics of law practice'.[117]

Sociolegal projects have, however, also provided evidence that the balance of power between lawyers and their clients varies according to particular contextual factors. These include the particular area of legal practice, the specific tasks lawyers are engaged in, the social status of client groups and respective resources. The balance of power also remains subject to ongoing processes of negotiation and mutual resistance.[118] For example, there can be a world of difference in wealth, power and prestige between the work of lawyers in small generalist practices, and that of commercial lawyers employed by large corporations.[119] Other studies have highlighted the impact of client resources upon the litigation process, particularly in relation to 'repeat players in major test cases'.[120] As Harris notes: 'interviews with legal practitioners are now a regular method of research adopted by researchers'.[121]

---

[111]Jolly, in Thomas, 1997 *op. cit.*, 344.

[112]Indeed, there is an extended tradition including D. McBarnet, 'Law and Capital: The Role of Legal Form and Legal Actors' (1984) 12 *IJSL* 223; S. Wheeler, 'Lawyer Involvement in Commercial Disputes', (1991) 18 *JLS* 241; C. Campbell, 'Lawyers and their Public' in N. MacCormick (ed.) *Lawyers in Their Social Setting*, (1976); I. Ramsay, 'What Do Lawyers Do? Reflections on the Market for Lawyers' (1993) 21 *IJSL* 355.

[113]Thibaut and Walker, *Procedural Justice: A Psychological Analysis*, (Hillsdale, NJ: Erlbaum, 1975); Lind and Tyler, *The Social Psychology of Procedural Justice*, (NY: Plenum Press, 1988).

[114]William Felstiner, 'Professional Inattention: Origins and Consequences', in Hawkins, 1997 *op. cit.*, 122.

[115]*Ibid.*, 122, 124-31.

[116]*Ibid.*, 128-31.

[117]*Ibid.*, 122.

[118]*Ibid.*, 124-5.

[119]Heinz and Laumann, *Chicago Lawyers: The Social Structure of the Bar*, (NY: Russell Sage Foundation, 1982).

[120]Mark Galanter, 'Why the Haves Come Out Ahead: Speculations on the Limits of Legal Change' (1974) 9 *Law & Society Review* 95; Levine, 1990 *op. cit.*, 26.

[121]Harris, 1983, *op. cit.*, 320.

The extent of citizens' access to 'appropriate' legal services relative to a range of problems and conflicts, including disputes over accidental compensation, has, from the 1970s onwards, become a well-established sociolegal topic.[122] This strand of research embraces the question of identifying 'unmet legal need',[123] and empirical studies of the perceived adequacy of existing systems of appeal and review against decisions denying citizens specific public sector services.[124] This strand of research has benefited from systematic comparisons between developments in the study of other professions, such as doctors and accountants.[125] Hazel Genn has published numerous sociolegal research projects on this theme. For example, her book *Mediation In Action*,[126] showed how rising cost of litigation meant that litigation had become a realistic possibility only for the very rich or, subject to legal-aid eligibility, the very poor. As an alternative, this research evaluated a legal mediation scheme operating at the Central London County Court for defended cases involving more than £5,000. American studies have indicated the important legal role that proactive groups can play in both mobilising and directing citizens' complaints against, for example, discriminatory practices.[127]

The theme of family law and policy, with its clear link to the sociology of the family and relevance to policy-makers, regularly features as a stream in sociolegal conferences and, perhaps, has been 'one of the more successful areas of the sociolegal enterprise'.[128] Unlike property law, it has been assisted by the relative novelty of the area, and the lack of having to compete with a longer-established and entrenched black-letter tradition of teaching and scholarship within law school.[129] A considerable degree of reform, including the Children Act 1989, has both prompted and, to some extent through the mediation of the Law Commission, been encouraged by,[130] a series of sociolegal studies. These have explored 'the ramifications of the changing nature of the family life, including patterns of divorce, family finance, domestic violence and child protection and care over the past three decades'.[131]

In addition to work conducted by the Oxford Centre, there are two other sociolegal centres producing studies: The Bristol Socio-Legal Centre for Family Studies and the

---

[122]The Royal Commission of Legal Services (1981) commissioned and funded a number of sociolegal projects on the legal profession, which also stimulated later research. See Thomas, *Law in the Balance: Legal Services in the Eighties* (Oxford: OUP, 1981), and various publications stemming from research carried out by the Institute of Judicial Administration at the University of Birmingham including Bridges *et al.*, *Legal Services in Birmingham*, (Birmingham: Institute of Judicial Administration, 1975).

[123]Abel-Smith, Zander and Brooks, *Legal Problems and the Citizen*, (London: Heinemann, 1973); Morris, White and Lewis, *Social Needs and Legal Action*, (London: Martin Robertson, 1973); Byles and Morris, *Unmet Need: The Case of the Neighbourhood Law Centre* (London: Routledge, 1977); Zander, *Legal Services for the Community* (London: Temple Press, 1978); Grace and Wilkinson, *Negotiating the Law: Social Work and Legal Services* (London: Routledge, 1978).

[124]Cowan and Halliday, *The Appeal of Internal Review*, (Oxford: Hart, 2003). This work uses homelessness law and practice as an empirical case study to explore the wider question of explaining why most welfare applicants decide not to challenge adverse bureaucratic decisions despite experiencing a continuing sense of relevant need.

[125]Dingwell and Lewis, *The Sociology of the Professions: Lawyers, Doctors and Others*, (Oxford: SSRC, 1983).

[126]Calouste Gulbenkian Foundation, 1999.

[127]Leon Mayhew, *Law and Equal Opportunity*, (Cambridge MA: Harvard University Press, 1968).

[128]Simon Jolly, 'Family Law' in Thomas, 1997 *op. cit.*, 342.

[129]*Ibid.*, 353–4.

[130]Jolly suggests that the criticism of existing law and policy by Davis and Murch's, *The Grounds for Divorce* (Oxford: Clarendon, 1988) and J. Eekelaar's, *Regulating Divorce* (Oxford: OUP, 1991) have been influential in prompting recent legislative reforms. *Ibid.*, 346.

[131]Jolly, 'Family Law' in Thomas (1997), 342.

Brunel Centre for the Study of Law, the Child and the Family. Family law, which has succeeded in attracting 'more than its fair share' of government funding,[132] was one of the first civil law areas where the routine operation of *substantive* doctrinal rules and procedures was studied through empirically grounded sociolegal research.[133]

From the mid-1970s, the Oxford Centre researched the outcomes of custody dispositions on divorce, and the way divorce registrars (now District Judges) exercised their discretion.[134] This broad theme has featured as 'a constant ingredient' in the Oxford Centre's programme from 1972 onwards.[135] Beyond Oxford, other researchers have concentred on the role played by the actions and discretionary decision-making of other legal actors, registrars, judges, barristers and solicitors.[136]

Once sociolegal researchers realised that regulators could not automatically prosecute all violations of applicable legal measures, the issue of the exercise of discretion within the necessarily selective process of enforcement became an important theme for sociolegal research. This remains the case where one of the factors determining the exercise of such discretion is a perceived need to confront the collective awareness of commercial sectors, as well as individual violators. Such confrontations often attempt to disrupt and deter unlawful activity in order to realise broader regulatory standards.[137] Thus, one influential aspect of law in action addresses complex issues in the *selective enforcement* of legal measures in those contexts where discretion exists but its exercise is conditioned and restricted by a range of interpersonal, institutional and contextual factors.[138] Sociolegal researchers have found that these can include imperatives derived from a regulator's need to use the publicity, which has been generated by selective prosecutions, to send out symbolic messages to deter actual and potential violators of regulatory regimes.[139] For instance, one study explored the basis on which a sample of eighty-one divorce registrars exercised their considerable scope for discretion in deciding property and income redistributions upon divorce.[140]

---

[132]*Ibid*. See also ESRC, 1994 *op. cit.*

[133]McGregor, Blom-Cooper and Gibson, *Separated Spouses: A Study of the Matrimonial Jurisdiction of the Magistrate's Courts*, (London: Duckworth, 1970); Harris, 1983 *op. cit.*, 322. The Finer Committee on One-Parent Families (1974, Cmnd. 5629) commissioned a number of sociolegal research projects and survey, thus starting a continuing trend amongst policy-makers to link the reform process with empirical research data and findings in relations to perceived difficulties within the operation of the present system, and then to monitor the 'effectiveness' of later reforms. See Harris, 1983 *op. cit.*, 322–3.

[134]Eekelaar and Clive, *Custody After Divorce*, (Oxford: Oxford Centre for Socio-Legal Studies, 1977); Barrington Baker *et al.*, 1977.

[135]Hawkins, 1997 *op. cit.*, vii–viii; Dingwell and Eekelaar, 'Families and the State: An Historical Perspective on the Public Regulation of Private Conduct,' (1988) 10 *Law and Policy*, 341–61; Mavis Maclean, *Surviving Divorce: Women's resources after Separation*, (London: Macmillan, 1991).

[136]Eekelaar, 1991 *op. cit.*; Richard Ingleby, *Solicitors and Divorce* (Oxford: OUP, 1992).

[137]Susan Shapiro, *Wayward Capitalists: Target of the Securities and Exchange Commission*, (New Haven CT: Yale University Press, 1984).

[138]On the existence of widespread discretion amongst regulators, see Lloyd-Bostock, 'The Psychology of Routine Discretion: Accident Screening by British Factory Inspectors', (1992) 14 *Law and Policy*, 45–76; Hawkins (ed.), *The Uses of Discretion*, (Oxford: OUP, 1992).

[139]Paterson, 1982, *op. cit.* – indicating that a range of rhetorical and extra-doctrinal features shape the judicial process, including a sense of collective responsibility to other members of the court and the senior bar. Regarding the symbolic dimensions of enforcement, see Hawkins, 1984.

[140]Barrington Baker *et al.*, *The Matrimonial Jurisdiction of Registrars*, (Oxford: Centre for Socio-Legal Studies, 1977).

Family law and policy is an area of sociolegal studies where the results of empirical projects, and to a lesser extent theoretical studies, are regularly cited by mainstream student textbooks and academic journals. In this way, they filter into undergraduate teaching to a far greater extent than in most other areas of the legal curriculum, a point that may reassure some dissertation students who wish to combine aspects of doctrinal analysis with the application of sociolegal approaches.[141] These empirical results have also been used, albeit selectively, by policy-makers and law reform bodies, including the Law Commission. A number of empirical studies have addressed the reallocation of family resources,[142] disputes over the custody of children,[143] and the role of welfare officers in divorce hearings.[144] Other projects have studied the use of separation as an alternative to divorce,[145] quasi-legal and legal reactions to alleged child abuse,[146] and the long-term economic consequences of divorce for different types of family, including 'reconstituted families', and the associated issues of step-parenting.[147]

Students looking for a blueprint of well-established and respected sociolegal work within family law and policy could do far worse than follow the lead, in a scaled down way, of John Eekelaar's *Regulating Divorce*. This work provides a broad-ranging, contextual account that both describes and analyses official ideologies with respect to the perceived significance of marriage and divorce. Eekelaar discusses current legal provisions, various official statements and the policy assumptions underpinning case law. This sociolegal work reviews national and international research findings. Eekelaar not only places recent proposals for divorce reform within an historical perspective, but also evaluates the grounds on which financial arrangements are made upon divorce. His work also explores how the rights and interests of children are legally determined. It provides a broad perspective on the evolution of divorce law in the UK, an evaluation of the present law and a basis for future debates on proposed reforms.

In other writings adopting a contextual approach, Eekelaar and his collaborators have highlighted how empirical research reveals that family law operates as a key factor in defining, shaping and regulating contemporary family life, including enabling specific

---

[141]Jolly, in Thomas, 1997 *op. cit.*, 323. This development, which contrasts markedly with for example Land Law and Trusts student textbooks, was clear even from textbooks published in the early 1980s including Cretney, *Principles of Family Law* (London: Sweet and Maxwell, 2003) and Hoggett and Pearl, *The Family, Law and Society: Cases and Materials* (Butterworths, 1996); J. Eekelaar, *Family Law and Social Policy* (London: Weidenfeld and Nicolson, 1978) However, this has prompted some strong criticism; see R. Deech, 'Divorce Law and Empirical Studies' (1990) 106 *LQR* 229 to which Eekelaar and Maclean replied (1990) 106 *LQR* 621.

[142]Eekelaar and Maclean, *Maintenance After Divorce*, (Oxford, Clarendon, 1986), which found that it was very rare for divorced spouses to be fully supported financially by their former partner, and when this did occur it was mainly in contexts where there were children requiring financial support. Most maintenance payments benefited the state in terms of reduced eligibility for social security payments.

[143]Barrington Baker *et al.*, 1977 *op. cit.*; Eekelaar and Clive, *Custody After Divorce*, (Oxford: Centre for Socio-Legal Studies, 1977). The latter survey of 855 cases found that the deeply entrenched judicial assumption that children should remain in their current family home to avoid further disruption prevailed in 95% of cases, even where this was contrary to the conclusions of social workers' reports and lengthy court testimony.

[144]Murch, *Justice and Welfare in Divorce* (1980).

[145]Maidment, *Judicial Separation*, (Oxford: Centre for Socio-Legal Studies, 1982).

[146]Dingwell, Eekelaar and Murray, *The Protection of Children: State Intervention and Family Life* (Oxford: Blackwell, 1983).

[147]Eekelaar and Maclean, *Children and Divorce: Economic Factors*, (Oxford: Centre for Socio-Legal Studies, 1983); Masson *et al.*, *Yours, Mine or Ours* (London; HMSO, 1983); Eekelaar and Maclean, 'Property and Financial Adjustment after Divorce in the 1990s – Unfinished Business', in Hawkins, 1997 *op. cit.*, 225–44.

interventions designed to protect and enforce the legal rights of individual family members. Law's social function is thus shown to be enmeshed in a number of politically sensitive areas of social policy related to the ideological significance afforded to 'family values'.[148]

A different but equally noteworthy illustration of the sociolegal approach to the legal regulation of families is a project into how individuals distribute their share of family assets after death. Given the rapid post-war expansion of home-ownership and the rise in property prices, this topic is clearly of relevance to a growing proportion of UK families. The project included an empirical study of eight hundred English wills in order to identify their role. The research examined the developing patterns of bequeathing and distributing inherited wealth across different generations. The bequests included property, sums of money and valuable items of personal property.[149] The results provided interesting clues regarding changing patterns of contemporary family and kin relationships across a broad cross-section of society.

A recent theme has been the connection between sexuality and the legal definition and regulation of family and familial relations, including the changing legal orientation towards same-sex parent families.[150] Students interested in the practical implications of decision-making within family law might want to note Eekelaar's summary of the impact of two decades of empirical sociolegal research in family law and policy:

> Empirical research tends to undermine old certainties. It draws hitherto excluded information into the judgemental process. The costs of child-care itself, the lost opportunity costs which fall on the child's carers, the evaluation of the contributions to family life: these are all matters which must now be factored in to an assessment of the fairness of post-divorce outcomes.[151]

Family research into post-divorce financial arrangements has also benefited from the link between empirical issues and feminist legal theories regarding the persistence of patriarchal ideologies and practices both within and beyond the operation of the legal system provided by the writings of Carol Smart[152] and Katherine O'Donovan.[153] Further interesting developments concern attempts to draw upon comparative analysis, including international comparisons of post-divorce financial settlements.[154] Jolly notes that future sociolegal research will have come to terms with the growing importance of quasi-legal decision-making taking place outside the formalised procedures of the courtroom adjudication via the roles of the child support agency and mediators.[155]

---

[148]John Eekelaar and Mavis Maclean, *Family Law* (Oxford: OUP, 1995).

[149]See Janet Finch, Lynn Hayes, Jennifer Mason, Judith Masson and Lorraine Wallis, *Wills, Inheritance, and Families* (Oxford: OUP, 1996).

[150]Belinda Brooks-Gordon *et al.*, (eds), *Sexuality Repositioned: Diversity and the Law*, (Oxford: Hart, 2003).

[151]John Eekelaar, 'Property Adjustment After Divorce', in Hawkins, 1997 *op. cit.*, 240–41.

[152]C. Smart, *The Ties that Bind*, (London: Routledge, 1984); C. Smart and S. Sevenhuijsen (eds), *Child Custody and the Politics of Gender*, (London: Routledge, 1989).

[153]K. O'Donovan, *Sexual Divisions in Law*, (London: Weidenfeld and Nicolson, 1985).

[154]M. Maclean, 1991 *op. cit.*

[155]Gwynn Davis, *Partisans and Mediators*, (Oxford: OUP, 1988); C. Piper, *The Responsible Parent* (Hemel Hempstead: Harvester, 1993); Dingwell and Greatbatch, 'The Virtues of Formality' in Eekelaar and Maclean (eds) 1994 *op. cit.*

The legal regulation of commercial enterprises via contracts and other legal devices[156] and the subject of compensation for industrial accidents[157] have remained popular areas of sociolegal research,[158] even permeating, to a limited extent, the pages of certain student textbooks.[159] One strand of research, which concerned the legal regulation of employment terms and conditions, has focused on the practical role of employment 'rights' as adopted by specific social movements. It considers how the deployment of a rights-based agenda can channel, but also restrict, their scope of action.[160] Campbell argues that the need for sociolegal rather than doctrinal approaches to employment contracts was recognised at an early stage by scholars:

> Following from the 'peculiar' qualities of labour-power as a commodity, the social dimensions of labour law are relatively manifest by comparison to other types of contract and the flat failures of trying to resolve labour issues by classical contractual reasoning are equally so. Under these circumstances, in which welfarist intervention (was, but even now) is the most obvious feature of labour law, the need for a broadly socio-legal approach relatively urgently impresses itself.[161]

Other projects focusing on the legal regulation of the workplace have addressed the role that specific organisations can play mediating between formal law and its practical enforcement in specific situations.[162] This general area of legal regulation is a field where multidisciplinary projects involving the collaboration of legal academics and economists has, in a number of cases, proved particularly fruitful. As with family law and policy, the establishment of Government Royal Commissions and related inquiries have resulted in official funding for sociolegal projects, which in turn have inspired later studies.[163]

Members of the Oxford Centre have conducted a multidisciplinary survey of 15,000 households to identify a representative sample of families affected by illness and injury. The survey concentrated on the actual workings of aspects of the tort of negligence, and of official social security and social services systems in relation to the diverse legal, social and economic consequences of injuries and illness. It also focused on the support offered to affected parties by employers, private insurance and community groups. This research revealed that only a fraction of those legally eligible to use the rights afforded

---

[156]The debate over the contribution of sociolegal studies to contract law addressed in more detail below is clearly relevant here as well. See Stuart Macauley, 28 *Amer Sociological Rev* 55 (1963); Beale and Dugdale, 2 *Brit J Law and Society* 45 (1975); Atiyah, *The Rise and Fall of Freedom of Contract* (Oxford: OUP: 1979).

[157]Atiyah, *Accidents, Compensation and the Law*, (London: Weidenfeld and Nicolson, 1970 and later editions).

[158]Ross Cranston, *Regulating Business, Law and Consumer Agencies*, (London: Macmillan, 1979); Bridget Hutter, *Compliance, Legal Regulation and the Environment*, (Oxford: Clarendon 1997); Baldwin, *Rules and Government*, (Oxford: Clarendon, 1995); Hawkins, *The Regulation of Health and Safety: A Socio-legal Perspective*, Report to Health and Safety Executive, (Oxford: Oxford Centre for Socio-Legal Studies, 1992); Lloyd-Bostock, 1992 *op. cit.*; S. Dawson *et al.*, *Safety at Work: The Limits of Self-Regulation*, (Cambridge: CUP, 1988).

[159]Tom Hadden, *Company Law and Capitalism* (London: Weidenfeld and Nicolson, 1972 and later editions).

[160]Levine, 1990 *op. cit.*, 28 addressing project work carried out at the University of Wisconsin by Michael McCann.

[161]Campbell, in Thomas 1997 *op. cit.*, 243.

[162]*Ibid.*, with reference to ongoing work by Lauren Edelman.

[163]The Pearson Royal Commission on Civil Liability and Compensation for Personal Injury (1978 Cmnd. 7054) accepted a significant role for empirical research and funded a variety of relevant sociolegal projects published in Vol. 11 of its final report. Other studies include Sally Wheeler, *Reservation of Title Clauses: Impact and Implications*, (Oxford: Clarendon, 1991b).

to them in theory by tort law made successful use of the legal system. The researchers were able to illustrate once again the considerable gap between legal rights in principle and those made available in practice.[164] This work complemented earlier American studies which had also highlighted the gap between rights 'in principle' under Tort Law, and the impact upon compensation of various institutional pressures operating within the insurance industry, including the imperative to 'close files quickly'.[165]

Sociolegal research has broken new ground in the field of company law, business finance and the law. Studies have addressed the role of insolvency lawyers,[166] the role of lawyers in commercial disputes,[167] the regulation of risk in the context of corporate finance and the development of a series of studies on 'creative compliance' in, for example, the fields of taxation.[168] Other sociolegal projects have studied the ideological aspects of the emergence of commercial law codes,[169] the use of contractual remedies between those involved in business transactions,[170] and the interaction of consumer agencies and business.[171] Wheeler suggests that, in the future, sociolegal studies 'can offer an empirically informed assessment of the impact of different legal structures and its links with policy formulators [to] . . . put the whole issue of wider [corporate] governance more firmly on the agenda in the age of accountability, which until now, in the context of company law in the UK, has centred on accountability to a relatively small and privileged group.'[172] With respect to creative compliance within the corporate sectors, McBarnet and Whelan's research suggests that:

> Creative compliance can be an expensive strategy, requiring major inputs in legal technicality and innovation. It is therefore characteristically – though not perhaps inevitably – a feature of the world of economic elites and large-scale corporations in corporate finance, taxation, takeovers and bankruptcy, or in battles for market share. In this context, legal control – both state regulations and the controls of private law – can become just another obstacle to be overcome in the pursuit of economic and competitive advantage.[173]

---

[164]Harris *et al.*, *Compensation and Support for Illness and Injury*, (Oxford: Clarendon, 1984); Hazel Genn, *Meeting Legal Needs? An Evaluation of a Scheme for Personal Injury Victims*, (Oxford: Centre for Socio-Legal Studies, 1982); Hazel Genn, *Hard Bargaining: Out of Court Settlements in Personal Injury*, (Oxford: Clarendon, 1987). The collaboration of academic lawyers with economists has also proved useful in the area of tort and personal injury.

[165]Laurance Ross, *Settled Out of Court: The Social Process of Insurance Claims Adjustments*, (NY: Aldine, 1970).

[166]Sally Wheeler, 'Capital Fractionalized: The Role of Insolvency Practitioners in Asset Distribution' in Cain and Harrington (eds), *Lawyers in a Postmodern World*, (Buckingham: Open University Press, 1994).

[167]Wheeler, 1991a *op. cit.*

[168]Doreen McBarnet, 'Law, Policy and Avoidance', (1988) 15 *JLS*, 113–21; 'Whiter than White Collar Crime: Tax, Fraud Insurance and the Management of Stigma', (1992) 52 *British Journal of Sociology*, 323–44; McBarnet and Whelan, 'The Elusive Spirit of the Law: Formalism and the Struggle for Legal Control', 54 (1991) *MLR*, 848–73; McBarnet and Whelan, 'Creative Compliance and the Defeat of Legal Control: The Magic of the Orphan Subsidiary', in Hawkins, 1997 *op. cit.*, 177–98.

[169]R. Ferguson 'Legal Ideology and Commercial Interests: The Social Origins of the Commercial law Codes' (1977) 4 *British J. of Law and Society*, 18.

[170]Beale and Dugdale, 'Contracts Between Businessmen: Planning and the Use of Contractual Remedies' (1975) 2 *British J. of Law and Society*, 45; R. Ferguson, 'The Adjudication of Commercial Disputes and the Legal System in Modern England' (1980) 7 *British J. of Law and Society*, 141.

[171]R. Cranston, 'Regulating Business: Law and Consumer Agencies', (London: Macmillan, 1979).

[172]Wheeler, in Thomas, 1997 *op. cit.*, 296.

[173]McBarnet and Whelan, in Hawkins, 1997 *op. cit.*, 178.

These writers provide a case study of the nature, risks and legal challenges posed by creative compliance. They focus on the use of one legal device in the context of a number of comparatively small companies who were able to raise very large sums for use in the mega-takeovers in the late 1980s.[174] One conclusion merits attention, not least because of its relevance to wider debates regarding the cat-and-mouse game played between legal regulators and regulated enterprises. Here, the legal prohibitions and requirements operate simultaneously as both a means for regulatory control, and a fertile source for ways of avoiding legal barriers to the realisation of economic goals:

> Creative compliance is directed at, and based on, current law, *whatever* that law may be. If legal control seems to be constantly lagging behind current practice, it is quite simply because current practice is geared to staying ahead of legal control and using the law in creative ways to achieve this. New laws may effectively control old devices, but new law will also stimulate attempts to find new devices based upon them. Creative compliance thus poses its own challenges for control. By complying with the letter of the law rather than breaching it, it poses a challenge for enforcement, while its inherent dynamism poses a challenge for those seeking to formulate laws comprehensive enough to capture all possible devices. Yet unless creative compliance can be effectively controlled, legal policies will be constantly vulnerable to being routinely nullified by legal creativity.... The courts have thwarted some devices, and caught in the enforcement net those using them, by rejecting literal interpretations of the requirements of the law in favour of a purposeful approach ... or by moving the goal-posts after the event by introducing a 'new approach'.[175]

Sally Wheeler has edited a collection of essays which provide students with examples of a sociolegal alternative to black-letter accounts of Company Law interpreted as a complex set of autonomous rules shaped by statute and common law.[176] This collection examines relevant *empirical* studies of the role played by company law measures within real instances of business enterprises of all sizes, including multinationals. It addresses the manner in which firms are organised, and their internal constitution in relation to the different roles played, in practice, by shareholders, directors, employees and managers. Other contributors have studied the gendered aspects of corporate law and practice.[177]

The field of criminal justice, criminology, policing and the sociology of deviance have, from the earliest developments onwards, been strongly represented in sociolegal conferences and publications.[178] One of the reasons why the Oxford Centre prioritised civil justice studies was to avoid duplicating the already well-established efforts of sociolegal

---

[174]*Ibid.*

[175]*Ibid.*, 196–7.

[176]Sally Wheeler, (ed.), *The Law of the Business Enterprise: Selected Essays* (Oxford: Clarendon Press, 1995).

[177]Smith, 'Women, the Family and Corporate Capitalism' in Stephenson (ed.) *Women in Canada*, (Toronto: General Publishing Co. 1977); Lahey and Salter, 'Corporate Law in Legal Theory and Legal Scholarship: From Classicism to Feminism' (1985) 23 *Osgoode Hall LJ* 543.

[178]The work of McBarnet, such as 'False Dichotomies in Criminal Justice Research', in Baldwin and Bottomley (eds), *Criminal Justice*, (Oxford: OUP, 1978), *Conviction: Law, State and Construction of Justice* (London: Macmillan, 1981) and Maureen Cain, *Society and the Policeman's Role* (London: Routledge, 1973) and Pat Carlen's *Magistrates' Justice* (London: Martin Robertson, 1976) were significant and influential milestones. See also K. Kusum, *Juvenile Delinquency: A Socio-Legal Study*, (New Delhi: KLM, 1979).

work in criminal justice areas.[179] Law and economics scholarship has developed a sociolegal model of 'optimal deterrence' under which 'individuals and firms will predictably comply with the law only if the expected cost to them of violation (the sanction and other costs from the criminal process, discounted by the probability of escaping detection and conviction) exceed the benefits of violation.'[180] This American model has, however, proved poor at predicting behaviour in British regulatory contexts. Hence, others have modified the model to explain the economic factors encouraging firms to bargain with regulators and to comply with less stringent standards that may approximate what is 'economically desirable behaviour'.[181]

More generally, Harris notes how one result of developments within qualitative social science approaches to the sociology of deviance 'was to question the definitions of crime, which in turn led analysts into the realm of law itself'.[182] For example, Ian Sanderson's work, *Criminal Justice*,[183] provides a critical analysis of the policy dimension with respect to different stages of the criminal justice system, including the exercise of police powers on the street, particularly stop and search and arrest, and the investigation and trial of suspected offenders. This law in action book sets doctrinal issues in wider sociolegal/sociological contexts, focusing on the manner in which formal legal rules are operated in practice, and the impact of their selective enforcement. This approach allows a critical review of possible reform initiatives.[184] American sociolegal literature on the criminal justice process is vast, including noteworthy studies on routine plea-bargaining within lower courts that challenged the received wisdom that such practices were necessitated by heavy urban caseloads.[185]

From the early 1970s onwards, studies of the changing patterns of the selective implementation of legal powers by various government or quasi-governmental bodies regulating industry and commerce have provided a well-developed, and continuing, strand of sociolegal research.[186] At its most comprehensive, the theme of regulation addresses the major phases of the regulatory process. These include such issues as:

- Who was responsible for exposing the hazards requiring regulation, and what were their motivations?[187]

- Through which stages did the legislative programme go through prior to enactment?

- Who were the main actors and interest groups engaging in a complex political process involving bargaining the measures through Parliament and overcoming various sources of resistance?

---

[179]Hawkins, 1997 *op. cit.*, Prologue, 8. However, the use of criminal law in the regulatory field was addressed in the 1970s precisely because criminology research centres had largely neglected this topic.

[180]Ogus, 1995 *op. cit.*, 30.

[181]*Ibid.* – citing Fenn and Veljanovski, 'A Positive Theory of Regulatory Enforcement' (1988) 98 *Economics J.* 1055.

[182]Harris, 1983, *op. cit.*, 317.

[183]Ian Sanderson, (London: Butterworths, 1997).

[184]See also the contextual and policy-oriented aspects of Katherine Doolin, *Criminal Justice*, 2nd edn, (London: Sweet and Maxwell, 2002).

[185]Malcolm Feeley, *The Process is the Punishment*: *Handling Cases in a Lower Criminal Court*, (NY: Russell Sage, 1979).

[186]Harris, 1983 *op. cit.*, 324.

[187]Bartrip and Hartwell, in Hawkins, 1997, 49, 59–60.

- How was the legislation creating the regulative policy goals justified?

- How were such goals translated into action through specific enforcement practices exhibiting varying degrees of discretion,[188] and resultant patterns of limited compliance[189] (or selective 'creative compliance'),[190] or 'regulatory capture',[191] by those whose behaviour is subject to such regulatory schemes?[192]

One question that a student dissertation in this field may usefully ask is whether the apparent compliance with the letter of regulatory law is, in practice, realising the standards and goals underpinning the regulatory scheme? This issue may become particularly clear if the rules are framed in ways that are either too broad or too narrow, such that conduct not intended to be regulated is encompassed or conduct intended to be regulated falls outside the measures.[193] Sociolegal work has addressed, in both empirical and theoretical ways, perceived problems in the efficiency and effectiveness of traditional 'command and control' forms of public sector regulation that exercise influence by imposing standards backed by criminal sanctions. Such works include recent critiques from those committed to free-market models of self-regulation, such as incentive-based regimes, disclosure regulation and market-harnessing controls, which are offered as alternatives to 'command and control' regulatory techniques.[194] These critical studies have highlighted discrepancies between the actual operation of regulatory schemes and their ostensible aims – and thus sources of legitimacy.[195] If student dissertations follow this strand of legal research, it may be possible to address questions not only of the instrumental 'efficiency' of various regulatory models, but also wider issues of fairness and accountability.[196] In addition to various historical studies, Carson, for instance, has studied the occupational health-and-safety aspects of the North Sea Oil industry.[197]

Students interested in how discretion operates in practice within a specific area of legal regulation might want to note that there have been a number of studies of the operation of discretion within the selective official enforcement of government regulation, particularly the enforcement of anti-pollution and environmental measures more generally, and with respect to consumer safety.[198] Such studies indicate the extent to which

---

[188]*Ibid.*; Baldwin (1995); Hutter 1988; Fenn and Veljanovski, 'A Positive Theory of Regulatory Enforcement', (1988) 98 *Economics Journal*, 1055.

[189]Bartrip and Hartwell, 1997 *op. cit.*, 49, 59–60; Keith Hawkins, 'Compliance Strategy, Prosecution Policy and Aunt Sally – a Comment on Peirce and Tombs', (1990) 30 *British Journal of Criminology*, 444.

[190]On creative compliance within the law in the fields of business finance involving using legal materials and devices to avoid law's requirements, to escape legal control, without actually contravening these requirements, see McBarnet and Whelan, 'Creative Compliance and the Defeat of Legal Control: The Magic of the Orphan Subsidiary', in Hawkins, 1997 *op. cit.*, 177–98.

[191]That is, the exertion of excessive influence over the regulatory process by those industries subject to regulation. See Bartrip and Hartwell, in Hawkins 1997 *op. cit.*, 48.

[192]*Ibid.*, 324.

[193]Robert Baldwin, 'Regulation After "Command and Control"' in Hawkins, 1997 *op. cit.*, 65–84, at 67–8.

[194]Baldwin, in Hawkins, 1997 *op. cit.* On market-oriented alternatives, see S. Breyer, *Regulation and Its Reform*, (Cambridge MA: Harvard University Press, 1982); Stewart, 'Regulation and the Crisis of Legislation in the United States', in T. Daintith, *Law as an Instrument of Social Policy*, (Berlin: Walter de Gruyter, 1988).

[195]Baldwin, in Hawkins, 1997 *op. cit.*

[196]*Ibid.*, 81.

[197]Carson, *The Other Price of Britain's Oil* (London: Martin Robertson, 1982).

[198]Gunningham, *Pollution, Social Interest and the Law* (London: Martin Robertson, 1974); Paulus, *The Search for Pure Food*, (London: Martin Robertson, 1974); Ross Cranston, *Regulating Business: Law and Consumer Agencies* (London: Macmillan, 1979); Harris, 1983 *op. cit.*, 324–5.

prosecution for regulatory enforcement frequently operates as a last resort where the regulator's preferred strategies of persuasion and negotiation have clearly failed to ensure broad compliance.[199] These and later studies suggest that regulators are subject to various internal organisational pressures to adapt patterns of law enforcement in the light of the interests of their employers' own institutional imperatives. These imperatives can be contradictory. Researchers may discover that this is particularly likely where, as in the case of water pollution, regulatory agencies need to strike a working balance between appearing effective to the wider public and still maintaining cooperative relations with actual and potential industrial polluters.[200] Indeed, studies of the enforcement of regulatory controls over water pollution in Britain caused by industrial enterprises have confirmed the existence of a wide range of discretion.[201]

Sociolegal research in this area could prompt students to raise wider-ranging questions. For example, the broadly focused study by Gunningham and Johnstone draws upon empirical evidence and recent developments in regulatory theory in order to explore the following question: how can legal measures influence the internal self-regulation of organisations to make their practices more responsive to occupational health-and-safety concerns?[202] This study suggests that occupational health-and-safety management systems have the potential to stimulate models of self-organisation within enterprises that prompt critical and self-reflective practices regarding their performance with respect to occupational health-and-safety standards. The authors propose a two-track system of regulation, under which firms are offered a choice between a continuation of traditional forms of legal regulation, and the adoption of a safety management system-based approach. Their book also includes a discussion of how criminal and administrative sanctions are able to provide enterprises with positive incentives to adopt effective occupational health-and-safety management systems.[203]

If such wide issues appear too daunting for a dissertation, students may wish to consider emulating studies into the legal profession. Unsurprisingly, another cluster of empirical sociolegal research projects concern the legal decision-making processes, particularly the structure, form and operation of legal procedures used within court and tribunal hearings during both civil and criminal justice systems.[204] A number of studies have used methods of direct observation and the tape-recording of proceedings, which has made possible the systematic analysis of patterns of verbal exchange between different

---

[199]See Bartrip and Hartwell, in Hawkins, 1997 *op. cit.*, 48; Peacock, (ed.), *The Regulation Game*, (Oxford: Blackwell, 1984); Bridget Hutter, *Regulation and Risk: Occupational Health and Safety on the Railways*, (Oxford: OUP, 2001), 104 – noting that prosecution for a breach was sometimes defined as a sign of individual failure by HSE inspectors.

[200]Hawkins, *Environment and Enforcement: Regulation and the Social Definition of Pollution* (Oxford: OUP, 1984).

[201]Richardson *et al.*, *Policing Pollution: A Study of Regulation and Enforcement*, (Oxford: Clarendon, 1983); Hawkins, 1984 *op. cit.*

[202]Neil Gunningham and Richard Johnstone, *Rethinking Occupational Health and Safety Regulation: Two Track Regulatory Reform*, (Oxford: OUP, 1999).

[203]For other contributions to sociolegal interpretations of regulation, see Ian Ayres and John Braithwaite, *Responsive Regulation: Transcending the Deregulation Debate* (Oxford: OUP, 1994).

[204]Pat Carlen, 1976 *op. cit.*; Bottoms and Maclean, *Defendants in the Criminal Process* (London: Routledge, 1976); Maxwell Atkinson, *Discovering Suicide* (London: Macmillan, 1978); Wilkinson, *Bibliography on the Social Organisation of Disputes and Dispute Processes*, (Oxford: Oxford Centre for Socio-Legal Studies, 1980); Harris, 1983 *op. cit.*, 322.

parties.[205] Projects at the Oxford Centre, for example, have sought to relate empirical analysis of the structuring of exchanges within civil and criminal proceedings both by rules of evidence and by less formal protocols to 'policy debates about the relative merits of alternative methods of dispute settlement'.[206]

It is arguable that sociolegal studies have not been sufficiently concerned to provide an alternative approach to the conduct of research within substantive areas of law and legal doctrine. Indeed, this approach to the conduct of legal research and analysis is not usually interested in the legal doctrine studied by researchers using the black-letter approach to analyse rules and principles. On the contrary, it is generally more interested in the social, economic and political factors that shape law-making on the input side of the equation, and, on the output side, the various cultural, economic and political consequences of the selective enforcement of different laws by officials, including the basis on which discretion is being exercised in practice. For example, within the sixteen chapters of Cownie and Bradney's *English Legal System in Context* there are extended analyses of the social and economic sources and impact of specific legal rules, combined with accounts of law as shaped by, but as also influencing, its historical and social context.

On the other hand, it is important to recall that aspects of legal doctrine can and have been studied by sociolegal scholars, and that research into doctrine does not have to be exclusively from a black-letter perspective. Indeed, one sociolegal oriented law journal has recently noted that:

> Thus while sociolegal studies may have first emerged and thrived by casting its eye elsewhere than on legal doctrine (the lawyer's terrain), the recent attention to cultural studies in almost all disciplines and fields of human life (from the arts to medicine, science, and politics, as well as law) has brought more legal doctrine within the purview of sociolegal studies. Our coding of 'content analysis' may reflect this shift.[207]

● The Emphasis on Law in Action

One feature of sociolegal research that may particularly appeal to students with a prior background in legal practice is its attention to law in action, to the practical impact of how law actually functions in society. We have already noted that a major early stimulus in the development of sociolegal studies in the UK was an attempt to remedy the negative consequences of the 'gap' between law in action and law in books. Sociolegal research frequently addresses law in action in the sense that it seeks to gain empirical knowledge of the actions, relationships and attitudes of parties affected by legal proceedings. Even in fields where there are many thousands of academic articles written from a black-letter perspective, there often remains a lack of empirical knowledge

---

[205]Atkinson and Drew, *Order in Court: The Organisation of Verbal Interaction in Judicial Settings* (London: Macmillan, 1979); Danet, 'Language in the Legal Process' 14 *Law and Society Review* 445 (1980); Levi, *Linguistics, Language and Law: A Topical Bibliography* (Bloomington: Indiana University Press, 1982); William O'Barr, *Linguistic Evidence: Language, Power and Strategy in the Courtroom*, (NY: Academic Press, 1982); Pomerantz and Atkinson, 'Ethnomethodology, Conversation Analysis and the Study of Courtroom Interaction', in Muller, Blackman and Chapman, *Topics in Psychology and Law*, (Chichester: Wiley, 1983).

[206]Harris, 1983 *op. cit.*, 322.

[207]'From the Editor,' (2000) 34 *Law and Soc'y Review* 859.

regarding what, for example, individuals involved in civil disputes at the 'pre-trial stage' are actually doing, how they are defining their situation and negotiating with other affected parties. This 'gap' has provoked sociolegal researchers.[208] A similar point applies to the routine actions, knowledge and orientations of different branches of, for instance, the legal profession faced with a variety of challenges. These challenges include those posed by clients' complaints of professional negligence,[209] and the involvement of lawyers in various types of commercial practice.[210]

In these, and many other areas, sociolegal research addresses what appears to be actually taking place on the ground. For example, one empirical project indicated that the percentage of divorced women having contact with at least one child was fewer among the remarried cohort, indicating that any public policy of encouraging remarriage cannot be based on the idea that this will always strengthen family ties and ensure improved childcare.[211] Other empirical sociolegal projects have also expressed caution about possible reform proposals, such as the reduction of the rights of the accused not to have their prior criminal record revealed to the jury.[212]

Another empirical sociolegal study of the experience of family breakdown focused on how parents cope financially on separation and divorce. This study sought to add to what is already known about the financial changes and difficulties that families undergo when parents separate, and how different family members respond to the issues these changes create. This initially descriptive aspect is supplemented by the researchers' concern for the specific policy implications of their empirical findings, particularly with respect to 'the continuing debate concerning the desirability of establishing a statutory objective and set of principles to guide those seeking to arrive at financial settlements on divorce'.[213]

Sociolegal researchers have reinterpreted many legal issues as essentially empirical in nature, which have traditionally been viewed as requiring either a formalist or jurisprudential analysis. This includes studies of the practical impact of enacting human rights measures in national contexts, which aim to 'penetrate the internal workings of domestic legal systems to see the law in action – as it is developed, contested, manipulated, or even ignored by actors such as judges, lawyers, civil servants, interest groups, and others'.[214] Dissertation students might find it interesting to note that Philip Lewis maintains that,

---

[208]Hawkins, 1997 *op. cit.*, vii.

[209]See William Felstiner, 'Professional Inattention: Origins and Consequences' and Philip Lewis, 1997; 'Knowing the Buzzwords and Clapping for Tinkerbell: The Context, Content and Qualities of Lawyers' Knowledge in a Specialised Industrial Field', both in Hawkins, 1997 *op. cit.*, 121–50 and 151–76 respectively.

[210]Ross Cranston, 'Doctrine and Practice in Commercial Law', in Hawkins, 1997 *op. cit.*, 199–224.

[211]See W. Solomou *et al.*, 'The Parent–Child Relationship in Later Life', in A. Bainham *et al.*, *What is a Parent? A Socio-Legal Analysis* (Oxford: Hart, 1999).

[212]Sally Lloyd-Bostock, 'The Effects on Juries of Hearing about the Defendant's Previous Record,' *Crim. L Rev.* (2000): 734 'This paper reports an experiment examining the effects of revealing a previous conviction to simulated jurors. The results indicate that the information evokes stereotypes of typical criminality, and that caution over revealing a defendant's criminal record is well justified. . . . If we assume that, amongst defendants with similar previous convictions, some are innocent of the current offence, we have good grounds to infer that routinely revealing previous convictions would indeed increase the risk of convicting an innocent man' *Ibid.*, at 755.

[213]Gillian Douglas and Alison Perry, 'How Parents Cope Financially on Separation and Divorce – Implications for the Future of Ancillary Relief', (2001) *CFam* 13.1(67).

[214]See Halliday and Schmidt (eds), *Human Rights Brought Home*, (Oxford: Hart, 2004) as described at http://www.hart.oxi.net/bookdetails.asp?id=539&bnd=0.

---

whilst it is possible to derive some understanding of legal topics from materials within law libraries, these are no substitute for detailed, empirical sociolegal studies. Such studies of law in action can address, for instance, the nature and use of legal knowledge. Lewis argues that by conducting interviews with those involved in participating in legal culture, legal researchers can reveal far more regarding the distribution of their topics, the extent to which they are deployed in practice, and the significance afforded to their practice use: 'Interviews, on the other hand, allowed an opportunity to ask what skills were actually used in practice, and which were most significant.'[215]

With respect to research into lawyer-client interactions, Felstiner's review of the empirical sociolegal literature concluded by arguing that, in addition to gathering empirical data through interviews, it can be worthwhile undertaking direct observations of law in action: 'One of the many things in life to be suspicious of is conventional wisdom. We only begin to approach what we know by going out into the field and looking at the questions as hard and systematically as we can ... [by] talking to lawyers and watching them work.'[216] With reference to the Oxford Centre's studies on compensation for illness and injury, Baldwin notes:

> Such research has manifested a concern that administrative and legal mechanisms should be tested for their appropriateness to particular tasks and a belief that the way such mechanisms operate on the ground should be the focus of attention.[217]

This emphasis on studying law in action meant sociolegal researchers posing a series of previously *unasked questions* regarding how law is actually operating in practice. This task can only be realised through researchers undertaking a rigorously empirical analysis of legal topics through the application of social scientific research methods capable of generating new data.[218]

Another particularly rich study of law in action is Keith Hawkins' *Law as a Last Resort*.[219] This work argues that prosecution decisions in the field of health and safety at work need to be understood not as individual responses to singular events, but rather in a wider institutional context. He develops an analytical framework, which students may find particularly helpful as a model for their own work. This framework consists of three broad organising ideas: surround, field and frame. Regulators typically deployed these to explain decision-making environments, formal structure and practice, and their own theories of compliance. By the idea of 'surround', Hawkins refers to the wider political and economic constraints and influences on regulators' behaviour as well as the local environments in different contexts. His category of 'field' denotes the set of boundaries shaping the range of actions a decision-maker can make. These include the legislative framework as well as less formal enforcement policy and public symbolism for a number of different audiences. Finally, the category of 'frame' relates to the interpretative work of regulators, their way of 'framing', or making sense and justifying, their decisions regarding compliance and punishment. Framing includes specific assumptions about the

---

[215]Lewis, 1997 *op. cit.*, 161.

[216]Felstiner, 1997 *op. cit.*

[217]Robert Baldwin, 'Regulation: After "Command and Control"', in Hawkins, 1997 *op. cit.*, 65.

[218]See Freeman's characterisation of sociolegal studies in *Lloyd's Introduction to Jurisprudence*, 6th edn, (London: Stevens, 1995), 538.

[219]Keith Hawkins, *Law as Last Resort: Prosecution Decision-Making in a Regulatory Agency*, (Oxford: OUP, 2002).

actual and likely effectiveness of different actions, how different levels of prosecution reflect on the perceived efficiency of the organisation and its employees.

The strong emphasis that sociolegal studies places on studying law in action is frequently justified by reference to the gap between law in books, such as rules and institutional protocols enshrined in cases and statutes, and the reality of law as it is actually selectively applied and experienced by different groups in society. For example, Hazel Genn and Alan Paterson conducted a wide-ranging survey of public use of, and attitudes towards, the civil justice system in Scotland. This study focused on the experiences of citizens in Scotland who were trying to handle the types of problems and disputes that could ultimately result in civil litigation.[220] Another recent study by Claire Archbold and others addressed the manner in which near-identical legislative schemes regarding divorce can, due to variations in the situation and context of regional legal cultures, operate differently in various parts of the UK. This work was structured around the stated belief that 'Roscoe Pound's 1910 observation that law in books and law in action are very different,'[221] is at the heart of sociolegal research.'[222] As a way of justifying their emphasis upon the informal influences exerted by lawyers and their clients, particularly the 'lawyers' shared view of law as founded as much upon fact-based argument and strategy, as upon legal doctrine . . . on the textbook law of the State which they negotiate and interpret in their day-to-day lives', these writers elaborated Pound's point as follows:

> Pound's statement that law in books is different from law in practice would today come as a surprise to few practising lawyers. In the academic world too, there are by now perhaps as many dissidents from as adherents to the positivist belief in law 'as a system of rules which can be applied to given facts in a courtroom', and the nature, extent and significance of the differences between book law and law in practice has been mapped by many contemporary legal academics, interested in the complex, dynamic nature of law and the way in which the making of 'legal' norms is inevitably influenced by the situation and context of the formal law. Some of the best-known socio-legal investigations into this process have put different relationships within it under the microscope.[223]

This sociolegal study places particular emphasis upon how a divorce system can develop and be reshaped less through formal state law than by means of informal processes of legal culture involving a complex dialogue between State officials, lawyers and clients, each of whom bring to this process their 'competing needs, agendas and perceptions'.[224] Many sociolegal researchers consider that the existence and demonstration of this 'gap' between law in books and law in action within many areas of legal regulation contradicts a central tenet of the black-letter approach. In short, one distinctive feature of sociolegal studies, which student dissertations may wish to emulate, is an emphasis on studying law in action. This can include focusing upon the question of how different types of

---

[220]Genn and Paterson, *Paths To Justice In Scotland*, (Oxford: Hart, 2001).

[221]See Roscoe Pound, 'Law in Books and Law in Action' (1910) 44 *American Law Review* 12.

[222]Claire Archbold *et al.*, 'Divorce Law and Divorce Culture – The Case of Northern Ireland' (1998) 10 *CFam* 377.

[223]*Ibid.*

[224]*Ibid.*

regulator exercise discretion in different contexts of application, and the factors shaping and guiding this and the practical implications for law enforcement.

● Policy and the Power of Ideologies

We noted in the previous chapter that one defining characteristic of the black-letter approach is the downplaying of policy aspects and other ideological dimensions of the legal process. By contrast, dissertation students who adopt a sociolegal methodology may well pay particular attention to how the policy underlying the application and enforcement of current law and forms of legal proceedings affect different groups in society.[225] Other sociolegal projects seek to influence policy either directly, as has been the case within family law particularly, or over time, within discussions over the adequacy of compensation for injuries in tort: 'by changing the nature of the debate so ideas and opinions begin to change'.[226] This link to policy is another sense in which sociolegal studies can be considered to focus on 'law in action'.[227] To take an extreme example, Richard Abel's work on the impact of apartheid laws in South Africa during the final decade of that racist regime has attracted positive reviews, noting that his adoption of a sociolegal methodology has resulted in an interesting new focus on the experienced impact of legal controls:

> Abel's methodology shifts the focus from the terms of the statutes themselves and the broad impact they have had, to struggles over their implementation in particular contexts. By detailing the specific steps in the application of these laws, including bureaucratic arrogance, ineptitude and viciousness as well as the countersteps of individuals, communities, and lawyers, Abel presents a picture of the law as it fares in the lives of those affected. So, for example, in discussing the pass laws – which formed one of the basic elements of colonial and apartheid control by denying freedom of movement to Africans – Abel does not describe and criticize the legislative design but rather focuses on the struggle of Veli Willie Komani to bring his wife to live with him in Cape Town . . . In so doing he not only reveals the complex and contradictory process of legal challenges to apartheid legislation, but provides a detailed and textured account of the ways in which the law operated in the

---

[225]See, for instance, Joan Hunt, 'A Moving Target – Care Proceedings as a Dynamic Process', (1998) *CFam* 10.3(281), an empirical study effectively contrasting the formal position on care proceedings as represented by black-letter textbooks with the great fluidity of law in action: 'The formal conceptualisation of care proceedings embedded in the Children Act 1989, as in the preceding statute law, remains the traditional one of trial and adjudication: the local authority as complainant brings an action to obtain compulsory powers, the family members, as respondents, have an opportunity to challenge, the court considers the evidence and determines whether the case has been made out and the remedy sought should be granted. The reality, however, is very different, as this article will seek to demonstrate. Research into proceedings both before and after the Children Act 1989 reveals a much more fluid and characteristically dynamic picture, which has major implications for policy and practice within the family justice system.' (abstract); David Cowan, *Housing: Participation and Exclusion. Collected Papers from the Socio-Legal Studies Annual Conference 1997, Cardiff University of Wales*, (Aldershot: Ashgate, 1998); Sally Wheeler, *Reservation of Title Clauses: Impact and Implications*, (Oxford: Clarendon, 1991).

[226]ESRC, 'Review of Socio-Legal Studies: Final Report (Swindon: ESRC, 1994), 17 – quoted in Wade Mansell, 'Tort and Socio-Legal Studies' in Thomas, 1997 *op. cit.*, 222.

[227]Gwynn Davis, Nick Wikeley and Richard Young, with Jacqueline Barron and Julie Bedward, *Child Support in Action*, (Oxford: Hart, 1999). The authors emphasised how individual claims to justice collide with the rigidities of formulaic assessment, and found that many people are not in supposedly 'typical' situations. The implication is that the formulaic approach to the assessment of child support cannot cope with the 'atypical'.

hands of the apartheid state and its opponents. . . . Abel has deployed a sociolegal methodology to produce a record of the multiple, ambiguous and at times contradictory roles of law under apartheid. This method reveals how the roles the law plays in the conflicts he discusses are formed and framed in a constant interaction with forms of power external to the law. Most striking of these interactions is the focus of the media and particularly the external or international media on the events and legal decisions that are at the center of these conflicts.[228]

Another example, within sociolegal approaches to the legal regulation of families, is the crucial question of 'whether the different balance in the welfare/rights approaches to child law leads to different practice and outcomes.[229]

A third useful illustration of the policy and ideological dimension which dissertation students may wish, on a reduced scale, to emulate is provided by a sociolegal project at Cardiff University. This project examined the role of grandparents in forty-four families in which their children had divorced, and the impact that the legal proceedings exerted upon prior family relationships. It represented 'an exploratory study of how grandparents, parents, and grandchildren view the role of grandparents in the divorced family, and what impact the divorce seems to have on that role'.[230] The policy dimensions in this project included exploring whether or not the empirical findings that emerged from the interviews of the various affected family members supported proposals that grandparents should be accorded specific legal rights simply by virtue of their status as grandparents. Its conclusion was that such proposals could not be supported because the empirical evidence regarding the willingness of all grandparents to provide support to divorced parents and their children indicated that this varied considerably from case to case.[231] The researchers concluded that the policy implications of proposed changes for increased formal status for grandparents in post-divorce childcare arrangements would be largely negative:

> What of the legal position of grandparents? Our evidence suggests that there is a need to be cautious about the idea that grandchild-grandparent contacts have some essential purpose or fundamental importance to grandparents or grandchildren in divorced families. . . . Moreover, given the matrilineal bias in grandparenting, and the gendered nature of grandparent involvement, what the call to mobilise grandparents would actually mean is likely to be the further feminisation of caring and the further alienation of paternal grandparents. For it will be grandmothers, primarily, who take the more active role in childcare, and it will be the maternal

---

[228]Heinz Klug, Review Essays, 'Law Under and After Apartheid: Abel's Sociolegal Analysis,' *Law & Social Inquiry*, Spring, 2000. (Review article address Richard L. Abel, *Politics by Other Means: Law in the Struggle Against Apartheid, 1980-1994*, (New York: Routledge, 1995).

[229]Christine Piper and Artem Miakishev, 'A Child's Right to Veto in England and Wales - Another Welfare Ploy?' (2003) *CFam* 15.1(57).

[230]Douglas, G. and Ferguson, N., 'The Role of Grandparents in Divorced Families,' (2003) 41 *International Journal of Law, Policy and the Family*; material reproduced by permission of Oxford University Press. Their project indicates that before divorce, 54 per cent of paternal grandparents met with their grandchildren at least 13 times a year. However, after these legal proceedings were concluded, this percentage fell to 44 per cent. Before divorce a third had contact more than once a week but after divorce, the figure fell to 14 per cent. In comparison, 58 per cent of maternal grandparents had seen their grandchildren on at least 13 occasions a year. This did not increase significantly after divorce but the percentage of those having contact more than once a week increased from 40 per cent to 48 per cent.

[231]*Ibid.*

grandmothers who do so. This is not a recipe for strengthening ties with the paternal grandparents in the post-divorce family. The long-term solution to this country's dearth of affordable childcare cannot be the conscription of grandparents.[232]

Within the field of criminal justice, a sociolegal project addressing sentencing discounts, whose data was based on questionnaire returns from magistrates, indicates that the use of such discounts and the award of larger discounts than official policy authorises, are far more common than was previously assumed within the mainstream literature on criminal law. This finding of a discrepancy between official policy and institutional activities in turn indicated that there is a need to revise underlying policy in this area out of a concern that it only adds to the already high pressure on defendants to plead guilty in magistrates' courts:

> The most significant finding was the unexpectedly high number of discounts which exceeded the conventional one-third level. Although it was not possible to examine specific reasons for each decision, the significance of this finding is increased by the fact that it emerged following analysis of a representative cross-section of virtually all the guilty plea cases sentenced in two busy urban magistrates' courts over a two-week period. Furthermore, given the emphasis on the stage when the plea was entered in section 48, it is also significant that (overall) just over half the sample cases only rated this variable as 'very important'. These two findings alone are sufficient to lead us to question the policy assumptions underlying the operation of sentence discounts in the magistrates' courts, and should provide the impetus for further research. As stated, the operation of the plea before venue system introduced by section 49 of the Criminal Procedure and Investigation Act 1996 is predicated on the notion of consistency in the application of sentence discounts by the courts and, indeed, the validity of section 48 itself rests firmly on crime control considerations which should be transparent in their operation. This research suggests that section 48 has done little to regulate the pragmatic nature of decision-making on sentence discounts and, in the absence of firm and relevant guidance for magistrates' courts by the Court of Appeal, confirms the absence of any coherent rationale or justification for continued reliance on this mechanism in the magistrates' courts where the pressures to plead guilty have become even stronger. As Ashworth has argued, more fundamental reform of the system of sentence discounts may be overdue, and there is no doubt that some fundamental reform is necessary if only on the basis that a number of fundamental rights and freedoms enshrined in the European Convention on Human Rights are breached. If the expedients of managerialism and financial constraint continue to be the driving force behind the practice of discounting sentences in return for guilty pleas in the magistrates' courts, eventual elimination of those principles of adversarial justice which purport to legitimise the operation of the sentencing process will inevitably result.[233]

In other words, sociolegal research addressing plea-bargaining has not only identified the operation of policy imperatives within the criminal justice system but also

---

[232]*Ibid.*

[233]Ralph Henham, 'Reconciling Process and Policy: Sentence Discounts in the Magistrates' Courts' 15 *Crim.L.R.* (2000) June 436.

highlighted discrepancies between the formal and actual positions, which themselves have policy implications. It is possible that student dissertations would discover similar discrepancies in other areas of the criminal justice system.

Another example of a sociolegal project that aims to produce findings that are relevant to policy debates, including those relating to law reform, is John Keown's work criticising the assumptions that inform the current law on the medical termination of life. He argues that, insofar as existing legal doctrine focuses on the distinction between positive acts and omissions, such as withdrawing life-preserving medication, fluids and treatment which, for example, results in death through dehydration, it results in clear inconsistencies. This distinction obscures what should be seen as the specific policy and moral issues: the extent, if any, to which doctors have a direct intention to end life. Arguing for the reversal of the Bland judgment,[234] Keown insists that it is the distinction between intention and foresight, rather than between acts and omissions, which judges should accept as key.[235]

There has also been sociolegal research focusing on specific case studies, which are then analysed in the context of a number of different policy factors. For example, Hazel Hartley has conducted extensive research into two disasters (the Hillsborough and Marchioness tragedies), whose implications are then critically analysed in their broader political, economic and policy contexts.[236] Mohd Sharifuddin *et al.*'s study of the legal regulation of water pollution brings together an environmental-geographic survey of water pollution with an analysis of its health and other impacts. The aim of this study is to provide a context for critically evaluating the adequacy of legislative and judicial responses at different official levels of regulation within India. In response to the alleged deficiency in the effectiveness of existing modes of legal regulation, the research advocates the adoption of 'community oriented environmental governance'.[237]

Policy-oriented studies of law in action have also contrasted the legal position in principle with that which empirical research indicates prevails in practice as a matter of fact. For example, whereas legal doctrine may insist that the victims of negligence have a right to compensation, sociolegal researchers may insist on examining the extent to which this theoretical right applies to different groups in society, such as employees whose health is seriously damaged by unsafe work practices.[238] In the field of family disputes, empirical research involving semi-structured interviews with Court Welfare Officers has also exposed specific discrepancies. Empirical research with respect to access disputes has suggested that it is the subjectively variable assumptions and orientations of these officials, as distinct from the formal legal position, that is often the

---

[234]*Airedale NHS Trust v Bland* [1993] AC 789.

[235]Keown in Bainham, Sclater, Richards, 2002 *op. cit.* See also George P Smith, *Bioethics and the Law Medical, Socio-Legal and Philosophical Directions for a Brave New World*, (NY: University Press of America, 2001).

[236]Hazel Hartley, *Exploring Sport and Leisure Disasters*, (London: Cavendish, 2001).

[237]Mohd Sharifuddin *et al.*, *Water Pollution and Law*, (New Delhi: Saloni, 2004). See also Y. Brittan, *The Impact of Water Pollution Control on Industry*, (Oxford: Centre for Socio-Legal Studies, 1984); Bridget Hutter, *The Reasonable Arm of the Law: The Law Enforcement Procedures of Environmental Health Enforcers*, (Oxford: Clarendon, 1988).

[238]See, for example, Sue Bowden and Geoffrey Tweedale, 'Poisoned by the Fluff: Compensation and Litigation for Business in the Lancashire Cotton Industry', *Journal of Law and Society* (2002) 12(4).

main factor in determining relevant rights and responsibilities within this form of legal decision-making.[239]

With respect to increased litigation between parents over contact with children following the end of their relationship, one sociolegal project critically examined proposals for a presumption of 'shared parenting'. The conclusion was that the introduction of such an idealistic presumption would not in practice 'achieve the aims of its proponents' by reducing conflict and litigation, and that prior sociolegal research indicates that its introduction would be 'fraught with practical and doctrinal problems'.[240] This type of policy-oriented research aims to resist proposals for law reform that, the authors maintain, would be counter-productive, even for those accepting the underlying values and goals of the measure in question.

Another variation on policy-oriented sociolegal studies are those that report on relative 'insider' developments within the law reform process. For instance, researchers have critically assessed the dangers of child abuse to which children are exposed on the internet, and the extent to which existing criminal laws fail to protect children. Having highlighted a perceived problem requiring legislative intervention, such research discusses the merits and potential dangers of proposed official responses. In the case of these child protection measures, sociolegal researchers have identified one key policy issue as: how best can new laws strike an appropriate balance between the need to prevent abuse through proactive policing and monitoring on the one hand, and civil liberty issues with respect to police entrapment on the other?[241]

A further variant on policy-relevant sociolegal research are those studies that are prompted by supposedly progressive judicial decisions that enlarge the rights of historically disadvantaged groups or groups subject to legal and social discrimination. This type of research will typically welcome the judicial innovation as an overdue corrective to past discriminatory policies enshrined in law, whilst also emphasising its contextual limitations and hence the perceived need for further legislative extension and entrenchment of the right in question.[242]

Another example is sociolegal work within the policy field of European asylum and immigration law in the context of recent enlargement, which argues that existing measures are in practice contradicting established principles of enhanced inclusiveness and free movement:

> It follows from the above analysis that what we are currently witnessing resembles the resurgence of a new Curtain replacing the Iron Curtain, but further to the East.

---

[239]Caroline Sawyer, 'Ascertaining the Child's Wishes and Feelings,' (2000) 30 *Fam LJ* 170: 'The CWO who found the children's perceived feelings of anger and betrayal at their father to be their own, and even justified (and the mother not necessarily to be obsessed with chasing the father), was rare. No one asked the father to compromise with the children's feelings. Indeed, the children's feelings were so recast and reattributed as to be ignored entirely, insofar as they dissented from the preconceived "proper" settlement. Clearly the CWOs' own assumptions drove not only the process of "settlement" but also the nature of the settlement pressed for, and the range of such assumptions was enormous, even amongst a small set of interviewees.'

[240]Felicity Kaganas and Christine Piper, 'Shared Parenting – a 70% Solution?' (2002) 14 *CFam* 365.

[241]Alisdair A. Gillespie, 'Child Protection on the Internet – Challenges for Criminal Law', (2002) 14 *CFam* 411. The author had been a member of The Home Office Internet Task Force On Child Protection.

[242]Lisa Glennon, '*Fitzpatrick v Sterling Housing Association Ltd* – An Endorsement of The Functional Family?' (2000) 14 *IJLP&F* 226; Mary Welstead, 'Case Commentary: Financial Support in Same-Sex Relationships – a Canadian Constitutional Solution', (2000) 12 *CFam* 73.

Europe's enlargement must not lead to the enlargement of 'Fortress Europe'. The Commission itself has warned that 'the future borders of the Union must not become a new dividing line'. In practice, whilst enlargement should be about inclusion, the hard border regime which is being imposed on candidate countries is about exclusion, 'about creating or recreating dividing lines in Europe'.[243]

A related research question on this form of sociolegal research is the question of whether any set of recent reforms have, in practice, achieved their stated objectives.[244] Consider, for example, a recent study on the position of disabled children in recent anti-discrimination legislation, which contrasts legal provisions with whatever would need to be introduced in order to realise more fully the stated goals of these measures:

We have sought to demonstrate here that, despite its evident improvements, SENDA has introduced a scheme that is imperfect. It is flawed by a number of deep inconsistencies, both at a conceptual and a practical level. These appear to lack a solid grounding in logic or fairness and, in some instances, could have been avoided completely had greater trust been placed in concepts such as reasonableness, already at work in the DDA. We have demonstrated how some of the inconsistencies identified above reveal a marked reluctance to confer on disabled children meaningful rights of their own in relation to their education. Improved participation rights in the SENDIST fall short of a right for children to be heard in legal proceedings or to bring such proceedings in their own name. Unlike older students, pupils will not be able to rely on a reasonable adjustments duty to call for auxiliary aids or services or physical alterations and will not be entitled to any compensation if they do manage to bring a successful disability discrimination claim. SENDA has recognised the benefits of a structured and planned approach to meeting need in this context. It has failed, however, to confer on children a fully-fledged right not to be discriminated against in their education and has failed to send out the clear message that schools (within the bounds of reasonableness) must always be responsive to the circumstances of a particular disabled pupil. Pupils have not been brought squarely within the framework of equality legislation. . . . There is still some way to go before disabled people can truly be said to be entitled to a system of comprehensive, enforceable, civil rights in education.[245]

In addition to a focus on the 'effectiveness' of policies, policy-relevant research can also be extremely critical of the nature, internal coherence and potential of current government policies, and insist that apparently benign measures can operate in ways that are distinctly problematic from the perspective of civil liberties. Students interested in this aspect of sociolegal studies should take heed of a sociolegal study of legislative reforms claiming to tackle antisocial behaviour:

Home-school agreements are a method of 'soft control' that sits alongside the more overtly disciplinary initiatives. In this case the project is pursued by trying to

---

[243]Catherine Phuong, 'Enlarging "Fortress Europe" ': EU Accession, Asylum, and Immigration in Candidate Countries, (2003) 52 *ICLQ* 641.

[244]See Robert Mosgrove and Anna Rowland, 'Are the Woolf Reforms a Success?', *Socio-Legal Newsletter*, No.38, (2002), 8; 'The Human Rights Act: Its impact on the Courts', *Socio-Legal Newsletter*, No.38, (2002), 8 (summarising empirical research published by the Lord Chancellor's Department entitled *The Impact on the Courts and the Administration of Justice of the Human Rights Act 1998*, (2002) 9/02.

[245]Blair and Lawson, 2003.

re-engage 'antisocial' parents with their civil obligations, and in doing so tries to make parents responsible for policing their own and other parents' conduct. This article intends to show that this particular initiative is riddled with internal incon-sistency, and that although the tone of the model of home-school agreement that the Department for Education and Employment (DfEE) is currently advocating is almost entirely benign the legislative framework that has been adopted is open to other less benign purposes, and worse might come about through minor shifts in government policy which would fit easily within the structures it creates. A further question is whether these agreements are capable of bringing about the effects the legislation has sought to achieve. . . . A preliminary question is that of why these home-school agreements have been seized with such enthusiasm by the current government? Are these reasons political and ideological rather than pragmatic or educational?[246]

This study is clearly critical of the ideological underpinnings of the topic. In particular, it criticises the alleged attempt to use legislative initiatives of a coercive nature to obtain party political advantage:

This article aims to show that home-school agreements are both instruments of participation and instruments of coercion. The question is whether the aim of using them to address the direct failings of the 'antisocial' parent and the problem of the 'antisocial' child is compatible with their use as an instrument of participation and community. However, one can see that their appeal for those converted to the New Labour mission is that these seemingly slight documents, and the obligations that surround them, hold the ability to touch multiple aspects of the Government's ideology and inclinations all at the same time. . . . If antisocial behaviour is to be addressed in part by engaging parents with their social responsibilities, it would perhaps be more fruitful to jettison compulsory home-school agreements with their coercive undertones and to concentrate on building genuine partnerships in a variety of ways that can be tailored to the needs of the individual school and com-munity. If coercion is then still required in relation to the minority of parents who are letting down their child and their community by failing in the duties of a 'good parent', then it is argued that a great deal more agreement is needed as to what exactly these duties are, and a great deal more transparency in the development of appropriate interventions.'[247]

Another variation on this theme is the fact that sociolegal research often includes studies and issues that take account of, and are relevant to, the policy dimension of legal topics. Such research, from the start, expressly advocates a reform in the law. Unlike reform proposals emerging from the black-letter tradition, the basis for arguing for reform is not that changes are needed to make current legal doctrine resemble more closely a coherent, clear and certain system of rules. On the contrary, the reform agenda will more often be that the operation of the present legal position is out of step with what a desirable policy should be attempting to bring about. Such proposals will, therefore, be supported by evidence that changes in social patterns, lifestyles, attitudes and economic circumstances now mean that the policy underlying a particular area of legal regulation

---

[246]Ann Blair, 'Home-School Agreements: A Legislative Framework for Soft Control of Parents,' (2001) 2 *Edu LJ* 79.
[247]*Ibid.*

has become outdated and anachronistic, even if it fully meets the aspirations of the black-letter model.

The author of one recent example of this type of sociolegal work argues that a number of post-war social and economic changes and developments in public policy have made the current legal provisions for distributing family property anachronistic. Hence, the courts should now use their discretion to develop an alternative response:

> [R]ecent history of the courts' decisions in the field of equity allows them to take the lead again in relation to 'family' property, using developments in the concept of parental responsibility for children in the context of social and economic changes. . . . There are several areas of change that so affect the operation of both property and personal law they must be fundamental to the making or main-tenance of social policy by the courts (for that is what their treatment of family resources amounts to). The social and economic situation in recent decades has leant more and more towards a requirement for individual capital wealth in order to lead a stable home life. An increasing number of people are home owner-occupiers; rented accommodation is often expensive and unpleasant. Moreover, . . . since the series of changes to residential tenancy regulation that began with the Housing Act 1988 there is little protection for families. Social housing becomes more rare and private tenancies are often nasty and short; they rarely provide the appropriate conditions in which to bring up a family. Home ownership is often closer to a necessity than a style choice; there is a considerable state interest in it too, for there is concern that the 'social exclusion' of some families is a breeze likely to lead to a whirlwind of future social disorder as dispossessed children grow into disaffected and even unemployable adults. A second but underlying considera-tion is that the social and economic outlook that vaunts the home-owning demo-cracy also demands that the state should not intervene in private arrangements save to provide a safety net. . . . The third major consideration is changing social attitudes to relationships, and especially the widespread possibility of divorce following the implementation of the Divorce Reform Act 1969.[248]

Sawyer concludes that developments in these various socio-economic and policy dimen-sions has now necessitated a specific law reform: incorporating a continuing obligation in equity to provide for children as a decisive factor in courts' decisions regarding the distribution of the family home of cohabiting couples whose relationship has ended.[249]

In short, a regular theme within sociolegal research has been the importance of researchers uncovering the operation of specific ideological dimensions to the interpretation and enforcement of legal measures in ways that contradict a central tenet of the more tradi-tional black-letter approach: namely, the strict separation of the analysis of law from social policy and wider political considerations. Students should note that there are many soci-olegal projects addressing the policy dimension to law in action, including the effective-ness of existing measures, their impact upon different groups in society, and the rationale for proposed law and policy reforms. Comparative studies of the link between policies and law enforcement also represent an important strand of this branch of research. Any of these themes could be taken as providing a suitable basis for a law dissertation.

---

[248]Caroline Sawyer, 'Equity's Children – Constructive Trusts for the New Generation,' (2004) 16 *CFam* 31.
[249]*Ibid.*

Not all sociolegal policy analyses are directly linked to a specific reform agenda. For instance, there has been sociolegal research within the field of environmental regulation, which has primarily been concerned to clarify tensions and contradictions between competing national, EC and international policy dimensions relevant, for example, in the regulation of the importation of live plants and animals.[250] However, much policy-oriented comparative legal research clearly rejects the positivist's strict separation of descriptive and evaluative analysis. Indeed, much research insists that legal analysis is inevitably related to questions of the moral and ethical validity of existing and proposed policies.[251]

● The Diversity of Research Methods Used in Sociolegal Studies

In addition to a diversity of topics addressed by contemporary sociolegal research, it is possible to identify a number of distinctive ways in which sociolegal researchers have approached their topics. Sociolegal researchers deploy numerous different methods. These research methods are used both individually, and in combination. For example, research on lawyer–client interactions have drawn on data stemming from interviews with specific segments of the profession, public opinion polls commissioned by lawyers' organisations and textual sources expressing reform programmes. They have also used published statements by professional leaders and their organisations, reports of lawyers' disciplinary bodies and internal professional conduct regulations, lawyers' membership polls, and lawyer–client focus groups.[252] Other studies have used sophisticated survey methods to gauge differences between the worlds of different categories of American lawyer.[253] Despite its importance, the practical conduct of empirical forms of sociolegal research can be far from straightforward. This is true not only concerning the generation of reliable data but also with respect to the best way to interpret such material:

> Empirical socio-legal research is challenging. It is difficult to obtain data and equally difficult to interpret the data obtained. As shown above, it also can be difficult to control variables and results can have more than one possible cause. Other limitations on and issues regarding empirical socio-legal research exist . . . For example, even if results are clear and unassailable, will courts and legislators abandon long-standing legal maxims? Will factual research prevail if instinct and emotion are contrary? Despite the obstacles and shortcomings, empirical research must be pursued and its methodologies further developed and refined. For it is only empirical research that can yield facts to reveal whether the assumptions upon which we base our laws may be specious.'[254]

---

[250]Robert Black, 'The Legal Basis for Control of Imports of Animal and Plant Material into the United Kingdom', 5 *Enviro LR* (2003) 179.

[251]For a discussion of comparative forms of contextual analysis see, M. Findlay, *The Globalisation of Crime*, (Cambridge: CUP, 1999), 6-8; for a brief example, see Mary Welstead, 'Case Commentary: Financial Support in Same-Sex Relationships – a Canadian constitutional solution', (2000) *CFam* 12.1(73). For more examples of comparative analysis within the sociolegal tradition, see Chapter 6 later.

[252]Felstiner, in Hawkins, 1997, *op. cit.*, 129.

[253]For an example of the application of survey methods to the work of the legal professional, see Heinz and Laumann, *Chicago Lawyers: The Social Structure of the Bar*, (NY: Russell Sage Foundation, 1982).

[254]Joyce Palomar, 'The War Between Attorneys and Lay Conveyancers – Empirical Evidence Says "Cease Fire!"', (1999) 31 *Conn. L. Rev*, 423.

Furthermore, many of the funding agencies for sociolegal research require that students attend a recognised research-training programme covering a wide range of qualitative[255] and quantitative methodologies.[256] The module on research methods at the University of Glasgow rightly notes that, under the broad banner of 'law in context', it is possible to distinguish a number of different approaches, noting that:

> The objective of this component is to distinguish socio-legal research from traditional legal research and philosophy of law, to outline the major debates about the scope and nature of the subject and to assess the relevance of the debate between sociology of law as a theoretical discipline, 'socio-legal studies' as applied social science and 'law-in-context' as a development of traditional legal scholarship.[257]

Law in context courses usually espouse an input–output model. The input of social, political and economic causation was manifested in the popularity of 'emergence studies' addressing how proposals for specific statutory measures first emerged and became developed through extended periods of consultation, lobbying and pressure-group politics. The 'output' side of the equation typically focuses on a 'social action model' of law conceived as a process with a number of key decision stages that are central to the enforcement of specific measures.

It is possible to distinguish, in broad-brush terms, the following contextual methods:[258]

- *Empirical* (the gathering and analysis of facts about law in action, experiences of the practical impact of legal proceedings upon different groups in society, such as criminal defendants[259] and consumers of legal services,[260] low-income families and grandparents of families affected by divorce).[261]

- *Theoretical* (debates over the validity of different concepts, and theoretical approaches, such as law as a social phenomena, law and globalisation, law and justice, law and morality, law and gender, law and sexuality, understanding law in terms of competing theories of society more generally). Students may need to appreciate the link between the definition of researchable topics and issues, and the intellectual foundations of sociolegal research, including positivism, empiricism, realism, idealism, post-structuralism, and feminist critiques.

---

[255]Qualitative research includes phenomenological, interactionist and ethnomethodological approaches to sociolegal studies.

[256]Quantitative analysis of differences in sentencing practices is a noteworthy example: see Hood, *Sentencing in Magistrates' Courts* (1962); Harris, 1983, *op. cit.*, 321. On the importance of quantitative research skills, see Loraine Gelsthorpe, 'How to get recognised,' Socio-Legal Newsletter 37 (2002), 3.

[257]http://www.lib.gla.ac.uk/courses/law/MacNeil2.shtml.

[258]Gelsthorpe, 2002 *op. cit.*, 4.

[259]Bottoms and Maclean, 1976 *op. cit.*

[260]Regarding the reported experiences of consumers of lawyer and mediation services, see G. Davis, *Partisans and Mediators* (Oxford: Clarendon Press, 1988); G. Davis, S. Cretney and J. Collins, *Simple Quarrels* (Oxford: Clarendon Press, 1994).

[261]See, for example, Ian Ramsay's contribution to *International Perspectives on Consumers' Access to Justice*. Charles E.F. Rickett and Thomas G.W. Telfer (eds), (Cambridge: CUP, 2003) is a clear example of sociolegal research addressing differential impact of individual redress mechanisms, noting that they serve the lower-income groups less well than the middle classes. He adopts a comparative approach to the various collective complaint mechanisms that have been developed to protect consumers.

- *Policy-oriented* (how does any existing area of legal regulation reflect changing government policies over, say, privatisation and nationalisation of land?).
- *Comparative* approaches (discussed later in Chapter 6).

Within these broad distinctions, it is clear that a variety of technical research methods are commonly applied within sociolegal types of legal research. Indeed, Levine has maintained that, ideally, sociolegal researchers acting individually but also within collaborative multidisciplinary teams, should attempt to employ a battery of research methods:

> To do it well, scholars would benefit from attending to micro and macro theory; examining data from different time periods, units of analysis, and locales; seeking explanation in specific contexts; and searching for coherent results through multiple methods, across long time spans, and in comparative perspective.[262]

This aspiration is clearly over-ambitious for an undergraduate and perhaps many types of postgraduate dissertation project, although possibly not for a well-focused PhD. Amongst the variety of possible research methods are included:

1. *Quantitative methods* using the official statistics, questionnaires and surveys to produce and then analyse statistical information about, say, the relationship between being the victim of different criminal offences in terms of both social class and gender.[263] The quantitative analysis of official statistics on road deaths have provided the raw material for a sociolegal project assessing the impact of the introduction of the breathalyser.[264] Questionnaires have also been used in research on the extent to which magistrates grant sentencing discounts in response to a guilty plea,[265] issues regarding the institutional and social 'construction' of litigation, crime and unemployment statistics. Quantitative research methods require an appreciation of a range of issues within the design of social surveys (factual, attitudinal, social psychological and explanatory survey technique), questionnaire schedules and experimental research. Other practical research issues arising here relate to the choice of different methods of sampling

---

[262]Levine, 1990 *op. cit.*, 24.

[263]See V. Jupp, *Methods of Criminological Research* (1989 *op. cit.*); Fitzgerald and Cox, *Research Methods in Criminal Justice* (Chicago, IL: Nelson-Hall, 1992), F. Caswell, *Success in Statistics* 2nd edn, (London: John Murray, 1989); W. Reichmann, *The Use and Abuse of Statistics*, (London: Pelican, 1964) and the wider-ranging T. Baker, *Doing Social Research* 3rd edn, (NY: McGraw Hall, 1999); Kidder and Judd, *Research Methods in Social Relations* (NY: Holt, Rinehart, 1986).

[264]H. Ross *et al.* 'Determining the Social Effects of a Law Reform' (1977) 13 *American Behavioral Scientist* 209, which by disaggregating the statistics, found that, once the measure was introduced, road casualties did reduce during or after peak drinking times.

[265]Ralph Henham notes that questionnaires can be a better tool than physical observation in this context: 'The research study was carried out in Leicester and Nottingham magistrates' courts . . . to assess whether, and to what extent, magistrates were taking the matters referred to in section 48(1) into account when deciding on the appropriate sentence discount. It was not considered appropriate to attempt an assessment of the rate of compliance with section 48(2) by attending relevant court hearings, since advance notice of the researcher's presence would invariably have influenced magistrates' sentencing behaviour to an unacceptable degree. It was, therefore, decided to obtain the cooperation of the magistrates themselves by asking the court chairman to complete a short questionnaire immediately after a guilty plea case had been sentenced. All guilty plea cases for a two-week period were included for all defendants who appeared in court and pleaded guilty, not just those appearing in plea courts. By including all defendants sentenced during the relevant period the study included all those who had pleaded guilty on the day or earlier. A total of 210 questionnaires were returned and subsequently analysed for guilty plea cases heard by both magistrates' courts during the relevant period (Leicester 102, Nottingham 108) and the data obtained constituted the empirical input subsequently analysed.' Ralph Henham, 'Reconciling Process and Policy: Sentence Discounts in the Magistrates' Courts' 15 *Crim.L.R.* 2000, 436.

(simple random sampling, systematic sampling, stratified random sampling, cluster/ multi-stage sampling and quota sampling);[266] interviewing and data collection. They also include conducting pilot studies. Quantitative methods including statistical analysis appear to have particular status amongst official bodies and public organisations.[267]

2. *Qualitative research* which may use in-depth interviews of either 'structured' or 'semi-structured' types.[268] The latter is where researchers ask different follow-up questions to explore the implications of earlier answers to the standardised questions asked to all interviewees).[269] Other qualitative methods include holding 'focus group' discussions,

---

[266]The study published by Douglas and Ferguson of the role of grandparenting in the context of divorce proceedings contained interesting information on both how the sampling was conducted and how this differed from earlier sociolegal projects relating to the role of grandparents in families affected by divorce proceedings: 'Since our study was intended to provide a broad range of family circumstances rather than focus on families in conflict, it is not surprising that few of the grandparents had had any direct involvement in legal proceedings concerning the parents' divorce. Nor had many been in the position where they had had to contemplate taking legal action to maintain or restore contact with their grandchildren. In this respect, our sample is importantly different from other previous socio-legal studies that have dealt with grandparents . . . Those [studies] have deliberately concentrated on grandparents who have had to resort to the courts, or who have tried and failed to seek legal remedies when blocked by the parents. . . . The families who took part in the study were recruited from two samples of parents on whom information was obtained from divorce court records. The first was a sample of parents who had been granted a decree nisi of divorce in the first half of 1997, who had participated in previous studies of divorce conducted by the University. The second was a randomly selected sample of parents who had been granted decree nisi between March and September 2000. The second sample was drawn because our approaches to parents in the first sample yielded insufficient numbers for the study.' Douglas and Ferguson, 2003, *op. cit.* See also the discussion of practical issues over sampling and concerns over issues of whether the sample is sufficiently 'representative' in Douglas and Perry, 2001 *op. cit.*

[267]See Gelsthorpe, 2002 *op. cit.*, 4.

[268]For an illustration of semi-structured interviewing in a sociolegal project, see Caroline Sawyer, 'Ascertaining the Child's Wishes and Feelings,' (2000) *Fam LJ* 30(170). See also, Douglas and Ferguson who report that: 'Our strategy was to use our initial contacts with the [divorcing] parents to help arrange interviews with other family members. Whenever possible, both parents, one of the divorced couple's children aged between 8 and 16 and the children's maternal and paternal grandparents were interviewed. Parents with care of children were asked if a member of the research team could talk to one of their children (selected at random where there was more than one such child) who was in the appropriate age range. The letter inviting parents and grandparents to take part offered them an interview fee of £20. Children were sent a certificate and a pen bearing the university logo. This activity resulted in a total of 115 interviews with family members who agreed to participate; these consisted of interviews with 33 mothers, 16 fathers, 30 children, 21 sets of maternal grandparents and 15 sets of paternal grandparents. A flexible "conversational-style" interview was chosen as the research tool. It was based on three interview guides that ensured that the two field-workers conducting the interviews covered the same ground. The interviews for adults usually lasted between 1 and 2 hours. Parents, grandparents and children were met in their own home, assured of the confidential nature of the interview and asked whether a tape recorder could be used. Grandparents who lived together were interviewed together. However, at the end of each interview they were interviewed separately for about 10 minutes so that the data could be explored for differences between grandmothers' and grandfathers' grandparenting practices and to provide an opportunity for individuals to provide opinions that were not influenced by the presence of their spouse. Parents were asked if the child could be interviewed alone and all agreed.' 2003, *op. cit.*

[269]For example, one sociolegal study into decision-making processes regarding the selective prosecution of breaches of health-and-safety measures involved the analysis of data from interviews with 16 senior HSE officials conducted in the mid-1980s, supplemented by interviews with 52 factory inspectors, also conducted in the mid-1980s. These were supplemented with a study of both 'infraction letters' issued by the former Industrial Air Pollution Inspectorate and a content analysis of the files in four HSE area offices relating to all workplace fatalities and cases prosecuted during the first six months of 1996. Keith Hawkins, *Law as Last Resort: Prosecution Decision-Making in a Regulatory Agency,* (Oxford: OUP, 2002). The empirical data generated by these interviews and other textual sources suggest that prosecution decision-making was being informed not only by legal considerations but also by three other main frames of reference, instrumental, organisational, and symbolic. Douglas and Ferguson, 2003, *op. cit.,* record some of the logistical difficulties in obtaining an ideal sample of interviewees: 'We identified families from two samples

field research based on observation of legal action (i.e. 'ethnography');[270] 'discourse analysis' (which is concerned with the link between identifiable power relationships and actual and potential legal decision-making); 'conversation analysis' of verbal interactions;[271] 'action research' (based on reflections upon previous practical engagements in the research field) and participant observation (where researchers immerse themselves in the subculture of the research subjects in order to better understand how these subjects experience the legal topic in question).[272] These methods attempt to understand the meaning, purpose and value that those who are involved in, or affected by, law attribute to their experiences.[273]

3. *Computer assisted analysis* using computer software analyses both quantitative (such as *GLIM*, *CAQDAS*), and qualitative data (such as *The Ethnograph*, *Qualpro* and *Kwalitanto*) generated by the application of different research methods.[274]

---

drawn at random from court files in courts in south Wales and south west England, in which decree nisi had been granted in the first half of 1997 and 2000 and wrote to the parents asking if they would agree to be interviewed. We also explained that we would wish to interview a child (aged between 8 and 16) and the child's grandparents. Because of the frequency with which divorced fathers moved home after divorce and became difficult to track down, it proved quite difficult to obtain interviews with them and with paternal grandparents. Our hope that we would be able to interview 'complete' family groups – comprising both parents, both sets of grandparents and the grandchild – was equally frustrated. However, we were able ultimately to conduct 115 interviews . . . amongst members of 44 families.'

[270]See Anita Kalunta-Crumpton, 1998 *op. cit.* for a study based on observation of trials in London Crown Court which suggests that the prosecution's use of racial imageries of crime and deprivation were themselves instrumental in classification of black defendants as drug traffickers.

[271]See Dingwell and Greatbatch, 1994 *op. cit.* (as a method for analysing the mediation interview in family proceedings).

[272]Hawkins' study of the selective enforcement of water regulations deployed this method to uncover the high tolerance afforded in practice to theoretically illegal levels of water pollution, particularly where there was an absence of clear fault, and a clear preference for strategies of negotiation and threat rather than automatic law enforcement. Enforcement was shown to be mediated by the specific values of the enforcers, including the idea that offences of 'strict liability' in particular should, in the absence of clear fault, be prosecuted only as a last resort. See Hawkins, 1984 *op. cit.*; Harris, 1983 *op. cit.*, 321; Jacqueline Hodgson, 'The Comparativist as Participant Observer', 2000 *op. cit.*

[273]For an overview of the key differences and disputes between qualitative and quantitative types of empirical social science research, see A. Dawe, 'The Two Sociologies' (1970) 21 *British J. of Sociology*, 207. See also, for example, C. Grace and P. Wilkinson, 'Social Action and a Methodology for the Sociology of Law', *BJLS* 1 (1974) 184-94: 'Engaging in sociology of law requires that our commitment flows from the nature of social action. What is at issue is an explanation or meaningful social action in respect of a legal phenomenon. Since legal propositions embody meanings and constitute the product of meaning endowed social action, as well as an interpreted object in terms of which men act, we must treat both the creation of the legal proposition, the proposition itself and application of the proposition, at the level of meaning.' 193. With respect to the importance of taking qualitative experiences seriously, Douglas and Ferguson, 2003, *op. cit.*, note that: 'Between 2000 and 2002 we conducted a study into the role of grandparents in families where their children (the 'parents') had divorced. The study's main aims were to contribute to knowledge of the role and function of grandparents and to shed light on the attitudes of three generations in a divorced family, to the contribution that grandparents make to the support and upbringing of children. We regarded it as particularly important to talk to grandchildren about their views and experiences, as the assumptions about the value and importance of grandparents to grandchildren appear to come from grandparents, parents or from the recollections of adult grandchildren.' The debate over the respective merits and deficiencies of qualitative and quantitative research bubbles up from time to time within sociolegal literature. See, for example, the various reactions to a piece by Carol Bohmer in *Law and Society Newsletter*, November 1995; Hutter and Lloyd-Bostock, 1997 *op. cit.*, 22-3.

[274]Fielding and Lee (eds), *Using Computers in Qualitative Research*, (London: Sage, 1991); Bradshaw, 1997 *op. cit.*, 116-20. Douglas and Ferguson used such software: 'All interviews were fully transcribed and analysed using the computer software programme ATLAS.ti. This reduces a large volume of text to a more manageable set of codes that can be elaborated into recurring themes and interpreted as sets of interrelated ideas. In this sense the data was 'grounded' in the utterances of the informants rather than predetermined or imposed as the result of some external body of formal theory.' 2003 *op. cit.*

Within fieldwork-based research, there was a series of practical, technical and theoretical issues associated with the collecting and analysing of sociolegal data in a manner that yields comparatively reliable and valid 'legal knowledge': the use of various inductive and deductive methods of data analysis, including for example 'critical social theory' and 'grounded theory'.[275]

Further details of the nature and application of these standard research methods and techniques is contained in any of the standard textbooks on social science methods, which are readily available from university libraries, and whose detailed content does not need to be repeated here. In our experience, students who adopt a sociolegal approach to their dissertations are most likely to use interview or comparative methods, rather than quantitative methods. Our experience is shared by Bradshaw, who notes that few students in law are sufficiently numerate to be able to grasp and respond positively to 'overtly technical issues (sampling, experimental design, computer software packages), some of which are quantitatively detailed (descriptive statistics) and/or apparently quantitatively mysterious (notably inferential statistics, i.e. the process of generalising from sample results to populations via hypothesis testing.'[276] Ideally, this should not be the case as researchers need to be able to assess the methodology of all types of published research relevant to their topic – even if they have no intention of using, for example, quantitative methods for their own dissertations and projects.

It might prove useful for present purposes to review how sociolegal researchers employed interview methods as a way of conducting research in three different empirical projects: small claims proceedings, the use of Family Assistance Orders (FAOs), and, finally, a comparative study. John Baldwin's extensive empirical study of the growth of use of Small Claims actions reports on research conducted over a two-year period.[277] In order to help assess the theoretical and practical implications of the expansion of 'DIY' or, more precisely lawyer-free, types of civil justice, Baldwin interviewed the district court judges who preside over small-claim hearings, the transcripts of which he included. Baldwin's project also includes discussion of interviews with litigants, many of whom experienced difficulties with the practical enforcement of court judgments.

The second example of interview-based research focused on three questions relevant to FAOs:

1. Why were FAOs being made, and specifically, why were so many being made in one specific area and for what purpose?
2. What was being done under an FAO?
3. What was the outcome?

This study eventually included all the FAOs which had been made in a selected area between July 1992 and March 1994, totalling 37 FAOs made on 35 families. This figure represented approximately 10 per cent of all referrals to the Court Welfare Service within that period. The bulk of the orders (32, or 86.5 per cent) were made in the County Court, with only a small number (5, or 13.5 per cent) in the Family Proceedings Court. The

---

[275]For an example of the contents of student-oriented course on sociolegal research methodologies at Essex and Leeds Universities, see: http://www.essex.ac.uk/methods/Archive/courses2002/1L.htm; http://www.le.ac.uk/law/pg/slrm.rtf.

[276]Bradshaw, in Thomas 1997 *op. cit.*, 103.

[277]John Baldwin, *Small Claims in the County Courts in England and Wales: The Bargain Basement of Civil Justice*, (Oxford: OUP, 1998). It was funded by the Lord Chancellor's Department, the Office of Fair Trading and the Economic and Social Research Council.

researchers were 'particularly interested in the perspectives of three key constituencies: the court welfare officers, those making the orders, and the parties'.[278] They thus collected data from four main sources:

1. The case records of all 37 orders in the sample, including previous welfare reports, and all documentation associated with the making, operation, and immediate aftermath of the FAO.

2. Interviews with the nine court welfare officers responsible for each of the orders in the sample. Officers were asked to describe and evaluate each case as well as to discuss FAO work in general.

3. Interviews with four judges and a clerk to the justices of the local family proceedings court. The four judges had made nine of the 32 county court FAOs. The leading local judge, who had made 15 orders, was unavailable for interview. These interviews centred on FAOs in general rather than on specific cases.

4. Interviews with six adults who had been named in an order (the 'parties').

The researchers analysed the profile of each case using the social science statistical package SPSS. Some variables, such as the number and type of meetings held, were derived straight from the case records; other variables, such as the presence of consent and outcome, were researcher-generated ratings based on case recordings and interviews with officers. Alongside the quantitative analysis, the researchers employed qualitative methods to analyse the fully transcribed interviews with judges, officers and parties. They derived the analytical categories at least partly from the qualitative data, rather than those pre-identified by the researchers themselves on the basis of a prior theory or model.[279]

A postgraduate student writing in the sociolegal newsletter has argued that the idea of research *training* (implying formal instruction) is a misnomer for a process designed 'to provide exposure to a range of theoretical and methodological approaches and perspectives, and to provide researchers with the space to consider the interconnectivity of different approaches'.[280] With respect to the use by sociolegal researchers of comparative methodologies, John Hopkins has analysed institutional processes of the devolution of powers in 15 member states of the EU. The aim was to assess the impact or potential impact of regional governments on policy-making in Europe.

Interestingly, the ESRC has produced a far wider list of research methods on which sociolegal and criminological dissertations could be based. Although a number of these points may, at first sight, appear to be of greater relevance to criminology than sociolegal studies, sociolegal studies of the criminal justice and punishment system overlap with criminological research:

Research training may include material such as the following:

● competing perspectives on what crime is, crime statistics, patterns and trends
● criminal and/or civil justice processes and legal regulation of behaviour in related organisations

---

[278]Liz Trinder and Nigel Stone, 'Family Assistance Orders – Professional Aspiration and Party Frustration,' (1998), *CFam* 10.3(291).
[279]*Ibid.*
[280]Morag McDermott, 'A View from the Coalface', *Socio-legal Newsletter* (1996) no.38, 5.

- critical reading of the contribution of research to understandings of crime and justice
- an appreciation of ways in which criminological research and theory might inform social policy
- the relationship between legal and criminological domains
- competing perspectives on criminal justice interventions
- different theoretical perspectives on deviance, crime and criminal justice (e.g. sociological, psychological, legal, historical, cultural and anthropological)
- the social history of the discipline of criminology and/or sociolegal studies
- the relevance of modern social theory for an understanding of crime and punishment
- competing perspectives on the intersection of criminal and or civil justice policy, practice and politics in local, national and global contexts
- critical appreciation of the expansion of international law in the context of globalisation
- competing political science and philosophical perspectives on the role of the state in legally regulating citizens' behaviour
- an appreciation of the distinctions between different fields of social scientific enquiry and different kinds of theoretical explanations about the form, content, processes and consequences of law (e.g. critical theory, feminist, socio-cultural, or economic theory)
- mastery of key jurisprudential concepts relating to the nature of law, legal ordering and legal process, and the categorisation of substantive law
- an ability to deploy and understand legal argumentation and the normative orientation of argument
- an appreciation of the potentiality and limits of combining legal and other kinds of social scientific analysis and the methodological problems confronting such inquiry
- a knowledge of and ability to evaluate existing literature and research in a sociolegal field.[281]

This provides an impressive (and perhaps for many students, daunting) list of competences that are required by the community of sociolegal researchers. In practice, students can reassure themselves by noting that, even amongst the leading researchers in sociolegal studies, few could claim to have mastered every one of these competences. Hence, even at LLM level, student dissertations may need only to demonstrate their practical competence in *a limited number of these research skills*.

Prior to their adoption and application in specific studies, it is necessary for students to appreciate how to define a research topic in a clear and well-focused manner and to develop an appropriate conceptual framework within which issues relevant to this topic can be developed. At some level, sociolegal researchers need to appreciate the possible interdependence of research methodology and sociolegal theory. The latter may include wider theories about the nature and functioning of existing social relationships. It is also necessary for students to identify issues in the field of law that can be answered by, for example, empirical and other forms of sociolegal research. As Campbell and Wiles note:

> The problems raised by socio-legal studies are clearly suited to empirical research methods, and the traditional range of social surveys, questionnaires, formal interviews and standard quantitative techniques are widely employed.[282]

---

[281]Http://www.esrc.ac.uk/esrccontent/postgradfunding/2000_Guidelines_f15.asp

[282]Campbell and Wiles, 'The Study of Law in Society in Britain' (1976) 10 *Law and Society Review* 547.

● Ethical and Other Normative Dimensions

Whatever methods are selected, sociolegal research may have to identify a range of possible significant ethical issues. These include, of course, protecting confidentiality with respect to how data is both used and published, obtaining fully-informed consent from research participants, avoiding interventions that damage the welfare of such participants, and ensuring that the contributions of fellow researchers are properly acknowledged and not misrepresented.

The question of ensuring informed consent to review records from affected parties was clear in a study of Family Assistance Orders. Here, ethical considerations required the researchers to approach the parties indirectly via the court welfare service, and to ask people to specifically 'opt in' to be interviewed, rather than to opt out.[283] Adherence to the ethical principle of obtaining informed consent can have a major effect on the conduct of research. In a recent sociolegal project investigating child support provision where both dependent children and the CSA were involved, ethical considerations meant that researchers were only able to study fully twenty cases from a potential total sample of 123 instances of relationship breakdown.[284]

A related issue is the question of how specific values can structure the research process, even in contexts where research claims to value-free. For example, the priorities of different funding agencies can influence the identification and development of sociolegal research, and the risk that research loses its objectivity by simply accepting as given the assumptions, goals and values that implicitly inform the agenda of these agencies.[285] Students also need to be aware of the various duties and responsibilities researchers owe towards funding bodies as well as respondents. These can include the manner in which research results are published, a topic which is addressed in the Sociolegal Studies Association's own code of practice.

The remainder of this section will draw upon and discuss research ethics guidelines drawn up by our own university, and intended as guidance for students and other researchers. Although these have been formulated by our own institution, they cover a broad range of issues, most of which should be applicable in any academic context. We have provided a statement of relevant general principles, as well as a more detailed checklist that students may wish to consult.

1. General Principles

This Code of Conduct prescribes standards of conduct expected of all persons engaged in research at the University. All such persons are expected to:

  (i) maintain professional standards;

 (ii) take steps to ensure and maintain good research practice, for example in relation to matters of policy, ethics, finance and safety;

(iii) observe legal and ethical requirements laid down by the University or other properly appointed bodies involved in the research project;

▶

---

[283]Trinder and Stone, 1998, *op. cit.*

[284]Gwynn Davis, Nick Wikeley and Richard Young, with Jacqueline Barron and Julie Bedward, *Child Support in Action* (Oxford: Hart, 1999), discussed by the authors in *NLJ* (1998) Vol.148, No 6840, 692.

[285]See the stream on methodology in the 2004 SLSA conference: http://www.law.gla.ac.uk/slsa2004/

(iv) recognise the importance of good leadership and cooperation in research groups;

(v) take special account of the needs of young researchers;

(vi) document results and keep secure primary data;

(vii) question findings;

(viii) attribute honestly the contribution of others;

(ix) take steps to ensure the safety of all those associated with the research;

(x) report any conflict of interest, actual or prospective, to the appropriate person.

2. Consents and Welfare of Participants

Where third parties participate in research projects, all researchers must ensure that:

(i) consent must be obtained from anyone invited to take part in a research project. This must be based on a knowledge and understanding of the risks, benefits and alternatives of taking part. Unless otherwise agreed by an ethics committee or other approved body, consent should be explicit and written (see sample consent form below);

(ii) the management of any organisation involved (and any other individual with relevant responsibilities) must be informed that the research project is planned, and that, where appropriate, their approval is given before the research commences. For example, in business research, it will be necessary to obtain the permission of the relevant manager;

(iii) where required, the approval of the external agencies' research ethics committee for the research must be obtained before this project commences;

(iv) researcher(s) will give priority at all times to the dignity, rights, safety and well-being of participants;

(v) when the research involves participants under the care of a specific professional, such as doctor, nurse or social worker, particular issues arise. These professionals must be informed that their clients or users are being invited to participate, and give their active and informed consent to retain overall responsibility for their care;

(vi) where the research involves a service user or carer or child, looked after or receiving services under the auspices of a local authority, researchers must recognise that specific issues arise. The agency director or his/her deputy must agree to the person (and/or their carer) being invited to participate, and must be fully aware of arrangements for dealing with the disclosure of information. This requirement could be particularly relevant for research that, for instance, interviews the clients of probation officers;

(vii) unless participants or the relevant Ethics Committee request otherwise, researchers should ensure that participants' welfare professionals are given information arising from the research that is specifically relevant to their welfare. This requirement could, for example, be relevant to social science research with disadvantaged or vulnerable individuals or groups.

Ethics Checklist

This checklist should be completed by the Principal Investigator/Supervisor/Student undertaking a research project which involves human participants. The checklist will identify whether a project requires an application for ethics approval, and whether it needs to be submitted directly to a relevant university ethics committee.

If the research involves contact with, observation of, or collection and storage of confidential information about human subjects, then you may need ethics approval. Complete the following questionnaire, and then follow the accompanying flow chart to help you decide.

	YES	NO
1. Does the study involve participants who are unable to give informed consent? (e.g., children, people with learning disabilities, unconscious patients)	☐	☐
2. Will participants be presented with high-intensity stimuli of various kinds including, for example, auditory, visual, electrical or other stimuli?	☐	☐
3. Is there any foreseeable risk of physical, social or psychological harm to a participant arising from the procedure?	☐	☐
4. Will deception of participants be necessary during the study?	☐	☐
5. Will the study involve invasion of privacy, or accessing confidential information about people without their permission?	☐	☐
6. Will the study involve NHS patients or staff?	☐	☐

➤ If you have answered 'Yes' to any of these questions, you should perhaps discuss with your supervisor whether it is necessary to submit your proposal to a relevant research ethics committee within your department or faculty.

➤ If you answered 'Yes' to question 6, then an application must also be submitted to the appropriate external health authority ethics committee.

➤ If you are undertaking your research as part of an undergraduate or taught postgraduate qualification, and you have answered 'No' to all the above questions, then generally it may not be necessary to submit your planned research for ethics approval. However, it is still incumbent on you to observe the University's rules on ethics in the conduct of your research.

➤ **NOTE:** When any doubt arises in relation to the above, always forward your proposal to the ethics committee.

Participant Information Sheet

Note to researchers:

- *PLEASE KEEP TO THE POINT*
- *USE CLEAR AND ACCESSIBLE LANGUAGE*
- *USE ONLY THE MOST NECESSARY TECHNICAL TERMS*

Section A: The Research Project

1. Title of project
2. Purpose and value of study
3. Invitation to participate
4. Who is organising the research
5. What will happen to the results of the study
6. Source of funding for the research
7. Contact for further information

Section B: Your Participation in the Research Project

1. Why you have been invited to take part
2. Whether you can refuse to take part
3. Whether you can withdraw at any time, and how
4. What will happen if you agree to take part (brief description of procedures/tests)
5. Whether there are any risks involved (e.g. side effects from taking part) and if so what will be done to ensure your well-being/safety
6. Agreement to participate in this research should not compromise your legal rights should something go wrong
7. Whether there are any special precautions you must take before, during or after taking part in the study
8. What will happen to any information/data/samples that are collected from you
9. Whether there are any benefits from taking part
10. How your participation in the project will be kept confidential

YOU WILL BE GIVEN A COPY OF THIS TO KEEP, TOGETHER WITH A COPY OF YOUR CONSENT FORM

NAME OF PARTICIPANT:

Title of the project:

Main investigator and contact details:

Members of the research team:

1. I agree to take part in the above research. I have read the Participant Information Sheet which is attached to this form. I understand what my role will be in this research, and all my questions have been answered to my satisfaction.

2. I understand that I am free to withdraw from the research at any time, for any reason and without prejudice.

3. I have been informed that the confidentiality of the information I provide will be safeguarded.

4. I am free to ask any questions at any time before and during the study.

5. I have been provided with a copy of this form and the Participant Information Sheet. Data Protection Act 1998: I agree to the University processing personal data which I have supplied. I agree the processing of such data for any purposes connected with the Research Project as outlined to me. I further agree to the University processing personal data about me described as Sensitive Data within the meaning of the Data Protection Act 1998.

Name of participant (print) . . . . Signed . . . . Date . . . .

Name of witness (print) . . . . Signed . . . . Date . . . .

YOU WILL BE GIVEN A COPY OF THIS FORM TO KEEP

. . . .

. . . .

If you wish to withdraw from the research, please complete the form below and return to the main investigator named above.

Title of Project:

I WISH TO WITHDRAW FROM THIS STUDY

Signed:_____ Date:_____

● Strengths and Criticisms of Sociolegal Approaches

The strengths of sociolegal approaches have, in one sense, already been discussed when we addressed the rationale for the development of this approach from the early 1960s onwards, and the difference that the adoption of this approach has made to topics previously dominated by black-letter models of analysis. These advantages were also examined when we sought to define the rationale for developing sociolegal studies as an expressly interdisciplinary and multidisciplinary type of research into law as a social phenomenon, which would remedy the difficulties created by the increasingly apparent 'gap' between 'law in books' and 'law in action'. We can summarise the claimed strengths of interdisciplinary forms of sociolegal studies:

1. It broadens the scope of legal research. This is possible not only by providing additional information but also expanding the conceptual framework within which such information can be interpreted and assessed.

2. It allows research topics to be addressed in their wider contexts of emergence, development and reform.

3. Sociolegal approaches enable researchers to address problems whose solution requires a combination of disciplinary approaches and perspectives merging legal with economic analysis, for example.

4. Where sociolegal researchers deploy the methods of applied social science, this can provide harder evidence about the state of play of law in action that would otherwise be available.

5. Through adopting the approaches and techniques of other disciplines, a sociolegal approach permits researchers to acquire and develop new and distinct research skills.

6. Researchers can derive new insights from appreciating how issues that relate to traditional legal themes, for instance war crimes, have been conceptualised in other disciplines, such as international relations and military history.

7. Sociolegal studies allows the dominant assumptions, theories and approaches of more traditional black-letter approaches to law as a distinct discipline to be critically assessed through comparison with the approaches and results of other social scientific disciplines.[286]

8. It transcends the disciplinary isolation of law from the other social sciences through adopting interdisciplinary approaches which are more adequate to the complex and multidimensional character of most forms of legal regulation.[287]

9. The application of this methodology expands the scope of legal analysis beyond law reports and statutes to include the social, economic, gender and political factors influencing the emergence and development of legal doctrine and decision-making.

10. It also requires researchers to address the varied impact of the application of law upon different social, economic, gender and political relations in society at large.

11. It allows a closer relationship between legal research and topical policy debates over the future direction of law reform, and hence an enhanced sense of 'relevance'.

---

[286]Vick, 2004 *op. cit.*, 181-2.

[287]Hutter and Lloyd-Bostock, 1997 *op. cit.*, 24.

12. Adopting a sociolegal approach allows empirical research to be conducted on the use, enforcement and actual workings of legal rules and legal institutional process in a range of new contexts.

13. Sociolegal studies also embraces a redefinition of legal topics, including personal injury compensation, environmental and industrial regulation, law and health care and policy aspects of family law.

14. This approach also allows dissertation students to draw connections between legal theory and wider social theories, which allow aspects of modern society as a whole to be studied in terms of how its characteristics, ideologies and interests permeate law in action.

15. It broadens the perspectives from that of lawyers' law (albeit of doubtful relevance to many legal practitioners) to include the lived experiences of any group in society whose actions or interests are affected by the operation of the legal system, whose interests and values help shape the emergence and enforcement of legal regulation.

Many of the points already made under the heading of the claimed strengths of the black-letter approach can be taken as direct or implicit criticisms of the relevance or practicality of adopting the sociolegal alternative approach to writing law dissertations. There is no need to repeat all of these again here. However, it is certainly arguable that those who claim that sociolegal research is best undertaken as a supplement to prior black-letter analysis of legal doctrine may have difficulty justifying how a single dissertation is expected to analyse the wider range of material at the required depth. The commendable objective of expecting a law dissertation to demonstrate proficiency in the 'intellectual range and provenance' of a wide range of material can shipwreck on the practical reality that the contextual factors are too vast and arcane for these ever to be addressed in sufficient depth to demonstrate adequate comprehension. There remains, however, a considerable number of other criticisms of variable degrees of credibility, many of which have emerged during the internal debates between representatives of different strands of sociolegal studies itself.

Criticism of different strands of sociolegal studies has been a pervasive feature of academic debate within contextual discussions of law and society.

1. Even influential tenets that first prompted the creation of sociolegal studies, such as the need to remedy identifiable gaps between law in books and law in action, have been challenged as insufficiently critical of legal doctrine. For example, critics have noted that the values, interests and ideologies contained within or underpinning judicial decisions and doctrinal commentaries can be just as questionable as the actual practices of the legal system.[288]

2. Politics and sociolegal studies: One potentially negative association of sociolegal studies is the accusation that, far from representing a systematic and objective social scientific approach to the study of law as an important social phenomena, this approach is tied inextricably to specific liberal and radical political agendas.

3. Failure to develop a positive identity: The various associations, academic law journals, and funding bodies promoting and supporting sociolegal studies have, as we

---

[288]*Ibid.*; McBarnet, 1978 *op. cit.*

have already discussed, failed to agree a positive definition of what sociolegal studies are, or aspires to be, other than as an oppositional movement to black-letter approaches.[289]

4. The failure to address theoretical assumptions: Empirical work within the sociolegal movement inevitably draws upon assumptions that, critics note, are not always expressly addressed, openly discussed or justified. As a result, such work repackages and digests law in action issues without necessarily questioning its own underlying assumptions.[290]

5. Uncritical approach to the benefits of existing or reform law: Empirical forms of sociolegal research rarely challenge either the dominance of law as a problem-solving institution, or the nature of the legal order as such.[291]

6. Capture by policy-makers and prevailing ideologies: One persistent concern, related to the difficulties already discussed above, is that empirical projects deploy assumptions regarding policy in an uncritical manner.

7. Naivety regarding the relevance of law reform to effective social change: A further criticism relates to the unduly restricted nature of the reforms endorsed by sociolegal research based on the 'interests and problems of social groupings or social classes that were previously ignored or seen as marginal . . . the relevance of legal determinations and legal procedures is taken for granted. Underpinning this determination is the idea that proper legal regulation is the panacea for all the iniquities identified by sociolegal research.'[292]

8. Underdeveloped conceptualisation of basic categories: All research into law cannot avoid putting into effect the concepts, assumptions, goals and values of a particular interpretative schema. Even in exclusively empirical variants of sociolegal studies, the viability of research depends, in part, upon the validity and appropriateness of this schema to the specific topic.

9. Institutional weakness and patchy coverage of areas of legal research: Another possible problem for law students attempting to undertake dissertation research from a sociolegal perspective is the relative lack of expertise in social science research methods amongst academics within many law schools.

10. Practical difficulties in achieving interdisciplinary research: There is empirical evidence that, outside the Oxford Centre, the sociolegal movement has been more successful in advocating full-blooded and collaborative forms of interdisciplinary research than in actually realising this goal in practice.

11. Failure to be recognised as an interdisciplinary social science: Another difficulty is that, arguably, sociolegal research needs to become at least as influential within each of the various social science departments as it has become in many law departments. This movement needs to shake off the charge that sociolegal studies has provided unwarranted intrusions of social science into law, as distinct from developing a broad-based social science *of* law.

---

[289]Wheeler, 1997 *op. cit.*, 285.

[290]Wheeler, 1997 *op. cit.*, 285 citing M. Salter, 'On the Idea of the Legal World' (1994) 1 *International Jnl. of the Legal Profession*, 283 at 289ff.

[291]Campbell and Wiles, 1975 *op. cit.*, 553.

[292]Hawkins, 1997 *op. cit.*, 11.

12. The failure to transcend a purely oppositional stance to black-letter practices by providing a viable alternative for law students.

There have, therefore, been a number of criticisms of sociolegal studies advanced from different perspectives, which are both internal and external to the sociolegal movement. One cluster of criticisms relates to the claims that sociolegal research amounts to objective social science, and points instead to the permeation of empirical research by the values of the researchers, which are typically liberal or leftist in some sense, and thereby predisposed towards a reform agenda. A related point is that the dependence on official funding also compromises the pretensions towards objectivity and conclusions based on an impartial account of the evidence. Furthermore, sociolegal research which claims to be policy-relevant may often underestimate the extent to which policy-makers will only be interested in conclusions which affirm their prior positions. Another cluster of criticism refer to the failure of this movement to replace the dominance of black-letter approaches within the core subjects of the legal curriculum, or even to provide a range of materials useful to undergraduate students studying such subjects. A further group of difficulties relates to its claims to represent an interdisciplinary form of scholarship which overcomes the isolation of law as a singular and autonomous academic discipline. It has been doubted whether the ideals of interdisciplinarity can be easily achieved in practice, at least outside the context of a team of researchers trained in different social sciences.

These criticisms are not, of course, entirely compatible with each other. It is arguable that, even if one fully accepts the critics' claims, the implications are not necessarily fatal for any form of student dissertation or other project which chooses this approach for its research. On the contrary, students adopting this approach need to be aware of these criticisms and qualify their conduct of research accordingly, particularly with respect to avoiding certain exaggerated and sweeping claims for the policy relevance and objectivity of their findings.

● Conclusion

This chapter has discussed the difficulties in providing a single and conclusive definition of the nature and scope of sociolegal studies. This problem stems from the sheer diversity of projects and types of research that have been conducted within this tradition, including the deployment of a broad range of research methods. Instead, we have suggested that there are some defining tendencies that distinguish sociolegal approaches to the conduct of dissertation research from those of the black-letter tradition. These tendencies include a movement away from studying 'law in books', that is, a close doctrinal analysis of cases and statutes, in favour of studies of 'law in action'. In other words, the emphasis upon studying 'law in action' involves a movement towards investigating the impact of legal regulation upon different groups in society. This includes studying the connection between such regulation and various ideological and policy factors.

We have also suggested that there are numerous possible justifications for students deciding to adopt this approach if, but only if, they have chosen certain types of research questions related to law in action. On the other hand, we have also pointed out and summarised numerous objections to the sociolegal approach which students should also consider before adopting it as the basis for their dissertation research. In both cases, students should satisfy themselves that, even where a criticism may be justified at a general level, it does not apply to their specific dissertation. Finally, we have argued that if students choose this approach, then they should be sensitive to the potential for a series of ethical issues arising, not least those concerned with confidentiality, privacy and informed consent. Such issues can rarely arise during black-letter forms of research because the source documents are exclusively public in nature. By contrast, sociolegal dissertations may deploy social science research methods, such as interviews and observation, where there are considerable risks of violating ethical standards especially if students do not recognise these. For this reason, we have included the statement of ethical principles for the conduct of research drawn up by our own university, which includes a helpful checklist.

6 Comparative and Historical Methods

● Introduction

This chapter introduces students to both comparative and historical methodologies. Students who have experienced the operation of law in another legal system may find comparative analysis particularly appealing because it affords the opportunity of 'cashing in' their own past experience and knowledge. Our analysis takes the form of a summary, rather than an extensive discussion of each of the different types of comparative and historical analysis, not least because this would require a book in its own right. We have, however, provided references to additional readings for Master's level students who wish to study these approaches in greater depth. In addition, we would recommend students inspecting the websites of recent legal history and comparative law academic conferences to appreciate the width of topics addressed and different combinations of methods. Finally, students should appreciate that neither of these approaches are unique to law, such that much 'legal history' has been written by historians as well as by legal academics.

This chapter will summarise aspects of comparative approaches as well as setting out certain advantages and disadvantages of these approaches at a general level. Once again, however, not all of these points will apply equally to every dissertation question and topic. In addition, we suggest that comparative analysis can be carried out in combination with both black-letter and sociolegal approaches depending upon whether the comparison is between 'law in books' (legal doctrine isolated as such and then contrasted), or between the practical operation and effects of 'law in action'. We will illustrate these and related points by reference to some examples of published work.

The section on comparative approaches is followed by one that addresses comparative histories of law. This in turn introduces historical approaches more generally in a way that highlights the differences between black-letter and sociolegal forms of historical analysis. This chapter discusses the arguments in favour of students adopting, or at least including some measure of, historical analysis in their dissertations. The points and arguments are illustrated by examples of historical analysis drawn from across the law syllabus, including property, public law and family policy. Many of the possible disadvantages of historical analysis within the black-letter and sociolegal traditions have already been discussed or at least implied by the points made in Chapters 4 and 5, and for this reason will not be repeated here.

● Comparative Approaches

Comparative approaches to the conduct of dissertation research have formed an increasingly popular option for many dissertation students, particularly as access to the cases, statutes and academic articles of other legal systems and cultures have become available online. Equally, a number of themes within European law lend themselves to a variety of different types of comparison, including comparative enforcement. Comparative research asks how different legal systems and legal cultures have addressed problems that our law faces but in a different way, and with what degree of perceived success or failure.[1]

Such research can include a policy aspect. This is particularly the case where law reform organisations attempt to learn lessons potentially available from the relative success and failure of reforms within other similar legal systems. These could include the introduction of, say, electronic forms of property conveyancing, or the replacement of damages for negligence through the courts with no-fault state compensation schemes, as was once the case in New Zealand. Another example is the question of whether civil law regimes have anything to teach us with respect to the rights of older children to veto their adoption.[2]

Law can be analysed as the expression of a continual social, political and economic debate concerning the appropriate balance between the frequently conflicting interests of, for example, employers, employees and the public. At the same time, the legal issues faced in one jurisdiction are rarely so unique that the experience of others remains entirely irrelevant. At least one other jurisdiction has probably been grappling with the same issues in law and policy. Other legal systems may have proposed, or even implemented, reforms as a consequence of the debate which forms part of the dissertation topic. For this reason, many dissertation topics lend themselves to comparative analysis. Kahn-Freund's seminal writing on the use of comparative approaches within labour law is instructive. He argued that an effective comparison had to take into account not merely the existing law in various jurisdictions under consideration but also, more importantly, the socio-political factors, which form the background against which that law has developed. Hence, a meaningful comparative analysis must consider the 'power structure,' which has influenced and formed the law.

Comparative analysis can be a particularly useful methodology for considering the desirability of introducing forms of legal regulation that have been successfully introduced in other jurisdictions as a response to analogous issues. For example, Price's work analysing organ transplants places the policy underpinning the UK system of regulation in the context of a number of international comparisons. He argues in favour of the UK adopting the statutory definition of brain death endorsed by the Law Reform Commission of Canada.[3] Another example is Thomas Spijkerboer's study of gendered aspects of

---

[1]R. Schlesinger 'The Past and Future of Comparative Law' (1995) 43 *AJCL* 477; O. Kahn-Freund 'On Uses and Misuses of Comparative Law' (1974) 37 *MLR* 1; P. Legrand, 'How to Compare Now' (1996) 16 *Legal Studies* 232; P. Legrand, 'The Impossibility of "Legal Transplants",' 4 *Maastricht J. Eur. & Comp. L.* 111 (1997); Vivian Grosswald Curran, 'Dealing In Difference: Comparative Law's Potential for Broadening Legal Perspectives', *American Journal of Comparative Law*, 657 Fall, 1998; D. Mattei, 'An Opportunity not to be Missed: The Future of Comparative Law in the United States,' 46 *Am. J. Comp. L.* 709–18 (1998); Reimann, 'Stepping Out of the European Shadow: Why Comparative Law in the United States Must Develop its Own Agenda,' 46 *Am. J. Comp. L.* 637–46 (1998).

[2]Christine Piper and Artem Miakishev, 2003 *op. cit.*

[3]See David Price, *Legal and Ethical Issues of Organ Transplantation*, (Cambridge: Cambridge University Press, 2000). See also David Downes, *Contrasts in Tolerance. Post War Penal Policy in the Netherlands and England and Wales*, (Oxford: Clarendon/OUP, 1993); Paul Rock, *A View from the Shadows: The Ministry of the Solicitor General of Canada and the Making of the Justice for Victims of Crime Initiative*, (Oxford: OUP, 1986); Carlo Guarnieri, Patrizia Pederzoli, Clive A. Thomas, *The Power of Judges: A Comparative Study of Courts and Democracy* (Oxford: OUP, 2002).

refugee status. This research has made use of empirical data with respect to Dutch asylum practice. This is then compared to other empirical findings and institutional practices in different Western legal regimes.[4] Harris and Tallon have also edited a collection of essays providing a systematic comparison between how the British and French legal systems address and respond to a series of analogous issues through the use of contracts or quasi-contractual devices.[5] Another policy-oriented, comparative study has drawn conclusions from its analysis of research conducted in North America, Europe and Australia. This indicates that different combinations of policy instruments, tailored to particular environmental goals, can produce effective forms of environmental protection without detriment to commercial enterprises.[6]

Comparative research is not necessarily purely at the service of official law reform agencies. Indeed, it can be carried out solely for academic reasons that fall outside the scope of official agencies altogether. For example, it is possible to compare and contrast the highest courts in two different jurisdictions in order to become more aware of the distinctive features of each. This can highlight differences in the distribution, commitment to, usage of and practical effects of precedent in, for instance, the House of Lords and the US Supreme Court.[7]

Alternatively such research has been employed in pursuit of constitutional and human rights agendas including comparisons of the state's reaction to political dissent in liberal democracies as opposed to totalitarian regimes.[8] This diversity of approaches and themes has been reflected in the ESRC review of sociolegal studies, which noted: 'Socio-legal Studies may also embrace a significant comparative methodology, investigating the social scientific context of law across and between legal systems, both spatially and temporally, including supra national developments.'[9]

Comparative legal research also raises a series of interesting methodological issues, which can prompt a degree of theoretical reflections regarding the nature of the comparative enterprise itself. Nelken draws attention to the problems created by the cultural origins, entrenched assumptions and starting points of comparative researchers that, in practice, make it difficult to understand another legal culture on its own terms. Nelken asks:

> How can we be sure that we are comparing 'like with like' both in terms of the distinctive elements of the criminal process and its place in the larger culture? How far does the idea of treating criminal justice as a series of decision stages which

---

[4] Thomas Spijkerboer, *Gender And Refugee Status* (Aldershot: Ashgate, 2000). For other gender-related comparative studies, see Umar Mohd, *Bride Burning in India: A Socio Legal Study*, (New Delhi: A P H Publishing, 1998), which addresses gendered social customs such as wife-beating and dowry-related violence, discriminatory divorce laws, and selective law enforcement.

[5] D. Harris and D. Tallon, *Contract Law Today: Anglo-French Comparisons* (Oxford: Clarendon, 1989).

[6] Neil Gunningham, Peter Grabosky, Darren Sinclair, *Smart Regulation: Designing Environmental Policy* (Oxford: OUP, 1998).

[7] Richard P. Caldarone, 'Precedent in Operation: A Comparison of the Judicial House of Lords and the US Supreme Court', *Public Law* (2004) 279. (Available in full text via Westlaw).

[8] See Jiri Priban, 'The Legacy of Political Dissent', *Socio-Legal Newsletter* 37 (2002), 7. See also G. Curran, 'The Legalization of Racism in a Constitutional State: Democracy's Suicide in Vichy France,' 50 *Hastings L.J.* (1999) 100; and D. Osiel, 'Dialogue with Dictators: Judicial Resistance in Argentina and Brazil,' 20 *L. & Soc. Inquiry* (1995) 481.

[9] Http://www.esrc.ac.uk/esrccontent/postgradfunding/2000_Guidelines_f15.asp.

can, and should, be studied empirically, reflect Anglo-American assumption and practices?[10]

Indeed, one particularly interesting result of comparative research can be to reveal some of the deeply entrenched and typically unnoticed parochial assumptions that members of one legal system and culture possess with respect to the nature of law. These can be highlighted precisely through the stereotypes used to categorise and interpret events in another legal culture.[11] Some of the more interesting comparative studies do indeed reflect upon the problem of whether it is possible to compare like with like. Consider the following reflections that formed part of a comparative study of the role of precedent in the US Supreme Court as contrasted to that in the House of Lords:

> Differences ranging from the way cases are selected for hearing to the opinion writing process remain, and these differences can impede the building of cross-national comparisons. . . . Variances in the ultimate decision-making process are, however, clearly relevant. For instance, the Supreme Court is much more collegial, arriving at a written decision of the court only after much communication between justices. The Law Lords, on the other hand, write separate judgments in the vast majority of cases, deliver their judgments orally, and have fewer cases overall. The general reasoning and justifications used in the opinions and the specific types of reason regarding precedents may also differ systematically between the countries. With these differences, we are back to the schism in the literature on judicial discretion: the reasoning in opinions can easily be viewed as a function of how judges see their jobs, which itself may be affected by the decision-making structures. . . . There is, however, one further problem separate from these constraints. The House of Lords' practice of sitting in panels of five or, exceptionally, seven Law Lords means that the reasons in the final opinions, and sometimes the disposition of the case itself, may depend on who happens to be assigned to which case. This means that, unlike the Supreme Court between appointments, the House of Lords cannot be treated as a stable institution. Indeed, the only way to account for constantly changing membership seems to be to trace the use of precedents by individual Lords across cases to test for systematic differences, and even then, any conclusions will be drawn from a small sample size and thus must be extremely tentative at best.[12]

Sociolegal research within law and economics has also engaged in comparative research. Here, Ogus has argued that the potential future development of economic analysis of law requires a systematic comparison of common law and continental civil law systems. An important project would be to use comparative methods to analyse the legal systems of national states with broadly comparable levels of economic development. This would allow researchers to test the 'theory that forces operating within a legal system . . . push substantive principles to allocatively efficient outcomes'.[13] He also argues that:

---

[10]Nelken, 2000 *op. cit.*, 4.

[11]For another example of sociolegal publications deploying comparative method, see Nader and Todd, *The Disputing Process: Law in Ten Societies*, (NY: Columbia University Press, 1978), which highlights how disputing can be interpreted as a dynamic process located within, and shaped by, the specific characteristics of the social relations of the parties.

[12]Caldarone, 2004 *op. cit.*, 769.

[13]Ogus, 1995 26.

Comparative analysis might ... demonstrate the universality of hypotheses generated within a particular institutional or cultural framework. On the other hand, it might lead to conclusions that legal institutions and their impact are in some important sense cultural-specific and that, therefore, the models of law and economics have to be adapted or refined to take account of cultural variables.[14]

Legal researchers have also deployed comparative analysis to highlight the discrepancy between how law appears in books and how it actually operates in practice. Comparative forms of sociolegal studies can be a particularly important way of highlighting and illustrating such tensions between law in books and law in action.[15] Consider, for example, the following critique of UK company law advocating that the British system import aspects of Germany's regime of corporate governance:

The separation of ownership from internal control, which resulted in, inter alia, agency costs and undermined efficiency and rationality, may have considerable effects on the functioning of corporate governance bodies. As Williamson rightly states, shareholders are disenfranchised and impotent; their representatives, the directors, are captured by management and no longer act as spokespersons for the shareholders. Thus, directors and managers are free to usurp control from its allegedly rightful possessors, and the exercise of their power is thus illegitimate and irresponsible. Several European, as well as non-European, countries have been trying to solve the above-mentioned problems of corporate governance. On the whole, however, the problems of corporate governance have not been solved yet. A proper form of employee participation scheme would solve some of the problems noted above. The German Public Companies Act of 1965 and various German co-determination laws are often put forward as a model and seem to have been taken as the model for the corporate governance structure proposed by the E.U. The E.U.'s proposals, which are substantially based on the German legislation, aim to give employees the control element of private property without property.[16]

The existence and demonstration of this 'gap' within many areas of legal regulation is considered within sociolegal circles to contradict a central tenet of the black-letter approach: its emphasis upon an abstract analysis of formal and precise rules. Consider, for instance, the following conclusions of the Braithwaites' empirical sociolegal study comparing rules versus standards in nursing home regulation:

Precise rules give more explicit guidance than vague standards. It would seem to follow that regulators will enforce precise rules more reliably than vague standards. This article demonstrates empirically that this is not necessarily so. ... We show how pursuit of reliability for a part of the law can increase the unreliability of a whole body of law.[17]

These researchers note that the British system has been more formalistic and black-letter in the sense of placing greater emphasis on strictly defined precise rules, (in

---

[14]*Ibid.*, 32.

[15]See, for example, Alan Watson, 'Law out of Context', *Edin. L.R.* 2000, 4(2), 147–67 which illustrates this discrepancy with examples from South African, German and US legal writings.

[16]Mahmut Yavasi, 2001.

[17]John and Valerie Braithwaite, 4 *Social and Legal Studies*, (1995), 307–41, 307.

circumstance X, does this or that particular rule apply) than upon open-ended and broad standards (e.g. setting the goal of improving the standards of care in nursing homes) prevalent in America.[18] However, in practice, any such distinction can be difficult to draw. This is because 'the divide [between rules and standards] is not a neat one, the world being full of rules about standards and standards about rules'.[19] In practice, it is frequently a question of the degree to which the goals of legal regulation are sought by means of the application of rules or standards. Furthermore, the formalistic emphasis upon rules in some areas at least can be empirically shown to be self-defeating.[20]

The Braithwaites' study noted that, if attention focuses exclusively on law in books, it might appear that British approach is more rule-dominated than the American. Yet if we examine the law in action in specific areas, then a very different pattern emerges. In other words, the switch of attention to the actual processes of enforcement can reveal that apparently standards-oriented measures are, in practice, enforced in a more rigidly formalistic way than ostensibly rule-based measures, whose enforcement may embody broader policy standards:[21]

> Data collected for the present study . . . [suggests] . . . that British Nursing regulation operates with more precise and formal rules than the more substantive standard-like American Nursing-home regulation, while British regulatory practice is more discretionary, more oriented towards securing improvement in the quality of care and less interested than in the USA in both collecting evidence for litigation concerning non-compliance with rules. While American law is more substantive and less formal than British law, British nursing home regulatory practice is less formal than is American practice.[22]

The explanation these researchers offered lies not in the positive 'legal' materials studied by researchers who have adopted the black-letter approach – instead, it lies in a cultural and political difference: the greater distrust of the state within American political culture and society compared to that which prevails within Europe and Asia:

> Distrust of the legislature by interest groups [litigants] and the courts has led them to pursue the limitation of administrative discretion, driving regulators to more formal regulatory enforcement.[23]

Sociolegal scholars have also conducted comparative studies in a wide range of areas, including those devoted to criminal justice. For example, Beverley Brown *et al.*'s work *Sex Crimes on Trial: The Use of Sexual Evidence in Scottish Courts*[24] claims that, following reforms in 1985, the Scottish experience of the legal treatment of rape victims contains lessons for common law and other systems. This sociolegal analysis of empirical evidence evaluates the implications of changes to the trial process designed to limit the intense scrutiny of women's prior sexual history. It also considers the effects such

---

[18]See Atiyah and Summers, *Form and Substance in Anglo-American Law* (Oxford: Clarendon, 1991).

[19]John and Valerie Braithwaite, 1995 *op. cit.*, 307.

[20]*Ibid.*

[21]*Ibid.*, 308.

[22]*Ibid.*

[23]*Ibid.*

[24]Beverley Brown *et al.*, (Edinburgh: Edinburgh University Press, 1993).

scrutiny has exerted in practice.[25] Peter Duff and Neil Hutton have edited a collection of essays providing a sociolegal account of Scotland's criminal justice processes and agencies. The essays bring together detailed description of legal rules and a sociological analysis of institutional structures that situate a number of contemporary criminal justice issues in Scotland. These include questions relating to gender, and the treatment of ethnic minorities and crime victims, within the broader policy processes and different forms of social, political, and cultural action.[26]

Another noteworthy example of comparative legal research within the criminal justice field is a study addressing the perceived need, in many national contexts, to develop new institutional strategies that embody principles of 'restorative justice'. These principles have been developed through practices of, for example, conferencing and victim-offender mediation. This collection analyses the current practice and potential of restorative justice with respect to young offenders in Australia, Canada, England, New Zealand, South Africa, the USA and various continental European countries.[27] Finally, David Nelken has edited and contributed to a collection of essays containing both sub-stantive and sophisticated methodological discussions of the potential difficulties of comparing how different legal cultures define and interpret various criminal justice issues, including covert and proactive policing.[28]

Within the field of family law and policy, Eekelaar has conducted comparative analysis of the legal position on post-divorce property adjustments in New Zealand, Scotland, Australia and the USA. The aim of this research was to evaluate the policy choices under-pinning current practices in England and Wales, and its results highlighted the relatively problematic and backward nature of British practices when compared to progressive developments within these other systems.[29] Sociolegal writers have also produced com-parative studies of the economic and social effects of divorce, including aspects that concern the redistribution of family property and income support of family members.[30] Such comparative forms of policy research clearly reject the positivist's strict separation of descriptive and evaluative analysis. Indeed, much research insists that legal analysis is inevitably related to questions of the moral and ethical validity of existing and proposed policies.[31]

As with previous chapters, it is useful to sum up various pros and cons of comparative analysis that are potentially relevant to dissertation students. A comparative approach

---

[25]Other examples of transnational analysis are Christopher Harding and Bert Swart, *Enforcing European Community Rules: Criminal Proceedings, Administrative Procedure and Harmonization*, (Aldershot: Ashgate, 1996); A. H. L. Shee, *Legal Protection of Children Against Sexual Exploitation in Taiwan: A Socio-legal Perspective* (Aldershot: Ashgate, 1998).

[26]Peter Duff and Neil Hutton (eds), *Criminal Justice in Scotland*, (Aldershot: Ashgate, 1999).

[27]Morris and Maxwell, *Restorative Justice for Juveniles*, (Oxford: Hart, 2003).

[28]Nelken, 2000 *op. cit*.

[29]John Eekelaar, 'Property Adjustment After Divorce', in Hawkins, 1997 *op. cit*.; Maclean, 1991 uses a pro-cess of international comparisons of post-divorce financial arrangements to cast new light on the issues raised, and range of possible policy responses.

[30]Lenore J. Weitzman and Mavis Maclean, *Economic Consequences of Divorce: The International Perspective*, (Oxford: OUP, 1991).

[31]For a discussion of comparative forms of contextual analysis see, M. Findlay, *The Globalisation of Crime*, (Cambridge: CUP, 1999), 6-8; for a brief example, see Mary Welstead, 'Case Commentary: Financial sup-port in Same-Sex Relationships - a Canadian Constitutional Solution', (2000) *CFam* 12.1(73).

to dissertation writing can be particularly appealing and useful to students for a number of reasons:

- A comparative approach facilitates more critical, questioning attitudes towards law by undermining the 'taken for granted' positions on legal provisions and practices. It does so by highlighting the relative peculiarities and distinctive features of a particular version of 'law' or a specific type of legal response to an issue. Too frequently – in long-established practices of law teaching or applications – these would often be simply accepted as 'given' without question.

- If a jurisdiction sharing English common law has reformed the topic in question, then students can usefully consider the details of those reforms. Where those reforms have been in place for long enough, it may be possible for a dissertation deploying a comparative methodology to assess how effective the operation of these reforms have been in practice.

- Although not binding on English courts, the decisions from other common law countries, such as Australia and the USA, can still be cited as authorities. Such cases are typically used where English authorities on a point are controversial, contradictory, weak or lacking altogether. To properly understand such a persuasive authority, in particular to ensure that the case does not turn on a statute or precedent peculiar to the source jurisdiction, students will almost certainly need to read more widely.

- In some areas of law, the subject matter of a legal dissertation may require a view broader than English law can give. For instance, studying the legal regulation of international trade or offshore trusts might be difficult if you refuse to look at the law of other jurisdictions.

- The development of EC law, particularly via the judgements and interpretations of the ECJ, signals a new era of convergence between the legal systems of EC member states.

- Adopting a comparative approach can provide dissertation students with a valuable framework through which researchers can explain conflicts and differences between legal concepts and particular provisions, and perhaps identify possible 'common ground' solutions.

On the other hand, it is equally important for students who are considering deploying a comparative methodology for their dissertations to be aware of the following possible pitfalls and disadvantages:

- It can be very time-consuming and, in particular, difficult to timetable accurately. Although British interlibrary loans can pick up many primary and secondary materials, some materials may be needed from the source jurisdiction, and this may take some time. If you intend to use comparative materials, we would recommend compiling the list of those materials you wish to consult as soon as possible.

- Although online databases and the internet have recently provided access to European, American, Irish and Canadian primary sources, the extent to which you make use of primary materials for many other comparator systems will almost inevitably be somewhat limited. Realistically most comparative research at this level involves students relying upon secondary sources, particularly as articles and textbooks. These will be out of date, and subject to all the limitations of secondary sources in the English jurisdiction.

- The posturing value of comparative law may provide a superficial cover for other weaknesses in a dissertation's analysis. It is common for students to feel that if they have a chapter on, say, 'United States and Australian Approaches to Reform.' they are automatically engaging in a serious and in-depth level of legal analysis. But the level of discussion in that chapter must still reach the appropriate level, albeit taking into account the special pressures of discussing a foreign jurisdiction. It is not appropriate to take a very critical approach to English law in the rest of your dissertation, and then simply narrate the law in a foreign jurisdiction in a purely descriptive and uncritical way, as if the lessons of comparison flow in an entirely one-way direction.

- Sometimes a dissertation will fall into a discussion of English law, a discussion of law in a foreign jurisdiction and a 'comparison' chapter. One danger is that none of them will really be enough to make the overall dissertation become a sound piece of work: all three elements might be carried out too sketchily or briefly. In particular, the 'comparison' chapters can become little more than a point-by-point comparison of the detail of the positive law in the two jurisdictions, with little or no critical analysis of the policy lessons to be learned.

● Comparative Historical Approaches

Historians of law and the legal process have published a number of comparative accounts of many different legal topics, including dispute resolution and criminal justice.[32] Within criminal justice scholarship, there have been a number of comparative historical projects.[33] For example, Petra De Vries's study entitled ' "White slaves" in a colonial nation: the Dutch campaign against the traffic in women in the early twentieth century' addresses, in a distinctly sociolegal manner, the issue of the Dutch campaign against trafficking in women for sexual exploitation within brothels and elsewhere. Interestingly, this is achieved without, in any sense, compromising its status as a contribution to early twentieth century history of the Dutch abolitionist movement and legal and other responses to such trafficking.[34] Another such comparative historical study has reconstructed the processes through which prohibition of alcohol was first introduced into nineteenth-century Hawaii.[35] This has highlighted the influence of a political agenda concerning race and identity with respect to both the colonised and the coloniser. The literature on sociolegal approaches to criminal justice includes other comparative histories of the youth justice systems in Scotland and England and Wales focusing on reasons why the two systems diverged during the 1970s until the late 1990s, and how the Scottish system developed techniques of punishment which had been established but then abandoned decades earlier in England and Wales.[36]

---

[32]See Robert Palmer, 'The Common Law and the French Connection', 4 *Anglo-Norman Studies*, (1982) 77-92; Paul Hyman, 'Norms and Legal Before 1150' 6 *Current Legal Issues*, 2004, 41-62; W. Davies and P. Fouracre, *The Settlement of Disputes in Early Medieval Europe*, (Cambridge: CUP, 1996); Thomas N. Bisson, (ed.) *Cultures of Power: Lordship, Status and Process in 12th Century Europe*, (Philadelphia, 1995).

[33]Leon Radzinowicz, *A History of the English Criminal Law and its Administration from 1750*, (London: Stevens, 1948); William Cornish *et al.*, *Crime and Law in Nineteenth Century Britain* (Dublin: Gov't Publications, 1978; Bailey, *Policing and Punishment in Nineteenth Century Britain*, (London: Croom-Helm, 1981). For limited exceptions, see A. Harding, *A Social History of English Law*, (London: Penguin, 1966).

[34]14(1), *Social & Legal Studies*, (2005) 39-60.

[35]Marilyn Brown 'Aina Under the Influence: The Criminalization of Alcohol in 19th-Century Hawai'i', *Theo. Crim.* (2003), 7(1), 89-110.

[36]Lesley McAra, 'The Cultural and Institutional Dynamics of Transformation: Youth Justice in Scotland, England and Wales', *Cambrian L.R.* (2004), 35, 23-54.

Another sociolegal project has identified five stages in the history of crime regulation within common law regimes through a comparative analysis of differences between US and Australian penal histories.[37]

A more obvious exception has been recent attempts to combine comparative analysis with historical contextualisation within the field of human rights, in particular the influence of national traditions upon the reception of newly-incorporated European human rights measures.[38] For instance Marie-Benedicte Dembour and Magda Krzyzanowska-Mierzewska's sociolegal analysis suggests that the European Convention's popularity within Poland needs to be understood in the context of this country's troubled national history, particularly the continuing legacy of life during the communist period and the historical lack of a developed legal culture, and the difficulties experienced during its transition to a modified form of capitalism.[39]

● Historical Methodologies More Generally

Some but not all forms of historical analysis are compatible with the sociolegal approach discussed above. For example, much sociolegal literature on the changing patterns of how law has come to regulate health-and-safety issues within industry has found a readership at least as much within journals specialising in social history and economic history, as within those devoted to the sociology of law. This lends support to the idea that such contextualisations do not necessarily belong within sociolegal studies.

In this context, should those students interested in applying an interdisciplinary analysis of the historical context of the emergence, development and change of law in action consider their dissertation research as aligned with the sociolegal movement? Alternatively, should such students consider their research as belonging more closely to the sub-discipline of 'legal history', which is more closely assigned with the black-letter approach to legal research?[40]

A strong case can be made for students including an element of historical contextualisation as part of their dissertation. A key argument here is that many, if not all, examples of legal research inevitably presuppose at least certain aspects of knowledge of the past. This remains true even where this is assumed, rather than subjected to detailed investigation and empirical reconstruction. Take, for instance, the popular theme of law and discrimination. One variant on policy-relevant sociolegal research are those projects by law students and academics that are prompted by supposedly progressive judicial decisions and legislative interventions that have enlarged the rights of historically

---

[37] John Braithwaite, 'Crime in a Convict Republic', *M.L.R.* 2001, 64(1), 11–50.

[38] Marie-Benedicte Dembour and Magda Krzyzanowska-Mierzewska, 'Ten Years On: The Popularity of the Convention in Poland', *E.H.R.L.R.* 2004, 4, 400–23.

[39] *Ibid.*

[40] K. J. M. Smith and J. P. S. McLaren, 'History's Living Legacy: An outline of 'Modern' Historiography of the Common Law', 21 *Legal Studies* (2001) 251–324, at 267. Professor Sir John Baker was knighted for his services to legal history in 2003. In, 'Why the History of English Law has not been Finished', 59 *The Cambridge Law Journal*, March [2000] pp. 62–84, at 64 – he laments that, after nearly 80 years of work on the series of Curia Regis Rolls, transcribers have only reached the year 1245. By contrast, Lobban claims that 'the legal historians' task "is not that of the antiquarian, gathering and recording all the data that can be recovered from the past"' Michael Lobban, 'Introduction: The Tools and Tasks of the Legal Historian' in 6 *Current Legal Issues*, (Oxford: OUP, 2004), 23.

disadvantaged groups and/or groups subject to continuing forms of legal and social discrimination.[41] This type of research will typically welcome judicial or legislative innovations as an overdue, if not necessarily sufficient, corrective to past discriminatory policies enshrined in legally-sanctioned or enabled practices. Such policy-oriented research also emphasises its contextual limitations, and hence the perceived need for further legislative extension and entrenchment of the right in question.[42] It is rarely informed by original historical reconstruction of events and patterns of change based on primary historical sources. Yet, such research nevertheless presupposes the truth of such reconstructions, if only to correctly identify the various ways in which specific groups have, in fact, been historically disadvantaged, and the continuing legacy of such disadvantage.

We would advance the following arguments in favour of the proposition that some element of historical analysis can be a useful, even necessary, element to many types of legal dissertation.

First, both generally and certainly with respect to many themes addressed by legal research, it is rarely possible to draw a clear-cut distinction between the past and present of the dissertation topic. This is because the present state of the topic remains encrusted with the legacy of all that it is perceived as having become over a sustained period of time. This, perhaps, explains why many legal researchers whose approaches are not exclusively historical nevertheless reconstruct, at least in an outline fashion, recent developments within their research fields.[43] Furthermore, within the materials studied by black-letter scholarship, it is important to recognise that a trial process will typically involve a degree of historical reconstruction. The trial lawyers who are engaged in this partial reconstruction will inevitably contest both the facts and their legal implications.

Contemporary war crimes trials are, for example, repeatedly defined as partial continuations and reactivation of the 'Nuremberg legacy'. The history of these trials is now being rewritten to reflect how recent developments, such as the creation of the Rwandan and former-Yugoslavia tribunals[44] and the emergence of a permanent International Criminal Court, have extended this increasingly 'contemporary' legacy.[45] A similar point applies to social welfare legislation that extends the legacy of the pioneering reforms creating the modern welfare state.

---

[41]Jennifer Brown, 'Discriminatory Experiences of Women Police: A Comparison of Officers Serving in England and Wales, Scotland, Northern Ireland and the Republic of Ireland', *Int. J. Soc. L.* (2000), 28(2), 91-111. This comparative study does, however, reconstruct the history of sexually discriminatory recruitment practices within both British and Irish police forces as well as reflecting on the experiences of a sample of affected officers, and therefore cannot be accused of simply presupposing the validity of what today many would identify as long-standing patterns of discriminatory treatment.

[42]Lisa Glennon, '*Fitzpatrick v Sterling Housing Association Ltd* – An Endorsement of The Functional Family?' (2000) 14 *IJLP&F* 226.

[43]Maureen O'Sullivan, 'Making Copyright Ambidextrous: An Exposé of Copyleft', *J.I.L.T.* 2002, 3, internet (providing a summary history of free and open source software).

[44]In 1993, the Security Council gave the International Criminal Tribunal for the former Yugoslavia (ICTY) jurisdiction over various crimes committed in civil wars - notably genocide, crimes against humanity, and 'violations of the laws or customs of war'. In 1994, the UN Security Council granted the International Tribunal for Rwanda jurisdiction over genocide, and crimes against humanity and other war crimes.

[45]Whitney Harris, *Tyranny on Trial*, 2nd edn, (Dallas: Southern Methodist University Press, 1998).

Individuals and groups, including lawyers, whose actions, omissions and achievements comprise the subject matter of many forms of legal enquiry, act on the basis of a certain historical explanation. This intuitive 'explanation' held by the research subjects can include how relevant events came about, their continuation and revision of earlier practices, and what is needed to alter them 'for the better'. It needs to be addressed and included within any legal analysis of the reasons behind actions and omissions of all participants within the legal field.

There is another cluster of arguments suggesting that the very process of studying law in action cannot forsake a historical form of analysis. The very idea of taking a particular event or process as the object of legal research necessarily requires scholars to enter into historical enquiries. This is needed in order to appreciate the extent to which the guiding ideas, beliefs and values contained within, or otherwise attributed to or associated with, the research topic have come to be constituted in their present but still developing form. The impact of changing contexts, and the resulting lessons of how and why things have changed, are positively enhanced by historical contextualisation. Such lessons can call in question the 'conventional wisdom' of the nature, purpose and scope of your dissertation topic.[46] Gordon, for example, has recognised that legal histories are capable of contributing to the wider tasks of critique of ideologies supportive of the status quo:

> that produces disturbances in the field – that inverts or scrambles familiar narratives of stasis, recovery or progress; anything that advances rival perspectives (such as those of the losers rather than the winners) for surveying developments, or that posits alternative trajectories that might have produced a very different present – in short any approach that unsettles the familiar strategies that we use to tame the past in order to normalise the present.[47]

It would be impossible for a dissertation to conduct research seriously into legal aspects of genocide, for example, without considering how this legal category first developed in response to a series of specific historical events and processes, and then became refined through a succession of measures within international and domestic law, such as the 1948 Genocide Convention. This legal response can only be properly understood through a close reconstruction of the factors underlying and explaining such changes.

As a number of sociolegal writers have recognised, a similar point demonstrably applies to the need to understand the recent history of aspects of contemporary housing law and policy. This includes how different interest groups have deployed key concepts within different ideological discourses concerning the direction of possible leasehold reform.[48] Furthermore, it may be impossible for students undertaking dissertations to study the operation of law without becoming conscious of, and working on, source materials and institutional settings, language patterns and protocols that clearly stem from the past. To make sense of these materials requires scholars to broaden the time-frame

---

[46]Leslie Sheinman, 'Ethical Practice or Practical Ethics? The Case of the Vendor-Purchaser Rule', *Legal Ethics* (2000), 3(1), 27-48; Shane Kilcommins, 'Context and Contingency in the Historical Penal Process: The Revision of Revisionist Analysis Using the Twelve Judges' Notebooks as One tool of Analysis', *Hold. L.R.* 1998, 19(1), 1-54.

[47]R. Gordon, 'Foreword: The Arrival of Critical Historicism' (1997) 49 *Stan L. R*, 1023, 1024.

[48]Sarah Blandy and David Robinson, 'Reforming Leasehold: Discursive Events and Outcomes 1984-2000'. *J. Law & Soc.* (2001) 28(3), 384-408.

they are using in their dissertation by interpreting such materials as the most recent phases of a long-standing, but still developing, process of historical evolution.

Consider, for example, published discussions of the legal regulation of lesbian sexual relations. These have included the expression of arguments for and against parity with heterosexual relationships concerning the age of consent, and the appropriateness of legal frameworks that claim to be not only universal but also gender-neutral. One sociolegal study addresses this issue through a historical reconstruction of the first criminal codification of the age of consent by the Offences Against the Person Act 1861, its subsequent interpretation by a cluster of evolving case law, through to more recent debate over sex between women, including the impact of lesbian feminist perspectives in the 1970s and contemporary policy debates regarding the limits of anti-discrimination measures.[49] This type of historical reconstruction can hardly be dismissed as falling outside the scope of sociolegal studies on the grounds that it is an example of 'history for its own sake'. This is because it draws lessons from this historical trajectory which culminate in a critical discussion of the policy dimensions of the Sex Offenders Act 1997 in the context of the relative advantages and costs to young lesbian women of campaigning for a standardised age of consent law, including a possible increase in the number of prosecutions for lesbian acts.[50] A similar point applies to sociolegal projects that have reconstructed the historical dynamics of those social and cultural transformations within France that have culminated in the recent 'normalisation' of how law regulates heterosexual and homosexual cohabitation, not least by introducing quasi marriage status for homosexual partnerships.

Once again, the importance of this type of historical contextualisation for dissertation students is that it provides an example of types of research that allow the significance of recent legal and policy reforms to be considered in a wider and more sophisticated manner. It makes it possible for the topic to be better understood by a form of analysis which locates such reforms within the context of a series of transformations whose patterns and trajectory have unfolded over many decades.[51] Such contextualisation interprets the past not for its own sake but rather to allow the significance and implications of current events to be more adequately understood than would otherwise be the case.

Even where the period of contextualisation does not extend to the present, as when a dissertation is confined to the period 1945–1979, a similar enhancement of our knowledge of present-day phenomena is still possible. For example, other sociolegal themes relating to law's definition and regulation of gender identities have benefited from historical scholarship, including studies of the British state's reaction to injuries caused by stereotypically masculine activities within the sixteenth and seventeenth centuries, such as duelling,[52] and reconstructions of early twentieth century attempts to censure the early suffragette movement.[53] A similar point applies to those studies of

---

[49]Matthew Waites, Inventing a 'Lesbian Age of Consent'? The History of the Minimum Age for Sex Between Women in the UK.' *S. & L.S.* 2002, 11(3), 323–42.

[50]*Ibid.*

[51]Claude Martin and Irene Thery, 'The PACS and Marriage and Cohabitation in France', *Int. J.L.P.F.* (2001) 15(1), 135–58.

[52]A. Mark Liddle, 'State, Masculinities and Law: Some Comments on Gender and English State-Formation', *Brit. J. Criminol.* (1996), 36(3), 361–80.

[53]Alison Young ' "Wild Women": The Censure of the Suffragette Movement', *Int. J. Soc. L.* (1988), 16(3), 279–93.

the changing historical treatment of women within, and by, the English criminal justice system.[54]

In addition, those studying the meaning and implications of even currently emerging events, such as the further development and refinement of the Nuremberg principles within the trial of Milosevic, still face a topic that remains determined, to a greater or lesser extent, by a certain understanding of the past. For example, the current meaning of most topics is influenced by whether they are perceived as being completely unprecedented, ('a radical departure'), or as modifications of earlier situations combining elements of novelty with the continuation of more traditional features, or as a simple repetition of familiar historical patterns. In each case, the interpretation of the meaning of an evolving dissertation topic necessarily draws, in part, upon a certain understanding of earlier developments, and hence a distinctly historical form of legal knowledge. Consider, for example, the analysis of the implications for policing and criminal justice systems of the British handover of Hong Kong to China in 1997. A viable dissertation on this topic would surely need to consider the tension between long-standing traditions of colonial and other forms of policing in a manner that included some measure of historical understanding of this relationship both generally and in the specific case of this particular colony. Clearly, any attempt by dissertation students or other researchers to justify one or more of these interpretations of such events is only possible by drawing upon a reliable and pre-existing type of historical knowledge.

Indeed, one of the claimed advantages of historical reconstruction of legal topics is the discovery that many reforms or supposedly 'new' approaches to the understanding of legal developments re-enact aspects of long-forgotten initiatives from past centuries. One example concerns supposedly 'novel' and ground-breaking theories of the 'risk society' formulated by criminal justice specialists and criminologists. These researchers deployed statistical analysis to classify and order criminal activity.[55] However, this 'breakthrough' can be shown to recapitulate the analysis of certain seventeenth-century economists.[56]

Even for those researchers whose focus remains resolutely fixed upon the present state of the law cannot ignore one element of the enduring presence of the past that continues to permeate their field of research. The history of developments whose most recent manifestations are studied by legal researchers can never become entirely settled. It can, and often does, constitute a battleground between competing perspectives on the topic in question that reinterpret the past to consolidate, revise or subvert the perceived legitimacy of aspects of the status quo. Indeed, one possible topic for legal research is precisely how authoritarian regimes act on their recognition that interpretations of national history, including the history of human rights developments and labour history, can represent threats to their own future. It is possible to study how such officially perceived threats are then censored and combated in favour of more 'official'

---

[54]Lucy Zedner, *Women, Crime and Custody in Victorian England* (NY: Oxford University Press, 1991); J. Kermode and G. Walker, eds, *Women, Crime and the Courts in Early Modern England*, (London: UCL Press, 1994).

[55]George S. Rigakos and Richard W. Hadden, 'Crime, Capitalism and the "Risk Society": Towards the Same Olde Modernity?' *Theo. Crim.* (2001), 5(1), 61-84.

[56]Pat O'Malley, 'Discontinuity, Government and Risk: A Response to Rigakos and Hadden', *Theo. Crim.* 2001, 5(1), 85-92.

and self-justificatory historical accounts supportive of the status quo. The opponents of such regimes may also mobilise a no less selective interpretation of the past to suggest that the present regime are trampling upon long-standing common law rights and liberties,[57] or that an officially 'suppressed' history of resistance exists, an underside social history, which should guide future struggles. Within the context of British legal education, a number of writers have detected a related justificatory and rationalisation strategy at play within aspects of the black-letter textbook tradition.[58] In short, the history of legal and constitutional developments is continually in the process of being rewritten and contested within present scholarship and beyond, and this contestation takes place with a view to its implications for the immediate future. This presence of competing interpretations and reinterpretations of the significance and implications of historical events remains a perennial feature of the contemporary manifestation of many, if not all, examples of legal dissertation topics. As such, it cannot be ignored without impoverishing your understanding of the issues under discussion.

The implication of these arguments is that even those legal researchers who claim to have no interest in undertaking historical enquiries as part of their dissertation project remain subject to a paradox. They cannot avoid being confronted by a number of aspects of their research field that remain unintelligible unless they are seen through the lens of specific assumptions about the continuation and modification of the past within the present. These points undermine the contention that legal scholarship can ever forsake historical enquiries by concentrating on the immediate present as if this could ever be fully isolated from the past.[59] Such arguments support the argument that an application of some form of historical methodology is required as an integral part of dissertation research.

Indeed, Smith and McLaren make a stark generalisation when they claim that 'legal historiography has relevance to, and the ability to insinuate itself into, practically every region and crevice of legal study and scholarship'.[60] However, even if this is true with respect to traditional legal scholarship, does this broad claim also apply to interdisciplinary historical work within sociolegal studies? Interdisciplinarity has become a feature that many leading commentators, such as Twining, have recognised as one of the distinctive tendencies of a type of legal scholarship 'that views almost everything through the multiple lenses of several disciplines'.[61] In both multi- and interdisciplinary legal scholarship, the aim is to 'transcend disciplinary boundaries by taking as the focus the subject area of law in society'.[62] Yet, those surveying contemporary legal history have implied that analysing historical contexts harmonises with the generally interdisciplinary and multidisciplinary character of sociolegal studies, with Smith and McLaren characterising 'contemporary legal historiography as the quintessence of a multidisciplinary pursuit, moving within the political and social sciences, the humanities, and beneficially borrowing

---

[57]The history workshop movement of socialist historians is a case in point.

[58]Alan Norrie, *Crime, Reason and History: A Critical Introduction to Criminal Law*, (Cambridge University Press, 2001), Doupe and Salter, 'Concealing the Past?: Questioning Textbook Interpretations of the history of Equity and Trusts', 2-3 (2000a) *Liverpool Law Review* 253; Doupe and Salter, 'The Cheshire World-View', 11(1) *Kings College Law Journal*, (2000b) 49.

[59]Tosh, *The Pursuit of History*, (London: Hutchinson, 1984), n.16, p. 1.

[60]Smith and McLaren, 2001 *op. cit.*, 252.

[61]William Twining, 'Remembering 1972' in D. J. Galligan, 1995, 43.

[62]Editorial, *BJLS* 1 (1974) 1.

from and drawing on the insights of each'.[63] If this is true, then perhaps it is still worth considering the place of historical contextualisation within student dissertations that deploy a sociolegal methodology.

In one sense, few types of academic analysis can claim to be as interdisciplinary or contextual in their approach to scholarly research as those academic studies using historical methodologies. This is a 'discipline' that includes conferences, sub-fields and specialist journals that positively embrace, amongst others, economic, social, political, institutional, social policy, gender and cultural contexts, and the complex and changing relationship within and between each of these contexts. It is arguable, therefore, that at least *certain types* of historical methods and analytical techniques could be included within any approach to legal research and scholarship that, like sociolegal studies, emphasises the importance of distinctly interdisciplinary forms of contextual analysis.[64]

Students who have a passing acquaintance with sociolegal approaches may suggest that legal history is not included within the methods frequently employed. For example, in the 2005 SLSA *Directory*, only seven members listed legal history as a particular research interest. Furthermore, not all of these researchers have published specifically on legal history. Of those who have, two are well known for their contributions to other sociolegal subjects. Lois Bibbings has published on conscientious objectors in the Great War,[65] as well as on gender, rights and the body; whilst Rebecca Probert, a convenor for Family Law and Policy at SLSA conferences, has been a regular contributor to legal history streams. She has widely published on the Marriage Act of 1753, including within a mainstream history journal.[66] Initial impressions of the lack of legal history scholarship within sociolegal studies can, however, be deceptive because, as we will illustrate below, the overwhelming majority of examples of historical contextualisation within sociolegal studies stem from scholars who do not list legal history as a particular interest but who include the reconstruction of past events and processes as an integral part of their wider interdisciplinary methodology.

In short, this brief reconstruction suggests that, providing those students interested in applying a sociolegal approach remain committed to an interdisciplinary approach to studying law in context, there is no reason, either in principle or in practice, why historical contextualisation must be excluded from the scope of the sociolegal research. On the contrary, we would endorse the more positive argument that contextualisation of legal topics over extended slices of space remains one-sided and incomplete if the equally important issue of their emergence, development and transformation over time is ignored through a 'parochialism of the present'. Indeed, it is possible to identify many

---

[63]Smith and McLaren, 2001 *op. cit.*, 252.

[64]Interdisciplinary legal research capable of embracing historical studies includes those projects in which the techniques and methods of law and at least one other discipline interact to produce a type of analysis and research findings that would not otherwise have been possible through the application of either discipline in isolation. J. Weinstein, 'Coming of Age: Recognising the Importance of Interdisciplinary Education in Law Practice' (1999) 74 *Washington Law Rev*. 319 at 353.

[65]L. S. Bibbings, 'Conscientious Objectors in the Great War: The Consequences of Rejecting Military Masculinities', in ed. Paul Higate, *Military Masculinities: Identity and the State* (London: Greenwood, 2003); 'Images of Manliness: The Portrayal of Soldiers and Conscientious Objectors in the Great War', *Social and Legal Studies* 12(3) 2003, 335-58; 'State Reaction to Conscientious Objection', in I. Loveland (ed.), *Frontiers of Criminality* (London: Sweet and Maxwell, 1995).

[66]Rebecca Probert, 2005.

examples of historically-oriented sociolegal research that have been generally accepted as comprising a vital part of this movement's analytical techniques. For example, a number of the early and ground-breaking works in the 'law in context' book series made a specific virtue of their commitment to, and practice of, historical contextualisation.[67] This commitment was evident even in traditionally unpromising areas of sociolegal scholarship, such as equity and trusts.[68]

By 1994, the ESRC's review of sociolegal studies rightly acknowledged the importance of at least social scientific forms of historical analysis when it noted: 'Socio-legal Studies may also embrace a significant comparative methodology, investigating the social scientific context of law across and between legal systems, both spatially and temporally, including supra national developments.'[69] A similar recognition is apparent within American sociolegal studies, which traditionally have been influential upon developments within Britain. Levine, for instance, has maintained that sociolegal researchers should attempt to examine 'data from different time periods, units of analysis, and locales; seeking explanation in specific contexts; and searching for coherent results through multiple methods, *across long time spans*, and in comparative perspective' (emphasis added).[70] Within the field of sociolegal studies, the American Law and Society Association have introduced an annual award, the Hurst Prize in Legal History.[71] Thus, with respect to historical contextualisation, there is some evidence that American forms of sociolegal studies may have become more receptive than British models. This is particularly the case concerning reconstructions of twentieth-century historical developments.[72] Within American sociolegal literature, there has been an explicit inclusion of historical methods, particularly 'locally based' types, (almost a sociolegal equivalent to

---

[67]Philip Harris, *An Introduction to Law* 5th edn (London: Butterworths, 1997) notes: 'I have tried to locate legal rules and institutions within the context of their historical background, taking into account the economic and political forces which have shaped – some might even say distorted – English law. To do this I have incorporated materials from disciplines other than that which is conventionally regarded as law'. xxxiii/Preface to 1997 edition. Harris's work reconstructs aspects of industrialisation and the role of law, the changing relationship between factories, social class, labour relations and employment contracts, and the impact of Thatcherism upon legal developments.

[68]Graham Moffat, *Trusts Law: Texts and Materials*, 2nd edn (London: Butterworths, 1994), whose opening two chapters contextualise the historical development of trusts as social devices deployed to achieve specific economic and other functions. Works in this series within other supposedly 'private law' areas include Hugh Collins, *The Law of Contract* 3rd edn (London: Butterworths, 1997) whose opening chapters consider, in a critical and contextual way, the activity of contracting within the specific context of laissez-faire policies of freedom of contract.

[69]Http://www.esrc.ac.uk/esrccontent/postgradfunding/2000_Guidelines_f15.asp. Whether this implies that the type of historical contextualisation practised within the humanities remains inappropriate will be examined further later.

[70]F. Levine, 'Presidential Address' (1990) *Law and Society Review*, 1–25 at 24.

[71]Sally Engle Merry, *Colonizing Hawai'i: The Cultural Power of Law* (Princeton: Princeton Univ. Press, 1999) won this prize in 2002. In writing this interdisciplinary work, Merry, an anthropologist, produced a careful historical study of the colonization of Hawai'i by New Englanders in the middle part of the nineteenth century. To produce this work, Merry examined sixty years of court records from the town of Hilo, covering roughly the period 1820–1880, in order to understand the ways in which Hawaiians both appropriated and transformed Anglo-American law as a means of resisting the European imperial project. But, she also conducted a significant amount of ethnographic research in Hawai'i in order to explore and understand the Hawaiian plantation system of the late nineteenth and early twentieth centuries.

[72]Don Harris, 'The Development of Socio-Legal Studies in the United Kingdom', (1983) 2 *Legal Studies*, 315, 332. For an argument for adopting historical approaches published in a non-specialist journal, see Nicola Lacey, 'In Search of the Responsible Subject: History, Philosophy and Social Sciences in Criminal Law Theory,' *M.L.R.* 2001, 64(3), 350–71.

local history) into aspects of sociolegal studies.[73] These include historical studies of legally-sanctioned punishment in areas as diverse as intellectual property, corporate securities, the regulation of drugs, and tax fraud.[74]

This brief reconstruction of a developing tendency within British and American sociolegal scholarship to increasingly recognise the value of historical studies suggests that at least certain types of such scholarship can no longer be excluded, or marginalized, as clearly falling outside the scope of this approach to legal research. Before this provisional conclusion can be accepted, it is now necessary to address the argument that those empirical studies that analyse legal topics by identifying and placing them within their developing historical contexts and onward trajectory represent contributions to the discipline of history, and therefore not to law. One irony of any such rejection of historical contextualisation from those within the sociolegal movement is that one of the pioneers of sociology of law, Roscoe Pound, is widely acknowledged to have derived many of his original insights from an extensive review and historical contextualisation of legal phenomena.[75] A similar point could be made with respect to a number of other pioneers and inspirations for social sciences, not least Max Weber and, to a lesser extent, Karl Marx.[76]

If the argument that only *certain types* of historical reconstruction can be assimilated into the toolkit of the research methods of sociolegal studies is correct, then this claim must be substantiated by reference to a far greater range of empirical supportive evidence than we have discussed to date. Fortunately, there are no shortages of examples of distinctly and recognisably sociolegal research that positively embrace historical contextualisation as part of their wider interdisciplinary or multidisciplinary mix. The inclusion of historical, as well as spatial contextualisation, has formed one part of the earliest contributions to British sociolegal studies. The pioneering studies by the Oxford Centre for Socio-Legal Studies involved, as a matter of principle, close collaboration between legal academics and social historians, as well as statisticians, economists, sociologists and others.[77] The commitment to include a distinctly historical type of contextualisation represented one of the multidisciplinary methodologies developed throughout this

---

[73]See, for an example of the relationship between legal developments and socio-economic changes, Willard Hurst, *Law and Economic Growth: The Legal History of the Lumber Industry in Wisconsin, 1936-1915*, (Cambridge MA: Harvard University Press/Belknap Press, 1964). Hurst's work represents a legal historian's empirical response to broader and instrumentalist forms of legal scholarship and offers an external history of American law-making agencies, which recognises the influence of external agencies, interests, events and ideas. In particular he examines local courts, legislatures, administrators and lawyers. His research focused on the relationship of private law to economic development in which the former operated as a 'rational tool' of specific interest groups bent on realising their particular goals.

[74]John Braithwaite, 'What's Wrong with the Sociology of Punishment?', *Theo. Crim.* 2003, 7(1), 5-28.

[75]Smith and McLaren note that Pound's *Interpretations of Legal History* (Cambridge: CUP, 1923) represents: 'a tour de force of historical survey, synthesis and jurisprudential speculation, striding across Germano-Romano and other ancient European legal systems as well as the common law, leading to Pound's own sociological legal history and jurisprudence.' 2001 *op. cit.*, 268-9. Pound made 'imaginative use of legal history' in *An Introduction to the Philosophy of Law* (New Haven: Yale UP, 1922) and *Law and Morals* (Chapel Hill: University of North Carolina, 1924). This was noted by legal historians, such as Pollock in his reviews of both these works in (1922) 38 *LQR* 509 and (1925) 41 *LQR* 108.

[76]Cain and Hunt, *Marx and Engels on Law*, (London: Academic Press, 1979).

[77]K. Hawkins (ed.) *The Human Face of Law: Essays in Honour of Donald Harris* (Oxford: Oxford University Press, 1997), prologue, 4. Vick considers such collaboration to be desirable in future interdisciplinary research projects to avoid basic mistakes in research design, data collection and data analysis, Douglas Vick, 'Interdisciplinarity and the Discipline of Law' 31 *JLS*, (2004) 163-93, 192-3.

centre's first two decades. Donald Harris, a former Director of the Oxford Centre, has confirmed this point.[78]

There are a number of examples of multi- and interdisciplinary studies that can be classified as illustrations of the benefits which can flow from the inclusion of historical contextualisation within the scope of sociolegal studies, which we discuss below. In 1994, the ESRC's wide-ranging review of the achievements of this movement concluded that historical studies clearly fall within topics allegedly ripe for future sociolegal research projects.[79] Furthermore, the recognition of the importance of historical contextualisation as part of the wider toolkit of sociolegal studies has, if anything, strengthened during the last decade. By 2000, the ESRC, an important source of sociolegal funding, suggested that: 'Research training may include material such as the following: . . . different theoretical perspectives on deviance, crime and criminal justice (e.g. sociological, psychological, legal, historical, cultural and anthropological) [and] the social history of the discipline of criminology and/or sociolegal studies'.[80]

Certainly, historical research has been increasingly included amongst the examples of papers presented at annual SLSA conferences. Moreover, legal history *per se* has recently made its appearance as a stream in its own right at the annual SLSA conference. For instance, at the SLSA conference held at Nottingham Trent University in 2003, seven sessions were dedicated to 'law and history'.[81] At the SLSA Conference held at the University of Liverpool in 2005, there were four 'legal history' sessions.[82] In addition, researchers whose work could be characterised as contributions to a distinctly sociolegal form of history have presented their findings at many of the earlier conferences. In other words, many regular speakers at the SLSA include an historical dimension to their papers, and contextualise their current sociolegal research within its historical perspective. These papers have appeared in an assortment of conference streams other than legal history, which reflect the subject matter researched, such as housing law and policy, rather than the particular methodological approach taken to the topic in question. These streams have included, amongst others, environmental law,[83] legal education,[84] tax,[85] and 'law and the question of identity'.[86] In short, it is clear that legal

---

[78]'We believe that in the immediate future, progress in socio-legal studies will best be made by building up a number of detailed studies of particular topics in the law, using as many relevant perspectives as our resources permit. If we bring together the insights of sociology, economics, psychology and history upon a particular problem area in society, we hope that the cumulative effect will be a deeper understanding than could be gained from any one discipline, given the all-pervasive nature of law in its social context.' Harris, 1983 *op. cit.*, 319. For more details on the pioneering Oxford Centre, see D. J. Galligan (ed.), *Socio-legal Studies in Context*, The Oxford Centre Past and Future, (Oxford: Blackwell, 1995).

[79]ESRC, *Review of Socio-legal Studies*, (Swindon: ESRC, 1994).

[80]Http://www.esrc.ac.uk/esrccontent/postgradfunding/2000_Guidelines_f15.asp

[81]See *Conference Brochure* (Nottingham: SLSA, 2003).

[82]See *Conference Brochure* (Liverpool: SLSA, 2005).

[83]See, for example, Ben Pontin's paper, 'Law and Science: An Historical Environmental Perspective', examining the role of the Alkali Acts 1863-1881 in leading scientific developments: *Conference Brochure* (Bristol: SLSA, 2001).

[84]Lorie Charlesworth and Andrea Loux, 'Gentlemen and Scholars in White Cotton Gloves: "Legal Education and the Reproduction of Hierarchy" in Legal History', SLSA, 2001.

[85]Margaret Lamb, 'Defining "Profits" for British Income Tax Purposes: A Contextual Study of the Depreciation Cases, 1875-1897', SLSA, 2001.

[86]Austin Chinhengo, 'Sons of the Soil - Land, Law and the Colonial Reconstruction of Indigenous Identities in Sub-Saharan Africa', Socio-legal Studies Conference, University of Bristol, 2001.

history, understood broadly as a reconstruction of the processes of emergence, consolidation and change over time, has exhibited a consistent, if partially concealed, presence within recent SLSA conferences.

Such analytical techniques of reconstruction have provided an important methodological tool for contextualising a wide range of otherwise disparate sociolegal themes. Within recent years, historical studies have become recognised as an important theme for sociolegal studies scholarship in its own right.[87] The following subsections will provide far more extensive evidence of the role that different forms of historical reconstruction have played within the development of sociolegal studies to date, starting with the largest area where this is the case: studies of the criminal justice system.

● Sociolegal Histories of Criminal Justice

Existing contributions to historical studies within sociolegal studies have concentrated largely in the field of criminal justice.[88] These have included studies of the overlap between criminalisation and other areas, such as the legal regulation of medicine in the field of the emergence of a defence to infanticide,[89] and the identification and regulation of the 'dangerous' offender within the penal system.[90] Much work since the 1970s bears direct or indirect testimony to influential works from two social historians, which stimulated an interest in the potential for critical historical work on the role of the state, ideology and criminal law.[91] These were Edward Thompson's *Whigs and Hunters*, which contextualised the eighteenth-century Black Act, and its companion work, *Albion's Fatal Tree* by Douglas Hay *et al.*[92] Hay's own chapter in this book, 'Property, authority and the criminal law', characterises England's eighteenth-century criminal justice system as an 'instrument of social hegemony, coercion and manipulation, exercised by the ruling class through legislative and sentencing practices.'[93]

Within British sociolegal scholarship, Nicola Lacey has reconstructed the concept of criminal responsibility, focusing particularly on the relationship between changes in legal frameworks and wider transformations in the process of criminalisation and punishment. Her work contextualises the latter by reference to wider patterns of social and economic change.[94] Other studies have reconstructed the social factors explaining the historical emergence and transformation of the legal regulation of blackmail within England and Wales.[95] There have also been attempts to re-examine nineteenth-century data to

---

[87]Rosemary Kruttschnitt, 'A Brief History of Doing Time: The California Institution for Women in the 1960s and the 1990s', *Law & Society* 38(2) (2004), 267.

[88]Henry Summerson, 'The Criminal Underworld of Medieval England', *J. Leg. Hist.* (1996), 17(3), 197-224.

[89]Tony Ward, 'The Sad Subject of Infanticide: Law, Medicine and Child Murder, 1860-1938', *S. & L.S.* (1999), 8(2), 163-80.

[90]John Pratt, 'Governing the Dangerous: An Historical Overview of Dangerous Offender Legislation', *S. & L.S.* (1996) 5(1), 21-36.

[91]See, for example, Alan Norrie, *Crime, Reason and History* (London: Weidenfeld and Nicolson, 1993).

[92]See E. P. Thompson, *Whigs and Hunters*, (London: Allen Lane, 1975; Douglas Hay *et al.*, *Albion's Fatal Tree* (London: Allen Lane, 1975). See also Robert Fine, *Capitalism and the Rule of Law* (London: Hutchinson, 1979).

[93]Smith and McLaren, 2001 *op. cit.*, 283.

[94]Nicola Lacey, 'In Search of the Responsible Subject: History, Philosophy and Social Sciences in Criminal Law Theory,' *M.L.R.* 2001, 64(3), 350-71.

[95]Peter Alldridge, ' "Attempted Murder of the Soul": Blackmail, Privacy and Secrets', *O.J.L.S.* 1993, 13(3), 368-87.

develop a specifically 'ecological analysis' of crime in early Victorian England.[96] One outstanding example merits particular discussion: Anette Ballinger's *Dead Women Walking: Executed Women in England and Wales 1900-1955*.[97] This work was recognised as an outstanding contribution to sociolegal studies work by its award of the Hart SLSA prize. It is a major critical and interdisciplinary study, in effect a social history, of the power of law and related institutions to subject women to capital punishment. It combines an account of biographical details, which are contextualised both by reference to an analysis of previously unpublished archival material, and existing feminist theories of law. Her work represents an interesting example of empirical historical analysis that has also been recognised as contributing to sociolegal studies of the institutional operation of the criminal justice system.

Aspects of Michel Foucault's work, which stresses the causal role played by modernisation, and the associated drive for greater efficiencies in institutional practices and strategies of control, have influenced a number of broadly sociolegal histories of criminal justice.[98] However, as Brown-Nagin recognises, there are multiple types of historical contextualision available to sociolegal scholars other than the Foucaultian type. Indeed, she specifically advocates in-depth case studies of local developments which identify the operation of broader structural factors within the topic in question:

> This approach to legal history combines an analysis of developments in litigation with a detailed discussion of the social dynamics in a single locality in order to highlight nuances overlooked in nationally oriented, case-law-driven legal history . . . In analyzing the social, political, and economic circumstances surrounding the Atlanta desegregation cases, I seek to demonstrate how locally based socio-legal history can help us more fully understand the human and structural factors that animate the success or failure of legal campaigns against inequality.[99]

● The Legal Regulation of Property and Housing

One of the most strikingly consistent areas of sociolegal research where writers have undertaken some measure of historical contextualisation is within the area of housing studies, including its human rights aspects. It has become almost *de rigeur* to locate any discussion of current themes concerning housing law and policy within the context of historical changes that have taken place over the last twenty years, and, in some cases, over a much longer period.[100] Within empirical research investigating the legal regulation of property relations more generally, explicitly sociolegal histories have analysed perceptions by dominant elites of legal measures of enclosure and other restrictions on access to land, particularly with reference to their impact upon working-class leisure

---

[96]Paul S. Maxim, 'An Ecological Analysis of Crime in Early Victorian England', *Howard Journal* (1989) 28(1), 37-50.

[97](Aldershot: Ashgate, 2000).

[98]See Martin Weiner *Reconstructing the Criminal - Culture, Common Law and policy in England 1830-1914* (NY: Cambridge University Press, 1990) and David Garland, *Punishment and Welfare: A History of Penal Strategies* (Aldershot: Dartmouth, 1985).

[99]Tomiko Brown-Nagin, 'Race as Identity Caricature: A Local Legal History Lesson in the Salience of Intraracial Conflict' (2003) 151 *U. Pa.L. Rev.* 1913.

[100]Since 1925 in the case of Emma Laurie's study, 'The Enduring Appeal of "Reasonable Preference" in Housing Allocations': *Conference Brochure* (Bristol: SLSA, 2001).

activities.[101] Related research has studied both the influence of national and local politics upon solicitors' traditional conveyancing monopoly.[102] Another piece of research in this area deals with questions concerning the relationship between eighteenth-century property settlements and issues concerning the social status and recognition for those aristo-cratic families who deployed this legal device to protect family capital.[103]

● International and Comparative Sociolegal Histories

Historians have published comparative accounts of many different legal topics including dispute resolution,[104] and same-sex adult relationships.[105] Sociolegal studies that have focused on nineteenth-century developments include research into aspects of the deployment of ideological doctrines and strategies of both orthodox and authoritarian liberalism through which Britain governed its empire partly by means of specific legisla-tive measures, taking the governance of the Mina tribe as a case study.[106] The estab-lished sociolegal theme of legal pluralism, which discusses the relationship between formal law and unofficial or lay understandings of law and justice, has also been sub-jected to historical reconstruction. For example, one study investigates the development of legal system under autocratic rule of a national governor in the British colony of New South Wales from 1788.[107]

● Public Law, Civil Liberties and Human Rights

There has only been a small number of sociolegal histories which could be classified under even a broad and elastic definition of this heading. Under the broad heading of studies of the emergence of public regulation, MacDonagh's work conceptualises and contextualises the historical development of English local and central governance.[108] Chantal Stebbings's research examines the growth of 'officialdom' in the nineteenth century, the compulsory administration of private affairs by state officials. It addresses the nature and ideology of the opposition from various social and political groups to these new regulatory frameworks.[109] Within the domestic realm, explicitly sociolegal forms of historical reconstruction have addressed changing patterns of extra-legal and

---

[101]David McCardle, '"A Ruling Class Conspiracy;" Law, Enclosure and the Politics of Leisure', *Nott. L.J.* (1999), 8(2), 69–78.

[102]Avron Offer, *Property and Politics 1870–1914* (Cambridge: CUP, 1981).

[103]Alain Pottage, 'Proprietary Strategies: The Legal Fabric of Aristocratic Settlements', *M.L.R.* (1998), 61(2), 162–87.

[104]See Robert Palmer, 'The Common Law and the French Connection', 4 *Anglo-Norman Studies*, (1982) 77–92; Paul Hyman, 'Norms and Legal Before 1150' 6 *Current Legal Issues*, 2004, 41–62; W. Davies and P. Fouracre, *The Settlement of Disputes in Early Medieval Europe*, (Cambridge: CUP, 1996); Thomas N. Bisson, (ed.) *Cultures of Power: Lordship, Status and Process in 12th Century Europe*, (Philadelphia, 1995).

[105]Mary Welstead, 'Case Commentary: Financial Support in Same-Sex Relationships – a Canadian Constitutional Solution,' (2000) 12 *CFam* 73.

[106]Mark Brown, 'Crime, Liberalism and Empire: Governing the Mina tribe of Northern India', *S. & L.S.* 2004, 13(2), 191–218.

[107]Bruce Kerche, 'Resistance to Law Under Autocracy', *M.L.R.* (1997), 60(6), 779–97.

[108]Oliver MacDonagh, *Early Victorian Government 1830–1870*, (London: 1977) and *A Pattern of Government Growth: 1800–1860. The Passenger Acts and their Enforcement*, (London: MacGibbon and Key, 1961).

[109]Chantal Stebbings, '"Officialism": Law, Bureaucracy, and Ideology in Late Victorian England', 6 *Current Legal Issues*, (2004) 316–42.

legal recognition of freedom of speech by reference, for example, to the regulation of Speakers' Corner in London's Hyde Park.[110] Sociolegal writers have also contextualised civil liberty issues arising from the controversial emergence in Northern Ireland of special control units within those prisons containing republican paramilitary prisoners.[111] There have also been distinctly sociolegal historical contextualisations of changing patterns of twentieth-century constitutional interaction, and in particular the emergence and development of institutional conflicts between the judges and different governments.[112]

As a supplement to domestic studies, within the field of human rights scholarship, there is also a distinctly comparative form of historical contextualisation, including studies of the influence of particular national traditions upon the reception of newly-incorporated European human rights measures.[113] For example Marie-Benedicte Dembour and Magda Krzyzanowska-Mierzewska's sociolegal analysis suggests that the European Convention's popularity within Poland needs to be understood in the context of this country's troubled national history, particularly the continuing legacy of life during the communist period and the historical lack of a developed legal culture, and the difficulties experienced during its transition to a modified form of capitalism.[114]

● Social Welfare and Family Policy

There has been a limited number of explicitly sociolegal histories under this heading. There are some generalist works of historians[115] supplemented by a series of more narrowly-focused specific studies. These include a series of studies into nineteenth-century occupational-health legislation, which have found outlets in both history and law publishing.[116] More generally, Alison Dunn has conducted historical research addressing the social, economic and political policy factors underpinning the regulation of charities

---

[110]John Michael Roberts, 'The Enigma of Free Speech: Speakers' Corner, the Geography of Governance and a Crisis of Rationality', *S. & L.S.* (2000), 9(2), 271–92.

[111]Jason M. Schone, 'Legacy of a Conflict: Special Secure Units, Penal Policy, and the Law', *Int. J. Soc. L.* (1999), 27(2), 207–28.

[112]Robert Steven's books are a good example. See his *Law and Politics: The House of Lords as a Judicial Body 1800–1976* (London: Weidenfeld and Nicolson, 1983); *The Independence of the Judiciary: The View from the Lord Chancellors' Office*, (Oxford: Clarendon, 1993); 'Judges, Politics, Politicians, and the Confusing Role of the Judiciary' in Hawkins, 1997 *op. cit.*, 245–89.

[113]Marie-Benedicte Dembour and Magda Krzyzanowska-Mierzewska, 'Ten Years On: the Popularity of the Convention in Poland', *E.H.R.L.R.* 2004, 4, 400–23.

[114]*Ibid.*

[115]David Roberts, *Victorian Origins of the British Welfare State*, (New Haven, 1960); Pat Thane, 'Histories of the Welfare State', W. Lament, ed., *Historical Controversies and Historians*, (London: UCL Press, 1998).

[116]Nob Doran, 'From Embodied "Health" to Official "Accidents": Class, Codification and British Factory Legislation 1831-1844', *S. & L.S.* (1996), 5(4), 523–46; Bartrip, '*Safety at Work: The Factory Inspectorate in the Fencing Controversy 1833-57*' (Oxford: Centre for Socio-Legal Studies, 1979); Bartrip, 'British Government Inspection 1832-1875', *Review of Social History* 77 (1980); Bartrip, 'The Conventionalization of Factory Crime: A Re-assessment', 8 *International Journal of the Sociology of Law* 175 (1980); Bartrip, 'British Government Inspection, 1832-1875', 25 *Historical Journal*, 605 (1982); Bartrip and Burman, *The Wounded Soldiers of Industry: Industrial Compensation Policy 1833-97*, (Oxford: Clarendon, 1983); Bartrip, 'Petticoat Pestering: The Women's Trade Union League and Lead Poisoning in the Staffordshire Potteries, 1890-1914', (1996) *Historical Studies in Industrial Relations*, 2, 3–25; Bartrip and Fenn, 'Factory Fatalities and Regulation in Great Britain, 1878-1913', 25 *Explorations in Economic History* (1980), 60–74; Bartrip and Hartwell, 'Profit and Virtue: Economic Theory and the Regulation of Occupational Health in Nineteenth and Early Twentieth Century Britain', in Hawkins 1997, *op. cit.*, 45-64.

created to relieve poverty.[117] The work of Peter Bartlett on the history of lunatic asylums during mid-nineteenth century England, which builds upon a broadly Foucaultian analysis, is another noteworthy example of critical accounts of social welfare provisions for those at the bottom of the social hierarchy.[118]

The narrower field of family law and policy continues to attract high-quality forms of historical contextualisation by John Eekelaar and various collaborators.[119] One serious wide-ranging historical and social contextual chapter addresses statistical and other evidence of changing patterns of adult and family relationships from 1886, such as marriage, cohabitation, illegitimacy, single parenthood, divorce and remarriage. Furthermore, such contextualisation includes a comparative dimension contrasting policy developments against a twentieth-century background in UK, Australia and Canada. Eekelaar's account also reconstructs the history of legal protection against domestic abuse, child abuse and neglect welfare measures. Historical dimensions are even more fully integrated in Katherine O'Donovan's path-breaking *Sexual Divisions in Law*,[120] which treats historical analysis as a pre-eminent way of explaining such divisions:

> Explanations for legal differentiation between women and men were sought in the structure for pre-industrial English society, in the material facts of biological reproduction, and in the organisation of home and work in modern industrialised society . . . The enquiry undertaken by the book is directed partly at social change. The model that underpins this analysis is a model of social change in which there is a movement from a community-based society . . . to an individualistic society.[121]

Her aim is to explain how the patriarchal family form, which flourished in medieval and early modern European culture, survives today in another guise, and she accounts for this by the emergence of an unregulated private realm. This work:

> puts forward a series of propositions about feudal law and the transition to market society . . . the object is to depict the controlling and shaping of lives in a gender order by the twin systems of feudal law and patriarchy, and to explain state intervention in family life and its limits. Law was fundamentally constructive of social relations in feudal society and it differentiated persons according to status and gender.[122]

Another, explicitly sociolegal collection of essays explores the question 'What is a parent?' from the disciplinary orientation of history, as well as those of sociology, psychology, biology and criminology.[123] The analysis of well-established themes within sociolegal studies, such as the relationship between family policy and the case-by-case legal regulation of marital breakdown, have also benefited from being located within their historical as well as other social contexts.[124] A similar point applies to certain studies within the overlap between studies of social welfare policy and the legal regulation of familial

---

[117] Alison Dunn, 'As "Cold as Charity"?: Poverty, Equity and the Charitable Trust' *L.S.* (2000), 20(2), 222–40.

[118] Peter Bartlett, *The Poor Law of Lunacy*, (Leicester: Leicester University Press, 1999).

[119] John Eekelaar, *Family Law and Social* Policy, 2nd edn (London: Weidenfeld and Nicolson, 1984).

[120] Katherine O'Donovan, *Sexual Divisions in Law* (London: Weidenfeld and Nicolson, 1985).

[121] *Ibid.*, preface, x.

[122] *Ibid.*, 21.

[123] Andrew Bainham, *et al.*, '*What is a Parent? A Socio-Legal Analysis*, (Oxford: Hart Publishing 1999).

[124] John Eekelaar's *Regulating Divorce* (Oxford: OUP, 1991).

relations,[125] and to comparative studies of the legal responses to unconventional family relations within broadly analogous common law regimes, such as Canada.[126]

● The Legal Regulation of Professions

Studies of the work and orientation of different branches of professions that are involved in the legal process, or which are regulated by legislative provisions are common within sociolegal studies. An example of distinctly sociolegal historical work is Russell Smith's reconstruction of the self-regulation of the professional conduct of doctors by the General Medical Council since its inception in 1858.[127] Smith's work deploys a historical methodology to analyse over 2,000 disciplinary cases involving a broad range of allegations made against different classes of doctors. This analysis casts light on the policy issue of whether, during this period, the GMC, which now includes lay assessors and lawyers, has been able to successfully balance its complex role. On the one hand, the GMC acts a representative of the sectional interests of doctors; yet, on the other, it has a public-interest role as a standard-setter and regulator of its own members' professional conduct and misconduct in order to protect the public from continuing misconduct. This sociolegal historical reconstruction casts light on the emergence of anomalies and problems within the present system, which in turn helps to provide a context for a discussion of the merits of possible future incremental or radical reform proposals.

Another example of historical contextualisation addressing the work of legal or law-related professional groups are studies of policing, including David Wall's impressive work on the social history of the chief constables between 1836 and 1996.[128] This study suggests that it is possible to identify recurring tendencies within the history of the police force.

● Black-Letter Versions of Legal History

It is not possible to explain the underdeveloped state of historical analysis within contemporary sociolegal studies by reference to the orientation of members of this movement alone. Instead, it is equally important to recognise that subscribers to certain types of 'legal history' have developed this particular sub-discipline in a distinctly black-letter manner. This has made such types of historical analysis distinctly unappealing to students and academics who are already committed to the main tenets of sociolegal studies:[129] that is, a commitment to interdisciplinary research, an emphasis on law in

---

[125]Julia Twigg, 'Carers, Families, Relatives: Socio-legal Conceptions of Care-Giving Relationships', *J. Soc. Wel. & Fam. L.* (1994), 3, 279–98, which provides an analysis of the history of care-giving and family relations as forming part of the 'liable relatives' tradition of poor law, for example, as well as inheritance laws; Josephine Reeves, 'The Deviant Mother and Child: The Development of Adoption as an Instrument of Social control', *J. Law & Soc.* (1993), 20(4), 412–26. The latter provides a historical reconstruction of legislative interventions from end of nineteenth century to 1990 to separate children from mothers deemed to be 'unfit' parents.

[126]Dorothy E. Chunn, 'Rehabilitating Deviant Families Through Family Courts: The Birth of "Socialized" Justice in Ontario, 1920-1940', *Int. J. Soc. L.* (1988), 16(2), 137–58.

[127]*Medical Discipline: The Professional Conduct Jurisdiction of the General Medical Council, 1858–1990* (Oxford: OUP, 1994).

[128]David Wall, *The Chief Constables of England And Wales: The Socio-Legal History Of A Criminal Justice Elite,* (Aldershot: Dartmouth, 1998).

[129]David Sugarman, 'Writing "Law and Society" Histories'. *M.L.R.* (1992), 55(2), 292–308.

action deployed as a device for achieving specific social functions, and a distinctly contextual methodology.

The overwhelming majority of papers presented within the biennial British legal history conferences lack any appreciation of, and hence citations to, the main achievements of sociolegal studies, including historical contextualistons of many of the topics and themes of this movement.[130] They remain rooted in a largely positivistic and black-letter approach to law as a more or less closed system of rules, principles and formal procedures, such as the writ system, whose exposition remains largely internal to the reasoning, culture and actions of lawyers. Biographical studies of 'great men of the law', such as Sir Henry Maine, Chief Justice Coke, Holdsworth, Hale, Pollock, Blackstone, Bentham, Vinogradoff and Austin, the complexity of the medieval writ system, and themes within Roman law seem to have a particular attraction for leading contributors.[131]

As such, most work within this tradition is resolutely opposed to these main tenets of the sociolegal movement discussed above. There is, for example, a widespread rejection of the idea that 'the task of historians is to provide the raw material for sociological theories, or simply to test such theories.'[132] The intellectual pedigree of traditional forms of legal history remains closer to that of black-letter conceptions of the nature, scope and role of doctrinal legal analysis, than to the form of historical contextualisation undertaken by trained historians. This can result in contributors to mainstream collections being required to 'take the history out' of their work as a precondition for publication, especially if this takes the form of social history written 'from the bottom up', as it were. With admirable clarity at least, Ibbetson sums up this policy of how those committed to strictly 'internal' forms of analysis typically seek to exclude so-called 'external history', including various institutional dimensions:

> I should begin by drawing the more or less conventional division between external legal history and internal legal history. External legal history is the history of law as embedded in its context, typically its social or economic context. . . . insofar as it might be said to be the history of law in action, it is the action that matters. It is the way that law operates in society, which seems to have law as the given and its operation as the thing that needs to be examined. . . . by no stretch of the imagination could we say that any of these constituted parts of the history of law. So far as external legal history is concerned, we could almost say that the one thing that it is *not* a history of is law.[133]

Students considering adopting a distinctly mainstream form of legal history will be required to reject as merely 'external' histories those contextualistons, exemplified in the works of Hurst and Lawrence Friedman, in which the social function of law is

---

[130]http://www.ucl.ac.uk/laws/history/documents/history_programme.pdf and http://www.ucd.ie/leghist/assets/downloads/papers.doc

[131]*Ibid*. Smith and McLaren, 2001 *op. cit.*, 253–64. For examples, see the collection of papers in 6 *Current Legal Issues*, (Oxford: OUP, 2004) by Andrew Lewis, Ray Cocks, Carl Landauer and Karuna Mantena (on Maine), and, Kaius Tuori, even discusses Max Weber's work in the context of his reception of Roman Law.

[132]Lobban, 2004 *op. cit.*, 24. However, Lobban does suggest in a more critical and pointed way, which targets those other members of this tradition who explicitly reject interdisciplinarity, that 'the perspectives of sociology, or anthropology or philosophy can generate questions which may help the historian to make sense of his material.' Lobban and Lewis (eds), 'Editor's Introduction' 6 *Current Legal Issues* (OUP, 2004).

[133]David Ibbetson, 'What is Legal History a History of?', in Lobban and Lewis (2004) *op. cit.* 33–4.

revealed as central to any understanding of how legal institutions operate and are shaped by general and specific goals, ideas and events.[134] Another generally excluded type of legal contextualisation is one that analyses the operation of law in the light of actual events taking place within its fields of application, such as plagues, famine, war, and general social unrest, and their impact upon both the creation and application of legal measures.[135] For example, in the field of the relief of poverty, historians of the poor law who contextualise the work of the inspectorate, which was set up to implement and then monitor the relevant statutory provisions, who examine the locally generated records of these meetings and negotiations, risk having their results dismissed as falling within the discipline of history but not legal history.[136] A similar point applies to historical reconstructions of how intelligence officials exerted political influence upon the Nuremberg prosecutors to ensure the success of various legal immunity deals they had negotiated with a number of senior Nazi leaders, including Himmler's former co-deputy.[137] Instead, students who adopt the mainstream position of legal history defined as part of the black-letter approach to legal research will be required to undertake a type of historical reconstruction which focuses on law as an intellectually autonomous professional culture. This means treating a dissertation topic 'on its own terms', addressing sources thrown up mainly by the legal process itself, that is, 'law that would have been recognised by lawyers in its time'.[138] In response to these requirements, the preface to Friedman's work is deliberately provocative to the central tenets of internal legal histories. It claims: 'This book treats American law, then, not as a kingdom unto itself, not as a set of rules and concepts, not as the province of lawyers alone, but as a mirror of society. It takes nothing as a historical accident, nothing as autonomous, everything as relative and moulded by economy and society.'[139]

It is possible, perhaps even likely, that students whose historical research is broad and contextual will experience resistance from supervisors committed to strictly internal, black-letter forms of historical analysis. Certainly, those who helped create sociolegal forms of historical contextualisation within the fields of private law found their contributions subjected to strong critiques by leading figures within the traditionalist internal school. For example, Patrick Atiyah's ground-breaking *Rise and Fall of Freedom of*

---

[134]Hurst, 1964 *op. cit.*; Lawrence Friedman, *A History of American Law* 2nd edn (NY: Simon and Schuster, 1985).

[135]For an exception, see the work of Robert C. Palmer, *English Law in the Age of the Black Death, 1348-1381: A Transformation of Governance and Law*, (London/Chapel Hill, Univ. of N. Carolina Press, 1993), which reconstructs institutional legal developments within their historical context.

[136]Cf. Lorie Charlesworth, 'Poor Law in the City: A Comparative Legal Analysis of the Anomalous Poor Relief Administration in the Cities of Liverpool and Chester After the 1834 Poor Law Amendment Act', paper presented at the 17th British Legal History Conference, London, 2005.

[137]See Michael Salter and Maggi Eastwood, 'Negotiating Nolle Prosequi at Nuremberg: The Case of Captain Zimmer', 3 *Jnl of International Criminal Justice*, (2005) 649-65; Michael Salter, 'Unsettling Accounts: Methodological Issues Within the Reconstruction of the Role of a US Intelligence Agency Within the Nuremberg War Crimes Trials, 6 *Current Legal Issues* (2004) 375-404; Kerstin von Lingen and Michael Salter, 'Contrasting Strategies Within the War Crimes Trials of Kesselring and Wolff', 26 *Liverpool Law Review*, (2005) 1-42.

[138]Ibbetson, 2004 *op. cit.*, 34. Ibbetson defines legal history as that of 'Sir John Baker's *Introduction* to the Subject' in Lobban and Lewis (2004) *op. cit.* For examples of supposedly 'internal' causal account of doctrinal developments, see Alan Watson, *The Evolution of Law*, (Oxford: Blackwell, 1985); *Legal Origins and Legal Change*, (London: Hambledon Press, 1991).

[139]Friedman, 1985 *op. cit.*, preface 12. See also Rubin and Sugarman, *Law Economy and Society Essays in the History of English Law 1750-1914* (Abingdon: Professional Books, 1984).

Contract[140] provoked severe critique from Baker, the doyen of internal history.[141] This work has, however, been applauded by others as providing 'intellectually rich, contextual accounts of legal developments, incorporating ideas spanning the fields of social, economic and political history'.[142] Such contextualisation, which violates this principle of exclusion discussed above, generates controversy precisely because it represents a contribution to sociolegal studies. Insofar as members of this tradition even discuss contextual writers, such as Max Weber and his sociology of law, they typically criticise their 'neglect' of the protocols of formal legal argument.[143] Furthermore, the claims of one member of this tradition, that in order to understand medieval legal devices one has to have already acquired a social theory of feudalism,[144] has rarely been taken up and followed by other subscribers to traditional legal history.

There is some evidence, however, that some legal academics within mainstream legal history, who continue to value purely internal legal histories of the traditional type, have recently become more receptive to the need for their supplementation by the type of external contextual historical reconstruction that form a key element of sociolegal studies. In a recent work, Lobban, for example, develops a cautious, if somewhat 'coded', critique of the purported self-sufficiency of traditional internal legal history:

> The legal historian who focuses only upon the superior courts may be led to assume that the rules emanating from these courts were the most important manifestation of law in the society, since they had the highest status, or the finest pedigree. But their wider importance cannot simply be presumed. These concerns which seek to place an 'external' history alongside the 'internal' history of the law are particularly pressing for the legal historian of the early modern era.[145]

Lobban's introductory editorial review of Wendie Schneider's study of Victorian perjury law further develops and illustrates this critique by endorsing the sociolegal view that legal materials remain unintelligible when interpreted in a non-contextual manner which excludes their social, political and policy dimension:

> As Schneider's piece shows, a proper understanding of the nature of the law of perjury requires an analysis not merely of the development of the rules of law, but also of the policy reasons which inform the process of reforming these rules, their implementation in courts throughout the country and the social and policy perspectives which influenced those who applied the rules. It is only with the aid of the 'external' perspective that we can make sense of the 'internal' developments.[146]

---

[140]Oxford: Clarendon Press, 1979.

[141]Baker in 'Review' (1980) 43 *MLR* 467 – where Atiyah is accused of 'misreading' central cases used to develop his wider thesis, where Baker's criteria for identifying a 'correct' reading seems to demand conformity to the central tenets of his own internalist position. The critique therefore presupposes precisely what first needs to be established. Baker's work includes his highly influential *An Introduction to English Legal History* 4th edn, (London: Butterworths, 2002); *The Law's Two Bodies* (Oxford: OUP, 2001).

[142]Smith and McLaren, 2001 *op. cit.*, 273.

[143]Joshua Getzler, 'Law, History and the Social Sciences: Intellectual Traditions of Late-Nineteenth- and Early Twentieth-Century Europe', 6 *Current Legal Issues*, *op. cit.*, 215.

[144]S. F. C. Milsom, 'The Legal Framework of English Feudalism', (Cambridge: CUP, 1976).

[145]Lobban, 2004 *op. cit.*, 26.

[146]*Ibid.*, 27–8.

In other words, there is a pressing need to open the closed doors and windows of this particular palace, to let in sufficient light from the world outside to illuminate what has actually taken place within and its implications for non-lawyers.

We would endorse a wider and more radical view of the centrality of contextualisation, which recognises that even those materials which mainstream legal history recognises as 'law' cannot be understood unless the social impact and influence of legal officials who interpret and apply these materials is also grasped. Contextualisation of social dimensions of law also requires the contextualisation of the impact of law upon society, and its pervasiveness as a social phenomenon. For example, the dramatic film, witness and documentary evidence of international war-crimes trials, including the Nuremberg and the Eichmann cases, have helped create, rewrite and even consolidate a certain view of the nature and operation of the Nazi regime within occupied Europe, which obstructs the project of contemporary neo-fascist revivalists.[147]

If students are looking for examples of traditional forms of legal historical analysis, where is a good place to begin a library search? Few, if any, of the leading writers of internal legal history, which is largely dominated by a close-knit group of academics who took their law degrees from the Universities of Cambridge and Oxford, attend, or other-wise contribute to, sociolegal conferences, or publish their work within associated publications. Hence, whilst sociolegal studies and other contextual journals have published a considerable number of explicitly historical studies of law in action, few if any of the self-styled 'legal historians' have published their research in these outlets. Instead, their attachment to the orthodox positivist project means that they find publishing in more mainstream and conservative journals, such as the *LQR* and *Cambridge Law Journal*, far more attractive than distinctly sociolegal outlets. This, combined with the preference for internal histories, shows that this genre is far more closely aligned with conventional 'law' than it is with any branch of either history or sociolegal studies.

From its earliest manifestation in the nineteenth century at Cambridge University, the mainstream versions of 'legal history' has developed its own niche outlets for publication and routes for academic appointment and promotions within the heart of the 'legal establishment', as it were. A comprehensive trawl of sociolegal history and the journals where researchers have found a receptive home for their work reveals that rarely do the six establishment legal journals appear on this list.[148] Only the American *Law and History Review* publishes a very wide spread of legal history, ranging from medieval studies to sociolegal and comparative legal history. It also includes a 'comments' section which sometimes engages in debate concerning historical topics of interest to sociolegal scholarship.

Students should be aware that, as already noted, there is some evidence that the exist-ing insulation of traditional black-letter forms of legal history from the interdisciplinary

---

[147]Alexander Cook, 'Settling Accounts: Law as History in the Trial of the Gang of Four' 6 *Current Legal Issues*, (2004) 413-31; Lawrence Douglas, 'The Holocaust, History and Legal Memory', in Lobban and Lewis (2004) *op. cit.* 405-12.

[148]These journals are *The Journal of Legal History; The American Journal of Legal History*, USA (the oldest founded in 1957); the *Law and History Review*; and to a lesser extent the *LQR* and the *Cambridge Law Journal*. One such exception is Rebecca Probert, 'The Judicial Interpretation of Lord Hardwicke's Act of 1753', *Journal of Legal History* 23 (2002) 129-51. The oldest established legal history journal is *The Legal History Review*; founded in 1918 in the Netherlands, it publishes a wide range of international legal history.

methodologies characteristic of sociolegal studies is beginning to break down, at least at the margins. Certainly in recent years, some researchers have developed a number of different approaches that transcend the traditional approach by formulating research agendas that are distinctly contextual.[149] The beginnings of a new movement for a more distinctly historical, comparatively 'deviant', and thus controversial, type of historical contextualisation can be discerned. A certain tension has long existed between legal history as the scholarly preserve of the Academy ('internal' legal history) and those whose more contextual approaches emphasise on law in society ('external' legal history).[150] Social historians, both drawn from law and mainstream history, are increasingly writing on many aspects of life in the past, ranging from the lives of women written from a feminist perspective, to law and literature.[151]

In the last few years, at conferences where groups of history researchers from many disciplines within the legal canon meet professional historians, there have been passionate discussions concerning the nature, scope and affiliations of contextual forms of legal history. At the Socio-Legal Studies Association annual conference at Nottingham Trent University in April 2003, there were seven legal history sessions with speakers from a wide variety of legal disciplines, from criminal justice and many professional historians.[152] The common factor was an interest in the legal past and an awareness of the need for a legal context in historical research, and a historical context for legal research.

In short, it would be naive for students to adopt a historical approach to their dissertations on the assumption that one type of historical contextualisation is pretty much the same as any other. On the contrary, students whose dissertation projects are more closely aligned to the types of analysis associated with the black-letter tradition would be well-advised to concentrate on producing a strictly internal form of legal history, as discussed above. By contrast, students whose questions concern the distinctly social aspects of law in action would be better advised to adopt a broader type of historical analysis of the type illustrated above, which is found more commonly within the sociolegal academic literature.

---

[149]For a discussion of the historiography of legal history see, K. J. M. Smith and J. P. S. McLaren, 'History's Living Legacy: An Outline of Modern Historiography of the Common Law', *Legal Studies* vol. 21 2(2001), 251–324.

[150]One marker can be found in Igor Stramignoni's article, published in *Legal Studies* in 2002. Igor Stramignoni, 'At the Margins of the History of English Law: The Institutional, The Socio-political and the "Blotted Out"', *Legal Studies*, vol.22, 2(2002) pp. 420–47. He reviews past and current legal historical writings that he characterises as 'institutional legal history' and he calls for a history of the 'blotted out'. In some sense, however, even the explicitly critical reading of Stramignoni has been 'captured' by the establishment dimension of legal history. His review is largely of *their* histories. He, perhaps, intends his work to be a call for sociolegal scholarship to take an interest in law's history, but he weakens his argument considerably, as he fails to take into account some 80 years of published research on legal and law-related themes by professional historians. These range from that of the Hammonds to the present day, researching the lives and history of what technically are referred to as the labouring classes, men, women, children, paupers, beggars, vagrants, criminals and the sick. He also neglects the vast body of work on protestors from the Chartists, the Rebecca rioters in Wales and the victims of the Peterloo massacre, to the Jarrow marchers and miners' strikes in the 1920s and 1980s.

[151]SOLON is a partnership between Nottingham Trent University Law School and History Department, Oxford Brookes University and Nottingham Museum of Law (known popularly as the Galleries of Justice) promoting Interdisciplinary Studies in Bad behaviour and Crime. See SOLON website for details: http://www.cheshire.mmu.ac.uk/ids/solon/.

[152]*Conference Catalogue* (Nottingham: SLSA, 2003).

● Conclusion

This chapter has summarised and illustrated by reference to published work aspects of both comparative and historical methodologies. It has not been possible in our short summary to do full justice to the width and variety of topics and approaches, and different combinations of methods, used by researchers in these traditions. This chapter has also set out certain advantages and disadvantages of comparative approaches at a general level which students may wish to consider before adopting this methodology as one aspect of black-letter or sociolegal analysis of their dissertation topic. This chapter has not repeated any of the possible disadvantages of historical analysis within the black-letter and sociolegal traditions but students can nevertheless formulate and evaluate these potential pitfalls for themselves. In other words, some of the general difficulties with sociolegal studies, for example, may well apply, to a greater or lesser extent, to comparative and historical variants of this methodology.

Conclusion

Each chapter of the present book has included a brief summary and conclusion, which it would be pointless to repeat again here. Instead, it may be useful to draw some more general conclusions from the work as a whole, supplemented by some additional observations of a more miscellaneous nature.

Drawing upon our own experiences as dissertation supervisors as well as those of our students, we have highlighted a number of practical issues concerning the process of carrying out dissertation research. Amongst these issues, choosing a viable research topic and identifying the key questions to explore are, at least initially, the most important. We have also emphasised the importance of negotiating, and then adhering to, a suitable framework of ground rules with your supervisor, of managing time effectively, and making the most of constructive feedback when revising successive draft chapters.

From our experience, students need to be forewarned of a number of possible pitfalls so that they can avoid these. For example, students will not impress their supervisors by failing to attend agreed appointments, adopting a casual attitude to their supervisory relationship (as evidenced by, for example, failing to switch off their mobile phones which even cinema attendance requires!), or by changing topic midway through the year. Students should also be aware that academics increasingly have to confront questions of plagiarism or near-plagiarism in which work, professed to be the student's own words and ideas, turns out to have been cut and pasted from a small number of internet sources, or even a single source, without full acknowledgement that this is the case. Very often this form of academic malpractice is evident from shifts in style: that is, from extremely formal to casual.

In too many cases, students lose marks by submitting dissertations that could have been substantially improved if the various chapters and sections had been better introduced and linked together, and by the addition of a more powerful conclusion that addresses the implications of the findings for existing academic literature. Frequently work is submitted that lacks a comprehensive bibliography, which has not been proofread adequately and which contains numerous inaccuracies of both content and style. Given the availability of electronic databases containing the abstracts and full text of academic articles, there is little excuse for students to ignore relevant and up-to-date academic literature discussing the issues addressed in their dissertations. In addition, supervisors are unlikely to be impressed by dissertations that claim to be objectively stating and analysing the law but which fail to consider any arguments other than those preferred by the student. The imperative to 'hear both sides' and make a balanced judgement applies equally to the researcher as it does to the jury.

On the other hand, students who genuinely engage in comprehensive library research, who conscientiously revise and improve their chapters over successive drafts, and who demonstrate that they have taken the research and supervisory processes seriously may well find that their supervisors will be sympathetic to their efforts, and perhaps even forgiving of minor imperfections in the final draft. Most academics take a pride in the process of conducting research and wish to transmit their enthusiasm to students. Consequently, they may resent attempts to bypass the skills and sheer hard work that is expected of undergraduate and postgraduate dissertations.

Having made these points regarding the process of completing a dissertation, we will now turn to specific methodological questions. There can be no single correct methodology that will suit every dissertation student, irrespective of their choice of topic and questions. Instead, law students need to think critically not only about their choice of topic but also regarding the particular questions that they want to explore within the research field. Furthermore, we would encourage students to think long and hard about the *implications* of their topics and research questions for their choice of methodologies, bearing in mind that some questions can only be answered through the adoption of a specific methodology. A student who, for instance, wants to restate what is the legal position on a certain issue (such as plea-bargaining in the criminal justice system) from cases and statutes alone, may have little choice but to adopt a black-letter approach, possibly in conjunction with some but not all elements of comparative and historical methodologies. By contrast, a student who chooses to study how, in practice, plea-bargaining within the lower courts operates as an example of the exercise of discretion that affects various groups in different ways must adopt a sociolegal methodology. This could be selected either in isolation or possibly supplemented by more contextual types of comparative and historical analysis. In other words, it is not the choice of research area which determines the choice of methodologies. On the contrary, it is the type of questions which you are interested in finding answers to which should act as your spur in selecting the most appropriate methodological tools for the task in hand.

We hope that our description and detailed illustration of the main features of black-letter, sociolegal, comparative and historical methodologies, together with a summary of their relative advantages and disadvantages, will help you make an appropriate and informed choice. If this has proven to be the case, then we have succeeded in one of the main aims of the present book.

Further Reading and Bibliography

● Further Reading and Bibliography for the Introduction

Cohen, L. and Manion, L. *Research Methods in Education* (London: Routledge, 2000)

Diener, E. and Crandall, R. Ethics in Social and Behavioral Research, (University of Chicago Press, 1978). Cited in L. Cohen and L. Manion, *Research Methods in Education*, (Routledge Press, 1994) at page 350

● Further Reading and Bibliography for Chapter 1

Cottrell, S. *The Study Skills Handbook*, (London: Palgrave MacMillan, 2003), at page 201

● Further Reading and Bibliography for Chapter 2

Hampson, L. 'How's Your Dissertation Going?'. Unit for Innovation in Higher Education, School of Independent Studies, Lancaster University. 1994 at page 37

● Further Reading and Bibliography for Chapter 3

Adams, J. N. and Brownsword, R. *Key Issues in Contract*, (London: Lexis Law Publishing, 1994), ch. 8 (Unfair Contract Terms)

Baldwin, J. and McConville, M. *Negotiated Justice: Pressures to Plead Guilty*, (London: Martin Robertson, 1977)

Balkan, J. M. 'Interdisciplinarity as Colonisation' (1996) 53 *Washington & Lee Law Rev.* 949, 954-6

Birks, P. (ed.), *Pressing Problems in the Law: What are Law Schools For?* (Oxford: Oxford University Press, 1996)

Bradshaw, A. 'Sense and Sensibility: Debates and Developments in Socio-Legal Research Methods' in Philip Thomas (ed.), *Socio-Legal Studies*, (Aldershot: Ashgate-Dartmouth, 1997), 107

Campbell, C. 'Legal Thought and Juristic Values' *British Jnl. of Law and Society* (1974)

Campbell, D. 'Socio-Legal Analysis of Contract' in P. Thomas, 1997 *op. cit.*, 271

Cane, P. and Stapleton, J. *Essays for Patrick Atiyah*, (Oxford: Clarendon, 1991), 17 at 23

Clark, E. and Tsamenyi, M. 'Legal Education in the Twenty-First Century: A Time of Challenge' in Peter Birks (ed.), *Pressing Problems in the Law: What are Law Schools For?* (Oxford: Oxford University Press, 1996), 17 at 23.

Clarke, M. 'A Black Letter Lawyer Looks at Bolero' (1999) *I.T.L.Q.*, 2 (May), 69-78

Collier, C. W. 'The Use and Abuse of Humanistic Theory in Law: Re-examining the Assumptions of Interdisciplinary Legal Scholarship' (1991) 41 *Duke Law J.* 191

Hawkins, K. *The Human Face of Law: Essays in Honour of Donald Harris*, (Oxford: OUP, 1997)

Hutter, B. M. and Lloyd-Bostock, S. in Keith Hawkins, *The Human Face of Law: Essays in Honour of Donald Harris*, (Oxford: OUP, 1997), 25

Jones, G. '"Traditional" Legal Scholarship: A Personal View' in Birks, 1996

Jupp, V. *Methods of Criminological Research*, (London: Routledge, 1989)

Kaye, J. S. 'One Judge's View of Academic Law Review Writing' (1989) *J. of Legal Education* 313

Lasson, K. 'Scholarship Amok: Excesses in Pursuit of Truth and Tenure' (1990) 103 *Harvard Law Rev.* 926

Lee, R. 'Socio-Legal Research – What's the Use?', in Thomas, 1997 *op. cit.*, 84

Leiter, B. 'Intellectual Voyeurism in Legal Scholarship' (1992) 4 *Yale J. of Law and Humanities* 79

Lilly, G. C. 'Law Schools Without Lawyers? Winds of Change in Legal Education' (1995) 81 *Virginia Law Rev.* 1421

McDermott, M. 'A view from the Coalface', *Socio-legal Newsletter* (1996) no.38, 5

Murphy, W. T. and Roberts, S. 'Introduction' (1987) 50 *MLR* 677, at 680

Tettenborn, A. 'The Critique of Wheeler and Shaw's *Contract Law*' in 54 *Cambridge Law Journal* (1995) 212

Thomas, P. (ed.), *Socio-Legal Studies*, (Aldershot: Ashgate-Dartmouth, 1997)

Twining, W. *Blackstone's Tower: The English Law School*, (London: Stevens, 1994), 80–81, 84–5

Vick, D. 'Interdisciplinarity and the Discipline of Law', 31 *JLS* (2004) 163 at 163–4

Ward, R. and Wragg, A. *Walker and Walker's English Legal System* 8th edition, (London: Butterworths, 1998), ch. 2 (Legislation) and ch. 3 (Law Reports and Precedents)

Weir, T. *Introduction to the Law of Contract* (1986) 45 *Cambridge Law Journal* 503

White, R. M. and Willock, I. D. *The Scottish Legal System*, 3rd edn (London: Lexis-Nexis, 2003)

Willock, I. 'Getting on with Sociologists' *British Jnl. of Law and Society* (1974)

Wilson, G. 'English Legal Scholarship' (1987) 50 *MLR* 818, at 824

Woolman, S. and Lake, J. *Woolman's Contract* (Edinburgh: W. Green, 2001)

● Further Reading and Bibliography for Chapter 4

Abel, R. 'Law Books and Books about Law' (1974) 26 *Stanford L. Rev.* 175

Abel-Smith, B. and Stevens, R. *Lawyers and the Courts: A Sociological Study of the English Legal System 1750-1965*, (London: Heinemann, 1967), 375

Aldridge, P. 'What is Wrong with the Traditional Criminal Law Course', (1990) 10 *LS* 38

Anderson, S. 'The 1925 Property Legislation: Setting Contexts' in Susan Bright and John Dewar (eds), *Land Law: Themes and Perspectives*, (Oxford: OUP, 1998), 126, n. 61

Atiyah, P. S. *The Rise and Fall of Freedom of Contract*, (Oxford: Clarendon, 1979), 388

Atiyah, P. 'Judges and Policy' (1980) 15 *Israel LR* 346

Atiyah, P. *Pragmatism and Theory in English Law*, (London: 1987)

Atiyah, P. S. and Summers, R. S. *Form and Substance in Anglo-American Law*, (Oxford: Clarendon, 1987)

Baldwin, R. *Rules and Government*, (Oxford: Clarendon 1995)

Balkan, J. M. 'Interdisciplinarity as Colonisation' (1996) 53 *Washington & Lee Law Rev.* 949

Banakar, R. 'Reflections on the Methodological Issues of the Sociology of Law', (2000) 27(2) *J. Law & Soc.* 273-95, 280

Becher, T. *Academic Tribes and Territories*, (Buckingham: Open University Press, 1989), 30

Bell, J. 'Conceptions of Public Policy', in Cane and Stapleton, *Essays for Patrick Atiyah*, (Oxford: Clarendon, 1991), 88-9, 105

Bingham, J. 'What is the Law?' (1912) 11 *Mich. LR*

Birks, P. (ed.), *Pressing Problems in the Law: What are Law Schools For?* (Oxford: Oxford University Press, 1996)

Blackstone, W. *Commentaries on the Laws of England*. 4 vols. Facsimile reprint edn of the 1st edn of 1765-69 (Chicago: University of Chicago Press, 1979)

Bottomley, A. 'Self and Subjectivities: Languages of Claim in Property Law', (1993) 20 *JLS*, 56ff

Bradney, A. 'Law as a Parasitic Discipline', (1998) 25 *JLS* 71 at 78

Bradney, A. and Cownie, F. 'Teaching Legal System' (National Centre for Legal Education Warwick University, 1999)

Bright, S. and Dewar, J. (eds), *Land Law: Themes and Perspectives*, (Oxford: OUP, 1998)

Cane and Stapleton, *Essays for Patrick Atiyah*, (Oxford: Clarendon, 1991)

Carrington, P. 'Of Law and the River' (1984) *Jo Leg Educ.* 437

Carrington, P. 'Aftermath' in Cane and Stapleton, 1991, 144-5

Collier, R. 'The Changing University and the (Legal) Academic Career - Rethinking the Relationship between Women, Men and the "Private Life" of the Law School' (2002) 22 *Legal Studies* 1, at 5

Collins, H. *The Law of Contract*, 3rd edn, (London: Butterworths, 1997), preface, v

Connaghan, J. and Mansell, W. 'Tort Law', in I. Grigg-Spall and P. Ireland, *Critical Lawyers Handbook*, Vol.1, (Oxford: Pluto Press, 1992), 83

Cotterrell, R. *Law's Community*, (Oxford: OUP, 1995)

Craig, P. 'Dicey: Unitary, Self-Correcting Democracy and Public Law' (1990) 106 *LQR* 105

Culley, A. and Salter, M. 'Why Study Legal Metaphors?' (2004) 15 *Kings College Law Review*, 347

Davis, K. *Discretionary Justice* (Chicago, IL: 1971)

Dicey, A. *Can English Law be Taught at the Universities?* (London: 1883), 20

Diduck, A. 'Ideologies of Motherhood, 2 *Social and Legal Studies*, (1993) 461

Doupe, M. and Salter, M. 'The Cheshire World-view', 11(1) *Kings College Law Journal*, (2000a) 49

Doupe, M. and Salter, M. 'Concealing the Past?: Questioning Textbook Interpretations of the history of Equity and Trusts', 2-3 (2000b) *Liverpool Law Review* 253

Dworkin, R. 'The Model of Rules', (1987) 35 *University of Chicago L. Rev.* 14

Edley, C. J. *Administrative Law: Rethinking Judicial Control of Bureaucracy* (New Haven, CT: Yale University Press, 1990), 217

Edwards, H. 'The Growing Disjunction Between Legal Education and the Legal Profession', (1992) 91 *Michigan Law. Rev*, 8

Lord Evershed, 'The Judicial Process in Twentieth Century England', (1961) 61 *Columbia Law Rev.* 761, n.1

Fish, S. *Doing What Comes Naturally*, (Durham, NC: Duke University Press, 1989)

Fitzpatrick, P. *Dangerous Supplements*, (London: Pluto, 1991)

Galligan, D. *Discretionary Powers* (Oxford: OUP, 1986) 4

Gilmore, G. *The Death of Contract* (Columbus, OH: 1974)

Lord Goff, 'Judge, Jurist and Legislature' [1987] *Denning Law J.* 79 at 92

Goff, R. 'The Search for Principle' (1983) 69 *Procs Brit Acad* 169 at 171; 'Judge, Jurist and Legislator', 87 *Denning Law J* 70, at 92

Goode, R. *Legal Problems of Credit and Security* (2003) 18 *Journal of International Banking Law and Regulation* 468-69

Goodrich, P. 'Of Blackstone's Tower: Metaphors of Distance and Histories of the English Law School' in Birks, 1996 *op. cit.*, 68

Griffiths, J. *The Politics of The Judiciary*, 4th edn, (London: Fontana, 1991)

Grigg-Spall, I. and Ireland, P. *Critical Lawyers Handbook*, Vol.1, (Oxford: Pluto Press, 1992)

Grossman, J. 'Social Backgrounds and Judicial Decision-Making' (1966) 79 *Harvard Law Review*, 1551-64

Harding, A. *A Social History of English Law*, (Harmondsworth: Penguin, 1966)

Harris, P. *Introduction to Law*, 3rd edn, (London: Weidenfeld and Nicolson, 1988), 42-4

Hart, H. L. A. *The Concept of Law* (Oxford: Clarendon, 1961)

Hawkins, K. (ed.), *The Use of Discretion* (Oxford: OUP, 1992)

Hawkins, K. General Editor's Introduction to B. Tamanaha, *Realistic Socio-Legal Theory*, (Oxford: Clarendon, 1997)

Hoeflich, M. H. 'The Americanisation of British Legal Education in the Nineteenth Century', (1987) 8 *J. of Legal History*, 244 at 245

Hofheinz, W. 'Legal Analysis': http://www.hofheinzlaw.com/LANLSYS.php #anchor47300 (accessed August 2005)

Holmes, O. 'The Path of the Law', (1897) 10 *Harv. LR* 451, 460-61

Horwitz, M. 'The Rise of Legal Formalism', (1975) 19 *American J. of Legal Hist.* 251

Hutchinson, A. 'Beyond Black Letterism: Ethics in Law and Legal Education', (1999) 33 *Law Teacher*, 301-9

Kahn-Freund, O. 'Reflections on Legal Education' (1966) 29 *MLR* 121, at 129

Kearys, D. (ed.), *The Politics of Law: A Progressive Critique* (NY: Pantheon Press, 1982)

Kennedy, D. 'The Structure of Blackstone's Commentaries' (1979) 28 *Buffalo L. Rev.* 205

Lacey, N. 'The Jurisprudence of Discretion: Escaping the Legal Paradigm' in K. Hawkins (ed.), 'The Use of Discretion' (Oxford: OUP, 1992), 362

Lacey, N. and Wells, C. *Reconstructing Criminal Law* (London: Butterworths, 1998) 1-90

Lawson, F. *The Rational Strength of English Law* (London: Stevens and Sons, 1952)

Lloyd, D. *Introduction to Jurisprudence*, 2nd edn, (Sweet and Maxwell, 1994) 262 (modified in later editions)

Look Chan Ho, 'Review of Roy Goode's, *Legal Problems of Credit and Security*' (2003) 18 *Journal of International Banking Law and* Regulation 468-9

McAuslan, P. 'Administrative Law, Collective Consumption and Judicial Policy' (1983) *MLR* 1

Macfarlane, J. 'Look Before You Leap: Knowledge and Learning in Legal Skills Education' (1992) 19 *Journal of Law & Society* 293, 298-301

Maudsley, R. H. and Burn, E. H. *Trust and Trustees: Cases and Materials*, (Lexis Nexis UK, 2002) preface

Megarry, R. E. 'The Deserted Wife's Right to Occupy the Matrimonial Home' in *LQR* 68 (1952), 379

Megarry, R. and Thompson, M. P. *Megarry's Manual of The Law Of Real Property*, 7th edn, (London: Maxwell, 1993)

Mensch, E. 'A History of Mainstream Legal Thought' in David Kearys (ed.), *The Politics of Law: A Progressive Critique* (NY: Pantheon Press, 1982)

Moffat, G. and Chesterman, M. *Trusts Law: Text and Materials*, (London: Weidenfeld, 1988)

Murphy, T. and Roberts, S. 'Introduction' (1987) 50 *MLR* 677

Murphy, T. 'Reference without Reality' (1990) 1 *Law and Critique*, 74

Murphy, W. T. 'The Oldest Social Science? The Epistemic Properties of the Common Law Tradition' (1991) 54 *MLR* 182, at 185-91

Murphy, W. T. and Rawlings, R. 'After the Ancient Regime' (1981) 44 *MLR* 617

Nelken, D. 'The "Gap Problem" in the Sociology of Law: A Theoretical Review' (1981) 1 *Windsor Yearbook of Access to Justice*, 35

Peritz, R. J. 'Exploring the Limits of Formalism: AI and Legal Pedagogy', (1999) *Law Technology Journal*, Vol.1, No.1

Pettit, P. *Equity and the Law of Trusts*, (London: Butterworths, 1989), 1

Posner, R. 'The Decline of Law as an Autonomous Discipline: 1962-1987', (1987) 100 *Harv. L. Rev* 761

Posner, R. 'Conventionalism: The Key to Law as an Autonomous Discipline', (1988) 38 *University of Toronto Law Jo*, 333

Pound, R. *Jurisprudence*, 5 vols, (St. Paul, MN: West Publishing, 1959), ii, 124

Purcell, E. American Jurisprudence Between the Wars: Legal Realism and the Crisis of Democratic Theory' (1969) 75 *Am Hist. Rev.* 424

Riddall, J. G. *Introduction to Land Law* 2nd edn, (London: Butterworths, 1988)

Salmond, J. W. *The Law of Torts* 14th edn, (Sweet and Maxwell, London: 1965)

Schauer, F. 'Formalism', (1988) 97 *Yale Law Jnl*, 509-48

Schauer, F. *Playing by the Rules*, (Oxford: Clarendon Press, 1991) ch.1

Schwartz, L. 'With Gun and Camera through Darkest CLS-land' (1984) 36 *Stanf L. Rev.* 413 at 431

Shaw, J. 'Socio-Legal Studies and the European Union', in Philip Thomas (ed.), *Socio-Legal Studies*, (Aldershot: Ashgate-Dartmouth, 1997), 310

Simpson, A. W. 'The Rise and Fall of the Legal Treatise: Legal Principles and Forms of Legal Literature' (1981) 48 *University of Chicago Law Rev.* 632

Simpson, A. W. 'Book Review', (1993) 56 *MLR* 608

Singer, J. 'The Player and the Cards: Nihilism and Legal Theory' 94 *Yale L.J.* 1, 65.

Stewart, R. 'The Reformation of American Administrative Law' (1975) 88 *Harv. L.R* 1667

Sugarman, D. 'A Hatred of Disorder: Legal Science, Liberalism and Imperialism', in P. Fitzpatrick, *Dangerous Supplements*, (London: Pluto, 1991), 34

Tamanaha, B. *Realistic Socio-Legal Theory*, (Oxford: Clarendon, 1997)

Thomas, P. (ed.), *Socio-Legal Studies*, (Aldershot: Ashgate-Dartmouth, 1997)

Thompson, M. 'The Textbook Approach to Modern Land Law' 21 *Conv.* (1989) 268

Tomlins, C. 'Framing the Field of Law's Disciplinary Encounters: A Historical Narrative' (2000) 34 *Law and Society Rev.* 911

Twining, W. 'Some Jobs for Jurisprudence', (1974) *Brit Jnl of Law and Society*, 149, 161-4

Twining, W. *Karl Llewellyn and the Realist Movement*, (London: Weidenfeld, 1985)

Twining, W. *Rethinking Evidence*, (Oxford: Blackwell) 1990

Twining, W. 'Reflections on Law in Context' in Cane and Stapleton, *Essays for Patrick Atiyah*, (Oxford: Clarendon, 1991), 1-30

Twining, W. *Blackstone's Tower: The English Law School*, (London: Stevens, 1994), 141

Twining, W. and Miers, D. *How to Do Things with Rules*, 3rd edition, (London: Weidenfeld and Nicolson, 1991), 131

Unger, R. *Law and Modern Society*, (NY: Free Press 1983), 1, 6ff

Unger, R. *The Critical Legal Studies Movement*, (Cambridge, MA: Harvard University Press, 1983), 2

Vick, D. 'Interdisciplinarity and the Discipline of Law' (2004) 31 *JLS*, n.86 at 77-8

Warrington, R. 'Land Law and Legal Education: Is There Any Justice or Morality in Blackacre?', [1984] *The Law Teacher*, 77-94, at 93

Webb, J. 'Extending the Theory-Practice Spiral: Action Research as a Mechanism for crossing the Academic/Professional Divide' [1995] 2 *Web JCLI*. http://webjcli.ncl.ac.uk/articles2/webb2.html

● Further Reading and Bibliography for Chapter 5

Abel, R. L. 'Sociolegal Analysis,' *Law & Social Inquiry*, Spring, 2000

Abel, R. L. *Politics by Other Means: Law in the Struggle Against Apartheid, 1980-1994*, (New York: Routledge, 1995).

Abel-Smith, B. Zander, M. and Brooks, R. *Legal Problems and the Citizen*, (London: Heinemann, 1973)

Archbold, C. *et al.*, 'Divorce Law and Divorce Culture - The Case of Northern Ireland' (1998) 10 *CFam* 377

Armstrong, K. 'Regulating the Free-Market of Goods, Institutions and Institutional Change' in Shaw, J. and More, G. (eds), *New Legal Dynamics of European Union*, (Oxford: OUP, 1996) 166

Atiyah, P. *Accidents, Compensation and the Law*, (London: Weidenfeld and Nicolson, 1970 and later editions)

Atiyah, P. *Introduction to the Law of Contract*, 2nd edn, (Oxford: Clarendon, 1971)

Atiyah, P. *The Rise and Fall of Freedom of Contract* (Oxford: OUP: 1979)

Atkinson, M. *Discovering Suicide*, (London: Macmillan, 1978)

Atkinson, J. M. and Drew, P. *Order in Court: The Organisation of Verbal Interaction in Judicial Settings*, (London: Macmillan, 1979)

Ayres, I. and Braithwaite, J. *Responsive Regulation: Transcending the Deregulation Debate*, (Oxford: OUP, 1994)

Bainham, A. Sclater, S. D. and Richards, M. (eds), *'What is a Parent? A Socio-Legal Analysis*, (Oxford: Hart Publishing, 1999)

Bainham, A. Sclater, S. D. and Richards, M. (eds), *Body Lore and Laws*, (Oxford: Hart Publishing, 2002)

Baker, B. *et al.*, *The Matrimonial Jurisdiction of Registrars*, (Oxford: Centre for Socio-Legal Studies, 1977)

Baker, T. *Doing Social Research* 3rd edn, (NY: McGraw Hill, 1999)

Baldwin, J. *Small Claims in the County Courts in England and Wales: The Bargain Basement of Civil Justice*, (Oxford: OUP, 1998)

Baldwin, R. *Rules and Government*, (Oxford: Clarendon, 1995), 9, ch.4

Baldwin, R. 'Regulation: After "Command and Control"', in Hawkins, 1997 *op. cit.*, 65–84

Baldwin, J. and Bottomley, K. (eds) *Criminal Justice*, (Oxford: OUP, 1978)

Baldwin, J. and McConville, M. *Negotiated Justice: Pressures to Plead Guilty*, (London: Martin Robertson, 1977)

Banakar, R. 'Reflections on the Methodological Issues of the Sociology of Law', (2000) 27(2) *J. La & Soc.* 273–95

Banakar, R. and Travers, M. (eds), *An Introduction to Law and Social Theory*, (Oxford: Hart Publishing, 2002)

Bartrip, P. and Hartwell, R. M. 'Profit and Virtue: Economic Theory and the Regulation of Occupational Health in Nineteenth and Early Twentieth Century Britain', in Hawkins, 1997 *op. cit.*, 48

Beale, H. and Dugdale, T. 'Contracts Between Businessmen: Planning and the Use of Contractual Remedies' (1975) 2 *British J. of Law and Society*, 45

Bennett, T. 'What's New in Evaluation Research? A Note on the Pawson and Tilley Article' (1996) 36(4) *Brit. J. Criminol.* 567–73

Bevan, G. *et al.*, 'Piloting a Quasi-Market for Family Mediation Amongst Clients Eligible for Legal Aid' (1999) 18 *Civil Justice Quarterly* 239

Bevan, G. *et al.*, 'Can Mediation Reduce Expenditure on Lawyers?' (2001) *Fam Law* 186

Black, R. 'The Legal Basis for Control of Imports of Animal and Plant Material into the United Kingdom', 5 *Enviro LR* (2003) 179

Blair, A. 'Home–School Agreements: A Legislative Framework for Soft Control of Parents,' (2001) 2 *Edu LJ* 79

Blair, A. and Lawson, A. 'Disability Discrimination Reforms in Education – Could Do Better? *C.F.L.Q.* 2003, 15(1), 41–55

Bohmer, C. in *Law and Society Newsletter*, November 1995

Bottoms, A. E. and Maclean, J. D. *Defendants in the Criminal Process*, (London: Routledge, 1976)

Bowden, S. and Tweedale, G. 'Poisoned by the Fluff: Compensation and Litigation for Business in the Lancashire Cotton Industry', *Journal of Law and Society* (2002) 12(4)

Bradney, A. and Cownie, F. 'Teaching Legal System' (National Centre for Legal Education Warwick University, 1999)

Bradshaw, A. 'Sense and Sensibility: Debates and Developments in Socio-Legal Research Methods' in Thomas, 1997 *op. cit.*, 99

Breyer, S. *Regulation and Its Reform*, (Cambridge, MA: Harvard University Press, 1982)

Bridges, L. *et al.*, *Legal Services in Birmingham*, (Birmingham: Institute of Judicial Administration, 1975)

Brittan, Y. *The Impact of Water Pollution Control on Industry*, (Oxford: Centre for Socio-legal Studies, 1984)

Brooks-Gordon, B. *et al.*, (eds), *Sexuality Repositioned: Diversity and the Law*, (Oxford: Hart, 2003)

Byles, A. and Morris, P. *Unmet Need: The Case of the Neighbourhood Law Centre*, (London: Routledge, 1977)

Cain, M. *Society and the Policeman's Role* (London: Routledge, 1973)

Cain, M. 'Realism, Feminism, Methodology, and the Law' *Int. J. Soc. L.* 1986, 14 (3-4), 255-67

Cain, M. and Harrington, C. B. (eds), *Lawyers in a Postmodern World*, (Buckingham: Open University Press, 1994)

Campbell, C. 'Lawyers and their Public' in N. MacCormick (ed.) *Lawyers in their Social Setting*, (W. Green, 1976)

Campbell, D. 'Socio-Legal Analysis of Contract' in Thomas, 1997 *op. cit.*, 252.

Campbell, C. and Wiles, P. 'The Study of Law in Society in Britain', (1976) 10 *Law & Society Review* 547

Carlen, P. *Magistrates' Justice* 1976 Law in Society Series. (London: M. Robertson, 1976)

Carson, W. G. *The Other Price of Britain's Oil* (London: Martin Robertson, 1982)

Caswell, F. *Success in Statistics* 2nd edn, (London: John Murray, 1989)

Cohen, S. and Taylor, L. *Psychological Survival: The Experience of Long Term Imprisonment*, (London: Penguin, 1972)

Cotterrell, R. *Law's Community*, (Oxford: OUP, 1995), 296, 314

Cotterrell, R. 'Subverting Orthodoxy, Making Law Central: A View of Sociolegal Studies, (2002) 29 *JLS*, 632-44, 632

Cowan, D. *Housing: Participation and Exclusion. Collected Papers From The Socio-Legal Studies Annual Conference 1997, Cardiff University Of Wales*, (Aldershot: Ashgate, 1998)

Cowan, D. and Halliday, S. *The Appeal of Internal Review*, (Oxford: Hart, 2003)

Cownie, D. *Housing Law and Policy*, (London: Palgrave Macmillan 1999)

Craig, P. and De Búrca, G. (eds), *The Evolution of EU Law*, (Oxford: OUP, 1999)

Cranston, R. *Regulating Business: Law and Consumer Agencies*, (London: Macmillan, 1979)

Cranston, R. 'Doctrine and Practice in Commercial Law', in Hawkins, 1997, 199-224

Cretney, S. M. *et al.*, *Principles of Family Law* (London: Sweet and Maxwell, 2003)

Daintith, T. *Law as an Instrument of Social Policy*, (Berlin: Walter de Gruyter, 1988)

Danet, B. 'Language in the Legal Process' 14 *Law and Society Review* 445 (1980)

Davis, G. *et al.*, 'Mediation and Legal Services – The Client Speaks' (2001) *Fam Law* 110

Davis, G. *et al.*, 'Family Mediation – Where do we go From Here?' (2001) *Fam Law* 265

Davis, G. Cretney, S. and Collins, J. *Simple Quarrels*, (Oxford: Clarendon Press, 1994)

Davis, G. *Partisans and Mediators*, (Oxford: OUP, 1988)

Davis, G. and Murch, M. *The Grounds for Divorce* (Oxford: Clarendon, 1988)

Davis, G. Wikeley, N. and Young, R. with Jacqueline Barron and Julie Bedward, *Child Support in Action*, (Oxford: Hart, 1999)

Dawe, A. 'The Two Sociologies' (1970) 21 *British J. of Sociology*, 207

Dawson, S. *et al.*, *Safety at Work: The Limits of Self-Regulation*, (Cambridge: CUP, 1988)

De Búrca, G. and Weiler, J. H. H. (eds), *The European Court of Justice* (Oxford: OUP, 2001)

Deakin, S. and Michie, J. (eds), *Contracts, Co-operation, and Competition*, (Oxford: OUP, 1997)

Deakin, S. Goodwin, T. and Hughes, A. 'Co-operation and Trust in Inter-Firm Relations: Beyond Competition Policy?' in Deakin and Michie (eds), *Contracts, Co-operation, and Competition*, (Oxford: OUP, 1997)

Deech, R. 'Divorce Law and Empirical Studies' (1990) 106 *LQR* 229

Dingwell, R. and Eekelaar, J. 'Families and the State: An Historical Perspective on the Public Regulation of Private Conduct,' (1988) 10 *Law and Policy*, 341–61

Dingwell, R. and Greatbatch, D. 'The Virtues of Formality' in Eekelaar and Maclean (eds) 1994 *op. cit.*

Dingwell, R. and Greatbatch, D. 'Family Mediators – What are They Doing?' (2001) *Fam Law* 378

Dingwell, R. and Lewis, P. *The Sociology of the Professions: Lawyers, Doctors and Others*, (Oxford: SSRC, 1983)

Dingwell, R. Eekelaar, J. and Murray, T. *The Protection of Children: State Intervention and Family Life*, (Oxford: Blackwell, 1983)

Doolin, K. *Criminal Justice*, 2nd edn, (London: Sweet and Maxwell, 2002)

Douglas, G. and Ferguson, N. 'The Role of Grandparents in Divorced Families,' (2003) 41 *Int Jo of Law, Policy and the Family*

Douglas, G. and Perry, A. 'How Parents Cope Financially on Separation and Divorce – Implications for the Future of Ancillary Relief', (2001) *CFam* 13.1(67)

Eekelaar, J. *Family Law and Social Policy*, (London: Weidenfeld and Nicolson, 1978)

Eekelaar, J. *Regulating Divorce* (Oxford: OUP, 1991)

Eekelaar, J. 'Property Adjustment After Divorce', in Hawkins, 1997 *op. cit.*, 240–41

Eekelaar, J. and Clive, E. *Custody After Divorce*, (Oxford: Oxford Centre for Socio-legal Studies, 1977)

Eekelaar, J. and Maclean, M. *Children and Divorce: Economic Factors*, (Oxford: Centre for Socio-Legal Studies, 1983)

Eekelaar, J. and Maclean, M. *Maintenance After Divorce*, (Oxford, Clarendon, 1986)

Eekelaar, J. and Maclean, M. 'Reply to Deech' (1990) 106 *LQR* 621

Eekelaar, J. and Maclean, M. (eds), *A Reader in Family Law* (Oxford: OUP, 1994) 2

Eekelaar, J. and Maclean, M. *Family Law*, (Oxford: OUP, 1995)

Eekelaar, J. and Maclean, M. 'Property and Financial Adjustment after Divorce in the 1990s – Unfinished Business', in Hawkins, 1997 *op. cit.*, 225–44

ESRC, *Review of Socio-legal Studies*, (Swindon: ESRC, 1994)

Farrington, D. *et al.*, (eds), *Psychology, Law and Legal Processes*, (London: Macmillan, 1979)

Faure, M. 'The Future of Social Legal Research with Respect to Environmental Problems', (1995) 22(1) *J. Law & Soc.* 127–32

Feeley, M. *The Process is the Punishment*: *Handling Cases in a Lower Criminal Court*, (NY: Russell Sage, 1979)

Felstiner, W. 'Professional Inattention: Origins and Consequences', in Hawkins, 1997 *op. cit.*, 122

Fenn, P. and Veljanovski, C. 'A Positive Theory of Regulatory Enforcement', (1988) 98 *Economics Journal*, 1055

Ferguson, R. 'Legal Ideology and Commercial Interests: The Social Origins of the Commercial law Codes' (1977) 4 *British J. of Law and Society*, 18

Ferguson, R. 'The Adjudication of Commercial Disputes and the Legal System in Modern England' (1980) 7 *British J. of Law and Society*, 141

Fielding, N. G. and Lee, R. M. (eds), *Using Computers in Qualitative Research*, (London: Sage, 1991)

Finch, J. Hayes, L. Mason, J. Masson, J. and Wallis, L. *Wills, Inheritance, and Families*, (Oxford: OUP, 1996)

Findlay, M. *The Globalisation of Crime*, (Cambridge: CUP, 1999)

The Finer Committee on One-Parent Families (1974, Cmnd. 5629)

Fitzgerald, J. D. and Cox, S. M. *Research Methods in Criminal Justice* (Chicago, IL: Nelson-Hall, 1992)

Fitzpatrick, P. 'Being Social in Socio-legal Studies', in D. J. Galligan (ed.), *Socio-legal Studies in Context*, The Oxford Centre Past and Future, (Oxford: Blackwell, 1995), 105

Flood, J. *Barristers' Clerks: The Law's Middle-Men*, (Manchester: Manchester University Press 1983)

Flood, J. 'Doing Business: The Management of Uncertainty in Lawyers' Work', (1991) 25 *Law and Society Review*, 41

Freeman, M. *Lloyd's Introduction to Jurisprudence*, 6th edn, (London: Stevens, 1995), 538

Friedmann, W. *Law in a Changing Society* (London: Stevens, 1959) 93ff (cf. Campbell, 1997 *op. cit.*, 240–42)

'From the Editor,' (2000) 34 *Law and Soc'y Review* 859

Galanter, M. 'Why the Haves Come Out Ahead: Speculations on the Limits of Legal Change' (1974) 9 *Law & Society Review* 95

Galligan, D. J. (ed.), *Socio-legal Studies in Context: The Oxford Centre Past and Future*, (Oxford: Blackwell, 1995)

Garth, B. and Sterling, J. 'From Legal Realism to Law and Society: Reshaping Law for the Last Stages of the Social Activist State' (1988) 32 *Law and Society Review* 409

Gelsthorpe, L. 'How to get recognised', Socio-Legal Newsletter 37 (2002), 3

Genn, H. *Meeting Legal Needs? An Evaluation of a Scheme for Personal Injury Victims*, (Oxford: Centre for Socio-Legal Studies, 1982)

Genn, H. *Hard Bargaining: Out of Court Settlements in Personal Injury*, (Oxford: Clarendon, 1987)

Genn, H. and Partington, M. unpublished paper presented to an ESRC conference in 1993: quoted in Philip Thomas, 1997 *op. cit.*, 2

Genn, H. and Paterson, A. *Paths To Justice In Scotland*, (Oxford: Hart, 2001)

Gerhard, U. 'Women's Experiences of Injustice: Some Methodological Problems and Empirical Findings of Legal Research' *Social & Legal Studies* 1993, 2(3), 303-21 (with reference to research in equal opportunities in employment)

Gillespie, A. A. 'Child Protection on the Internet – Challenges For Criminal Law', (2002) 14 *CFam*

Gilligan, G. P. 'The Potential of Socio-legal Approaches in the Development of Company Law' (2000) 21 *Company Lawyer* 127

Glennon, L. *'Fitzpatrick v Sterling Housing Association Ltd* – An Endorsement of The Functional Family?' (2000) 14 *IJLP&F* 226

Grace, C. and Wilkinson, P. 'Social Action and a Methodology for the Sociology of Law', *BJLS* 1 (1974) 184–94

Grace, C. and Wilkinson, P. *Negotiating the Law: Social Work and Legal Services* (London: Routledge, 1978)

Grounds, A. and Jamieson, R. 'No Sense of an Ending: Researching the Experience of Imprisonment and Release Among Republican ex Prisoners', *Theo. Crim.* 2003, 7(3), 347–62

Gunningham, N. *Pollution, Social Interest and the Law* (London: Martin Robertson, 1974)

Gunningham, N. and Johnstone, R. *Rethinking Occupational Health and Safety Regulation: Two Track Regulatory Reform*, (Oxford: OUP, 1999)

Hadden, T. *Company Law and Capitalism* (London: Weidenfeld and Nicolson, 1972 and later editions)

Hadden, T. *Compulsory Repair and Improvement*: *A Study of the Operation of the Housing Acts 1957–1974* (Oxford: Centre for Socio-Legal Studies, 1978)

Halliday, S. and Schmidt, P. (eds), *Human Rights Brought Home*, (Oxford: Hart, 2004)

Harding, C. 'Who Goes to Court in Europe: An Analysis of Litigation Against the European Community' (1992) 17 *E.L.Rev.*

Harlow, C. 'A Community of Interests: Making the Most of European Law' (1992) 55 *MLR* 331

Harlow, C. 'Towards a Theory of Access for the European Court of Justice' (1992) 12 *Y.E.L.* 213

Harris, D. *et al.*, *Compensation and Support for Illness and Injury*, (Oxford: Clarendon, 1984)

Harris, D. 'The Development of Socio-Legal Studies in the United Kingdom', (1983) 2 *Legal Studies*, 315

Hartley, H. *Exploring Sport and Leisure Disasters*, (London: Cavendish, 2001)

Hawkins, K. *Environment and Enforcement: Regulation and the Social Definition of Pollution*, (Oxford: OUP, 1984)

Hawkins, K. 'Compliance Strategy, Prosecution Policy and Aunt Sally – a Comment on Peirce and Tombs', (1990) 30 *British Journal of Criminology*, 444

Hawkins, K. *The Regulation of Health and Safety: A Socio-legal Perspective*, Report to Health and Safety Executive, (Oxford: Oxford Centre for Socio-Legal Studies, 1992)

Hawkins, K. (ed.), *The Uses of Discretion*, (Oxford: OUP, 1992).

Hawkins, K. *The Human Face of Law: Essays in Honour of Donald Harris*, (Oxford: OUP, 1997), 20

Hawkins, K. General Editor's Introduction to B. Tamanaha, *Realistic Socio-Legal Theory*, (Oxford: Clarendon, 1997)

Hawkins, K. *Law as Last Resort: Prosecution Decision-Making in a Regulatory Agency*, (Oxford: OUP, 2002)

Heinz, J. and Laumann, E. *Chicago Lawyers: The Social Structure of the Bar*, (NY: Russell Sage Foundation, 1982)

Hendrick, H. *Children, Childhood and English Society*, (Cambridge: Cambridge University Press, 1990), at 97–9

Henham, R. 'Reconciling Process And Policy: Sentence Discounts in the Magistrates' Courts' 15 *Crim.L.R.* (2000) June 436

Hillyard, P. 'Invoking Indignation: Reflections on the Future Directions of Socio-legal Studies', (2002) 29 *JLS* 645–56

Hillyard, P. 'What is Socio-legal Studies?' ESRC Review of Socio-Legal Studies, (Swindon: ESRC, 1994)

Hillyard, P. and Sim, J. 'The Political Economy of Socio-Legal Research', in Thomas, 1997 *op. cit.*, 45

Hodgson, J. 'The Comparativist as Participant Observer', in D. Nelken (ed.), *Contrasting Criminal Justice*, (Aldershot: Ashgate Publishing, 2000) 139–56.

Hoggett, B. M. and Pearl, D. *The Family, Law and Society*: *Cases and Materials* (Butterworths, 1996)

Hood, R. *Sentencing in Magistrates' Courts* (London: Stevens, 1969)

Hunt, J. 'A Moving Target – Care Proceedings as a Dynamic Process', (1998) *CFam* 10.3(281)

Hutter, B. *The Reasonable Arm of the Law: The Law Enforcement Procedures of Environmental Health Enforcers*, (Oxford: Clarendon, 1988)

Hutter, B. *Compliance, Legal Regulation and the Environment*, (Oxford: Clarendon 1997)

Hutter, B. (ed.) *A Reader in Environmental Law*, Oxford Readings in Socio Legal Studies, (Oxford: Oxford University Press), 1999

Hutter, B. *Regulation and Risk: Occupational Health and Safety on the Railways*, (Oxford: OUP, 2001), 104

Hutter, B. and Lloyd-Bostock, S. 'Law's Relationship with Social Science: The Interdependence of Theory, Empirical Work and Social Relevance in Socio-legal Studies', in K. Hawkins (ed.), *The Human Face of Law: Essays in Honour of Donald Harris* (Oxford: Oxford University Press, 1997), 29

Ingleby, R. *Solicitors and Divorce* (Oxford: OUP, 1992)

Jolly, S. 'Family Law' in Thomas, 1997 *op. cit.*, 342

Jupp, V. *Methods of Criminological Research* (London: Unwin Hyman, 1989)

Kaganas, F. and Piper, C. 'Shared Parenting – A 70% Solution?' (2002) 14 *CFam* 365

Kalunta-Crumpton, A. 'Claims Making and the Prosecution of Black Defendants in Drug Trafficking Trials: The Influence of Deprivation,' (1998) 3(1), *International Journal of Discrimination and the Law*, 29–49

Kemp, C. 'The Uses of Abstraction; Remarks on the Interdisciplinary Efforts in Law and Philosophy' (1997) 74 *Denver University Law Rev.* 877

Keown, J. in Bainham, A. Sclater, S. D. and Richards, M. 2002 *op. cit.*

Kidder, L. and Judd, C. *Research Methods in Social Relations*, (NY: Holt, Rinehart, 1986)

Klug, H. Review Essays, 'Law Under And After Apartheid: Abel's Sociolegal Analysis', Law and Social Inquiry, Spring 2000

Kusum, K. *Juvenile Delinquency: A Socio-Legal Study*, (New Delhi: KLM, 1979)

Lahey, K. and Salter, S. 'Corporate Law in Legal Theory and Legal Scholarship: From Classicism to Feminism' (1985) 23 *Osgoode Hall LJ* 543

Levi, J. N. *Linguistics, Language and Law: A Topical Bibliography*, (Bloomington: Indiana University Press, 1982)

Levine, F. 'Presidential Address' (1990) 25 *Law and Society Review*, 1-25

Lewis, P. 'Knowing the Buzzwords and Clapping for Tinkerbell: The Context, Content and Qualities of Lawyers' Knowledge in a Specialised Industrial Field', in Keith Hawkins, *The Human Face of Law: Essays in Honour of Donald Harris*, (Oxford: OUP, 1997) 151-76

Lewis, R. 'Making Justice Work: Effective Legal Interventions for Domestic Violence' *Brit. J. Criminol.* 2004, 44(2), 204-24 (with reference to researching restorative justice in the UK)

Lind, E. A. and Tyler, T. R. *The Social Psychology of Procedural Justice*, (NY: Plenum Press, 1988)

Lloyd-Bostock, S. 'The Psychology of Routine Discretion: Accident Screening by British Factory Inspectors, (1992) 14 *Law and Policy*, 45-76

Lloyd-Bostock, S. 'The Effects on Juries of Hearing About the Defendant's Previous Record,' *Crim. L Rev.* (2000)

Macauley, S. 28 *Amer Sociological Rev* 55 (1963)

McBarnet, D. 'False Dichotomies in Criminal Justice Research', in Baldwin and Bottomley, *Criminal Justice*, (Oxford: OUP, 1978)

McBarnet, D. *Conviction: Law, State and Construction of Justice* (London: Macmillan, 1981)

McBarnet, D. 'Law and Capital: The Role of Legal Form and Legal Actors' (1984) 12 *IJSL* 223

McBarnet, D. 'Law, Policy and Avoidance', (1988) 15 *JLS*, 113-21; 'Whiter than White Collar Crime: Tax, Fraud Insurance and the Management of Stigma', (1992) 52 *British Journal of Sociology*, 323-44

McBarnet, D. and Whelan, C. 'The Elusive Spirit of the Law: Formalism and the Struggle for Legal Control', 54 (1991) *MLR*, 848-73

McBarnet, D. and Whelan, C. 'Creative Compliance and the Defeat of Legal Control: The Magic of the Orphan Subsidiary', in Hawkins, 1997 *op. cit.*, 177-98

MacCormick, D. N. (ed.), *Lawyers in their Social Setting*, (W. Green, 1976)

McDermott, M. 'A View from the Coalface', *Socio-legal Newsletter* (1996) no.38, 5

McGregor, O. R. Blom-Cooper, L. and Gibson, C. *Separated Spouses: A Study of the Matrimonial Jurisdiction of the Magistrate's Courts*, (London: Duckworth, 1970)

Maclean, M. *Surviving Divorce: Women's Resources After Separation*, (London: Macmillan, 1991)

Maclean, M. and Genn, H. *Methodological Issues in Social Surveys*, (Atlantic Highlands, NJ: Humanities Press, 1979

Maidment, S. *Judicial Separation*, (Oxford: Centre for Socio-Legal Studies, 1982)

Mansell, W. 'Tort and Socio-Legal Studies' in Thomas, 1997 *op. cit.*, 222.

Mare, T. de la, 'Article 177 EC in Social and Political Context: Perspective on the Key Procedure for EC Legal Integration' in Craig and De Búrca (eds), *The Evolution of EU Law* (Oxford: OUP, 1999)

Marshall, K. *Children's Rights in the Balance: The Participation-Protection Debate* (London: The Stationery Office, 1997)

Masson, J. et al., Yours, Mine or Ours (London; HMSO, 1983)

Mayhew, L. Law and Equal Opportunity, (Cambridge, MA: Harvard University Press, 1968)

Moran, J. The New Critical Idiom: Interdisciplinarity, (London: Routledge, 2001)

Morris, P. White, R. and Lewis, P. Social Needs and Legal Action, (London: Martin Robertson, 1973)

Mosgrove, R. and Rowland, A. 'Are the Woolf Reforms a Success?', Socio-Legal Newsletter, No.38, (2002), 8; 'The Human Rights Act: Its impact on the courts', Socio-Legal Newsletter, No.38, (2002)

Muller, D. J. Blackman, D. E. and Chapman, A. J. (eds) Topics in Psychology and Law, (Chichester: Wiley, 1983)

Murch, M. Justice and Welfare in Divorce (Sweet and Maxwell, 1980)

Nazroo, J. 'Uncovering Gender Differences in the Use of Marital Violence: The Effect of Methodology', (1995) 29 Sociology, 475

Nelken, D. 'The "Gap Problem" in the Sociology of Law: A Theoretical Review' (1981) 1 Windsor Yearbook of Access to Justice, 35

Nelken, D. 'Just Comparing; Virtually There, Researching There, Living There and Telling Difference; Of Crime and Criminal Justice in Italy' in Contrasting Criminal Justice (David Nelken, ed.), (Aldershot: Ashgate Publishing, 2000)

O'Barr, W. Linguistic Evidence: Language, Power and Strategy in the Courtroom, (NY: Academic Press, 1982)

O'Donovan, K. Sexual Divisions in Law, (London: Weidenfeld and Nicolson, 1985)

Ogus, A. 'Law and Economics in the UK: Past, Present, and Future' (1995) 22 J. Law and Society, 28

Ogus, A. 'Exemplary Damages and Economic Analysis', in Hawkins 1997

Palomar, J. 'The War Between Attorneys and Lay Conveyancers – Empirical Evidence Says "Cease Fire!" ', (1999) 31 Conn. L. Rev, 423

Partington, M. 'Socio-Legal Research in Britain: Shaping the Funding Environment', in Thomas, 1997 op. cit., 23–44

Passas, N. and Nelken, D. 'The Thin Line Between Legitimate and Criminal Enterprises: Subsidy Frauds in the EC' (1993) 18 Crime, Law and Social Change, 223

Paterson, A. The Law Lords: How Britain's Top Judges See Their Role, (London: Macmillan, 1982)

Paterson, J. and Teubner, G. 'Changing Maps: Empirical Legal Autopoiesis' (1998) 7(4) Social & Legal Studies, 451–86

Paulus, I. The Search for Pure Food, (London: Martin Robertson, 1974)

Peacock, A. (ed.), The Regulation Game, (Oxford: Blackwell)

Phuong, C. 'Enlarging "Fortress Europe": EU Accession, Asylum, and Immigration in Candidate Countries', (2003) 52 ICLQ 641

Piper, C. The Responsible Parent, (Hemel Hempstead: Harvester, 1993)

Piper, C. and Miakishev, A. 'A Child's Right to Veto in England and Wales – Another Welfare Ploy?' (2003) CFam 15.1(57)

Pomerantz, A. and Atkinson, J. M. 'Ethnomethodology, Conversation Analysis and the Study of Courtroom interaction', in Mueller, Blackman and Chapman, Topics in Psychology and Law, (Chichester: Wiley, 1983)

Pound, R. 'Law in Books and Law in Action' (1910) 44 *American Law Review* 12

Ramsay, I. M. 'What Do Lawyers Do? Reflections on the Market for Lawyers' (1993) 21 *IJSL* 355

Reichmann, W. *The Use and Abuse of Statistics*, (London: Pelican, 1964)

Richardson, G. *et al.*, *Policing Pollution: A Study of Regulation and Enforcement*, (Oxford: Clarendon, 1983); Hawkins, K. 1984 *op. cit.*

Rickett, C. E. F. and Thomas G. W. Telfer (eds), *International Perspectives on Consumers' Access to Justice*. (Cambridge: CUP, 2003)

Roche, J. and Piper, C. in S. Day Sclater and C. Piper (eds), *Undercurrents of Divorce*, (Aldershot: Ashgate Publishing Ltd, 1999)

Ross, H. *et al.* 'Determining the Social Effects of a Law Reform' (1977) 13 *American Behavioural Scientist* 209

Ross, L. *Settled Out of Court: The Social Process of Insurance Claims Adjustments*, (NY: Aldine, 1970)

Sanderson, I. *Criminal Justice*, (London: Butterworths, 1997)

Sarat, A. *et al.*, *Crossing Boundaries: Traditions and Transformations in Law and Society Research*, (Evanston, IL: Northwestern University Press, 1998), Part One

Sawyer, C. 'Ascertaining the Child's Wishes and Feelings,' (2000) 30 *Fam LJ* 170

Sawyer, C. 'Equity's Children – Constructive Trusts for the New Generation,' (2004) 16 *CFam* 31

Schepel, H. and Blankenburg, E. 'Mobilising the European Court of Justice' in De Búrca and Weiler (eds), *The European Court of Justice*, (Oxford: OUP, 2001)

Sclater, S. Day and Piper, C. (eds), *Undercurrents of Divorce*, (Aldershot: Ashgate Publishing, 1999)

Shapiro, S. *Wayward Capitalists: Target of the Securities and Exchange Commission*, (New Haven, CT: Yale University Press, 1984)

Sharifuddin, M. *et al.*, *Water Pollution and Law*, (New Delhi: Saloni, 2004)

Shaw, J. 'Socio-Legal Studies and the European Union' in Thomas, 1997 *op. cit.*, 310

Shaw, J. and More, G. (eds), *New Legal Dynamics of European Union*, (Oxford: OUP, 1996)

Smith, D. E. 'Women, the Family and Corporate Capitalism' in Stephenson (ed.) *Women in Canada*, (Toronto: General Publishing, 1977)

Smith, G. P. *Legal and Healthcare Ethics for the Elderly*, (London: Taylor & Francis, 1996)

Slaughter, A. M. Stone Sweet, A. and Weiler, J. H. H. (eds), *The European Court and National Courts: Legal Change in its Social Context* (Oxford: Hart Press, 1998)

Smart, C. *The Ties that Bind*, (London: Routledge, 1984)

Smart, C. and Sevenhuijsen, S. (eds), *Child Custody and the Politics of Gender*, (London: Routledge, 1989)

Smith, G. P. *Legal and Healthcare Ethics for the Elderly*, (London: Taylor & Francis, 1996)

Smith, G. P. *Bioethics and the Law: Medical, Socio-Legal and Philosophical Directions for a Brave New World*, (NY: University Press of America, 2001)

Solomou, W. *et al.*, 'The Parent–Child Relationship in Later Life', in A. Bainham *et al.*, *What is a Parent? A Socio-Legal Analysis* (Oxford: Hart, 1999)

Stevens, R. 'Judges, Politics, Politicians and the Confusing Role of the Judiciary,' in Hawkins, 1997 *op. cit.*, 245–90

Stewart, R. B. 'Regulation and the Crisis of Legislation in the United States', in T. Daintith, *Law as an Instrument of Social Policy*, (Berlin: Walter de Gruyter, 1988)

Thibaut, J. and Walker, L. *Procedural Justice: A Psychological Analysis*, (Hillsdale, NJ: Erlbaum, 1975)

Thomas, P. *Law in the Balance: Legal Services in the Eighties* (Oxford: OUP, 1981)

Thomas, P. 'Curriculum Development in Legal Studies' (1986) 20 *Law Teacher* 110 at 112.

Thomas, P. (ed.), *Socio-Legal Studies*, (Aldershot: Ashgate-Dartmouth, 1997)

Thomas, P. 'Socio-Legal Studies: The Case of Disappearing Fleas and Bustards', in Philip Thomas (ed.), *Socio-Legal Studies*, (Aldershot: Ashgate-Dartmouth, 1997), 4

Tomlins, C. 'Framing the Field of Law's Disciplinary Encounters: A Historical Narrative' (2000) 34 *Law and Society Rev.* 911

Trinder, L. and Stone, N. 'Family Assistance Orders – Professional Aspiration And Party Frustration' (1998), *CFam* 10.3(291)

Twining, W. 'Law and Anthropology: A Case-study of Interdisciplinary Collaboration' (1973) 7 *Law & Society Review* 561

Twining, W. 'Remembering 1972' in D. J. Galligan, (ed.), *Socio-legal Studies in Context: The Oxford Centre Past and Future*, (Oxford: Blackwell, 1995)

Vick, D. 'Interdisciplinarity and the Discipline of Law' (2004) 31 *JLS*, 163–93

Weinstein, J. 'Coming of Age: Recognising the Importance of Interdisciplinary Education in Law Practice' (1999) 74 *Washington Law Rev.* 319 at 353

Welstead, M. 'Case Commentary: Financial Support in Same-Sex Relationships – a Canadian Constitutional Solution', (2000) 12 *CFam* 73

Wheeler, S. 'Lawyer Involvement in Commercial Disputes', (1991a) 18 *JLS* 241

Wheeler, S. *Reservation Of Title Clauses: Impact and Implications*, (Oxford: Clarendon, 1991b)

Wheeler, S. 'Capital Fractionalized: The Role of Insolvency Practitioners in Asset Distribution' in Cain and Harrington (eds), *Lawyers in a Postmodern World*, (Buckingham: Open University Press, 1994)

Wheeler, S. 'The Business Enterprise: A Socio-Legal Introduction' in Sally Wheeler (ed.), *A Reader on the Law of the Business Enterprise: Selected Essays* (Oxford: OUP, 1994)

Wheeler, S. (ed.), *A Reader on the Law of the Business Enterprise: Selected Essays* (Oxford: OUP, 1995)

Wheeler, S. 'Company Law' in Thomas, 1997 *op. cit.*, n.8 / 285

Wheeler, S. 1997 *op. cit.*, 285 citing M. Salter, 'On the Idea of the Legal World' (1994) 1 *International Jnl. of the Legal Profession*, 283 at 289ff

Whelan, C. and McBarnet, D. 'Lawyers in the Market: Delivering Legal Services in Europe' (1992) 19 *J. Law and Society* 49

Wilkinson, P. J. *Bibliography on the Social Organisation of Disputes and Dispute Processes*, (Oxford: Oxford Centre for Socio-legal Studies, 1980)

Yavasi, M. 'A Socio-Legal and Economic Introduction to Corporate Governance: Problems in the E.U,' (2001) 22(6) *Company Lawyer*, 162

Zander, M. *Legal Services for the Community* (London: Temple Press, 1978)

● Further Reading and Bibliography for Chapter 6

Alldridge, P. '"Attempted Murder of the Soul": Blackmail, Privacy and Secrets', *O.J.L.S.* 1993, 13(3), 368–87

Atiyah, P. *Rise and Fall of Freedom of Contract* (Oxford: Clarendon Press, 1979)

Atiyah, P. and Summers, *Form and Substance in Anglo-American Law*, (Oxford: Clarendon, 1991)

Bailey, V. *Policing and Punishment in Nineteenth Century Britain*, (London: Croom-Helm, 1981)

Bainham, A. *et al.*, *What is a Parent? A Socio-Legal Analysis*, (Oxford: Hart Publishing 1999)

Bainham, A. Shelley Day Sclater, Martin Richards (eds), *Body Lore and Laws*, (Oxford: Hart Publishing, 2002)

Baker, J. H. *The Law's Two Bodies* (Oxford: OUP, 2001)

Baker, J. H. *An Introduction to English Legal History* 4th edn, (London: Butterworths, 2002)

Baker, J. 'Why the History of English Law has not been Finished', 59 *The Cambridge Law Journal*, March [2000] pp. 62–84

Ballinger, A. *Dead Women Walking*: *Executed Women in England and Wales 1900–1955*, (Aldershot: Ashgate, 2000)

Bartlett, P. *The Poor Law of Lunacy*, (Leicester: Leicester University Press, 1999)

Bartrip, P. W. J. *Safety at Work*: *The Factory Inspectorate in the Fencing Controversy 1833–57* (Oxford: Centre for Socio-Legal Studies, 1979)

Bartrip, P. W. J. 'The Conventionalization of Factory Crime: A Re-assessment', 8 *International Journal of the Sociology of Law* 175 (1980)

Bartrip, P. W. J. 'British Government Inspection 1832–1875', *Review of Social History* 77 (1980)

Bartrip, P. W. J. 'British Government Inspection, 1832–1875', 25 *Historical Journal*, 605 (1982)

Bartrip, P. W. J. 'Petticoat Pestering: The Women's Trade Union League and Lead Poisoning in the Staffordshire Potteries, 1890–1914', (1996) *Historical Studies in Industrial Relations*, 2, 3–25

Bartrip, P. W. J. and Burman, S. B. *The Wounded Soldiers of Industry: Industrial Compensation Policy 1833–97*, (Oxford: Clarendon, 1983)

Bartrip, P. W. J. and Fenn, P. T. 'Factory Fatalities and Regulation in Great Britain, 1878–1913', 25 *Explorations in Economic History* (1980), 60–74

Bartrip, P. W. J. and Hartwell, R. M. 'Profit and Virtue: Economic Theory and the Regulation of Occupational Health in Nineteenth and Early Twentieth Century Britain', in Hawkins 1997, *op. cit.*, 45–64

Bibbings, L. S. 'State reaction to Conscientious Objection', in I. Loveland (ed.), *Frontiers of Criminality* (London: Sweet and Maxwell, 1995)

Bibbings, L. S. 'Conscientious Objectors in the Great War: The Consequences of Rejecting Military Masculinities,' in Paul Higate (ed.), *Military Masculinities: Identity and the State* (London: Greenwood, 2003)

Bibbings, L. S. 'Images of Manliness: The Portrayal of Soldiers and Conscientious Objectors in the Great War', *Social and Legal Studies* 12(3) 2003, 335-58

Bisson, T. N. (ed.) *Cultures of Power: Lordship, Status and Process in 12th Century Europe*, (Philadelphia, 1995)

Blandy, S. and Robinson, D. 'Reforming Leasehold: Discursive Events and Outcomes 1984-2000'. *J. Law & Soc.* (2001) 28(3), 384-408

Braithwaite, J. 'Crime in a Convict Republic', *M.L.R.* 2001, 64(1), 11-50

Braithwaite, J. 'What's Wrong with the Sociology of Punishment?', *Theo. Crim.* 2003, 7(1), 5-28

Braithwaite, J. and V. 4 *Social and Legal Studies*, (1995), 307-41, 307

Brown, B. *et al.*, *Sex Crimes on Trial: The Use of Sexual Evidence in Scottish Courts*, (Edinburgh: Edinburgh University Press, 1993)

Brown, J. 'Discriminatory Experiences of Women Police: A Comparison of Officers Serving in England and Wales, Scotland, Northern Ireland and the Republic of Ireland', *Int. J. Soc. L.* (2000), 28(2), 91-111

Brown, M. 'Aina Under the Influence: The Criminalization of Alcohol in 19th-Century Hawai'i', *Theo. Crim.* (2003), 7(1), 89-110

Brown, M. 'Crime, Liberalism and Empire: Governing the Mina Tribe of Northern India', *S. & L.S.* 2004, 13(2), 191-218

Brown-Nagin, T. 'Race as Identity Caricature: A Local Legal History Lesson in the Salience of Intraracial Conflict' (2003) 151 *U. Pa.L. Rev.* 1913

Cain, M. and Hunt, A. *Marx and Engels on Law*, (London: Academic Press, 1979)

Caldarone, R. P. 'Precedent in Operation: A Comparison of the Judicial House of Lords and the US Supreme Court', *Public* Law (2004) 279

Charlesworth, L. 'Poor Law in the City: A Comparative Legal Analysis of the Anomalous Poor Relief Administration in the Cities of Liverpool and Chester After the 1834 Poor Law Amendment Act', paper presented at the 17th British Legal History Conference, London, 2005

Charlesworth, L. and Loux, A. 'Gentlemen and Scholars in White Cotton Gloves: "Legal Education and the Reproduction of Hierarchy" Legal History', (Bristol SLSA, 2001)

Chinhengo, A. 'Sons of the Soil – Land, Law and the Colonial Reconstruction of Indigenous Identities in Sub-Saharan Africa', (Bristol SLSA, 2001)

Chunn, D. E. 'Rehabilitating Deviant Families Through Family Courts: The Birth of "Socialized" Justice in Ontario, 1920-1940', *Int. J. Soc. L.* (1988), 16(2), 137-58

Collins, H. *The Law of Contract* 3rd edn (London: Butterworths, 1997)

Cook, A. 'Settling Accounts: Law as History in the Trial of the Gang of Four' 6 *Current Legal Issues*, (2004) 413-31

Cornish, W. *et al.*, *Crime and Law in Nineteenth Century Britain* (Dublin: Gov't Publications, 1978)

Curran, V. G. 'Dealing in Difference: Comparative Law's Potential for Broadening Legal Perspectives', 46 *Am. J. Comp. L* 657 Fall, (1998)

Curran, V. G. 'The Legalization of Racism in a Constitutional State: Democracy's Suicide in Vichy France,' 50 *Hastings L.J.* (1999) 100

Davies, W. and Fouracre, P. *The Settlement of Disputes in Early Medieval Europe*, (Cambridge: CUP, 1996)

Dembour, M-B and Krzyzanowska-Mierzewska, M. 'Ten Years On: The Popularity of the Convention in Poland', *E.H.R.L.R.* 2004, 4, 400-423

De Vries, P. ' "White Slaves" in a Colonial Nation: The Dutch Campaign Against the Traffic in Women in the Early Twentieth Century' 14(1), *Social & Legal Studies*, (2005) 39-60

Doran, N. 'From Embodied "Health" to Official "accidents": Class, Codification and British Factory Legislation 1831-1844', *S. & L.S.* (1996), 5(4), 523-46

Douglas, L. 'The Holocaust, History and Legal Memory', 6 *Current Legal Issues*, (2004) 413-31

Doupe, M. and Salter, M. 'Concealing the Past?: Questioning Textbook Interpretations of the History of Equity and Trusts', 2-3 (2000a) *Liverpool Law Review* 253

Doupe, M. and Salter, M. 'The Cheshire World-view', 11(1) *Kings College Law Journal*, (2000b) 49

Downes, D. *Contrasts in Tolerance: Post War Penal Policy in the Netherlands and England and Wales*, (Oxford: Clarendon/OUP, 1993)

Duff, P. and Hutton, N. (eds), *Criminal Justice in Scotland*, (Aldershot: Ashgate, 1999)

Dunn, A. 'As "Cold as Charity"?: Poverty, Equity and the Charitable Trust' *L.S.* (2000), 20(2), 222-40

Eekelaar, J. *Family Law and Social Policy*, 2nd edn, (London: Weidenfeld and Nicolson, 1984)

Eekelaar, J. *Regulating Divorce*, (Oxford: OUP, 1991)

Eekelaar, J. 'Property Adjustment After Divorce', in Hawkins, 1997 *op. cit.*

ESRC, *Review of Socio-legal Studies*, (Swindon: ESRC, 1994)

Findlay, M. *The Globalisation of Crime*, (Cambridge: CUP, 1999)

Fine, R. *Capitalism and the Rule of Law* (London: Hutchinson, 1979)

Friedman, L. *A History of American Law* 2nd edn (NY: Simon and Schuster, 1985)

Galligan, D. J. (ed.), *Socio-legal Studies in Context*, The Oxford Centre Past and Future, (Oxford: Blackwell, 1995)

Garland, D. *Punishment and Welfare: A History of Penal Strategies*, (Aldershot: Dartmouth, 1985)

Getzler, J. 'Law, History and the Social Sciences: Intellectual Traditions of Late-Nineteenth- and early Twentieth-Century Europe', 6 *Current Legal Issues*, 215

Glennon, L. 'Fitzpatrick v Sterling Housing Association Ltd – An Endorsement of the Functional Family?' (2000) 14 *IJLP&F* 226

Gordon, R. 'Foreword: The Arrival of Critical Historicism' (1997) 49 *Stan L. R*, 1023, 1024

Grosswald Curran, V. 'Dealing in Difference: Comparative Law's Potential for Broadening Legal Perspectives', *American Journal of Comparative Law*, 657 Fall, 1998

Guarnieri, C. Pederzoli, P. and Thomas, C. A. *The Power of Judges: A Comparative Study of Courts and Democracy*, (Oxford: OUP, 2002)

Gunningham, N. Grabosky, P. and Sinclair, D. *Smart Regulation: Designing Environmental Policy*, (Oxford: OUP, 1998)

Harding, A. *A Social History of English Law*, (London: Penguin, 1966)

Harding, C. and Swart, B. *Enforcing European Community Rules: Criminal Proceedings, Administrative Procedure and Harmonization*, (Aldershot: Ashgate, 1996)

Harris, D. 'The Development of Socio-Legal Studies in the United Kingdom', (1983) 2 *Legal Studies*, 315

Harris, D. and Tallon, D. *Contract Law Today: Anglo-French Comparisons* (Oxford: Clarendon, 1989)

Harris, P. *An Introduction to Law*, 5th edn (London: Butterworths, 1997)

Harris, W. *Tyranny on Trial*, 2nd edn, (Dallas: Southern Methodist University Press, 1998)

Hawkins, K. (ed.) *The Human Face of Law: Essays in Honour of Donald Harris*, (Oxford: Oxford University Press, 1997)

Hay, D. *et al.*, *Albion's Fatal Tree* (London: Allen Lane, 1975)

Higate, P. (ed.), *Military Masculinities: Identity and the State* (London: Greenwood, 2003)

Hurst, W. *Law and Economic Growth: The Legal History of the Lumber Industry in Wisconsin, 1936-1915*, (Cambridge MA: Harvard University Press/Belknap Press, 1964)

Hyman, P. 'Norms and Legal Before 1150' 6 *Current Legal Issues*, 2004, 41-62

Ibbetson, D. 'What is Legal History a History of?', in Lobban and Lewis, 6 *Current Legal Issues*, (Oxford OUP, 2004)

Kahn- Freund, O. 'On Uses and Misuses of Comparative Law' (1974) 37 *MLR* 1

Kerche, B. 'Resistance to Law Under Autocracy', *M.L.R.* (1997), 60(6), 779-97

Kermode, J. and G. Walker (eds), *Women, Crime and the Courts in Early Modern England*, (London: UCL Press, 1994)

Kilcommins, S. 'Context and Contingency in the Historical Penal Process: The Revision of Revisionist Analysis Using the Twelve Judges' Notebooks as One Tool of Analysis', *Hold. L.R.* 1998, 19(1), 1-54

Kruttschnitt, R. 'A Brief History of Doing Time: The California Institution for Women in the 1960s and the 1990s', *Law & Society* 38 (2) (2004), 267

Lacey, N. 'In search of the Responsible Subject: History, Philosophy and Social Sciences in Criminal Law Theory,' *M.L.R.* 2001, 64(3), 350-71

Lamb, M. 'Defining "profits" for British Income Tax Purposes: A Contextual Study of the Depreciation Cases, 1875-1897'

Lament, W. (ed.), *Historical Controversies and Historians*, (London: UCL Press, 1998)

Laurie, E. 'The Enduring Appeal of "Reasonable Preference" in Housing Allocations': *Conference Brochure* (Bristol: SLSA, 2001)

Legrand, P. 'How to Compare Now' (1996) 16 *Legal Studies* 232

Legrand, P. 'The Impossibility of Legal Transplants' 4 *Maastricht J. Eur & Comp. L.* 111 (1997)

Levine, F. 'Presidential Address' (1990) 25 *Law and Society Review*, 1-25

Lewis, A. Cocks, R. Landauer, C. and Mantena, K. 6 *Current Legal Issues*, (Oxford: OUP, 2004)

Liddle, A. M. 'State, Masculinities and Law: Some Comments on Gender and English State-Formation', *Brit. J. Criminol.* (1996), 36(3), 361-80

Lobban, M. 'Introduction: The Tools and Tasks of the Legal Historian', 6 *Current Legal Issues*, (Oxford: OUP, 2004)

Loveland, I. (ed.), *Frontiers of Criminality* (London: Sweet and Maxwell, 1995)

von Lingen, K. and Salter, M. 'Contrasting Strategies Within the War Crimes Trials of Kesselring and Wolff', 26 *Liverpool Law Review*, (2005) 1-42

McAra, L. 'The Cultural and Institutional Dynamics of Transformation: Youth Justice in Scotland, England and Wales', *Cambrian L.R.* (2004), 35, 23-54

McBarnet, D. 'False Dichotomies in Criminal Justice Research', in Baldwin and Bottomley, *Criminal Justice*, (Oxford: OUP, 1978)

McCardle, D. '"A Ruling Class Conspiracy": Law, Enclosure and the Politics of Leisure', *Nott. L.J.* (1999), 8(2), 69-78

MacCormick, D. N. (ed.), *Lawyers in their Social Setting*, (W. Green, 1976)

MacDonagh, O. *A Pattern of Government Growth: 1800-1860. The Passenger Acts and their Enforcement*, (London: MacGibbon and Key, 1961)

MacDonagh, O. *Early Victorian Government 1830-1870*, (London: Holmes and Meier, 1977)

Maclean, M. *Surviving Divorce: Women's Resources After Separation*, (London: Macmillan, 1991)

Martin, C. and Thery, I. 'The PACS and Marriage and Cohabitation in France', *Int. J.L.P.F.* (2001) 15(1), 135-58

Mattei, D. 'An Opportunity Not to Be Missed: The Future of Comparative Law in the United States', 46 *Am. J. Comp. L.* 709-18 (1998)

Maxim, P. S. 'An Ecological Analysis of Crime in Early Victorian England', *Howard Journal* (1989) 28(1), 37-50

Merry, S. E. *Colonizing Hawai'i: The Cultural Power of Law* (Princeton: Princeton Univ. Press, 1999)

Milsom, S. F. C. *The Legal Framework of English Feudalism*, (Cambridge: CUP, 1976)

Moffat, G. *Trusts Law: Texts and Materials*, 2nd edn (London: Butterworths, 1994)

Mohd, U. *Bride Burning in India: A Socio Legal Study*, (New Delhi: A P H Publishing, 1998)

Morris, A. and Maxwell, G. (eds), *Restorative Justice for Juveniles*, (Oxford: Hart, 2003)

Muller, D. J. Blackman, D. E. and Chapman, A. J. (eds) *Topics in Psychology and Law*, (Chichester: Wiley, 1983)

Nader, L. and Todd, H. F. *The Disputing Process: Law in Ten Societies*, (NY: Columbia University Press, 1978)

Nelken, D. 'Just Comparing; Virtually There, Researching There, Living There and Telling Difference; Of Crime and Criminal Justice in Italy' in *Contrasting Criminal Justice* (David Nelken, ed.), (Aldershot : Ashgate Publishing, 2000)

Norrie, A. *Crime, Reason and History*, (Cambridge University Press, 2001)

O'Donovan, K. *Sexual Divisions in Law*, (London: Weidenfeld and Nicolson, 1985)

Offer, A. *Property and Politics 1870-1914*, (Cambridge: CUP, 1981)

Ogus, A. 'Law and Economics in the UK: Past, Present, and Future' (1995) 22 *J. Law and Society*, 28

O'Malley, P. 'Discontinuity, Government and Risk: A Response to Rigakos and Hadden', *Theo. Crim.* 2001, 5(1), 85-92

Osiel, D. 'Dialogue with Dictators: Judicial Resistance in Argentina and Brazil', 20 *L. & Soc. Inquiry* (1995) 481

O'Sullivan, M. 'Making Copyright Ambidextrous: An Exposé of Copyleft', *J.I.L.T.* 2002, 3

Palmer, R. 'The Common Law and the French Connection', 4 *Anglo-Norman Studies*, (1982) 77-92

Palmer, R. C. *English Law in the Age of the Black Death, 1348-1381: A Transformation of Governance and Law*, (London/Chapel Hill: Univ. of N. Carolina Press, 1993)

Piper, C. and Miakishev, A. 'A Child's Right to Veto in England and Wales – Another Welfare Ploy?' (2003) *CFam* 15.1(57)

Pontin, B. 'Law and Science: An Historical Environmental Perspective', Examining the Role of the Alkali Acts 1863-1881 in Leading Scientific Developments. *Conference Brochure* (Bristol: SLSA, 2001)

Pottage, A. 'Proprietary Strategies: The Legal Fabric of Aristocratic Settlements', *M.L.R.* (1998), 61(2), 162-87

Pound, R. *An Introduction to the Philosophy of Law*, (New Haven: Yale UP, 1922)

Pound , R. *Interpretations of Legal History* (Cambridge: CUP, 1923)

Pound, R. *Law and Morals*, (Chapel Hill: University of North Carolina, 1924)

Pratt, J. 'Governing the Dangerous: An Historical Overview of Dangerous Offender Legislation', *S. & L.S.* (1996) 5(1), 21-36

Priban, J. 'The legacy of Political Dissent', *Socio-Legal Newsletter* 37 (2002)

Price, D. *Legal and Ethical Issues of Organ Transplantation*, (Cambridge: Cambridge University Press, 2000)

Probert, R. 'The Judicial Interpretation of Lord Hardwicke's Act of 1753', *Journal of Legal History* 23 (2002) 129-51

Probert, R. 'Chinese Whispers and Welsh Weddings', *Continuity and Change* 20 (2005) 2

Radzinowicz, L. *A History of the English Criminal Law and its Administration from 1750*, (London: Stevens, 1948)

Reeves, J. 'The Deviant Mother and Child: The Development of Adoption as an Instrument of Social Control', *J. Law & Soc.* (1993), 20(4), 412-26

Reimann, M. 'Stepping Out of the European Shadow: Why Comparative Law in the United States Must Develop Its Own Agenda,' 46 *Am. J. Comp. L.* 637-46 (1998)

Rigakos, G. S. and Hadden, R. W. 'Crime, Capitalism and the "Risk Society": Towards the Same Olde Modernity?' *Theo. Crim.* (2001), 5(1), 61-84

Roberts, D. *Victorian Origins of the British Welfare State*, (New Haven, 1960)

Roberts, J. M. 'The Enigma of Free Speech: Speakers' Corner, the Geography of Governance and a Crisis of Rationality', *S. & L.S.* (2000), 9(2), 271-92

Rock, P. *A View from the Shadows: The Ministry of the Solicitor General of Canada and the Making of the Justice for Victims of Crime Initiative*, (Oxford: OUP, 1986)

Rubin, G. R. and Sugarman, D. *Law Economy and Society Essays in the History of English Law 1750-1914*, (Abingdon: Professional Books, 1984)

Salter, M. 'Unsettling Accounts: Methodological Issues Within the Reconstruction of the Role of a US Intelligence Agency Within the Nuremberg War Crimes Trials, 6 *Current Legal Issues* (2004) 375-404

Salter, M. and Eastwood, M. 'Negotiating Nolle Prosequi at Nuremberg: The Case of Captain Zimmer', 3 *Jnl of International Criminal Justice*, (2005) 649-65

Schlesinger, R. 'The Past and Future of Comparative Law' (1995) 43 *AJCL* 477

Schone, J. M. 'Legacy of a Conflict: Special Secure Units, Penal Policy, and the Law', *Int. J. Soc. L.* (1999), 27(2), 207-28

Shee, A. H. L. *Legal Protection of Children Against Sexual Exploitation in Taiwan: A Socio-legal Perspective*, (Aldershot: Ashgate, 1998)

Sheinman, L. 'Ethical Practice or Practical Ethics? The case of the Vendor–Purchaser Rule', *Legal Ethics* (2000), 3(1), 27–48

Smith, K. J. M. and McLaren, J. P. S. 'History's Living Legacy: An Outline of Modern Historiography of the Common Law', *Legal Studies* vol. 21 2(2001), 251–324

Smith, R. G. *Medical Discipline: The Professional Conduct Jurisdiction of the General Medical Council, 1858–1990* (Oxford: OUP, 1994)

Spijkerboer, T. *Gender And Refugee Status*, (Aldershot: Ashgate, 2000)

Stebbings, C. '"Officialism": Law, Bureaucracy, and Ideology in Late Victorian England', 6 *Current Legal Issues*, (2004) 316–42

Steven, R. *Law and Politics: The House of Lords as a Judicial Body 1800–1976*, (London: Weidenfeld and Nicolson, 1983)

Steven, R. *The Independence of the Judiciary: The View from the Lord Chancellors' Office*, (Oxford: Clarendon, 1993)

Steven, R. 'Judges, Politics, Politicians, and the Confusing Role of the Judiciary' in Hawkins, 1997 *op. cit.*, 245–89

Stramignoni, I. 'At the Margins of the History of English Law; the Institutional, the Socio-political and the "Blotted Out"', *Legal Studies*, vol.22, 2(2002) pp. 420–47

Sugarman, D. 'Writing "Law and Society" Histories', *M.L.R.* (1992), 55(2), 292–308

Summerson, H. 'The Criminal Underworld of Medieval England', *J. Leg. Hist.* (1996), 17(3), 197–224

Thane, P. 'Histories of the Welfare State', in W. Lament (ed.), *Historical Controversies and Historians*, (London: UCL Press, 1998)

Thompson, E. P. *Whigs and Hunters*, (London: Allen Lane, 1975)

Tosh, J. *The Pursuit of History*, (London: Hutchinson, 1984)

Twigg, J. 'Carers, Families, Relatives: Socio-legal Conceptions of Care Giving Relationships', *J. Soc. Wel. & Fam. L.* (1994), 3, 279–98

Twining, W. 'Remembering 1972' in D. J. Galligan, (ed.), *Socio-legal Studies in Context: The Oxford Centre Past and Future*, (Oxford: Blackwell, 1995)

Vick, D. 'Interdisciplinarity and the Discipline of Law' 31 *JLS*, (2004) 163–93, 192–3

Waites, M. 'Inventing a "Lesbian Age of Consent"? The History of the Minimum Age for Sex Between Women in the UK' *S. & L.S.* 2002, 11(3), 323–42

Wall, D. *The Chief Constables of England And Wales: The Socio-Legal History Of A Criminal Justice Elite*, (Aldershot: Dartmouth, 1998)

Ward, T. 'The Sad Subject of Infanticide: Law, Medicine and Child Murder, 1860–1938', *S. & L.S.* (1999), 8(2), 163–80

Watson, A. *The Evolution of Law*, (Oxford: Blackwell, 1985)

Watson, A. 'Law out of Context', *Edin. L.R.* 2000, 4(2)

Watson, A. *Legal Origins and Legal Change*, (London: Hambledon Press, 1991)

Weiner, M. *Reconstructing the Criminal: Culture, Common Law and Policy in England 1830–1914*, (NY: Cambridge University Press, 1990)

Weinstein, J. 'Coming of Age: Recognising the Importance of Interdisciplinary Education in Law Practice' (1999) 74 *Washington Law Rev.* 319

Weitzman, L. J. and Maclean, M. *Economic Consequences of Divorce: The International Perspective*, (Oxford: OUP, 1991)

Welstead, M. 'Case Commentary: Financial Support in Same-Sex Relationships: A Canadian Constitutional Solution', (2000) *CFam* 12.1(73)

Wheeler, S. 'The Business Enterprise: A Socio-Legal Introduction' in Sally Wheeler (ed.), *A Reader on the Law of the Business Enterprise: Selected Essays* (Oxford: OUP, 1994)

Yavasi, M. 'A Socio-Legal and Economic Introduction to Corporate Governance Problems in the E.U' (2001) 22(6) *Company Lawyer*, 162

Young, A. '"Wild women": The Censure of the Suffragette Movement', *Int. J. Soc. L.* (1988), 16(3), 279–293

Zedner, L. *Women, Crime and Custody in Victorian England*, (NY: Oxford University Press, 1991)

Index

Abel, Richard, 156-7
academic discipline, law as distinct and
        separate, 86, 94-9
access to legal services, 142
anti-social behaviour, 161-2
Archibald, Claire, 155
asylum and immigration law, 160-1
Atiyah, P. S. 65, 66-7, 84, 208-9

Ballinger, Anette, 202
Baldwin, Robert, 125, 126, 154, 169
Becher, Tony, 47
Bell, J., 80
benefits of writing dissertations, 1-2, 7
black-letter approach to doctrinal research,
        44-118
    advantages and disadvantages of approach,
        108-18
    argumentative and linguistic techniques, 57
    alternative methodologies, 49
    authority of, 75
    bias against, 46
    cases, 63-4
        interpretation of, 48-51, 64-77, 83-8
        legal principles, 64-72
        system of rules, relationship with, 50-1,
            70-1
    characteristics of black-letter approach, 49
    coherence and systematic order, searching
        for, 68-75, 99, 100
    combinations of approach, 40
    common sense, discarding, 85
    comparative approach, 186-7
    consistency and predictability, 78-9
    context, 80, 82
    criminology, 99
    critical legal studies, 49, 108
    criticism, 99-108, 112-18
    cross-referencing rules to underlying
        principles, 45, 51, 70
    deductive methods of legal reasoning, 45,
        90-4
    defensiveness and sensitivity of supervisors
        with regard to, 47-8
    distinct and unique discipline, law as, 86,
        94-9
    doctrine, 48-50, 63, 67, 80, 84-6, 89,
        98-101, 118
    equity, 51
    explanatory factors, exclusion of, 84

external factors, exclusion of, 44-5, 62-3,
        84-9, 93
generalizations, 50, 57
historical methods of research, 196, 206-11
individual rights, 81-3, 101-8
interpretation, 42, 46, 48-51, 57, 64-77,
        83-90
judicial decision-making, 51, 66
jurisprudence, 48
justification for, 108-9, 112
law and economics, 42
legal categories, 45
legal formalism, 51-6, 68, 85-7, 102-4
legal history, 48
legal positivism, 48
legal principles, 67-79, 90-4, 118
legal profession and legal studies, close
        relationship with, 97-8
legal reasoning, 80, 83-7
liberalism, 51, 101-8
marriages, validity of, 44-5
meaning, 44, 45-56
methodologies of research, 34-43, 214
moral and ethic values, exclusion of, 62-3,
        86
policy, 80, 84-5, 105-6
precedent, 42
primary sources, 64, 80-1, 89-90
public interest, 106-7
purpose of, 44-5
relevant law and material facts, 87
rules, 49-50, 52, 56-7, 64-80, 101-4, 108
selective exclusion, 80-9
self-image of legal profession, as endorsing
        the, 96
setting and answering the question, 63-4
social institutions, criticism of, 45
social sciences, 98, 118
sociolegal studies, 119-21, 126-31, 134-5,
        155-6, 162-4, 178, 180
    criticism of black-letter approach, 112-13
    doctrine, 152
    exclusions from black-letter approach,
        139-40
    tensions between black-letter approach
        and, 34-43
sources of law, 48-51
standpoint of black-letter analysis, 79-80
statutes, interpretation of, 48-9, 50
supervisors, 35